ASENETH OF EGYPT

EARLY JUDAISM AND ITS LITERATURE

Rodney A. Werline, General Editor

Editorial Board:
Randall D. Chesnutt
Kelley N. Coblentz Bautch
Maxine L. Grossman
Carol Newsom

Number 53

ASENETH OF EGYPT

The Composition of a Jewish Narrative

Patricia D. Ahearne-Kroll

SBL PRESS

Atlanta

Copyright © 2020 by Patricia D. Ahearne-Kroll

All rights reserved. No part of this work may be reproduced or transmitted in any form or by any means, electronic or mechanical, including photocopying and recording, or by means of any information storage or retrieval system, except as may be expressly permitted by the 1976 Copyright Act or in writing from the publisher. Requests for permission should be addressed in writing to the Rights and Permissions Office, SBL Press, 825 Houston Mill Road, Atlanta, GA 30329 USA.

Library of Congress Cataloging-in-Publication Data

Names: Ahearne-Kroll, Patricia D., author.
Title: Aseneth of Egypt : the composition of a Jewish narrative / by Patricia D. Ahearne-Kroll.
Description: Atlanta : SBL Press, 2020. | Series: Early Judaism and its literature ; 53 | Includes bibliographical references and index.
Identifiers: LCCN 2020012820 (print) | LCCN 2020012821 (ebook) | ISBN 9781628372830 (paperback) | ISBN 9780884144571 (hardback) | ISBN 9780884144588 (ebook)
Subjects: LCSH: Joseph and Aseneth—Criticism, interpretation, etc. | Judaism—Egypt—Heliopolis (Extinct city).
Classification: LCC BS1830.J62 A44 2020 (print) | LCC BS1830.J62 (ebook) | DDC 229/.91—dc23
LC record available at https://lccn.loc.gov/2020012820
LC ebook record available at https://lccn.loc.gov/2020012821

To my parents

Contents

Acknowledgments ix
Abbreviations xi

Introduction 1

1. The Reconstructed Texts of *Aseneth* and Their Limitations:
   The Analysis of Standhartinger and Kraemer 25
   The Textual Witnesses of *Aseneth* 26
   The Reconstructions of Burchard and Philonenko 33
   The Revival of Philonenko's Reconstruction:
      Standhartinger's Analysis 36
   The Revival of Philonenko's Reconstruction:
      Kraemer's Analysis 56
   The Limitations of Comparing the Reconstructed Texts
      of *Aseneth* 74

2. The Reconstructed Texts of *Aseneth* and Their Limitations:
   The Texts of Burchard and Fink 77
   Transmission History of the *Aseneth* Witnesses:
      Burchard's and Fink's Assessments 79
   The Limitations of Fink's Reconstructed Text and the
      Inherent Flaws of Burchard's Reconstructed Text 105
   A New Path to the Earliest *Aseneth* 117

3. The *Fabula* of *Aseneth* 123
   Thomas's Study of the Acts of Peter 126
   Thomas's Model and the Textual Witnesses of *Aseneth* 134
   The *Fabula* of *Aseneth* 139
   The Implications of a *Fabula* of *Aseneth* 184

4. *Aseneth* and the Landscape of Ptolemaic and Early
   Roman Egypt 187
   Rewriting Ancestral Identity into the Pharaonic Past   188
   The Narrative Landscape of *Aseneth* and the Environment
      of Ptolemaic Egypt   210
   Conclusion   240

5. Conclusion 243

Bibliography...249
Ancient Sources Index..269
Greek Words Index 280
Subject Index..281
Modern Authors Index...283

Acknowledgments

> If you wish to make an apple pie from scratch, you must first invent the universe.
> —Carl Sagan

This work has been twenty years in the making. I have benefitted greatly from innumerable conversations and correspondences I have had over the years with colleagues, scholars, students, and friends, but I wish to call attention to those who considerably supported me along the way. It was in John J. Collins's seminar on Hellenistic Judaism at The University of Chicago Divinity School where I was first introduced to *Aseneth*, and John advised my dissertation on the topic. I am grateful for his ongoing encouragement of my work on *Aseneth*, and I am also grateful to Randall Chesnutt and Angela Standhartinger who remained interested in my project these many years. As the reader will see, my analysis required detailed examination of minutiae that sometimes could be dizzying to organize; I would have lost steam if it were not for the support of these senior scholars. Special mention must also be given to Harold and Jan Attridge, whose incredible generosity provided me a tranquil space to do considerable textual work during my dissertation-writing years, which set me on my path of critiquing the reconstructions of *Aseneth*. I also wish to thank the editor of the Early Judaism and Its Literature series, Rodney Werline, whose patience and support in the completion of my project made this monograph possible. I wrote the bulk of this book in my current position in the Classical and Near Eastern Studies Department at the University of Minnesota, so I also offer thanks to Nita Krevans and Christopher Nappa, who each as department chair supported the rearrangement of my teaching schedule, and to the College of Liberal Arts, which granted me a semester course-release, for providing me time to work on this book. I am also grateful for feedback offered by Angela Standhartinger (who read through on an earlier rendition of my text-critical chapters), Melissa Harl

Sellew (who read through my final chapters), and Randall Chesnutt (who read through the entire manuscript at its final stage). Of course, any errors discovered in this work are my own.

By far, the people who have stayed the course with me are my family. Steve Ahearne-Kroll steadily supported me amid the various challenges that I have faced in completing this project; my gratitude to him is beyond words. My children, Kieran and Marin, can now see the product of this never-ending book, and I am thankful to them for their understanding for all the times I had to work on it. Finally, my parents, John and Barbara Ahearne, have been an enduring, encouraging presence in my life, and they have been unwavering in their support of my intellectual interests, going as far back as my college years when I first started dabbling in the study of religion. The words of Carl Sagan above was my father's favorite quote; for him, as a physicist, Sagan's summary best describes how to examine the world: comprehensively, in-depth, and with an open and critical mind. My father passed away in 2019, and I have come to realize how much my own academic perspective has been influenced by him; I am grateful to him for that gift. Both my mother and father have supported me in my work on *Aseneth* and in my career overall, and I could not have produced this monograph without them. It is to them that I dedicate this book.

Abbreviations

AB	Anchor (Yale) Bible
Ag. Ap.	Josephus, *Against Apion*
AGJU	Arbeiten zur Geschichte des antiken Judentums und des Urchristentums
ANRW	Temporini, Hildegard, and Wolfgang Haase, eds. *Aufstieg und Niedergang der römischen Welt: Geschichte und Kultur Roms im Spiegel der neueren Forschung*. Part 2, Principat. Berlin: de Gruyter, 1972–.
APFB	Archiv für Papyrusforschung Beiheft
Apos. Con.	Apostolic Constitutions and Canons
ARelG	*Archiv für Religionsgeschichte*
Asen.	Aseneth
Arm	Armenian
BASP	*Bulletin of the American Society of Papyrologists*
BBVO	Berliner Beiträge zum Vorderen Orient
BCH	*Bulletin de correspondance hellénique*
BCHSup	Bulletin de correspondance hellénique Supplément
BETL	Bibliotheca Ephemeridum Theologicarum Lovaniensium
BGU	Berliner griechische Urkunden
BHL	Blackwell Handbooks in Linguistics
Bib. hist.	Diodorus Siculus, *Bibliotheca historica*
BIFAO	*Le Bulletin de l'Institut français d'archéologie orientale*
BNJ	Worthington, Ian, ed. *Brill's New Jacoby*. Leiden: Brill, 2006–.
BRS	Biblical Resource Series
Bu	Reconstructed text in Burchard, Christoph. *Joseph und Aseneth*. Assisted by Carsten Burfeind and Uta Barbara Fink. PVTG 5. Leiden: Brill, 2003.
Bu/F	Adaptation of Burchard's reconstructed text in Fink, Uta Barbara. *Joseph und Aseneth: Revision des griechischen*

	Textes und Edition der zweiten lateinischen Übersetzung. FSBP 5. Berlin: de Gruyter, 2008.
CBET	Contributions to Biblical Exegesis and Theology
CE	*Chronique d'Egypte*
CEJL	Commentaries on Early Jewish Literature
CHANE	Culture and History of the Ancient Near East
ClAnt	*Classical Antiquity*
ClQ	*Classical Quarterly*
CNI	Carsten Niebuhr Institute Publication
C.Ord.Ptol.	Lenger, Marie-Thérèse, ed. *Corpus des Ordonnances des Ptolémées.* Brussells: Palais des Académies, 1964.
CPJ	Tcherikover, Victor A., ed. *Corpus Papyrorum Judaicarum.* 3 vols. Cambridge: Harvard University Press, 1957–1964.
CRINT	Compendia Rerum Iudaicarum ad Novum Testamentum
CrStHB	Critical Studies in the Hebrew Bible
CSCO	Corpus scriptorum christianorum Orientalium
CurBR	*Currents in Biblical Research*
CW	*Classical World*
DBAT	*Dielheimer Blatter zum Alten Testament Testament und seiner Rezeption in der Alten Kirche*
DMOA	Documenta et Monumenta Orientis antiqui
EJL	Early Judaism and Its Literature
EPRO	Études préliminaires aux religions orientales dans l'Empire Romain
FJB	*Frankfurter judaistische Beiträge*
FGrHist	Jacoby, Felix, et al., eds. *Die Fragmente der griechischen Historiker.* 1923–.
FSBP	Fontes et subsidia ad Bibliam pertinentes
GM	*Göttinger Miszellen*
GRBS	*Greek, Roman, and Byzantine Studies*
HCS	Hellenistic Culture and Society
Hist.	*Historiae*
HSCL	Harvard Studies in Comparative Literature
HTR	*Harvard Theological Review*
HUCA	*Hebrew Union College Annual*
Il.	Homer, *Iliad*
JAOS	*Journal of the American Oriental Society*
JARCE	*Journal of the American Research Center in Egypt*
JBL	*Journal of Biblical Literature*

JEA	*Journal of Egyptian Archaeology*
JHebS	*Journal of Hebrew Studies*
JHS	*Journal of Hellenic Studies*
JJS	*Journal of Jewish Studies*
JNES	*Journal of Near Eastern Studies*
JRS	*Journal of Roman Studies*
JSHRZ	Jüdische Schriften aus hellenistisch-römischer Zeit
JSJ	*Journal for the Study of Judaism in the Persian, Hellenistic, and Roman Period*
JSJSup	Journal for the Study of Judaism in the Persian, Hellenistic, and Roman Period Supplement Series
JSP	*Journal for the Study of the Pseudepigrapha*
JSPSup	Journal for the Study of the Pseudepigrapha Supplement Series
JTS	*Journal of Theological Studies*
Lam. Rab.	Lamentations Rabbah
LCL	Loeb Classical Library
LDAB	Leuven Database of Ancient Books; https://www.trismegistos.org/ldab/
LSJ	Liddell, Henry George, Robert Scott, and Henry Stuart Jones. *A Greek-English Lexicon*. 9th ed. with revised supplement. Oxford: Clarendon, 1996.
MIFAO	Mémoires publiés par les membres de l'Institut Français d'Archéologie Orientale du Caire
MSU	Mitteilungen des Septuaginta-Unternehmens
NovTSup	Supplements to Novum Testamentum
NPAJ	New Perspectives on Ancient Judaism
NTS	*New Testament Studies*
OCT	Oxford Classical Texts
Od.	Homer, *Odyssey*
OEAE	Redford, Donald B., ed. *The Oxford Encyclopedia of Ancient Egypt*. 3 vols. New York: Oxford University Press, 2005.
OG	Old Greek
OGIS	Dittenberger, Wilhelm, ed. *Orientis Graeci Inscriptiones Selectae: Supplementum Sylloges Inscriptionum Graecarum*. Leipzig: Hirzel, 1903–1905.
OLA	Orientalia Lovaniensia Analecta
OLZ	*Orientalistische Literaturzeitung*

OTP	Charlesworth, James H., ed. *Old Testament Pseudepigrapha*. 2 vols. New York: Doubleday, 1983–1985.
P.Cair.Zen.	Edgar et al., C. C., ed. *Zenon Papyri*. Cairo: l'Institut français d'archéologie orientale, 1925–1940.
P.Carlsberg	Carlsberg papyrus
P.Col.	Columbia papyrus
P.Corn.	Westermann, W. L., and C. J. Kraemer Jr., eds. *Greek Papyri in the Library of Cornell University*. New York: Columbia University Press, 1926.
P.Dion.	Boswinkel, E., and P. W. Pestman, eds. *Les archives privées de Dionysios, fils de Kephalas*. Leiden: Brill, 1982.
P.Dryton	Vandorpe, K., ed. *The Bilingual Family Archive of Dryton, His Wife Apollonia and Their Daughter Senmouthis*. Brussels: Koninklijke Vlaamse Academie van België voor Wetenschappen en Kunsten, 2002.
P.Enteux.	Guéraud, Octave, ed. *Ἐντεύξεις: Requêtes et plaintes adressées au roi d'Égypte au IIIe siècle avant J.-C.* Cairo, 1931–1932.
P.Erasm.	Sijpesteijn, P. J., and P. A. Verdult, eds. *Papyri in the Collection of the Erasmus University (Rotterdam)*. Brussels: Fondation Égyptologique Reine Élisabeth, 1986–1988.
P.Fay.	Frenfell, B. P., A. S. Hunt, and D. G. Hogarth, eds. *Fayum Towns and Their Papyri*. London: Egypt Exploration Society, 1900.
P.Giss.Univ.	Kling, Hans, et al., ed. *Mitteilungen aus der Papyrussammlung der Giessener Universitätsbibliothek*. Giessen: Töpelmann, 1924–1975.
Ph	Reconstructed text in Philonenko, Marc. *Joseph et Aséneth: Introduction, texte critique, traduction et notes*. SPB 13. Leiden: Brill, 1968.
P.Haun.	Larsen, T., et al., ed. *Papyri Graecae Haunienses*. Bonn: Habelt, 1942–1985.
P.Heid.	Siegmann, E., et al., ed. *Veröffentlichungen aus der Heidelberger Papyrussammlung*. Heidelberg: Winter, 1956–2006.
P.Hib.	Grenfell, B. P., et al., ed. *The Hibeh Papyri*. London, 1906, 1955.
P.Köln	Kramer, B., et al., ed. *Kölner Papyri*. 1976–.
P.Lond.	Kenyon, Frederic G., et al., ed. *Greek Papyri in the British Museum*. London: British Museum, 1893–.

pl(s).	plate(s)
P.Münch.	Heisenberg, A., et al., ed. *Die Papyri der Bayerischen Staatsbibliothek München*. Stuttgart: Teubner, 1986.
P.Oxy.	Grenfell, B. P., et al., ed. *The Oxyrynchus Papyri*. London: Egypt Exploration Society, 1898–.
P.Petr.	Mahaffy, J. P., ed. *The Flinders Petrie Papyri*. Dublin: Royal Irish Academy, 1891–1905.
P.Polit.Iud.	Cowey, James M. S., and Klaus Maresch, eds. *Urkunden des Politeuma der Juden von Herakleopolis (144/3–133/2 v.Chr.) (P.Polit.Iud.)*. Abhandlungen der Nordrhein-Westfälischen Akademie der Wissenschaften, Sonderreihe Papyrologica Coloniensia 29. Wiesbaden: Westdeutscher, 2001.
Praep. ev.	Eusebius *Praeparatio evangelica*
P.Rein.	Reinach, Théodore, et al., ed. *Papyrus grecs et démotiques recueillis en Égypte*. Paris: Leroux, 1905–1940.
P.Rev.Laws	Papyrus revenue laws
P.Ryl.	Hunt, A., et al., eds. *Catalogue of the Greek and Latin Papyri in the John Rylands Library, Manchester*. Manchester: Manchester University Press, 1911–1952.
PSI	Vitelli, G., M. Norsa, et al., eds. *Papiri greci e latini*. Florence: Pubblicazioni della Società Italiana per la ricerca dei papiri greci e latini in Egitto, 1912–.
P.Sorb.	Cadell, H., ed. *Papyrus de la Sorbonne*. Paris: Presses Universitaires de France, 1966–.
P.Tebt.	Grenfel,l B. P., et al., eds. *The Tebtunis Papyri*. London: Egypt Exploration Society, 1902–1979.
P.Tor.Choach.	Pestman, Pieter Willem, ed. *Il Processo di Hermias e altri documenti dell'archivio dei choachiti, papiri greci e demotici conservati a Torino e in altre collezioni d'Italia*. Torino: Soprintendenza al Museo delle Antichità Egizie, 1992.
P.Vindob.	Papyrus Vindobonensis
PVTG	Pseudepigrapha Veteris Testamenti Graece
P.Yale	Oates, J. F., et al., ed. *Yale Papyri in the Beinecke Rare Book and Manuscript Library*. Oxbow, 1967–2001.
QUCC	*Quaderni Urbinati di Cultura Classica*
RBL	*Review of Biblical Literature*
Resp.	Plato, *Respublica*
RN	*Revue Numismatique*

SAOC	Studies in Ancient Oriental Civilization
SAPERE	Scripta Antiquitatis Posterioris ad Ethicam Religionemque pertinentia
SB	Preisigke, F., et al., ed. *Sammelbuch griechischer Urkunden aus Aegypten*. 1915–.
SBLDS	Society of Biblical Literature Dissertation Series
SBLSPS	Society of Biblical Literature Seminar Paper Series
SBLTT	Society of Biblical Literature Texts and Translations
SC	Sources chrétiennes
SCS	Septuagint and Cognate Studies
SPB	Studia Post-Biblica
SPhA	Studies in Philo of Alexandria
STAR	Studies in Theology and Religion
Strom.	Clement of Alexandria, *Stromateis*
SubBi	Subsidia Biblica
Svonoros	Svoronos, I. N. $Τα\ νομίσματα\ του\ κράτους\ των\ Πτολεμαίων$. 4 vols. Athens, 1904–1908.
SVTP	Studia in Veteris Testamenti Pseudepigrapha
SWR	Studies in Women and Religion
Syr	Syriac
TED	Translations of Early Documents
Th	Theodotian
TSAJ	Texts and Studies in Ancient Judaism
UPZ	Wilcken, Ulrich, ed. *Urkunden der Ptolemäerzeit: Ältere Funde*. 2 vols. Berlin: de Gruyter, 1900–1999.
VCSup	Supplements to Vigiliae Christianae
VTSup	Supplements to Vetus Testamentum
WUNT	Wissenschaftliche Untersuchungen zum Neuen Testament
ZNW	*Zeitschrift für die neutestamentliche Wissenschaft und die Kunde der älteren Kirche*

Introduction

Morpheus: I imagine that right now you're feeling a bit like Alice, tumbling down the rabbit hole?... Unfortunately, no one can be told what the Matrix is. You have to see it for yourself.
This is your last chance. After this there is no turning back.
You take the blue pill, the story ends. You wake up in your bed and believe whatever you want to believe.
You take the red pill, you stay in Wonderland, and I show you how deep the rabbit hole goes.

—*The Matrix*

The phenomenon of Neo taking the red pill resonates very much with my experience of studying Joseph and Aseneth (hereafter referred to as *Aseneth*).[1] Twenty years ago, I was introduced to this fascinating story in a course I took with John J. Collins at The University of Chicago Divinity School. I eventually chose that narrative for my dissertation, but early

---

In the 1999 film, *The Matrix*, the protagonist, Neo, meets Morpheus, the leader of a group of human beings who had escaped enslavement in a futuristic, machine society that uses human bodies as a biological energy source. To maintain order and the subjugation of humanity, this robotic system (the Matrix), psychologically deceives human beings by plugging their minds into a virtual reality that simulates what we today would think to be the real world. Some humans, like Neo, are onto this scheme, and Morpheus (a liberated human) seeks out Neo to show him the truth. Morpheus offers Neo two pills, one that would allow him to continue living as is and the other to reveal the unpleasant reality of the Matrix. Neo, of course, chooses the red pill, and the rest of the film reveals a series of rude awakenings.

1. Although the *SBL Handbook of Style* dictates that the story should be referred to as Joseph and Aseneth, I agree with Ross Shepard Kraemer that a more fitting reference to this narrative should be centered on the protagonist of the story, Aseneth (*When Aseneth Met Joseph: A Late Antique Tale of the Biblical Patriarch and His Egyptian Wife, Reconsidered* [New York: Oxford University Press, 1998], 3). I will refer to the narrative as *Aseneth* throughout, and I use the narrative title in italics to distinguish it from the times I discuss the character, Aseneth.

on in my work I found myself tumbling down a rabbit hole. I dug rather deeply into the reconstructed texts of Christoph Burchard and Marc Philonenko (creating my own comparative chart of the textual discrepancies), and I very much felt like I had swallowed the red pill that opened my eyes to textual deceptions. As helpful as the reconstructions of Burchard and Philonenko were, I found both to consist of unexplained or poorly defended textual choices, and I noticed discrepancies between the textual witnesses that may indicate significant scribal choices in time and place. In addition, even though reconstructed texts reflect no actual, known manuscript, scholars continued to build theories off of those reconstructions, most making claims about the meaning and/or origin of this narrative without considering the more difficult problems of a reconstructed text. I could not get past how these academic theories were built off of a virtual *Aseneth* whose sources were mostly hidden.

At the time I worked on my dissertation, *Aseneth* scholars depended upon the reconstructions of either Burchard or Philonenko. These reconstructions were compiled from the textual groups that Burchard had established in the 1960s (the four textual families of *a*, *b*, *c*, and *d*).[2] Early on, Burchard had argued that family *b* was closest to the original *Aseneth*, and in 1979, he produced a reconstructed text that was supposedly based primarily on the *b* witnesses.[3] In contrast, Philonenko argued for the prominence of family *d*, and in 1968 he published a reconstructed text that supposedly was based on that family.[4] Burchard's text and argument for *b* convinced most scholars for the next two decades, but in the 1990s, Angela Standhartinger and Ross Shephard Kraemer resurrected Philonenko's argument and offered pointed challenges to the study of *Aseneth*. Back when Philonenko had produced his text, several scholars identified how, for unexplained reasons, Philonenko had relied on other textual families when he had claimed that his text reflected the

---

2. First proposed in his 1961 dissertation and then more fully explained in *Untersuchungen zu Joseph und Aseneth: Überlieferung-Ortsbestimmung*, WUNT 8 (Tübingen: Mohr, 1965). For a succinct summary of Burchard's initial work, see Randall D. Chesnutt, *From Death to Life: Conversion in "Joseph and Aseneth,"* JSPSup 16 (Sheffield: Sheffield Academic, 1995), 36–39.

3. Burchard, "Ein vorläufiger griechischer Text von Joseph und Aseneth," *DBAT* 14 (1979): 2–53.

4. Marc Philenko, *Joseph et Aséneth: Introduction, texte critique, traduction et notes*, SPB 13 (Leiden: Brill, 1968).

text of the *d* family.⁵ Standhartinger outlined this particular critique of Philonenko's text, and she deleted those non-*d* additions from his text in her analysis of *Aseneth*. Standhartinger also exposed how Burchard's text is flawed in a similar way; Burchard's text incorporates non-*b* material, most notably from family *a*.⁶ In their monographs, both Standhartinger and Kraemer provided key differences in the characterization of Aseneth in Burchard's and Philonenko's reconstructions, and they argued that those differences revealed purposeful redactions that altered the presentation of Aseneth. Yet, their hypotheses relied on the reconstructions and not on the manuscripts, and I began to see more problems that went beyond their observations. Not only did the reconstructions of Philonenko and Burchard contradict the intentions of each scholar (to construct a text from primarily family *d* or *b*, respectively), but also the manuscripts of the individual textual families suggested a more complicated transmission process than what a linear, chronological genealogy of families implied (which was, at the time, families $b \rightarrow [c$ and $d] \rightarrow a$ for Burchard and $d \rightarrow b \rightarrow c \rightarrow a$ for Philonenko).

For my dissertation, I resolved the problem of the reconstructions by proposing a *fabula* of Aseneth. I borrowed the idea from the work of Christine Thomas on the Acts of Peter, in which she applied this concept from Russian formalism to explain the different yet connected textual traditions about the apostle Peter.⁷ Given the scholarly discussion at the time, my *fabula* for *Aseneth* relied on the commonalities between the textual families *b* and *d*, since at that time in scholarship, families *a* and *c* were considered to represent redactions. Near the end of my completion of the dissertation, Burchard adjusted his view of the textual witnesses and published a critical edition of *Aseneth*.⁸ It was too late for me to incorporate

---

5. Sebastian P. Brock, review of *Joseph et Aséneth: Introduction, texte critique, traduction et notes*, by Marc Philonenko, *JTS* 20 (1969): 588–91; Christoph Burchard, "Zum Text von 'Joseph und Aseneth,'" *JSJ* 1(1970): 3–34; Traugott Holtz, review of *Joseph et Aséneth*, by Marc Philonenko, *OLZ* 67 (1972), 49–55; and E. W. Smith, review of *Joseph et Aséneth*, by Marc Philonenko, *JBL* 89 (1970): 257.

6. Angela Standhartinger, *Das Frauenbild im Judentum der hellenistischen Zeit: Ein Beitrag anhand von "Joseph und Aseneth,"* AGJU 26 (Leiden: Brill, 1995), 42–45.

7. Thomas, *The Acts of Peter, Gospel Literature, and the Ancient Novel: Rewriting the Past* (New York: Oxford University Press, 2003).

8. Christoph Burchard, *Joseph und Aseneth*, assisted by Carsten Burfeind and Uta Barbara Fink, PVTG 5 (Leiden: Brill, 2003). Burchard also provides a summary of his new classification in "Ein neuer Versuch zu Textgeschichte von Joseph und Aseneth,"

Burchard's analysis into my dissertation, but I knew that I had to revisit my understanding of the manuscript evidence. Still unbeknown to many scholars who analyze *Aseneth*, Burchard's critical edition with the assistance of Carsten Burfeind and Uta Barbara Fink changed the playing field.

Burchard reclassified the textual families, which has led me to alter the value of textual witnesses I had left out of my initial analysis. First, Burchard dissolved the category, "family *b*," and instead divided it into five units: three individual families of versions (Syriac, Armenian, and a group of Latin texts identified as L2), one new family consisting of Greek and Latin witnesses (family *f*), and a single Greek manuscript in its own category (MS E).[9] Second, building off of the work of Carsten Burfeind on palimpsest M, Burchard included M with his original family *c* textual group and elevated the significance of this new group M*c*.[10] In particular, M demonstrates that family *c* descends from a fuller narrative (one that went beyond ch. 16), and M complicates the textual relationship between *c* and former *b* witnesses, most notably seen in the shared readings between M, Syr, Arm, and L2.[11] The critical edition also provided extensive annotations that gathered and improved upon all the noted variants that had been dispersed in various publications. Before this edition, scholars had to consult several sources to gather all the evidence (in several works by Burchard as well as by Philonenko, Pierre Batiffol, and E. W. Brooks).[12] The reason why I had compiled my own chart was due to the difficulty of keeping track of all the evidence. The critical edition produced by Burchard, Burfeind, and Uta Barbara Fink considerably improved the study

---

in *Der Freund des Menschen: Festschrift für Georg Christian Macholz zur Vollenung des 70. Lebensjahres*, ed. Aarndt Meinhold and Angelika Berlejung (Neukirchen-Vluyn: Neukirchener Verlag, 2003), 237–46.

9. Burchard, *Joseph und Aseneth*, 1–48.

10. Carsten Burfeind, "Der Text von *Joseph und Aseneth* im Palimpsest Rehdiger 26 der Universitätsbibliothek Wroclaw (Breslau)," *JSJ* 32 (2001): 42–53.

11. Burchard, *Joseph und Aseneth*, 20–22.

12. Burchard, *Untersuchungen zu Joseph und Aseneth*; Burchard, "Ein vorläufiger griechischer Text," 2–53; Burchard, *Unterweisung in erzählender Form: Joseph und Aseneth*, JSHRZ 2.4 (Gütersloh: Mohn, 1983), 631–720; Burchard, "Joseph and Aseneth," *OTP* 2:177–247; Philonenko, *Joseph et Aséneth*; Pierre Batiffol, *Le Livre de la Prière d'Asenath*, Studia Patristica 1–2 (Paris: Leroux, 1889–1890), 1–87 (Greek text) and 88–115 (Latin text); and E. W. Brooks offers a Latin translation of the Syriac in *Historia ecclesiastica Zachariae Rhetori vulgo adscripta*, CSCO 87, Scriptores Syri 41 (Leuven: Peeters, 2003).

of *Aseneth* manuscripts, and this was a resource that was not available to Standhartinger or Kraemer. While producing my translation and commentary of *Aseneth* for the anthology, *Outside the Bible*, I began to rework my rendering of the *fabula* given Burchard's reorganization and recalibration of the evidence as well as the critical edition's presentation of the textual variants.[13]

By now I felt I was definitely in Wonderland, and I reworked my analysis of the textual traditions and began to rethink how to put together the textual evidence while still talking about the narrative and its possible meaning in Hellenistic times. Then in 2008, when I had submitted my translation of and commentary on *Aseneth* for *Outside the Bible*, Fink published her important work, *Joseph und Aseneth*.[14] Fink presents a systematic critique of Burchard's reconstructed text, a revised reconstructed text with the questionable portions removed, and full explanations for her textual choices. Notable in her work is her deletion of all the passages from Burchard's text that were solely taken from family *a*, which in essence created a new reconstructed text that, even today, not all scholars recognize.[15] Very similar to the critique of Philonenko's text, Fink definitively

---

13. Patricia Ahearne-Kroll, "Joseph and Aseneth," in *Outside the Bible: Ancient Jewish Writings Related to Scripture*, ed. Louis H. Feldman, James L. Kugel, and Lawrence H. Schiffman (Lincoln: University of Nebraska Press, 2013), 3:2525–89.

14. Uta Barbara Fink, *Joseph und Aseneth: Revision des griechischen Textes und Edition der zweiten lateinischen Übersetzung*, FSBP 5 (Berlin: de Gruyter, 2008).

15. E.g., the following recent studies on *Aseneth* continue to use Burchard's critical edition and not Fink's text: Nina Braginskaya, "*Joseph and Aseneth* in Greek Literary History: The Case of the 'First Novel,'" in *The Ancient Novel and Early Christian and Jewish Narrative: Fictional Intersections*, ed. Marília P. Futre Pinheiro, Judith Perkins, and Richard Pervo (Groningen: Barkhuis Publishing & Groningen University Library, 2012), 79–106; Nicholas A. Elder, "On Transcription and Oral Transmission in *Aseneth*: A Study of the Narrative's Conception," *JSJ* 47 (2016): 119–42; Maria S. Kasyan, "The Bees of Artemis Ephesia and the Apocalyptic Scene in *Joseph and Aseneth*," in *Intende, Lector: Echoes of Myth, Religion and Ritual in the Ancient Novel*, ed. Marília P. Futre Pinheiro, Anton Bierl, and Roger Beck (Berlin: de Gruyter, 2013), 251–71; Joseph Verheyden, "A Jewish King in Egypt? A Note on the So-called *History of Joseph*," in *Old Testament Pseudepigrapha and the Scriptures*, ed. Eibert J. C. Tigchelaar, BETL 270 (Leuven: Peeters, 2014), 449–61; and Meredith Warren, "A Robe Like Lightning: Clothing Changes and Identification in *Joseph and Aseneth*," in *Dressing Judeans and Christians in Antiquity*, ed. Kristi Upson-Saia, Carly Daniel-Hughes, and Alicia J. Batten (Surrey: Ashgate, 2014), 137–53. The following scholars mention Fink's monograph but work with Burchard's text: René Bloch, "Take Your

demonstrates that variants solely in *a* should be removed from Burchard's text. In addition, Fink provided the deciphered portions of palimpsest M and reproduced two Latin texts representing the two strands of the textual family L2. Fink also made a convincing argument for the importance of MS E in reconsidering the transmission of this narrative. The combination of Burchard's critical edition and Fink's monograph made it even more possible to see the particulars of the manuscript evidence, and as a result, I reworked the *Aseneth fabula* yet again. Instead of relying on families *b* and *d*, I went back to the drawing board and built up a core narrative and linguistic links that incorporated the textual families in their current configurations (Syr, Arm, L2, E, *f*, Mc, *a*, and *d*). I no longer depended on solely *b* and *d* texts, although I did maintain the general argument for a *fabula* from my dissertation.[16]

There are two important distinctions between the *fabula* of my dissertation and the one I present in this monograph. The inclusion of all the textual families in creating a core narrative has altered the basic storyline from what I had proposed in my dissertation. For some readers, my core narrative may seem to weaken *Aseneth*; to these readers, the dynamic parts of the story are washed away as they are particular to only some (or one) of the textual families. I sympathize with those who experience this disappointment, and I suspect that all who have looked closely at the

---

Time: Conversion, Confidence and Tranquility in *Joseph and Aseneth*," in *Anthropologie und Ethik im Frühjudentum und im Neuen Testament*, ed. Matthais Kondradt and Esther Schläpfer, WUNT 322 (Tübingen: Mohr Siebeck, 2014), 77–96; Andrei Orlov, "Unveiling the Face: The Heavenly Counterpart Traditions in *Joseph and Aseneth*," in *The Embroidered Bible: Studies in Biblical Apocrypha and Pseudepigrapha in Honour of Michael E. Stone*, ed. Lorenzo DiTommaso, Matthias Henze, and William Adler, SVTP 26 (Leiden: Brill, 2018), 771–808; and Tyson L. Putthoff, "Aseneth's Gastronomical Vision: Mystical Theophagy and the New Creation in *Joseph and Aseneth*," *JSP* 24 (2014): 96–117. Finally, Rivka Nir's work continues to use Burchard's critical edition (representing the long text) and Philonenko's (representing the short text); as far as I can tell, she does not consider the revisions of Fink (Nir, *Joseph and Aseneth: A Christian Book*, Hebrew Bible Monographs 42 [Sheffield: Sheffield Phoenix, 2012]; and Nir, "'It Is Not Right For a Man Who Worships God to Repay His Neighbor Evil for Evil': Christian Ethics in *Joseph and Aseneth* [Chapters 22–29]," *JHebS* 13 [2013]: art. 5, http://dx.doi.org/10.5508/jhs.2013.v13.a5).

16. I presented a preliminary account of my revised response to the text-critical issues of *Aseneth* at the Annual Meeting of the Society of Biblical Literature, Chicago, IL, 20 November, 2012 ("Multiple Witnesses, the 'Original Text,' and the Historian's Challenge: How to Make Sense Out of 'Joseph and Aseneth'").

manuscript evidence of *Aseneth* would echo this sentiment. At the start of my dissertation, I fixated on particulars like Aseneth's ensemble, the role of Metanoia, and the allusion to Song of Songs in chapter 18, only to discover that the textual families vary too greatly to identify a shared set of details. Neo's awakening after taking that red pill is an apt image; what is first so exciting about the narrative is gone when we rely on the *fabula*, and at first, the story loses its shine. I argue, however, that the *fabula* is the only way to posit the initial creation of this narrative, which even at this base level conveys meaning that is worth discussing.

What makes creating a *fabula* possible from the *Aseneth* evidence is the fact that despite the variants, the core narrative shared by the textual families is still quite extensive. This is why in my dissertation I also proposed a common set of images and linguistic expressions along with my *fabula*. Since I had relied only upon families *b* and *d*, I had a considerable amount of common material to work with, which included the ability to discuss in detail the literary genre of *Aseneth*. In my dissertation, then, I presented a thorough explanation of how *Aseneth* was composed in the genre of the ancient Greek novel, and I provided an extensive discussion as to how *Aseneth* in particular interacted with LXX Gen 37–50 to produce its particular take on that genre.[17] I provided my own definition of the genre in terms of literary form, plot, and what I referred to as a set of expectations that extend from the genre's design.[18] I then provided a

---

17. Patricia Ahearne-Kroll, "*Joseph and Aseneth* and Jewish Identity in Greco-Roman Egypt" (PhD diss., University of Chicago Divinity School, 2005), 88–143.

18. I stated that the literary form and plot of *Aseneth* was: "a narrative in which two characters, a female and a male, fall in love, marry, and spend the rest of their lives in happiness after encountering a series of obstacles that prevent the success of this union" ("*Joseph and Aseneth* and Jewish Identity," 89). I listed the following set of expectations that the ancient Greek novel genre works with: "(1) an emphasis on human emotions, (2) the characterization of the protagonists with high-quality traits (e.g., nobility, beauty, and knowledge), (3) the love shared by the protagonists as a significant plot element, (4) separation as the main obstacle faced by the protagonists, (5) the focus on the private lives of the characters, especially of the female protagonist, and (6) the use of paradoxical characters and/or scenarios" (91). I pointed out that this was not an exhaustive list but that they were features I had identified in the five fully surviving Greek novels: *Chaereas and Callirhoe* by Chariton of Aphrodisias, the *Ephesiaka* by Xenophon of Ephesus, *Leucippe and Clitophon* by Achilles Tatius of Alexandria, *Daphnis and Chloe* by Longus, and the *Aithiopika* by Heliodorus of Emesa. Catherine Hezser also compares these ancient Greek novels with *Aseneth*, but

detailed comparison of how Chariton's novel, *Chaereas and Callirhoe*, and *Aseneth* worked with these expectations to demonstrate how well *Aseneth* fit the genre of an ancient Greek novel. In a separate chapter of my dissertation, I also presented how *Aseneth*—in depicting the typical expectation in ancient Greek novels to portray the nobility of the protagonists—utilized LXX material for its characterizations of Joseph and Aseneth (using Gen 37–50 and Dan 10–16, respectively).¹⁹ My new *fabula*, however, is more limited in its linguistic scope. I no longer work primarily from Burchard's and Philonenko's reconstructions nor do I argue for the genre of *Aseneth* in particular.

So what is worth discussing about the *Aseneth fabula*? In my dissertation, I had argued that *Aseneth* gave meaning to the lives of Jews in Hellenistic Egypt by creating an ancestral narrative that was rooted in Egypt's past and that instructed them how to negotiate living in their

---

unlike Hezser, I focused on defining the genre and defending how *Aseneth* utilized that genre (Hezser, "'Joseph and Aseneth' in the Context of Ancient Greek Novels," *FJB* 24 [1997]: 1–40; cf. Ahearne-Kroll, "*Joseph and Aseneth* and Jewish Identity," 88–143). Independent from my own work, Meredith Warren also compares *Aseneth* and Chariton's novel ("Robe Like Lightning," 137–53).

19. My discussion about LXX Gen 37–50 and the characterization of Joseph ("*Joseph and Aseneth* and Jewish Identity," 218–25) was based on a paper I had presented at the New England Regional Society of Biblical Literature meeting in May 2003 ("The Use of the Septuagint in *Joseph and Aseneth*," Andover-Newton Theological School, Boston, MA). Susan Docherty presents similar observations about the relationship between Gen 37–50 and *Aseneth*, although she focuses on the narrative as "rewritten bible," which I did not ("*Joseph and Aseneth*: Rewritten Bible or Narrative Expansion?," *JSJ* 35 [2004]: 27–48). Many scholars have noted the use of Dan 10:5-6 in ch. 14 of *Aseneth*, but I extended the relationship between the book of Daniel and the characterization of Aseneth (Ahearne-Kroll, "*Joseph and Aseneth* and Jewish Identity," 226–39; and further developed in Ahearne-Kroll, "The Portrayal of Aseneth in Joseph and Aseneth: Women's Religious Experience in Antiquity and the Limitations of Ancient Narratives," in *Women and Gender in Ancient Religions: Interdisciplinary Approaches*, ed. Stephen P. Ahearne-Kroll, Paul A. Holloway, and James A. Kelhoffer, WUNT 263 [Tübingen: Mohr Siebeck, 2010], 41–58). For previous references to Dan 10:5-6 and *Asen.* 14, see Burchard, "Joseph and Aseneth," 2:225; Gerhard Delling, "Einwirkungen der Sprache der Septuaginta in 'Joseph und Aseneth,'" *JSJ* 9 (1978): 48; Kraemer, *When Aseneth Met Joseph*, 33–35; and Angela Standhartinger, "From Fictional Text to Socio-historical Context: Some Considerations from a Text Critical Perspective on Joseph and Aseneth," in *Society of Biblical Literature 1996 Seminar Papers*, SBLSPS 35 (Atlanta: Scholars Press, 1996), 306–7.

contemporary, diverse environment.²⁰ This argument was presented in two ways. First, based upon Susan Stephens's analysis of the *Argonautica*, I extended the concept that epics "endowed their present with a heroic past" to the ancestral story of *Aseneth*; I argued that *Aseneth* endowed the present for Hellenistic Jews in Egypt with a heroic past that predated the Ptolemies. In particular, the character Aseneth rises to a status equal to that of Joseph, and in so doing, the two then echo the power of Ptolemaic couples in Egypt, and Joseph's kingship over Egypt prior to the Hellenistic age elevated the self-worth of Jews under Ptolemaic rule. Second, I applied Fredrik Barth's analysis of ethnic identity to my analysis of the boundary markers in *Aseneth*, and I discussed how *Aseneth* "produces distinct points of contact within the narrative that clearly instruct the audience how to act in their present setting."²¹ In this monograph, I complement my earlier reasoning, but I do not employ the same argumentation. I maintain the essential point that heroic, ancestral stories were valued in the Hellenistic period, which I have also expanded upon elsewhere, but instead of comparing the *Argonautica* with *Aseneth*, I focus on the narrative choices of Hecataeus of Abdera and Artapanus in constructing stories about the Egyptian past.²² I had treated Artapanus in my dissertation, but I expand upon its narrative design considerably in this monograph. I also highlight the importance of explicit instructions in *Aseneth*, most especially regarding appropriate responses to grievances or violence.

At the time of my dissertation, there was a renewed debate about the date, provenance, and designation of *Aseneth* (whether it was a Jewish or Christian text). Spearheaded by Kraemer's book, *When Aseneth Met Joseph*, scholars began to question whether *Aseneth* was best discussed as a late antique, Christian text. In my dissertation, I responded in detail to Kraemer's argument and then defended my position that *Aseneth* could still be understood as a Jewish text from Hellenistic Egypt.²³ I do not repeat my critique of Kraemer's argument in this monograph, nor do I engage in

---

20. Ahearne-Kroll, "*Joseph and Aseneth* and Jewish Identity," 198–265. Susan Stephens's work that I reference is from *Seeing Double: Intercultural Poetics in Ptolemaic Alexandria*, HCS 37 (Berkeley: University of California Press, 2003), 171–237.

21. Ahearne-Kroll, "*Joseph and Aseneth* and Jewish Identity," 216.

22. The value of heroic, ancestral stories is expanded in Ahearne-Kroll, "Portrayal of Aseneth in Joseph and Aseneth," 41–58.

23. Ahearne-Kroll, "*Joseph and Aseneth* and Jewish Identity," 149–69; 176–97.

detail with the more recent argument by Rivka Nir to place *Aseneth* in a late antique, Christian setting.[24] Other scholars have addressed their arguments, and I will briefly comment on their work in my conclusion.[25] Suffice it to say, both Kraemer and Nir fail to convincingly contextualize the entire narrative into the historical settings that they propose as opposed to a Hellenistic, Jewish environment.

In my dissertation, I defended the Hellenistic Egyptian setting for *Aseneth* in three ways. First, I argued that the particular way *Aseneth* employs the LXX/OG echoed interpretation techniques of other Hellenistic Jewish writers, specifically Artapanus, Philo, Demetrios the Chronographer, Philo the Epic Poet, and the author of the Wisdom of Solomon.[26] I argued that these writers rewrote Joseph's significance in Egypt, and I identified two themes that *Aseneth*'s rendition of Joseph shared with them (Joseph's association with wisdom and Joseph's authoritative status).[27] Second, I argued that particular images in *Aseneth* reflected Ptolemaic representations of imperial rule in Egypt and that *Aseneth* utilized these images purposely in creating its heroic past. I specifically identified Aseneth's headwear (diadem and head covering) as reminiscent of representations of Ptolemaic queens, and I presented the correlation between

---

24. Nir, *Joseph and Aseneth*.

25. Responses to Kraemer's monograph can be found in George J. Brooke, "Men and Women as Angels in Joseph and Aseneth," *JSP* 14 (2005): 159–77; Randall D. Chesnutt, review of *When Aseneth Met Joseph: A Late Antique Tale of the Biblical Patriarch and His Egyptian Wife, Reconsidered*, by Ross Shepard Kraemer, *RBL* 119 (2002): 760–62; John J. Collins, "*Joseph and Aseneth*: Jewish or Christian?," *JSP* 14 (2005): 97–102; Angela Standhartinger, review of *When Aseneth Met Joseph: A Late Antique Tale of the Biblical Patriarch and His Egyptian Wife, Reconsidered*, by Ross Shepard Kraemer, *JAOS* 120 (2000): 488–89; and J. Tromp, "Response to Ross Kraemer: On the Jewish Origin of Joseph and Aseneth," in *Recycling Biblical Figures: Papers Read at a NOSTER Colloquium in Amsterdam, 12–13 May 1997*, ed. Athalya Brenner and J. W. van Henten, STAR 1 (Leiden: Deo, 1999), 266–71. For responses to Nir's monograph, see Jill Hicks-Keeton, "Aseneth between Judaism and Christianity: Reframing the Debate," *JSJ* 49 (2018): 194–96; Hicks-Keeton, *Arguing with Aseneth: Gentile Access to Israel's Living God in Jewish Antiquity* (New York: Oxford University Press, 2018), 24–26; Angela Standhartinger, "Recent Scholarship on *Joseph and Aseneth* (1988–2013)," *CurBR* 12 (2014): 368–69; and Jonathon Wright, review of *Joseph and Aseneth: A Christian Book*, by Rivka Nir, *JTS* 66 (2015): 330–32.

26. Ahearne-Kroll, "*Joseph and Aseneth* and Jewish Identity," 176–89.

27. Hicks-Keeton expands on my argument in "Aseneth between Judaism and Christianity."

Joseph's Helios crown and coin portraits of particular Ptolemaic kings.²⁸ Finally, I argued that the particular instructions dictated in *Aseneth*, especially with regard to intermarriage, made sense as guidelines for Jews negotiating the diverse environment of Hellenistic Egypt.

In this monograph, I maintain my general point that *Aseneth* reflects hermeneutical choices that we find in other Jewish writings of Hellenistic Egypt and that it utilizes Ptolemaic rhetoric of power in its characterizations of Aseneth and Joseph. Yet, my argument is distinct from the dissertation. My comparison of Jewish writings with *Aseneth* in my dissertation was at a linguistic level I no longer can do (given my recalibrated *fabula*), although my basic point about the attention on Joseph can still be argued. For this monograph, I focus instead on the general narrative design of Artapanus (who was influenced by Hecataeus of Abdera) to present the suitability of *Aseneth* in Hellenistic Egypt. My recalibrated *fabula* also changes what I can propose in terms of how *Aseneth* replicates Ptolemaic images of royalty, but I also present new evidence that bolsters my claim that *Aseneth* utilizes connections to imperial authority. Finally, I incorporate more evidence into the discussion about the possible lives of Jews in Hellenistic Egypt.

At the time of this writing, there has been no other scholar to propose a *fabula* of *Aseneth*, and no other scholar has proposed the set of connections of *Aseneth* to Ptolemaic Egypt that I do in chapter 4. Philonenko was the first to provide an extensive presentation of the associations between *Aseneth* and Egyptian traditions, arguing for the author's knowledge of Egyptian cosmology as well as of traditions involving the goddess, Neith.²⁹

---

28. Ahearne-Kroll, "*Joseph and Aseneth* and Jewish Identity," 189–94. Jürgen Zangenberg also recognized similarities between Ptolemaic queens and Aseneth ("*Joseph und Aseneths* Ägypten, oder: Von der Domestikation einer 'gefährlichen' Kultur," in *Joseph und Aseneth*, ed. Eckart Reinmuth, SAPERE 15 [Tübingen: Mohr Siebeck, 2009], 172–75), to which Martina Hirschberger also refers ("Aseneths erstes Brautkleid, Symbolik von Kleidung und Zeit in der Bekehrung Aseneths [JosAs 1–21]," *Apocrypha* 21 [2011]: 179–202). See also, Standhartinger, "Recent Scholarship," 374. Several scholars have recognized the clear reference in *Asen.* 5 of Joseph's crown and chariot to Helios, however: John M. G. Barclay, *Jews in the Mediterranean Diaspora: From Alexander to Trajan (323 BCE–117 CE)*, HCS 33 (Berkeley: University of California Press, 1996), 212; Burchard, "Joseph and Aseneth," 208 n. 5k; Kraemer, *When Aseneth Met Joseph*, 163–67; and Philonenko, *Joseph et Asénéth*, 79–81.

29. E.g., Philonenko argues that the phrase, ὁ ὑψώσας τὸν οὐρανόν in 12:3 (Philonenko's versification) reflects knowledge of Egyptian cosmological traditions

He also posited a Hellenistic Egyptian environment for the narrative, which led him to explore Hellenistic influences of astrological imagery (concerning Helios and Hecate), initiation rituals for mystery religions, and Hellenistic Jewish thought in Egypt (particularly expressed by Philo, such as his philosophical discussion of wisdom and logos).[30] As others have demonstrated, Philonenko's precise correlations are difficult to defend, but I am in agreement with him that *Aseneth* was composed in an environment where Jews encountered both Egyptian and Greek religious practices and cultural traditions.[31] Sabrina Inowlocki has made a similar argument to mine (that *Aseneth* creates a foundation myth for Jews in Egypt living in a multicultural environment), but her discussion primarily focuses on Aseneth's transformation and she argues for a different set of associations.[32] Fundamentally, the cultural adaptation that I iden-

---

in which certain gods "raise the heavens" (59–60), and he provides a comprehensive summary of the traditions of Neith at Sais and Esna and relates those traditions with the etymology of the name "Aseneth" as well as with scenes in *Aseneth* (*Joseph et Aséneth*, 61–79).

30. Philonenko, *Joseph et Aséneth*, 79–89.

31. See Dieter Sänger who refutes Philonenko's associations of Neith with *Aseneth* ("Bekehrung und Exodus: Zum jüdischen Traditionshintergrund von 'Joseph und Asenteh,'" *JSJ* 10 [1979]: 11–36) and who highlights the problems of interpreting *Aseneth* through the lens of mystery religions (Sänger, *Antikes Judentum und die Mysterien: Religionsgeschichtliche Untersuchungen zu Joseph und Asenteh*, WUNT 2/5 [Tübingen: Mohr, 1980]). Chesnutt also provides a definitive correction on the ritual meal language (bread-cup-[ointment]) in *Aseneth* and clarifies what can be gleaned by comparing Aseneth's conversion scene with initiation rituals into the mysteries (*From Death to Life*, 96–150, and 217–53, respectively). Because *Aseneth* was composed in an environment where Jews encountered both Egyptian and Greek religious practices and cultural traditions, Philonenko particularly locates the creation of this narrative in the *chora* and not Alexandria (*Joseph et Aséneth*, 107). Scholarship on Hellenistic Egypt no longer sees a stark divide between the *polis* and the *chora* in Egypt, so *Aseneth* could have been composed in either setting. On multicultural interaction and identity in Hellenistic Egypt, see Ian Moyer, *Egypt and the Limits of Hellenism* (Cambridge: Cambridge University Press, 2011); Stephens, *Seeing Double*; and Dorothy J. Thompson, *Memphis under the Ptolemies*, 2nd ed. (Princeton: Princeton University Press, 2012).

32. Inowlocki, *Des idoles mortes et muettes au dieu vivant: Joseph, Aséneth et le fils de Pharaon dans un roman du judaïsme hellénisé* (Turnhout: Brepols, 2002). Inowlocki mentions the importance of Joseph's royal status in *Aseneth*, but she primarily collects a host of literary associations from Greek and some Egyptian traditions that may help to explain parts of the story. In particular, she offers a unique and interesting

tify in *Aseneth* relates to juridical practices in Ptolemaic Egypt and to the Ptolemaic rhetoric of power that replicated Egyptian pharaonic imagery. I do not, however, promote more specific, historical allusions in *Aseneth*, whether it be to Alexandrian tensions, Onias IV and the temple in Leontopolis, or other historical events.[33] Working with a *fabula* prohibits any comprehensive allegorical reading of the narrative, but even so, I am not convinced that the story was meant to be an encoded commentary on particular historical events.

The recent monograph by Jill Hicks-Keeton builds off of the work I had done on *Aseneth*, especially from my dissertation.[34] In particular, she adopts (1) my earlier method of textual analysis by focusing on the common denominators of the two (then labeled) textual families *b* and *d*; (2) my argument that *Aseneth* shares affinities with other Hellenistic writers in their expansions about Joseph, and she discusses many of the same texts that I had in my dissertation (Artapanus, Philo, Demetrius the Chronographer, and Josephus, to name a few); and (3) my argument that both the combination of *Aseneth*'s literary techniques and its reflection of Hellenistic Egyptian imagery support the claim that *Aseneth* was composed in Hellenistic Egypt.[35] Hicks-Keeton, however, is interested in

---

comparison between the bee scene in *Aseneth* and Marcel Detienne's analysis of bee traditions in classical literature and Greek religious practices (Detienne, "Orphée au miel," QUCC 12 [1971]: 7–23).

33. Dieter Sänger proposes detailed connections between the characters in *Aseneth* and Alexandrian politics in the first century CE ("Erwägungen zu historischen Einordnung und zur Datierung von 'Joseph und Aseneth,'" ZNW 76 [1985]: 86–106). Gideon Bohak was the first to argue for explicit connections between *Aseneth* and the Leontopolite temple (*"Joseph and Aseneth" and the Jewish Temple in Heliopolis*, EJL 10 [Atlanta: Scholars Press, 1996]), and his position more recently has been developed by Martina Hirschberger ("Aseneths erstes Brautkleid," 179–202) and incorporated by Livia Capponi (*Il tempio di Leontopoli in Egitto: Identità politica e religiosa dei Giudeidi Onia [c. 150 a.C.–73 d.C.]*, Pubblicazioni della Facoltà di Lettere e Filosofia dell'Università di Pavia 118 [Pisa: ETS, 2007]). Noal Hacham proposes that the latter half of *Aseneth* (chs. 22–29) reflects societal tensions that arose from Jewish support of Cleopatra III and Ptolemy Alexander (her son) against Ptolemy Lathyrus (107–88 BCE) ("*Joseph and Aseneth*: Loyalty, Traitors, Antiquity and Diasporan Identity," JSP 22 [2012]: 53–67). See also, Standhartinger, "Recent Scholarship," 371–74.

34. Hicks-Keeton, *Arguing with Aseneth*.

35. (1) The first chapter of my dissertation outlines my text-critical approach ("*Joseph and Aseneth* and Jewish Identity," 14–89); (2) in the fourth chapter of my dissertation, I compared the characterization of Joseph in *Aseneth* and other Hellenistic

Aseneth as a gentile, and she argues that *Aseneth* is, in part, a narrative that promotes gentile inclusion through individual affiliation with the "living God" of Joseph. The story, then, does not advocate for association with a Jewish community or even in self-ascribing as a Ἰουδαία or Ἰουδαῖος; as a "city of refuge," Aseneth becomes "a proleptic mediator" of God's inclusion of all those who repent, Jew or gentile.[36] I find convincing some of the septuagintal connections that Hicks-Keeton identifies with the *fabula* of *Aseneth* (such as the descriptor "life-giving God' in ch. 8), but I disagree with her assessment about Aseneth's identity after she marries Joseph.[37] Hicks-Keeton focuses on the individual choice that Aseneth makes ("choosing life") and the reward that she receives ("becoming covenanted," and thus receiving life and protection from death), but in reading this narrative within an ancient Mediterranean setting, I cannot divorce Aseneth's religious affiliation from her familial association. I still find Jonathan M. Hall's definition of ethnicity salient when thinking about identity during the Hellenistic period, and I highlight here what Hall identifies as the core elements of ethnic identity: that members of the group share "a putative subscription to a myth of common descent and kinship, an association with a specific territory and a sense of shared history."[38] In the ancient Mediterranean world, most people identified

---

Judean texts from Egypt (176–89); (3) Hicks-Keeton clearly indicates that she builds off of my basic argument for the provenance of *Aseneth*, but I disagree with her claim that my dissertation focused on the "celebrated past" of Joseph as characterized by the narrative and not to the "contested present" of the audience ("Aseneth between Judaism and Christianity," 199 n. 42). The final chapter of my dissertation fundamentally argues that *Aseneth* constructs a heroic past for Jews in Egypt while simultaneously providing specific guidance as to how to navigate the polyethnic environment of Hellenistic Egypt ("*Joseph and Aseneth* and Jewish Identity," 198–265).

36. Hicks-Keeton, *Arguing with Aseneth*, 57–58, 133–40.
37. Hicks-Keeton, *Arguing with Aseneth*, 44–66.
38. Hall summarizes his full definition of ethnic identity as follows: "(i) The ethnic group is a self-ascribing and self-nominating social collectivity that constitutes itself in opposition to other groups of a similar order. (ii) Biological features, language, religion or cultural traits may appear to be highly visible markers of identification but they do not ultimately define the ethnic group. They are, instead, secondary indicia (the operational set of distinguishing attributes that tend to be associated with membership in an ethnic group) or 'surface pointers.' (iii) Ultimately, the definitional criteria or 'core elements' which determine membership in an ethnic group—and distinguish the ethnic group from other social collectivities—are a putative subscription to a myth of common descent and kinship, an association with

with their familial group, which had particular connections to geographical spaces and ancestral traditions, and which participated in religious activities that venerated particular gods and reaffirmed the importance of those spaces and traditions. As I will argue, Aseneth joins a new kinship group that Judean communities in Hellenistic Egypt would have identified as their ancestors; her value in the story is not that she is a gentile but that she is one of *them*, that her noble story is a part of *their* history. The gentile inclusion that *Aseneth* promotes only has to do with the prerequisites for Judean marriages, that a non-Judean can marry a Judean if she/he changes allegiances to Joseph's god. In the end, though, Aseneth models proper Judean behavior as she becomes fully incorporated into the household of Joseph.

My reference to "Judean" brings me to my last point, which is how I will be referring to the social group(s) behind the initial composition and reception of *Aseneth*. As stated above, identity in *Aseneth* is best portrayed in ethnic terms or, better put, in terms rooted in ancient connotations of *ethnos* (ἔθνος). If we start with how Hellenistic writers referred to *ethnos*, Steve Mason offers a helpful summary:

> Each *ethnos* had its distinctive nature or character (φύσις, ἦθος), expressed in unique ancestral traditions (τὰ πάτρια), which typically reflected a shared (if fictive) ancestry (συγγενεία); each had its charter stories (μῦθοι), customs, norms, conventions, mores, laws (νόμοι, ἔθη, νόμιμα), and political arrangements or constitution (πολιτεία).[39]

Mason's definition is quite similar to Hall's articulation of ethnicity; the *ethnos* of a person was associated with a geographical space, a particular

---

a specific territory and a sense of shared history. (iv) The ethnic group is neither static nor monolithic and is often subject to processes of assimilation with, or differentiation from, other groups. (v) Since individuals possess a broad repertoire of social identities and roles that they adopt in varying circumstances and for specific goals and purposes, membership in an ethnic group will not always be the most salient dimension of identification, though it tends to assume greater importance at times when the integrity of the ethnic group is threatened. (vi) Finally, ethnicity often emerges in the context of migration, conquest or the appropriation of resources by one group at the expense of another" (*Hellenicity: Between Ethnicity and Culture* [Chicago: University of Chicago Press, 2002], 9–10).

39. Mason, "Jews, Judaeans, Judaizing, Judaism: Problems of Categorization in Ancient History," *JSJ* 38 (2007): 484.

group ("ancestors"), and traditions that members of that *ethnos* shared.⁴⁰ Mason's definition also summarizes well how Josephus discusses Ἰουδαῖοι as an *ethnos* in *Contra Apionem*; he describes it in terms of ancestry, territory, language, and constitution (the latter which is how Josephus frames customs and religious practices along with organizational structures). But Josephus's discussion echoes how other Hellenistic writers referred to *ethnoi*, and John M. G. Barclay argues that everyday people in the Hellenistic world viewed the *ethnos* category differently.⁴¹ For Barclay, most ancients had a polythetic understanding of ethnic identity, in that no one association was essential for being included in that so-called *ethnos*, and, instead, most individuals shared a "cluster of characteristics" in common that were associated with an *ethnos*.⁴² The polythetic reading of *ethnos* neither convinces Hall, who argues for the centrality of the myth of common descent, nor fits Mason's rendering, which places the geographical space of Judea as central to the ethnic reference Ἰουδαῖος.⁴³ Qualifying these three positions, however, yields what I think best illustrates how Ἰουδαῖοι in Hellenistic Egypt possibly viewed themselves.

First and foremost, a basic reference point for most ancients was the connection to a particular geographical space that was associated with a particular god(s) and with a particular household(s) (one's ancestors).⁴⁴ I agree with Mason that an *ethnos*-designation implied connection to a particular territory, whether or not the person ever lived there, but I would add that geography mattered because of its perceived association with the

---

40. In a footnote, Mason contends that his position differs from Hall's, but his rebuttal is not detailed ("Jews, Judaeans, Judaizing, Judaism ," 483 n. 57). As I will note further below, Mason and Hall differ on the core elements, but they share very similar ideas as to identity construction in the Hellenistic period.

41. John M. G. Barclay, "Ἰουδαῖος: Ethnicity and Translation," in *Ethnicity, Race, Religion: Identities and Ideologies in Early Jewish and Christian Texts, and in Modern Biblical Interpretation*, ed. Katherine M. Hockey and David G. Horrell (London: T&T Clark, 2018), 48.

42. Barclay, "Ἰουδαῖος: Ethnicity and Translation," 49.

43. Hall, *Hellenicity*, 11–12; Mason, "Jews, Judaeans, Judaizing, Judaism."

44. As Mason describes ("Jews, Judaeans, Judaizing, Judaism," 484), but see also Fritz Graf, "Sacred Times and Spaces: Introduction," in *Religions of the Ancient World: A Guide*, ed. Sarah Iles Johnston (Cambridge: Harvard University Press, 2004), 243–44; and Karel van der Toorn, "Religious Practices of the Individual and Family: Introduction," in Johnston, *Religions of the Ancient World*, 423–24.

divine.⁴⁵ For any ancient *ethnos*, their supposed ancestors encountered a patron deity or family of gods in a particularly identified "there," where stories evolved, rituals were performed, and traditions were passed down for generations.⁴⁶ By "there," I do not simply mean the location of sacred sites, but the perceived protections of a territory those sites guaranteed as well as the perceived relationships forged between the ancestors and the gods in that space. In this way, I do not think that prior to 70 CE, Ἰουδαῖοι in diaspora ever considered their identity as separated from or irrelevant to the temple in Jerusalem and the territory of Judea (broadly defined). For the most part, the God of Israel touched down in only one place, and for that reason, connection to that place mattered. I agree, then, with Mason that "Judean" is an apt translation of Ἰουδαῖος, especially prior to the fall of Jerusalem and its temple in the late first century CE.

I differ here, then, from the analysis of Daniel R. Schwartz on how best to translate Ἰουδαῖος.⁴⁷ I consider the *ethnos* categories in ethnographic or historical works by non-Judeans (such as those compiled by Menahem Stern in *Greek and Latin Authors on Jews and Judaism*) a different matter than the emic renderings of ethnic identity in Josephus's works or in the documentation of Ἰουδαῖοι in Hellenistic Egypt.⁴⁸ I agree with Schwartz, however, that the destruction of the Jerusalem temple in the late first century CE changed how the ethnic term Ἰουδαῖος was understood from

---

45. Mason, "Jews, Judaeans, Judaizing, Judaism," 503–4. Epigraphical and papyrological evidence from Ptolemaic Egypt also provide further support, where military personnel are referred to by their ethnic designations but were likely born in Egypt (this is unrelated to the pseudoethnic terms such as *Persēs* or *Makedōn*) (Christelle Fischer-Bovet, *Army and Society in Ptolemaic Egypt* [Cambridge: Cambridge University Press, 2014], 160–98).

46. Mason ("Jews, Judaeans, Judaizing, Judaism," 484–86) makes a similar point in that every ancient ethnos typically had a national cult, with its own cultic organization, ritual practices, and sacred spaces. My rendering differs from Hall's, whose ethnic definition cited above provides an underdeveloped construct of religion (however defined) and its relationship to ethnic identity. My thinking here is highly influenced by J. Z. Smith's *To Take Place: Toward Theory in Ritual*, Chicago Studies in the History of Judaism (Chicago: University of Chicago Press, 1987).

47. Schwartz, "'Judaean' or 'Jew'? How Should We Translate *Ioudaios* in Josephus?," in *Jewish Identity in the Greco-Roman World*, ed. Jörg Frey, Daniel R. Schwartz, and Stephanie Gripentrog, AGJU 71 (Leiden: Brill, 2007), 1–27.

48. Even though much of the evidence is fragmentary, Stern's collection continues to be a valuable resource (*Greek and Latin Authors on Jews and Judaism*, 3 vols. [Jerusalem: Israel Academy of Sciences and Humanities, 1974]).

that point onward. Adele Reinhartz argues against Mason's rendering, claiming that "Judean" erases "Jews" from the first century CE and circumvents addressing anti-Semitic and anti-Jewish sentiments in ancient literature, such as in the Gospel of John.[49] I agree that scholars need to think about the academic consequences of how they translate Ἰουδαῖος, that their decisions may aid supersessionist conclusions by scholars and lay readers alike. In the case of *Aseneth*, however, envisioning the audience as "Jewish" in scholarship has actually inserted late-antique notions of "Jewish" versus "Christian," and, in effect, the audience scholars have perceived does not necessarily reflect how Ἰουδαῖοι in Hellenistic Egypt understood themselves. Judean better represents what the papyrological evidence from Egypt seems to indicate; Ἰουδαῖος was an *ethnos* much in the ways that Mason discusses.[50] I grant that, by the time of Philo, Judean elite in Alexandria started to change their self-perceptions in response to Alexandrian hostilities; Rome's new division of the population created friction among the different elite, *ethnos* groups.[51] In disagreement with Dieter Sänger, though, *Aseneth* does not clearly demonstrate any references to Alexandrian conflicts in the early first century CE.[52] I argue in this monograph that *Aseneth* best reflects an environment where Ἰουδαῖοι understood themselves in *ethnos*-like terms while living in Egypt.

---

49. Especially in Reinhartz, "Jew and Judean: A Forum on Politics and Historiography in the Translation of Ancient Texts," *Marginalia*, https://marginalia.lareviewofbooks.org/jew-judean-forum/.

50. A strong case in point is the Herakleopolite papyrus, P.Polit.Iud. 4, in which Philotas of the Judean *politeuma* uses septuagintal language from the book of Deuteronomy to accuse Lysimachos of proceeding without a "writ of separation" (ἀποστασίου [τὸ] βυβλίον) when Lysimachos had reneged on a negotiated marriage between Philotas and Lysimachus's daughter, Nikaia (cf. LXX Deut. 24:1–4). Later on in the document, Philotas also seems to appeal to norms about oath-giving from LXX Num. 30:3. In this legal document, then, the Torah appears to be customary νόμοι used by an ethnic group identified as Ἰουδαῖοι (Robert A. Kugler, "Dispelling an Illusion of Otherness? Juridical Practice in the Heracleopolis Papyri," in *The "Other" in Second Temple Judaism: Essays in Honor of John J. Collins*, ed. Daniel C. Harlow et al. [Grand Rapids: Eerdmans, 2011], 461–65).

51. A helpful summary is provided by Jane Rowlandson, "Dissing the Egyptians: Legal, Ethnic, and Cultural Identities in Roman Egypt," in *Creating Ethnicities and Identities in the Roman World*, ed. Andrew Gardner, Edward Herring, and Kathryn Lomas, Bulletin Supplement 120 (London: Institute of Classical Studies, 2013), 219–24.

52. Sänger, "Erwägungen zu historischen Einordnung," 86–106.

I also agree with Hall that ancients often expected an *ethnos*-designation to include a common story that traced back to ancestors, and so in disagreement with Barclay's model, the myth of common descent cannot fall into a polythetic pot of resemblances from which individuals would sometimes choose. At the very least, when it comes to understanding the designation of Ἰουδαῖος in the Hellenistic period, it is quite demonstrable from Jewish/Judean writings that ancestral stories were, what Hall would call, a "core element" of this particular *ethnos*. Yet, Barclay's distinction between the rhetoric of *ethnos* in our intellectual material and the use of *ethnos* designations in everyday life must be noted. Instead of a polythetic model, however, I propose that we apply an acoustic one. Depending upon the social setting, some features were amplified more than others; sometimes association with land mattered more, other times the shared history was emphasized, and other times particular practices were highlighted. Regardless, the core elements of geographical association, ancestral connections, traditions, and affiliations with the divine all constituted what it meant to be a member of an *ethnos*.

Although, on the surface, *Aseneth* resides in the narrative world of the Joseph novella (LXX Gen 37–50), both stories resonate with Hellenistic *ethnos* designations. In LXX Genesis, Joseph is identified as the "Hebrew servant" (ὁ παῖς ὁ Ἑβραῖος; LXX Gen 39:14,17; 41:12); the eating practices of Joseph and his brothers as "Hebrews" are kept separate from those of "Egyptians" (Ἑβραῖοι and Αἰγύπτιοι; LXX Gen 43:32); and while in prison, Joseph refers to himself as a Hebrew in that he was stolen from "the land of the Hebrews" (ἐκ γῆς Ἑβραίων; LXX Gen 40:15). Furthermore, the drama of the entire story partakes in the ancestral metanarrative of Ἰουδαῖοι (when the descendants of Abraham become enslaved in Egypt and are ransomed by their god so to serve their god in Abraham's homeland), and although Jerusalem's temple has not been established yet in Genesis, the God of Abraham as the patron god of the Hebrews has been. In fact, Joseph's success derives from his affiliation with his patron god (LXX Gen 39:5, 21, 23; 41:16, 39; 45:4–11). The identity of Joseph and Jacob's household, then, are interconnected with a homeland, ancestral kin, customs and tradition, and a patron deity, not to mention that the story itself is a portion of the Hebrew narrative of descent.

The story of *Aseneth* complements how the Joseph novella constructs *ethnos*-identity. It reflects the Egyptian and Hebrew distinctions of the Genesis story, but it also legitimates new ways to be a Ἰουδαία or Ἰουδαῖος in Egypt. *Aseneth* repeats the Genesis account's separation of Joseph's eating practices from that of the Egyptians (Bu/F 7:1), but it expands the Genesis narrative in that Aseneth affiliates with Egyptian gods and then switches her allegiance to the god of the Hebrews (Αἰγύπτιοι [Bu/F 2:3; 12:5] and Ἑβραῖοι [Bu/F 11:10]).[53] Much of *Aseneth* takes pains to demonstrate how Aseneth could become a Ἑβραία. She looks more like Hebrew women than Egyptian women (Ἑβραῖαι and Αἰγύπτίαι; Bu/F 1:5); she is different than those crazed Egyptian women who fawn over Joseph (αἱ γυναῖκες καὶ αἱ θυγατέρες τῶν Αἰγυπτίων; Bu/F 7:3); and, of course, she uniquely is visited by an angelic copy of Joseph (Bu/F 14–17). But the sole reason that Aseneth can join Joseph's kinship group is that she commits her allegiance to Joseph's god (Bu/F 8:5–7). Once she does, Aseneth becomes a member of Joseph's *ethnos*; once married, her kinship relations all concern Jacob's household (and not Pentephres's), and she bears progeny who will later participate in the Hebrew ancestral history (e.g., Ephraim and Manasseh) (Bu/F 20–29).

Even in hearing this story, however, I do not think that Ἰουδαῖοι in Hellenistic Egypt would have forgotten the geographical connection of Joseph and the household of Jacob to Judea. The epic past of *Aseneth* carves out a way to hold Jerusalem and its temple in the distant future, while at the same time affirming Joseph's god. The god of the Hebrews is not local in *Aseneth* because the Hebrews are outsiders. As assimilated as Joseph is, he is a foreigner (Bu/F 4:9), his kindred come from another land (Bu/F 22:1–2), and he never becomes an adopted heir to the pharaonic throne (in that he abdicates his power in favor of another male in Pharaoh's household; Bu/F 29:9). *Aseneth* also provides much commentary on what constituted inclusion in the *ethnos* of Joseph. Women and men of non-Hebrew descent could join if they gave sole allegiance to Joseph's god (Bu/F 8:5–7, 19–20), and no matter the offense, those who feared the God Most High did not commit evil for evil (Bu/F 23–28).

I argue that *Aseneth* was written by and for Ἰουδαῖοι in Hellenistic Egypt. Documentary evidence from this time period demonstrates that ethnic designations of Ἰουδαῖος or Ἰουδαία were common yet not alone among other ethnic identifiers, and I argue that *Aseneth* is an example of how Ἰουδαῖοι were reconceiving their *ethnos* in Egypt.[54] Even though

---

53. As I will explain below, "Bu/F" refers to the reconstructed text of Fink, who adapts Burchard's original reconstructed text of *Aseneth*.

54. Documentation that provide Ἰουδαῖοι designations during the Ptolemaic and early Roman periods in Egypt including the following: James M. S. Cowey and Klaus

the story itself does not use the ethnic terms Ἰουδαία or Ἰουδαῖος, *Aseneth* focuses on *ethnos* delineations that echo the Joseph novella (LXX Gen 37–50) and reflect realistic negotiations of identity in Hellenistic Egypt.[55] I will refer to Ἰουδαῖοι in Hellenistic Egypt and their *ethnos* designations as "Judean" for the reasons I state above, that Judean best reflects the core elements with which Ἰουδαῖοι in Hellenistic Egypt associated. I am sympathetic to Barclay's decision to use "Jew/Judean" or the Greek term, Ἰουδαῖος, instead of simply the term "Judean," but the first is too unwieldy and the second produces more complications when adjectival modifiers are needed.[56] I will only refer to the terms "Jew" or "Jewish" when repeating the arguments of scholars who use those terms, or when referring to after the first century CE.

The monograph is divided into four chapters. The first two review and critique the nature of the reconstructed texts by Burchard, Philonenko, and Fink. In the first chapter, I review the manuscript evidence and the two ways Burchard has organized the evidence (his pre-2003 and 2003 classifications), and I provide a critique of the analyses by Standhartinger and Kraemer on the reconstructed texts of both Burchard and Philonenko. The debate about how best to organize the textual witnesses of *Aseneth* has formed the foundational principles behind the reconstructed texts of Burchard, Philonenko, and Fink, and chapter 1 reviews important contributions to the first thirty years of that debate. In the second chapter, I deconstruct Burchard's primary argument for the chronological history of how *Aseneth* was transmitted and critique Fink's reconstructed text. Burchard's "two-majuscule" hypothesis is the linchpin that holds his prioritization of the witnesses in place, and I argue that his theory is not substantiated enough and there are other legitimate ways to view the transmission of the evidence. There is a direct relation-

---

Maresch, ed., *Urkunden des Politeuma der Juden von Herakleopolis (144/3–133/2 v.Chr.) (P.Polit.Iud.)*, Abhandlungen der Nordrhein-Westfälischen Akademie der Wissenschaften, Sonderreihe Papyrologica Coloniensia 29 (Wiesbaden: Westdeutscher, 2001); William Horbury and David Noy, ed., *Jewish Inscriptions of Graeco-Roman Egypt* (Cambridge: Cambridge University Press, 1992); Victor A. Tcherikover, ed., *Corpus Papyrorum Judaicarum*, 3 vols. (Cambridge: Harvard University Press, 1957–1964). For more comprehensive discussions about the ethnic-designations in Ptolemaic Egypt, see Willy Clarysse and Dorothy J. Thompson, *Counting the People in Hellenistic Egypt*, 2 vols. (Cambridge: Cambridge University Press, 2006).

55. A point that Mason also identifies ("Jews, Judaeans, Judaizing, Judaism," 508).
56. Barclay, "Ἰουδαῖος: Ethnicity and Translation," 56.

ship between the prioritization of the witnesses and the ultimate choices one makes to produce a reconstructed text, and my main point in this chapter is to show how the weaknesses in the two-majuscule hypothesis should make us question the reliability of Burchard's reconstructed text. Fink's reliance on Burchard's hypothesis produces similar problems for her text, and I close the chapter summarizing the limitations of both of Fink's and Burchard's reconstructed texts. Most scholars who analyze and discuss *Aseneth* do not seem to know the details of the reconstructions, the challenges posed by Standhartinger and Kraemer about the text-critical problems of these reconstructions, or the corrections and advances proposed by Fink. A fundamental point of my monograph is that in order to say something about *Aseneth*, one must deal with the evidence in a more substantial and comprehensive way.

Having argued that none of the reconstructions are sufficient, my third chapter presents my solution for talking about the historical significance of *Aseneth*. I propose a *fabula* for *Aseneth* as well as the linguistic touch points that I argue can still be used to discuss the earliest forms of this narrative. To be clear, I am not proposing that the *fabula*-method would work for all pseudepigrapha-like texts. The nature of the *Aseneth* evidence in particular allows for a demonstrable *fabula*; I do not make any claims about other texts. In my final chapter, I explore the value of *Aseneth* in the Hellenistic Egyptian environment. I focus on comparable literary traditions in Egypt, and I present documentary and material evidence that situates the content of this narrative in the context of Judean life in Hellenistic Egypt. My goal is to demonstrate how the entire narrative, and not just the conversion scene of chapters 10–17, would have resonated for Judeans in Egypt.

When referring to particular passages in the textual reconstructions of *Aseneth*, "Bu" will stand for Burchard's reconstruction as represented in his 2003 critical edition, "Ph" will stand for Philonenko's reconstruction, and "Bu/F" will stand for Fink's 2008 adaptation of Burchard's text. When discussing textual variations, I rely most heavily on the annotations of Burchard's critical edition, but they are incomplete. Since many of the manuscripts are not easily available, I supplement the evidence of textual variants from Batiffol's Greek text (which replicates MS A of family *a*), Batiffol's Latin text (which is a reconstruction of L1), Brooks's Latin translation of *Aseneth* from the Syriac, Fink's transcriptions of palimpsest M (portions of chs. 16–29) and the two renditions of L2 (MS 436 and a reconstruction of MSS 435&), and Jonathon Stuart Wright's recent dissertation, which provides complete renditions of the Greek manuscripts FW and E as well as from families *c*, *a*, and *d*.[57] Even so, my presentation of any particular witness may be incomplete or incorrect. As the reader will see, however, I have utilized the available resources extensively, and I am transparent about the variations that exist in the manuscripts.

So now, let me take you to Wonderland...

---

57. Batiffol, *Le Livre de la Prière d'Aséneth*; Brooks, *Historia ecclesiastica Zachariae Rhetori*; Fink, *Joseph und Aseneth*, 38–44 and 198–325, respectively; and Wright, "After Antiquity: *Joseph and Aseneth* in the Manuscript Transmission; a Case Study for Engaging with What Came After the Original Version of Jewish Pseudepigrapha," 2 vols. (PhD diss., University of Oxford, 2018). Burchard has criticized Batiffol's text, and Burchard sometimes translates the Syriac differently than Brooks does (*Joseph und Aseneth*), so I am more careful with how I supplement my analysis with Batiffol's and Brooks's texts.

1
The Reconstructed Texts of *Aseneth* and Their Limitations: The Analysis of Standhartinger and Kraemer

Ever since Philonenko and Burchard published reconstructions of the earliest textual form of *Aseneth*, scholars have favored one of these reconstructions over the other.[1] For decades, most scholars preferred Burchard's edition, but then Standhartinger and Kraemer challenged the authority of Burchard's text and endorsed that of Philonenko's instead.[2] At issue for them was the question whether Burchard's reconstruction revealed ideologically driven emendations of and/or alterations to Philonenko's reconstruction, which was seen to represent an earlier telling of *Aseneth*. This debate placed Burchard's edition in a more tentative position (one which he seems to have intended from the beginning) and has problematized the reconstruction of the earliest, retrievable text.[3] For his part, Burchard revised his theory about the manuscript families and the history of this narrative's transmission, but he has kept his reconstructed text largely unchanged. Most recently, Fink altered Burchard's reconstruction, resolving problems inherent in his work, but she too maintains much of his text.[4] Although reconstructed texts have served a helpful purpose in the study of *Aseneth*, the focus on the earliest text has obscured the manuscript evidence. The transmission of *Aseneth* may have been more fluid and various than what

---

1. Philonenko, *Joseph et Aséneth*; Burchard, "Ein vorläufiger griechischer," 2–53; Burchard *Joseph und Aseneth*.

2. Standhartinger, *Das Frauenbild im Judentum*; Kraemer, *When Aseneth Met Joseph*.

3. The initial title of Burchard's published reconstruction itself expresses his cautious position, "Ein *vorläufiger* griechischer Text," 3 (emphasis added). Kraemer also offers this reminder (*When Aseneth Met Joseph*, 8).

4. Fink, *Joseph und Aseneth*.

Burchard's transmission history allows, and even Fink's adaptation relies upon a distinct genealogy of transmission that the witnesses do not clearly demonstrate. Standhartinger's and Kraemer's analyses would also be better served by foregoing the reconstructed texts altogether and instead by offering close readings of individual witnesses.

My critique of the reconstructed texts of *Aseneth* by Burchard, Philonenko, and Fink will cover two chapters. In this chapter, I introduce the reader to the textual evidence, and then I present how Burchard's and Philonenko's reconstructions, in the end, undermine Standhartinger's and Kraemer's arguments. I highlight the work of Standhartinger and Kraemer, though, because their attention to the two reconstructions should have issued a more definitive shift in *Aseneth* studies, a shift that this monograph promotes. In the next chapter, I address the problems inherent in Burchard's and Fink's perception of the textual transmission of *Aseneth*, and I argue that their reconstructions inevitably mislead scholarly conclusions about the creation and use of this narrative.

The Textual Witnesses of *Aseneth*

Burchard's classification of the textual witnesses has remained standard in the study of *Aseneth*, but in his 2003 critical edition, he slightly altered his former classification of the manuscripts that had dominated scholarship for over thirty years.[5] In the interest of clarity, I present the textual evidence below according to Burchard's most recent classification but I also identify the relationship between Burchard's 2003 and pre-2003 classifications. In addition, I present the textual units in the order that Burchard ranks them in terms of each units' usefulness for producing a reconstruction of the earliest *Aseneth* text. I highlight Burchard's position here so that the reader can understand the critiques of it that I will discuss in this chapter and the next. For every family unit, I also provide the abbreviation that Burchard uses in his critical edition, and I maintain the same abbreviations in this monograph.

For Burchard, the most valuable witnesses are the Syriac (Syr), Armenian (Arm), and a particular set of Latin versions of *Aseneth* (L2). The Syriac translation is the only manuscript known to provide a scribal reference to the narrative. Preserved in a church chronicle attributed to

---

5. Burchard, *Joseph und Aseneth*, 1–34.

Pseudo-Zacharias and composed by the mid-sixth century CE, the manuscript contains two letters that precede the text of *Aseneth*. The first letter reports that an anonymous person sent Moses of Aggel "a small book, very old, which was called 'Of Asyath' [or: '(book) of Asyath'], written in the Greek language," and asked that he translate and explain it. The second letter, which is damaged, preserves part of Moses's interpretation of the narrative.[6] Two Syriac manuscripts exist; MS 2071 (dated ca. 600 CE) provides a rather complete manuscript, although parts are missing due to folio damage (1:1–2:1a and 13:15 [after "in saptientia"] to 16:17 [before "et invenies"]), and MS 221 (dated to the twelfth or thirteenth centuries) is a copy of manuscript 2071 that also lacks 13:15–16:17.[7] Burchard suggests that the Armenian translation (Arm) of a Greek miniscule (Arm[Gr]) occurred between the tenth to eleventh centuries CE, during the "Golden Age" of Armenia, and he divides the Armenian witnesses into two groups: one manuscript (Arm[f] or MS 332) was copied from an Armenian exemplar that contained the pairing of *Aseneth* with a homily on the life of Joseph (referred to by Burchard as the LJos-JosAs archetype), and the remaining manuscripts (Arm[a–e, g–h], amounting to about forty-nine witnesses) descended from an Armenian exemplar that contained The Testament of the Twelve Patriarchs followed by LJos-JosAs (or the TestXII-LJos-JosAs subarchetype).[8] The actual Armenian manuscripts date from the thirteenth to the nineteenth centuries.[9] Finally, Burchard assigns a group of Latin manuscripts as "L2," which consists of (1) one manuscript (MS C 37) designated as "436," and (2) group 435&, composed of four manuscripts plus the primary witness (MS 136, designated as "435").[10]

---

6. Christoph Burchard, "Der jüdische Asenethroman und seine Nachwirkung: Von Egeria zu Anna Katharina Emmerick oder von Moses aus Aggel zu Karl Kerényi," *ANRW* 20.1:574–77; and Burchard, *Joseph und Aseneth*, 29.

7. Burchard, *Joseph und Aseneth*, 29. MS 221 provides 1:1–2a but lacks 26:6b–29:9.

8. For reference to Armenia's Golden Age, see Burchard, *Joseph und Aseneth*, 14. For the manuscripts, see Burchard, *A Minor Edition of the Armenian Version of 'Joseph and Aseneth,'* (Leuven: Peeters, 2010), 8–14; and Burchard, "Character and Origin of the Armenian Version of *Aseneth*," in *Apocryphes arméniens: Transmission— traduction—création—iconographie; actes du colloque international sur la littérature apocryphe en langue arménienne, Genève, 18–20 septembre, 1997*, ed. Valentina Calzolari Bourvier, Jean-Daniel Kaestli, and Bernard Outtier (Lausanne: Zèbre, 1999), 73–90. See also Burchard, *Joseph und Aseneth*, 11–15.

9. Burchard, *Joseph und Aseneth*, 3–6.

10. Burchard, *Joseph und Aseneth*, 7.

The L2 translation of a Greek miniscule (L2^{Gr}) could have occurred as early as the ninth century CE but, according to Burchard, certainly by the twelfth century, and the actual L2 witnesses date to the thirteenth century.[11] Fink provides a transcription of MS 436 and a reconstruction of MSS 435& in her critical edition of *Aseneth*.[12]

The next valuable set of textual witnesses for Burchard is family *f* (FWRum, GNgr, and L1), which is a new designation by Burchard.[13] He suggests that the ancestor of *f* was probably a miniscule, and it existed at the latest in the twelfth century but perhaps as early as the eleventh century.[14] Greek MS F and MS W date from the seventeenth century, but they attest to a longer form of *Aseneth* (as do Syr, Arm, L2 and perhaps Mc [see below]), and Burchard identifies MS F and MS W as the most significant witnesses of group *f*. The Romanian witnesses (Rum) reflect a condensed version of what FW provide, but the version was independent from FW and all three (F, W, and Rum) descended from a common text. The Romanian version, however, is text-critically useless.[15] The Greek MS G and MS Ngr (the latter in modern Greek) date from the sixteenth and seventeenth centuries and are heavily adapted, but they descend from an eleventh or twelfth century archetype that was roughly as long as the archetype of

---

11. Burchard, *Joseph und Aseneth*, 15–16. Burchard's hypothesis that L2^{Gr} was a miniscule is based on Bu 2:2, in which L2 reads *culmen*, a likely translation of ἡ κορυφή (attested in family *c* and Greek witness MS W). The other witnesses read ἡ ὀροφή. Burchard suggests that since in miniscules, the letters κ and η were easily confused (and not in majuscules), a transcriber wrote κορυφη in place of ἡ ὀροφη (Christoph Burchard, "Überleiferung, Gestalt und textkritischer Wert der zweiten lateinischen Übersetzung von Joseph und Aseneth," in *Religionsgeschichte des Neuen Testaments: Festschrift für Klaus Berger zum 60. Geburtsag*, ed. Axel von Dobbeler, Jurt Erlemann, and Roman Heiligenthal [Tübingen: Francke, 2000], 14; Burchard, *Joseph und Aseneth*, 16).

12. Fink, *Joseph und Aseneth*, 198–325.

13. As will be explained below, the former family *b* consisted of Syr, Arm, L2, *f*, and E.

14. Burchard, *Joseph und Aseneth*, 19. The eleventh century date is based on Gary K. Vikan's proposal that the miniature cycle preserved in G and Ngr descend from an archetype from the eleventh century in Constantinople (Vikan, "Illustrated Manuscripts of Pseudo-Ephraem's 'Life of Joseph' and the 'Romance of Aseneth'" [PhD diss., Princeton University, 1976]; Burchard, *Joseph und Aseneth*, 18). See also Burchard, "Ein neuer Versuch," 243.

15. Burchard, *Joseph und Aseneth*, 17, 19. See also Burchard, "Ein neuer Versuch," 239–40.

FWRum.¹⁶ Burchard identifies another group of Latin translations as "L1" (dating from the twelfth to the fourteenth centuries), and they descend from a modest, twelfth century translation of a Greek text (L1^Gr) that was orthographically poor and defective in places.¹⁷ In Burchard's opinion, the large gaps of the narrative in these Latin witnesses render L1 unhelpful, text-critically speaking.¹⁸

The fifth category of valuable witnesses consists solely of Greek MS E, which dates to the fifteenth century. Although MS E paraphrases often and exposes very long omissions, Burchard argues that it demonstrates links to a longer text like that of Syr, Arm, and L2, and possibly its archetype also shared commonalities with that of Mc.¹⁹ Burchard does not comment upon the likely date of E's exemplar, but Fink's stemma of the manuscript tradition suggests that the source of MS E was the same majuscule (or copy of it) from which, in Burchard's and her opinions, families *f*, Mc, *a*, and *d* descend.²⁰ As will be discussed in the next chapter, Burchard and Fink date this majuscule to the ninth or tenth centuries CE and Fink elevates the textual value of this witness.

These five manuscript classifications (Syr, Arm, L2, *f*, and E) constituted Burchard's former textual family *b*. Despite Burchard's reorganization of the manuscripts, his assigned textual value of the witnesses remains the same; for Burchard, these witnesses are still the most significant witnesses for reconstructing the earliest text, although as we will see, his reconstructed text does not always demonstrate his position.

---

16. MS G paraphrases and expands often as well as has several omissions. Ngr witness MS 671 also paraphrases by adding and omitting much, and Ngr witness MS 661 is an epitome that uses new words in its rendition (Burchard, *Joseph und Aseneth*, 17–18; Burchard, "Ein neuer Versuch," 239–40). They are as long as FWRum with the exception of having passage Bu 21:10–21, which in the Greek is only preserved in MSS F and W (Burchard, *Joseph und Aseneth*, 18; Burchard, "Ein neuer Versuch," 240).

17. Burchard, *Joseph und Aseneth*, 18–19; Burchard, "Ein neuer Versuch," 240.

18. Burchard, *Joseph und Aseneth*, 18–19.

19. Burchard, *Joseph und Aseneth*, 19–20. Burchard gives one example of the connection between MS E and the common denominator of Syr-Arm-L2: in Bu 9:1 of *Aseneth*, the witnesses attest to the following: 9:1 ἀσθμένουσα (<ἀσθμαίνουσα) E (Syr) (Arm) L2 against ἀσθενοῦσα FW, L1, Mc, *d*, and *a*; unattested in G (*Joseph und Aseneth*, 20).

20. Fink, *Joseph und Aseneth*, 17. Building on Burchard's assessment of MS E, Fink argues that it has been undervalued in the text-critical study of this narrative (26–28).

The sixth classification of manuscripts in Burchard's taxonomy is Mc (Greek witnesses HJK and the palimpsest M), and all but M date from the seventeenth to the nineteenth centuries. Up until recently Burchard contended that c ended at 16.17y, but Burfeind's examination of the eleventh century palimpsest (M) has changed his position.[21] The textual commonalities between c and M suggest that they are related, and since M seemed to have contained the entire narrative of *Aseneth*, the archetype of c likely had the longer narrative as well.[22] Burchard proposes that the archetype dates back to the eleventh century, and together with M, these witnesses descend from a common Greek miniscule that contained LJos-JosAs.[23] The relationship of Mc with the rest of the manuscripts is the most complex. Against families a and d (see below), Mc often correlates with all or some of the following witnesses: Syr, Arm, L2, f, and E; it especially corresponds with attestations in MS E and more significantly in the witnesses Syr, Arm and L2.[24] However, c and family a share many other readings in common, which complicates how best to understand

---

21. For ending at 16.17y, see Burchard, *Joseph und Aseneth*, 21. For his revised opinion, see Burfiend, "Der Text von *Joseph und Aseneth*." See also Fink, who reproduces the decipherable parts of palimpsest M in Greek (16:14–17:3; 18:7–21:4; 24:18–28:3; and 29:3–9; *Joseph und Aseneth*, 38–44).

22. Burchard, *Joseph und Aseneth*, 21.

23. Burchard, *Joseph und Aseneth*, 21–22. Burchard does not posit a date for the Mc Vorlage. The argument for the Vorlage of Mc being a miniscule is based on the same argument for L2^{Gr}. In 2:2, family c reads ἡ κορυφή when the dominant reading in the rest of the witnesses is ἡ ὀροφή. Common confusion in deciphering κ and η in miniscule script explains the different readings. For L2^{Gr}, see n. 11 above.

24. Burchard provides the following examples for the correspondence between (M)c and E: Bu 5:3; 13:15; and 15:1, 8. He cites the following examples regarding Mc correlations with Syr-Arm-L2: (1) Bu 2:8, where c (unreadable in M) has στρωμνήν, and Syr, Arm, and L2 have the plural form of this word in translation; (2) Bu 12:8, where Syr, Arm, L2, and Mc (with an absence in M probably due to homoioteleuton) share four phrases that otherwise are lacking or are present with gaps in the other witnesses; and (3) Bu 19:10, where the phrase attested in Syr, Arm, and L2 (in translation), τῷ νεύματι τῶν ὀφθαλμῶν αὐτοῦ, also is attested in M (in Greek) (Burchard, *Joseph und Aseneth*, 22; Burfeind, "Der Text von *Joseph und Aseneth*," 52–53). For (formerly) b-c attestations against a-d, see Burchard, "Zum Stand der Arbeit am Text von Joseph und Aseneth," in *Das Ende der Tage und die Gegenwart des Heils: Begegnungen mit dem Neuen Testament und seiner Umwelt*, ed. Michael Becker and Wolfgang Fenske, AGJU 44 (Boston: Brill, 1991), 16–24.

1. The Reconstructed Texts of *Aseneth*: Standhartinger and Kraemer   31

the transmission of Mc in comparison with the other witness groups.²⁵ For these reasons, Burchard (in theory) raises the significance of Mc in terms of its textual value in reconstructing the earliest retrievable text of *Aseneth*. Because of folio damage, the following parts of the narrative are lost in M: 14:14 (from τη ζωνη τη διπλη)–16:13 (ending at την χειρα του αγγελου); and 21:4 (from διοτι κυριος ο θεος του Ιωσηφ)–24:15 (ending at προστεταχας ημιν ακ).²⁶

The seventh valuable witness group is family *a* (Greek witnesses A, PQ, CR, and O), which consists of manuscripts that date from the tenth to the sixteenth centuries (MS A, dated to the eleventh/twelfth century is the best and longest witness).²⁷ Manuscripts P and Q (fifteenth century) were independent of A and probably shared a common ancestor; P is the second most textually valuable manuscript in this family.²⁸ Manuscripts C and R (fifteenth to sixteenth centuries) appear to be independent of each other, but they are also closely related textually speaking. Burchard surmises that they shared a common ancestor which was faulty and filled with gaps, but the ancestor nonetheless reflected a text (Textform) that was older than what the rest of the *a* manuscripts indicate (e.g., the archetype of CR apparently consisted of LJos-JosAs).²⁹ Manuscript O (tenth century) consists only of the title and incipit of the narrative; the title is similar to that of A and the incipit to that of Q.³⁰ Family *a* exhibits long gaps in two places and several small expansions, but most significantly *a* demonstrates an adaptation of the Greek syntax.³¹ There is a decrease of paratactical clauses connected by και and an increase in the use of other conjunctions or adverbs, subordinate clauses, and participial constructions.³² For Burchard, the archetype of *a* did not exhibit these Greek adaptations because

---

25. Burchard provides the following examples of *c* and *a* readings held in common: Bu 1:2, 5–6; 3:3; 5:5–6; 6:1; 7:5; 8:8; 9:2; 10:2; 11:4, 9, 13; 12:8; 13:11; 14:4; 16:9, 13; and 16:16x–17x (*Joseph und Aseneth*, 22).

26. Fink, *Joseph und Aseneth*, 34–36; Fink, "Anhang: Erläuterung zum Stemma," in Reinmuth, *Joseph und Aseneth*, 48–49.

27. Burchard, *Joseph und Aseneth*, 2 and 22.

28. Burchard, *Joseph und Aseneth*, 22. Q abbreviates much and exhibits many extra readings and gaps (22–23).

29. Burchard, *Joseph und Aseneth*, 23.

30. Burchard, *Joseph und Aseneth*, 22.

31. Burchard, *Joseph und Aseneth*, 23.

32. Although independent from *a* and each other, families Mc and L2 also reveal similar syntactical tendencies (Burchard, *Joseph und Aseneth*: L2 [15], Mc [21], *a* [23]).

it was also the ancestor of family *d*, which does not indicate these syntactical tendencies.³³ Since the oldest manuscripts (O and A) are menologia, Burchard suggests that the earliest form of *a* (i.e., lacking the Greek adaptations) was made for a menologium (of which MSS O and A were a part), and therefore it was written in miniscule script.³⁴ As for the origin of the Greek-adapted *a* tradition, Burchard surmises that it could have arisen in Byzantium during the "Macedonian Renaissance" (ca. 867–1081) when the production of hagiographies increased for both ecclesiastical and private use.³⁵ It is possible that at this stage, *a* had been reduced because it is shorter than *f*, Mc, Syr, Arm, and L2 but longer than *d*.³⁶

The final witness group, and therefore the least textually valuable in Burchard's opinion, is family *d* (BD and Slav). Greek MS B (eleventh century) is in a hagiographical collection, and Burchard suggests that it could have been contaminated by scribal reference to a witness from the *a* family.³⁷ Fink has since provided more extensive evidence that demonstrates the likelihood of the ancestor of MS A (what Fink designates as Vorfahr λ) being used in the production of the ancestor of M B (Vorfahr ξ).³⁸ Greek MS D (fifteenth century) exhibits Modern Greek influences (which Burchard contends does not go back to the *d* archetype), and it also contains the sequence LJos-JosAs.³⁹ Although B and D differ in details in several places and vary in gaps, they apparently share a common ancestor that existed no later than the eleventh century and contained LJos-JosAs.⁴⁰ The Slavic manuscripts (551 and 552, dated to the fifteenth century) are longer than BD, and their extensions match what other witnesses support (e.g., 21:2–8) but their exemplar had larger gaps than what B and D demonstrate.⁴¹ The Greek *Vorlage* of the Slavic witnesses (Slav^Gr) descended

---

33. Burchard, *Joseph und Aseneth*, 23.
34. Burchard, *Joseph und Aseneth*, 23–24. Explained and less confidently stated in Burchard, "Der jüdische Asenethroman," 563.
35. Burchard, *Joseph und Aseneth*, 23–24.
36. Burchard, *Joseph und Aseneth*, 23.
37. Burchard cites 12:2 and 14:6 as examples (*Joseph und Aseneth*, 24).
38. Fink, *Joseph und Aseneth*, 53–57. Fink includes Bu 14:6, but not 12:2 in her evidence.
39. Burchard, *Joseph und Aseneth*, 24.
40. Burchard, *Joseph und Aseneth*, 24.
41. Burchard, *Joseph und Aseneth*, 24.

independently from the same ancestor of B and D and also supposedly contained LJos-JosAs.[42]

These eight manuscript categories (Syr, Arm, L2, *f*, E, Mc, *a*, and *d*) represent the viable textual evidence of *Aseneth*, and Burchard has slightly altered his original classifications based on the decipherment of palimpsest M and on reconsiderations from comparing the witness units (such as between Syr/Arm/L2 and *f* or Syr/Arm/L2 and E). Yet despite his reassessment of the evidence, Burchard has made few changes to his reconstructed text, and as we will see, his ranking of the witnesses in terms of their respective value has not altered in any significant way. Previous debates about identifying the earliest, retrievable text, then, still pertain to Burchard's work. Most pressing is the question about which reconstruction—Burchard's, Fink's slight alteration of Burchard's, or Philonenko's—represents the earliest, retrievable text. To best address this debate, I will review the major text-critical arguments in chronological order. In the next sections of this chapter, I will review Philonenko's and Burchard's (original) positions, and then I will address the significant contributions of Standhartinger and Kraemer. For this chapter, I will be referring to the witnesses in terms that Burchard had initially classified them, since these were the terms that Philonenko, Burchard, Standhartinger, and Kraemer had used (see "Pre-2003 Critical Edition Classifications" in table 1.1). In the next chapter, I will address Burchard's revision of his position and Fink's adaptation of Burchard's reconstruction. For that chapter and the remainder of the monograph, I will refer to the witnesses according to Burchard's 2003 classifications (see table 1.1 on page 34).

The Reconstructions of Burchard and Philonenko

Up until 2003, Burchard had placed his primary textual witnesses into one category, family *b*. As the next chapter will demonstrate, Burchard ultimately became convinced that translated versions in family *b* (Syr, Arm, and L2) were the most reliable in constructing the earliest retrievable text of *Aseneth*, but in his early work, he had focused on all the witnesses of family *b*, as demonstrated in his preliminary work on reconstructing the narrative in 1965.[43] At that time, previous scholarly publications of

---

42. Burchard, *Joseph und Aseneth*, 24–25.
43. Burchard, *Untersuchungen zu Joseph und Aseneth*.

Table 1.1. Burchard's classification of the textual evidence of *Aseneth*

Pre-2003 Critical Edition Classifications	2003 Critical Edition Classifications
Family *b* =	Syr
Syr	Arm
Arm	L2
L2	Family *f* = FW, G, Ngr, and L1
FW, G, and Ngr (Greek)	E
L1	
E (Greek)	
Family *c* = HJK (Greek)	Family M*c* = HJK and palimpsest M (Greek)
Family *a* = A, CR, O, PQ (Greek)	Family *a* = A, CR, O, PQ
Family *d* = BD (Greek) and Slav	Family *d* = BD and Slav

Aseneth had not incorporated many of the *b* manuscripts, such as Batiffol's edition, which focused on family *a*, and V. M. Istrin's edition of family *d*.[44] For Burchard, families *a*, *d*, and *c* represented later developments in the transmission of *Aseneth*, with *a* reflecting what was farthest away from the

---

44. Batiffol was the first to publish a full Greek text of *Aseneth* ("ΠΡΟΣΕΥΧΗ ΑΣΕΝΕΘ," in *Le Livre de la Prière d'Aseneth*, 1–87). He primarily based his translation on MS A from Burchard's later classification family *a*. Batiffol also supplied attestations from Burchard's family *d* in his apparatus, and he provided a Latin text of *Aseneth* that became classified by Burchard in his category L1, which was also in Burchard's family *b* (Batiffol, "Liber de Aseneth," in *Le Livre de la Prière d'Aseneth*, 89–115). Istrin's Greek edition printed the Palatine Greek manuscript (or MS B) of the *d* group and a modern Greek manuscript (Bodlein Library, Oxford, MS Roe 5, 1614), and he supplies variant readings of one manuscript in the *a* group (MS Q, Vatican Library, Vatican City, MS Palatinus Graecus 364, fifteenth century) ("Aprokrif ob Iosefě i Asenefě," in *Drevnosti: Trudy slavjanskoj kommissii imperatorskago moskovskago archeologičeskago obščestva* [Moscow: Lissner & Geschel, 1898]). Chesnutt notes that "this text had negligible impact on the study of *Aseneth*, in part because of the scathing review in Germany (K. Krumbacher, *ByzZ* 8 [1899]: 22–23) and in part because it was published in Moscow under a Russian title so that it was never as widely known nor as readily accessible in Western Europe as Batiffol's text" (*From Death to Life*, 25 n. 40). Burchard criticized Istrin's edition of the modern Greek manuscript and published his own edition of this witness ("Joseph und Aseneth neugriechisch," *NTS* 24 [1977]: 68–79).

earliest text; *d* presenting a condensed form of that; and *c* being designated as the least helpful of the three since this family preserved the narrative only up to Bu 16:17y.⁴⁵ Burchard's initial reconstruction also depended on attestations from manuscript families other than family *b* when he deemed those readings superior.⁴⁶ Most notable was (and is) his reliance on family *a* when it stands in contrast with family *b*, and as we will see in this chapter and the next, several arguments have been made against this reliance. Burchard published his full reconstructed text in 1979 and provided German and English translations shortly thereafter.⁴⁷

In 1968, Philonenko agreed with Burchard's initial arrangement of the textual witnesses (families *a*, *b*, *c*, and *d*) but presented a different chronological order of the transmission history. Philonenko argued that family *d* preserves the oldest rendition of *Aseneth*, and families *b*, *c*, and *a* represent longer recensions that were produced sequentially (thus, *b* is a revision of *d*; *c* is a revision of *b*; and *a* is a revision of *c*).⁴⁸ Philonenko presented his reconstructed text as an attempt to produce the most ancient text (therefore, the ancestor of family *d*), but he admitted that he had incorporated readings from the other families when he considered those readings to preserve what the *d* ancestor most likely had provided.⁴⁹

In 1970, Burchard responded to Philonenko's assessment and defended his own position, which dominated *Aseneth* scholarship for over twenty years.⁵⁰ In 1987, Burchard summarized his and Philonenko's conclusions in the following way. In the comment below, Burchard presumes that the family groups of *a*, *b*, *c*, and *d* derived from hypothetical text-forms α, β, ζ, and δ, which all descended from a common text (ω).

> Philonenko opines that δ comes closest to ω. It is about one third shorter than α and even more than the other two families. 11:1x–18, most of chs. 18 and 19, 21:10–21 (read by some **b** witnesses only), 22:6–9a and

---

45. Articulated most succinctly in Burchard, "Zum Text von 'Joseph und Aseneth,'" 3–34.

46. Burchard first discusses this approach in his monograph, *Untersuchungen zu Joseph und Aseneth*, 18–23, 45–49.

47. Burchard, "Ein vorläufiger griechischer Text," 2–53; Burchard, *Unterweisung in erzählender Form*, 631–720; and Burchard, "Joseph and Aseneth," 177–247.

48. Philonenko, *Joseph et Aséneth*, 3–26.

49. Philonenko, *Joseph et Aséneth*, 23–26.

50. Burchard, "Zum Text von 'Joseph und Aseneth,'" 3–34. See also Chesnutt, *From Death to Life*, 65–69.

> a series of verses and clauses extending over the whole range of the narrative are lacking.... Philonenko proceeded to reconstruct a critical text on the base of δ touching it up now and then with the aid of other witnesses, mainly of the b group. The outcome is not quite what it might have been. Philonenko ought to have made more of the Serbo-Slavonic ["Slav"] which he himself admits is often superior to the two Greek manuscripts. Furthermore, if the b group is an offshoot of δ or a related text which branched off very early, it should have been taken into account in a systematical way, after some effort to determine the original β and its *Vorlage*. Finally, whereas Philonenko registers all variants from the d group he is eclectic as to the rest. Most of the excess matter from β, ζ, and α over against δ does not appear in the apparatus. So his reconstruction cannot be judged on his edition alone.[51]

In the same article, Burchard began to raise reservations about his configuration of family *b*, but he remained convinced that *b* preserves readings that are superior to what is found in the *d* family. In the 1990s, Standhartinger and Kraemer revived Philonenko's critique of whether *b* or *d* preserve the earliest readings, and their arguments remain pertinent because Burchard's recent dissolution of family *b* does not change much his prioritization of Syr, Arm, L2, *f*, and E manuscripts (the formerly designated *b* family).[52] For the most part, Burchard depends upon the same witnesses as he did before. Both Standhartinger and Kraemer construct their positions by comparing the reconstructed texts of Burchard and Philonenko, presuming that, in general, Burchard's text favors the *b* readings and Philonenko's text favors the *d* readings. The next two sections outline important challenges raised by Standhartinger and Kraemer and address the limitations of their arguments.

The Revival of Philonenko's Reconstruction: Standhartinger's Analysis

In her monograph, *Das Frauenbild im Judentum der hellenistischen Zeit: ein Beitrag anhand von "Joseph und Aseneth,"* Standhartinger reviews the textual problems of both Philonenko's and Burchard's reconstructions.

---

51. Christoph Burchard, "The Present State of Research on Joseph and Aseneth," in *Religion, Literature, and Society in Ancient Israel, Formative Christianity and Judaism*, ed. Jacob Neusner, NPAJ 1–2 (Lanham, MD: University Press of America, 1987), 2:33 (emphasis original).

52. Which Burchard admits, *Joseph und Aseneth*, 11, 47–48.

Although she agrees with Philonenko's assessment about the precedence of the *d* family, she identifies inconsistencies in his reconstruction and she presents a cautious approach by limiting the extent to which she uses both reconstructions. After establishing her texts, Standhartinger argues that Burchard's reconstruction reveals alterations to the characterization of Aseneth as presented in Philonenko's reconstruction, and each text's respective portrayal of the female reflects Second Temple ideas.[53] But as we will see, the dependence on reconstructions alone restricts Standhartinger's examination; the individual witnesses portray even more alterations to the story than what the reconstructions suggest. In this section, I will review Standhartinger's critique of Philonenko's text; she builds upon other scholars' evaluations but also highlights the problem of reconstructed texts which few scholars of *Aseneth* seem to appreciate. Then I will discuss Standhartinger's argument that *d* is not an abridgment of the longer narrative of family *a*; this is a fundamental position for those who advocate for the priority of *d* against Burchard's preference for *b*. When examining the individual textual witnesses, and not just the manuscript families, it becomes clear that Standhartinger's position cannot be defended, but I will argue that Burchard's (and now also Fink's) position is not definitive either. The relationship between families *d*, *a*, and *b*, whether close or distant, does not get us closer to the earliest *Aseneth* text.

In agreement with previous critics, Standhartinger outlines how Philonenko's text of *Aseneth* does not correlate with the stated purpose of his work, which was to reconstruct the earliest form of the *d* family group.[54] In a number of places, Philonenko disregarded the witnesses of the *d* family and instead selected verses from other witnesses or even ignored the attestations in *d*. Some of these changes made sense (alterations based on grammatical, orthographical, or stylistic reasons), but some were untenable, as in the case of Ph 10:15 where Philonenko omit-

---

53. See Standhartinger's summary of her findings, *Das Frauenbild im Judentum*, 205–39.

54. Philonenko states, "Notre ambition n'est donc pas de reconstituer un texte original, tentative utopique à nos yeux, mais seulement d'établir, autant que faire se peut, le texte de la recension la plus ancienne, le texte court" (*Joseph et Aséneth*, 23). Standhartinger's argument can be found in *Das Frauenbild im Judentum*, 42–45; and a similar argument was also made by Holtz, "Rezension zu Philonenko," 49–55; to which Standhartinger refers (*Das Frauenbild im Judentum*, 45 n. 211); and Brock, review of *Joseph et Aséneth*, 588–91. Burchard makes a similar point in his critique, "Present State of Research," 33.

ted δέρρις against BD for no apparent reason (Slav does not attest to this phrase).⁵⁵ Philonenko's text reads: καὶ μετὰ ταῦτα ἔλαβε τὴν τέφραν καὶ κατέχεεν αὐτὴν ἐπὶ τὸ ἔδαφος ("and after these matters, she took the ashes and poured them on the floor"), but MS B attests to τὴν τέφραν τῆς δέρρις and MS D attests to τὴν δέρριν τῆς τέφρας.⁵⁶ In contrast, Burchard's text (10:14) reads: καὶ μετὰ ταῦτα ἔλαβεν Ἀσενὲθ <u>τὴν δέρριν τῆς τέφρας</u> καὶ κατέχεεν αὐτὴν ἐπὶ τὸ ἔδαφος ("and after these matters, Aseneth took <u>the leather (curtain) of ashes</u> and poured it on the floor"). Either a curtain or hide full of ashes is attested in the following witnesses: families *b* (specifically, Arm, L2, Syr, *f* [MSS FW, G, and L1]), *c*, *a*, and *d* (MSS B and D mentioned above).⁵⁷ Given the common rendering of δέρρις within family *d* (and not just across the textual families), Philonenko needed to defend why he chose to leave it out of his reconstruction.

Most problematic in Philonenko's reconstruction are the places where his disregard for BDSlav and dependence upon the other witnesses inevitably altered the meaning of the *d* narrative. At these times, Standhartinger argues, Philonenko seemed more interested in reconstructing the earliest text of *Aseneth* based on *all* the witnesses instead of just focusing on the *d* tradition.⁵⁸ Philonenko should have first considered the content of a possible form of the *d* ancestor, that it was an understandable text in and of itself, before comparing the witnesses of *d* with other textual groups. According to Standhartinger, the following verses are problematic alterations of the *d* tradition (all Philonenko's versification): 1:7; 8:5; 8:10; 15:4; 15:7; 21:3; 28:2.⁵⁹ Using Ph 15:4 (Bu 15:5) as an example, the following chart displays Philonenko's text, and the particular readings from the BDSlav witnesses:⁶⁰

---

55. Standhartinger, *Das Frauenbild im Judentum*, 43–44 n. 209. Standhartinger lists the following examples as sensible alterations: Ph 15:6 (grammatical reason), Ph 1:14 (orthographical reason), and Ph 9:1 (stylistic reason). See also Burchard, *Joseph und Aseneth*, 136 (Ph 10:15 = Bu 10:14).

56. Philonenko, *Joseph et Aséneth*, 164. Unless otherwise noted, all translations into English are mine.

57. Burchard, *Joseph und Aseneth*, 136–37.

58. Standhartinger, *Das Frauenbild im Judentum*, 42 n. 206.

59. Standhartinger, *Das Frauenbild im Judentum*, 43–45 n. 210. For no apparent reason, she deletes 15:4 from her list in "From Fictional Text to Socio-historical Context," 304 n. 11.

60. If none of my main sources for the textual evidence suggest otherwise (see introduction), I assume that B, D, and Slav share the same reading of the passage in question. When one witness is distinguished from the other two, I assume that

1. The Reconstructed Texts of *Aseneth*: Standhartinger and Kraemer 39

Ph 15:4	D	B	Slav
ἰδοὺ ἀπὸ τῆς σήμερον ἀνακαινισθήσῃ καὶ ἀναπλασθήσῃ	ἰδοὺ ἀπὸ τῆς σήμερον ἀνακαινισθήσῃ	ἰδοὺ ἀπὸ τὴν σήμερον ἀνακαινισθήσῃ	ἰδοὺ ἀπὸ τὴν σήμερον ἀνακαινισθήσῃ
καὶ ἀναζωοποιηθήσῃ καὶ φάγῃ ἄρτον ζωῆς	καὶ ζωοποιηθήσῃ φαγεῖς ἄρτον ζωῆς	καὶ ἀναζωοποιηθήσῃ καὶ φάγῃ ἄρτον ζωῆς	καὶ ἀναζωοποιηθήσῃ [you will eat][61] ἄρτον ζωῆς
καὶ πίεσαι ποτήριον	καὶ πιεῖς ποτήριον	καὶ πίεσαι ποτήριον	[and you will drink][61] ποτήριον
ἀθανασίας καὶ χρισθήσῃ χρίσματι τῆς ἀφθαρσίας	τῆς ἀφθαρσίας	ζωῆς ἀφθάρτου	ἰατρείας (MS 551) [(of) immortality (MS 552)][62]

The witnesses of BDSlav do not attest to ἀναπλάσσω ("to form anew"), ἀθανασία ("immortality"), other than in Slav MS 552, apparently, or any suggestion of ointment, but for some reason Philonenko included these portions from other textual family groups.[63] The MS 552 read-

---

the other two read the same or a similar passage, unless it is noted otherwise. As for the presentation of the Slavonic version, the Greek equivalent is given when provided in Philonenko's or Burchard's annotations; otherwise, an English translation is provided.

61. According to Burchard, Slav agrees with BD in these places (he lists "manducabis" and "bibes" for Slav; *Joseph und Asenath*, 189). Philonenko does not offer what the Slavonic version reads.

62. Philonenko (*Joseph et Asénath*, 182) provides the reading from the Slavonic witness, MS 551, according to Burchard (*Joseph und Asenath*, 190). Perhaps MS 552 translated ἀθανασίας, but Burchard does not speculate on this point.

63. Standhartinger, *Das Frauenbild im Judentum*, 43–45, especially n. 209. Burchard also notes that Philonenko's reconstruction of this phrase is questionable (marking Philonenko's attestation with an asterisk [Phil*] (*Joseph und Asenath*, 189). The word ἀθανασία is attested in the following witnesses: Arm, 436 (from L2), FW, E, *c*, A(P), and Slav MS 552 (see preceding note). Manuscripts F and W, however, appear to use this word to modify ἄρτον; there is no blessed cup to drink from in these witnesses.

ing, "of immortality," was not clear in the critical editions prior to Burchard's 2003 critical edition (which came out after Standhartinger's book), but Standhartinger's critique still holds since Philonenko only cites ἰατρείας as the Slavonic attestation.[64] He, too, apparently did not think that the Slavonic witnesses attested to a translation of ἀθανασία. Philonenko seemed to add the verb ἀναπλάσσω in 8:11 (Bu 8:9) as well to provide the threefold verbal blessing again (ἀνακαίνισον ... ἀνάπλασον ... ἀναζωοποίησον; "renew ... form anew ... restore to life"), but BDSlav only provide ἀνακαίνισον in that verse.[65] Philonenko inserts these additions into his reconstruction for unidentified reasons.[66] He appears to be searching for the underlying common text of all the witnesses, and his non-*d* additions to these verses weaken his argument that the *d* family is not an abbreviated tradition of *Aseneth*.[67]

Philonenko's rendition of *Asen.* 1:7 (Bu: 1:5) reveals another dependence upon non-*d* witnesses that changes the portrayal of Aseneth. Philonenko's text and the BDSlav witnesses read as follows:[68]

Ph 1:7	D	B	Slav
καὶ αὕτη οὐδένα εἶχεν ὅμοιον τῶν θυγατέρων τῶν Αἰγυπτίων	καὶ αὐτὴ οὐδένα εἶχεν ὅμοιον τῶν θυγατέρων τῶν Αἰγυπτίων καὶ	καὶ αὐτὴ οὐδένα εἶχεν ὅμοιον τῶν θυγατέρων τῶν Αἰγυπτίων καὶ	[because no one was similar to her][69] τῶν θυγατέρων τῶν Αἰγυπτίων καὶ

L1 reads *incorruptionis* and MS G reads εὐλογημένον only (i.e., "blessed cup"). Anointing with ointment appears in Arm, 436 (from L2), G, L1, *c*, and AP, but it is lacking in 435& (from L2), FW, E, Q, and *d* (the Syriac attestation for this verse is missing) (Burchard, *Joseph und Aseneth*, 189).

64. Philonenko, *Joseph et Aséneth*, 182.

65. Burchard, *Joseph und Aseneth*, 120; Philonenko, *Joseph et Aséneth*, 158; and Standhartinger, *Das Frauenbild im Judentum*, 44–45 n. 210. Both families *d* and *a* lack the phrase, καὶ ἀνάπλασον αὐτὴν τῇ χειρί σου τῇ κρυφαίᾳ καὶ ἀναζωοποίησον αὐτὴν τῇ ζωῇ σου. Greek MSS E and G (of former family *b*) also lack this phrase.

66. Standhartinger, *Das Frauenbild im Judentum*, 44–45 n. 210.

67. Many have offered a similar critique; see Brock, review of *Joseph et Aséneth*, 588–91; Smith, review of *Joseph et Aséneth*, 257; and Chesnutt, *From Death to Life*, 66.

68. For more details, see Burchard, *Joseph und Aseneth*, 72–73.

69. According to Burchard, the Slavonic version reads some form of "denn keine war ähnlich ihr von" (*Joseph und Aseneth*, 72).

1. The Reconstructed Texts of *Aseneth*: Standhartinger and Kraemer

Ph 1:7	D	B	Slav
ἀλλὰ ἦν κατὰ πάντα ὁμοία ταῖς θυγατράσι			
τῶν Ἑβραίων	τῶν Ἑβραίων	τῶν Ἑβραίων	τῶν Ἑβραίων

Not attested in BDSlav, the modifying clause, ἀλλὰ ἦν κατὰ πάντα ὁμοία ταῖς θυγατράσι ("but was in every way like the daughters [of the Hebrews]"), alters the meaning of the verse and should be discarded from a reconstruction of the earliest *d* text.[70] This phrase is attested in the majority of the textual families, but clearly not in *d*.[71] Philonenko most likely added this clause to make sense of the next line (1:8/Bu 1:5): καὶ ἦν μεγάλη ὡς Σάρρα καὶ ὡραία ὡς Ῥεβέκκα καὶ καλὴ ὡς Ῥαχήλ ("and she was tall like Sarah, attractive like Rebecca and beautiful like Rachel"). He possibly concluded that the discord between 1:7 and 1:8 in BDSlav is illogical, and so he added the clause from other textual families to resolve the problem. In these cases, however, more consideration of the possible meaning in BDSlav is needed before smoothing out the perceived inconsistencies in the text. I would add that the reading of BDSlav makes sense within the storyline of *Aseneth*. Within the logic of the narrative, it is fitting that the woman who would soon marry Joseph would be "in no way like Egyptian and Hebrew women" but stunning like the Hebrew matriarchs. Greek MS G (of Burchard's family *b*) provides a similar rendering. Aseneth is neither like the Egyptians nor the Hebrews, but she is associated with Sarah, Rebecca, and Rachel as well.[72]

---

70. Standhartinger, *Das Frauenbild im Judentum*, 44 n. 210.

71. The following witnesses attest to some form of Ph 1:7/Bu 1:5: Arm, L2 (435&), FW, L1, *c* (and possibly M), and *a*. Manuscript E presents the following for the entire verse: μὴ διαφέρουσα ταῖς αἰγυπτίαις ἀλλὰ μᾶλλον ταῖς θυγατράσι τῶν Ἑβραίων; and Syriac and Latin MS 436 (from L2) lack any part of this phrase (Burchard, *Joseph und Aseneth*, 73).

72. For the same line in Ph 1:7/Bu 1:5, MS G reads: οὐδεμίαν αὐτῆς ὅμοιαν ἦχεν ποτὲ ἐν αἰγύπτῳ ἐκ τῶν θυγατέρων τῶν μεγιστάνων γῆς αἰγύπτου οὐδὲ ἦν ὅμοια αὐτῆς εἰς τὰς θυγατέρας τῶν Ἑβραίων, and then in the next verse it retains some form of the line: καὶ ἦν μεγάλη ὡς Σάρρα καὶ ὡραία ὡς Ῥεβέκκα καὶ καλὴ ὡς Ῥαχήλ (Burchard, *Joseph und Aseneth*, 73). This example complicates Fink's theory that an exemplar of G (what she calls "Vorfahr ρ") contaminated the Greek *Vorlage* of Slav. She lists sev-

Standhartinger restricts how she uses Philonenko's reconstruction, and she explicitly deletes the non-*d* material from the most problematic passages cited above.[73] She also raises concerns about the two places in Philonenko's edition where he had reconstructed portions solely from the Slavonic version (portions of Ph 21:2–7 and 27:8 [Bu 21:4–8 and 27:10–11, respectively]).[74] The example from chapter 21 highlights further difficulties not only in Philonenko's reconstruction but also in Standhartinger's argument about the ranking of *d*. The following presents the attestations for this pericope from chapter 21:[75]

Ph 21:1–8	Slav	B	D
(1)			
Καὶ ἀνέστη Ἰωσὴφ τῷ πρωῒ καὶ ἀπῆλθε πρὸς Φαραὼ καὶ ἐλάλησεν αὐτῷ περὶ Ἀσενέθ.	Καὶ ἀνέστη Ἰωσὴφ τῷ πρωῒ καὶ ἀπῆλθε πρὸς Φαραὼ καὶ ἐλάλησεν αὐτῷ περὶ Ἀσενέθ.	Καὶ ἀνέστη Ἰωσὴφ τῷ πρωῒ καὶ ἀπῆλθε πρὸς Φαραὼ	Καὶ ἀνέστη πρωῒ ὁ Ἰωσὴφ καὶ ἀπῆλθε πρὸς Φαραὼ
(2)			
Καὶ ἀπέστειλε Φαραὼ καὶ ἐκάλεσε τὸν Πεντεφρῆ καὶ τὴν Ἀσενέθ.	Καὶ ἀπέστειλε Φαραὼ καὶ ἐκάλεσε τὸν Πεντεφρῆ καὶ τὴν Ἀσενέθ.		καὶ ἐκάλεσε Φαραὼ τὸν Πεντεφρῆ καὶ τὴν Ἀσενέθ
(3)			
Καὶ ἐθαμβήθη Φαραὼ ἐπὶ τῷ κάλλει αὐτῆς καὶ εἶπεν· εὐλογήσει σε κύριος ὁ θεὸς	Καὶ ἐθαμβήθη Φαραὼ ἐπὶ τῷ κάλλει αὐτῆς καὶ εἶπεν· εὐλογήσει σε κύριος ὁ θεὸς		

---

eral examples that demonstrate this possibility (*Joseph und Aseneth*, 57–63), but she does not explain the similarities that MS G shares with BDSlav in Bu 1:5/Ph 1:7 noted above.

73. Standhartinger, *Das Frauenbild im Judentum*, 45.
74. Standhartinger, *Das Frauenbild im Judentum*, 45.
75. For more details, see Burchard, *Joseph und Aseneth*, 256–63.

1. The Reconstructed Texts of *Aseneth*: Standhartinger and Kraemer

Ph 21:1-8	Slav	B	D
τοῦ Ἰωσήφ, ὃς ἐξελέξατό σε εἰς νύμφην αὐτοῦ, ὅτι	τοῦ Ἰσραήλ, ὃς ἐξελέξατό σε εἰς νύμφην αὐτῷ, ὅτι		
αὐτός ἐστιν ὁ υἱὸς τοῦ θεοῦ ὁ πρωτότοκος καὶ			
ἡ θυγάτηρ τοῦ ὑψίστου κληθήσει καὶ Ἰωσὴφ ἔσται σου νυμφίος εἰς τὸν αἰῶνα χρόνον.	σὺ ἡ θυγάτηρ τοῦ ὑψίστου κληθήσῃ καὶ Ἰωσὴφ ἔσται [to you][76] νυμφίος εἰς τὸν αἰῶνα χρόνον.		
(4-6) Καὶ ἔλαβε Φαραὼ στεφάνους χρυσοῦς καὶ ἔπεθηκε ἐπὶ τὰς κεφαλὰς αὐτῶν καὶ εἶπεν· εὐλογήσει	Καὶ ἔλαβε Φαραὼ στεφάνους χρυσοῦς καὶ ἔπεθηκε ἐπὶ τὰς κεφαλὰς αὐτῶν καὶ εἶπε Φαραώ· εὐλογήσει		
ὑμᾶς ὁ θεὸς ὁ ὕψιστος καὶ πληθυνεῖ ὑμᾶς εἰς τὸν αἰῶνα χρόνον.	ὑμᾶς ὁ θεὸς ὁ ὕψιστος καὶ πληθυνεῖ ὑμᾶς εἰς τὸν αἰῶνα χρόνον.		
Καὶ ἀπέστρεψεν αὐτοὺς Φαραὼ πρὸς ἀλλήλους καὶ κατεφίλησαν ἀλλήλους.	Καὶ [(he) turned one to another][77] καὶ κατεφίλησαν ἀλλήλους.		

---

76. Burchard translates the Slavonic version here as "dir," so supposedly reading σοι of a Greek witness (*Joseph und Aseneth*, 259).

77. Burchard translates the Slavonic version here as "[er] wandte um einen zu[r] anderen" (*Joseph und Aseneth*, 261 n. 21.6).

Ph 21:1-8	Slav	B	D
Καὶ ἐποίησε Φαραὼ γάμους αὐτῶν καὶ δεῖπνον καὶ πότον πολὺν ἐν ἡμέραις ἑπτά.	Καὶ ἐποίησε [them]⁷⁸ Φαραὼ γάμους καὶ δεῖπνον καὶ πότον [great]⁷⁹ [after seven days].⁸⁰		
(7) Καὶ ἐκάλεσε πάντας τοὺς ἄρχοντας τῆς γῆς Αἰγύπτου καὶ ἐκήρυξε λέγων·	Καὶ συνεκάλεσε πάντας τοὺς ἄρχοντας τῆς γῆς Αἰγύπτου [and he issued a command, saying]:⁸¹		καὶ ἐπιφωνήθη Φαραὼ λέγων·
πᾶς ἄνθρωπος ὃς ποιήσει ἔργον ἐν ταῖς ἑπτὰ ἡμέραις τοῦ γάμου τοῦ Ἰωσὴφ καὶ τῆς Ἀσενὲθ	πᾶς ἄνθρωπος ὃς τις ποιήσει ἔργον ἐν ταῖς ἑπτὰ ἡμέραις τοῦ γάμου τοῦ Ἰωσὴφ καὶ τῆς Ἀσενὲθ [or works a little]⁸²	πᾶς ἄνθρωπος ὃς ποιήσει ἔργον ἐν ταῖς ἑπτὰ ἡμέραις τοῦ γάμου Ἰωσὴφ καὶ τῆς Ἀσενὲθ	ὅτι εἴ τις ἄνθρωπος ποιήσει ἔργον ἐν ταῖς ἑπτὰ ἡμέραις τοῦ γάμου τοῦ Ἰωσὴφ καὶ τῆς Ἀσενὲθ
θανάτῳ πικρῷ ἀποθανεῖται.	θανάτῳ πικρῷ ἀποθανεῖται ὁ ἄνθρωπος ἐκεῖνος.	θανάτῳ ἀποθανεῖται πικρῷ ὁ ἄνθρωπος ἐκεῖνος.	θανάτῳ πικρῷ ἀποθανεῖται

78. Burchard translates the Slavonic as "ihnen" (*Joseph und Aseneth*, 262 n. 21.8).
79. Burchard provides "magnam" (*Joseph und Aseneth*, 262 n. 21.8).
80. Burchard is uncertain about the adverb "after" in the Slavonic version ("nach [?] 7 Tagen") (*Joseph und Aseneth*, 262 n. 21.8).
81. Burchard provides "und erließ Befehl sagend" (*Joseph und Aseneth*, 262 n. 21.8).
82. Burchard notes that the Slavonic version adds "oder arbeitet etwas" (*Joseph und Aseneth*, 263 n. 21.8).

Ph 21:1-8	Slav	B	D
(8) Καὶ γενομένων τῶν γάμων καὶ τοῦ δείπνου τελεσθέντος εἰσῆλθεν Ἰωσὴφ πρὸς Ἀσενὲθ καὶ συνέλαβεν Ἀσενὲθ ἐκ τοῦ Ἰωσήφ. Καὶ ἔτεκε τὸν Μανασσῆ καὶ τὸν Ἐφραὶμ τὸν ἀδελφὸν αὐτοῦ ἐν τῷ οἴκῳ Ἰωσήφ.	Καὶ γενομένων τῶν γάμων καὶ τοῦ δείπνου τελεσθέντος [and] εἰσῆλθεν Ἰωσὴφ πρὸς Ἀσενὲθ [and (she) conceived]⁸³ʰ ἐκ τοῦ Ἰωσήφ. ἔτεκε τὸν Μανασσῆ καὶ τὸν Ἐφραὶμ τὸν ἀδελφὸν αὐτοῦ ἐν τῷ οἴκῳ Ἰωσήφ.	Καὶ γενομένων τῶν γάμων καὶ τοῦ δείπνου τελεσθέντος εἰσῆλθεν Ἰωσὴφ πρὸς Ἀσενὲθ καὶ συνέλαβεν Ἀσενὲθ ἐκ τοῦ Ἰωσήφ. καὶ ἔτεκε τὸν Μανασσῆ καὶ τὸν Ἐφραὶμ τὸν ἀδελφὸν αὐτοῦ ἐν τῷ οἴκῳ Φαρα.	Καὶ γινομένων τῶν γάμων καὶ τοῦ δείπνου τελεσθέντος εἰσῆλθεν Ἰωσὴφ πρὸς Ἀσενὲθ καὶ συνέλαβεν Ἀσενὲθ ἐκ τοῦ Ἰωσήφ. καὶ ἔτεκε τὸν Μανασσῆ καὶ τὸν Ἐφραὶμ τὸν ἀδελφὸν αὐτοῦ ἐν τῷ οἴκῳ Ἰωσήφ.

Philonenko depended heavily on the Slavonic version, and Standhartinger questions his addition to verse 3 (Bu 21:4) with a phrase that is mostly attested in witnesses from family *b* (αὐτός ἐστιν ὁ υἱὸς τοῦ θεοῦ ὁ πρωτότοκος καί, "he is the firstborn son of God and").[84] In the same verse, Philonenko ignored the Slavic attestation, εὐλογήσει σε κύριος ὁ θεὸς τοῦ Ἰσραήλ ("May the Lord God of Israel bless you"), and instead provided, εὐλογήσει σε κύριος ὁ θεὸς τοῦ Ἰωσήφ ("May the Lord God of Joseph bless you") according to family *b* witnesses 436 (L2), FW, L1, and MS A of family *a*.[85] For Standhartinger, estimating what the Greek exemplar of the Slavonic translation provided is an approximation at best, and she warns

---

83. Burchard provides "schwanger geworden" (*Joseph und Aseneth*, 263 n. 21.9).

84. Standhartinger, *Das Frauenbild im Judentum*, 44–45. From the *b* family: witnesses Syr, L2, and MS F all attest to some form of αὐτός ἐστιν ὁ υἱὸς τοῦ θεοῦ ὁ πρωτότοκος, and witnesses Arm, MS W, and L1 (minus MSS 424 and 431) attest to some form of αὐτός ἐστιν ὁ υἱὸς τοῦ θεοῦ. The only other witness to attest to a similar phrase is Greek MS A (from family *a*), which reads: ὡς γὰρ υἱὸς ὑψίστου ἐστὶν Ἰωσήφ (Burchard, *Joseph und Aseneth*, 259). Burchard agreed with Standhartinger that this phrase should not be included in Philonenko's reconstruction (Burchard, "Zum Stand der Arbeit," 6; Burchard, *Joseph und Aseneth*, 259).

85. The following *b* witnesses lack "of Joseph" or "of Israel": Syr, 435& (L2), MSS G and E; the Armenian does not seem to have this attestation either. From family *a*, MSS P and Q show a similar rendition to that of MS A (εὐλογητὸς ὁ θεὸς τοῦ Ἰωσήφ καὶ εὐλογήσει σε) (Burchard, *Joseph und Aseneth*, 259).

that all reverse translations (from translated versions back to the supposed Greek exemplar) should be treated with caution.[86] Yet there are other challenges related to chapter 21.

The relationship between families *a* and *d* in this chapter poses a more pressing problem in Standhartinger's analysis. Fundamental to her argument is that *d* is not textually related to *a*, and therefore is not a later representation of *Aseneth*. For Burchard, *d* is an abridged rendition of *Aseneth* because the other textual families attest to longer passages that are missing in *d* but are essential to the plot of the story (especially in chs. 11–22).[87] Standhartinger contends that what Burchard identified as omissions in *d* can be rendered differently, that much of the *d* tradition reads as a coherent narrative.[88] But Burchard in particular sees *d* as an abbreviated version of the *a* recension, and by linking *a* more closely to *d* than to the other family groups, he challenged Philonenko's hypothesis that *a* is a stylized recension of *c* and former *b* (and thus, is far removed from *d*).[89] The example above from Ph 21:2-7 supports Burchard's argument, but let us look at it further.

The Greek manuscripts of *d* clearly reduce the scene from chapter 21; MS B appears to be incomplete (i.e., there is no introduction to the line beginning with πᾶς ἄνθρωπος), and MS D offers a less elaborate scene than that of the Slavonic. The Slavonic witnesses provide the lengthier marriage scene, as do also families *a* and *b* (see Ph 21:3-7; Bu 21: 4-8), but MS B and MS D do not provide a marriage ceremony at all.[90] The Greek manuscripts of *d* simply refer to the marriage in Ph 21:8, but the beginning of this verse, καί γενομένων (D: γινομένων) τῶν γάμων καὶ τοῦ δείπνου τελεσθέντος ("after the wedding occurred and the feast was finished"), is only attested in BDSlav and family *a* (MSS AP, and partially

---

86. This includes the times when Burchard proposes Greek words/phrases based on the translations alone (Standhartinger, *Das Frauenbild im Judentum*, 46, esp. nn. 217-18).

87. Burchard, *Joseph und Aseneth*, 41-42, 341-45. Burchard identifies the following gaps in *d* that are attested in his reconstruction and thus, according to Burchard, are necessary to the plot: Bu 11:1x-18; 12:14-15a; 13:9 end-12; 16:15 καὶ εἶπεν αὐτῇ-16x; 18:3-5a, 7, 9b-11; 19:3-8, 11; 21:10-21; and 22.6b-9a ("Zum Stand der Arbeit," 12-15).

88. Standhartinger, *Das Frauenbild im Judentum*, 40.

89. Burchard, "Zum Stand der Arbeit", 16-27; Burchard, *Joseph und Aseneth*, 36-37, 39-46.

90. See Burchard, *Joseph und Aseneth*, 258-63 for particular attestations in *a* witnesses as compared to what is found in *b* witnesses.

Q).⁹¹ Since (1) *a* preserves the longer wedding scene *and* this participial phrase that only *d* shares, and (2) Slav preserves the longer wedding scene, it appears that the marriage scene was condensed in MS B and MS D. It is also striking that *d* and *a* share a phrase in common against the rest of the witnesses. Burchard (and now also Fink) identifies the distinct readings in Ph 21:8/Bu 21:8-9 as proof that *a* and *d* share a common ancestor that produced a secondary reading.⁹²

Even though *a* and *d* may share similarities at times against the other witnesses, Standhartinger argues that the attestations of *a* and *d* are not always distinct from *b*, and she suggests that *a* and *b* share more passages that alter the narrative than what *a* and *d* share.⁹³ She provides two examples in which MS A (the primary witness of family *a*) and family *b* read

---

91. In agreement with MS D, MS A also provides γινομένων. Burchard's reconstruction instead relies on several witnesses from family *b* that read: καὶ ἐγένετο μετὰ ταῦτα (Syr, Arm, 436 [from L2], FW, and L1). Manuscript G provides καὶ παραχρῆμα ἐγένοντο τὰ πάντα (Burchard, *Joseph und Aseneth*, 263).

92. Burchard, "Zum Stand der Arbeit," 24; and Fink, *Joseph und Aseneth*, 86.

93. Standhartinger introduced this point with a breakdown of how MS A (from family *a*), *b* (as represented by Burchard's reconstruction), and *d* (as represented by Philonenko's reconstruction) compared in ch. 6 of *Aseneth*. According to Standhartinger, *d* corresponds with MS A thirteen times against *b* (not including the versification order of a/d in 6:2-7, which will be discussed further in this chapter), and MS A agrees with *b* nine times against *d*. Standhartinger admitted, however, that overall in ch. 6, *a* shares more in common with *d* than with *b*, and she acknowledged that among the a/b correspondences in this chapter, only one attests to a significant addition (Bu 6:2/Batiffol 46:18-19, καὶ λάμπει εἰς αὐτὴν ὡς φῶς ἐπὶ τῆς γῆς), whereas the rest of the correspondences consist of smaller insertions or alterations. But according to Standhartinger, the a/b correspondences are more dominant throughout the entire narrative, and she cited an example from Bu 14:1-9a/Ph 14:1-8a (citing Burchard's synopsis of Bu 14:1-9/Ph 14:1-8 in, "Zum Text der Arbeit," 30-34), but she did not explain this reference any further (*Das Frauenbild im Judentum*, 38-39). According to Burchard's comparison in "Zum Text der Arbeit," MSS A/*b* appear to read seven times against *d*, and MSS A/*d* appear to read six times against *b*. In his critical edition of *Aseneth*, however, Burchard has partially changed his reconstructed text from what he presented of ch. 14 in "Zum Text der Arbeit," so the comparison of A/*d* and *b* vs. A/*b* and *d* is not as stark. From what I can detect, A/*d* read against *b* four times (three of which are substantial, one of which is just the inclusion of the copular use of εἰμί [14:1]; see also Burchard, "Zum Stand der Arbeit," 17), and A/*b* read against *d* four times. Incidentally, *d*/*b* read against A at least three times in this passage. Standhartinger also refuted Burchard's claim that MS B is closely related to MS A, but recently Fink has provided substantial evidence to the contrary. See Standhartinger,

against family *d* to demonstrate this point. The examples are: (1) Bu 2:7 and Batiffol 41,18 (MS A) compared with Ph 2:13; and (2) Bu 20:4 and Batiffol 70,11–13 compared with Ph 20:3.[94] Although the second example defends Standhartinger's point, the first exposes further complications.[95] I will first present why Standhartinger provides this first example from *Asen.* 2, but I will then outline the finer details from the manuscript evidence that inevitable weakens her argument. Comparing *a* versus *d* as related to *b* will not help us reconstruct the earliest *Aseneth* text.

Chapter 2 of *Aseneth* describes the windows in Aseneth's room, and Standhartinger cites the following lines:[96]

Family *a* (Batiffol 41,18) and family *b* (Bu 2:7)
καὶ ἡ δευτέρα [θυρὶς] ἦν ἀποβλέπουσα εἰς [MS A: ἐπὶ] μεσημβρίαν καὶ ἡ τρίτη ἦν ἀποβλέπουσα εἰς (βορρᾶν)[97] ἐπὶ τὸ ἄμφοδον
And the second (window) was facing <u>south</u> and the third was facing (<u>north</u>) *toward the street.*

Family *d* (Ph 2:13)
καὶ ἡ δευτέρα [θυρὶς] ἦν ἐπιβλέπουσα πρὸς βορρᾶν πρὸς τὸ ἄμφοδον καὶ ἡ τρίτη πρὸς μεσημβρίαν.
And the second (window) was facing <u>north</u> *toward the street* and the third (was facing) <u>south</u>.

The main distinction between the two renditions is the direction each window faces. The majority of witnesses from families *a* and *b* portray

---

Das Frauenbild im Judentum, 39; Burchard, "Der jüdische Asenethroman," 564; and Fink, *Joseph und Aseneth*, 53–57.

94. Standhartinger, *Das Frauenbild im Judentum*, 39.

95. In Standhartinger's second example, the *b* witnesses that attest to this line (Syr, Arm L2, *f* [F and L1]) share what *a* provides (Burchard, *Joseph und Aseneth*, 252). Bu 20:4/Batiffol 70, 11–13 vs. Ph 20:3

b/A: διότι οἱ πόδες σου πόδες μού εἰσι καὶ αἱ χεῖρές σου χεῖρές μου (*b*: εἰσι) καὶ ἡ ψυχή σου ψυχή μου,

d: διότι αἱ χεῖρές μου χεῖρές σου καὶ οἱ πόδες σου πόδες μου (Standhartinger, *Das Frauenbild im Judentum*, 39)

96. Standhartinger, *Das Frauenbild im Judentum*, 39.

97. All Burchard's primary witnesses and most of the witnesses of family *a* (but not MS A) attest to this phrase (*Joseph und Aseneth*, 81). Standhartinger indicates this point in her comparison with MS A (*Das Frauenbild im Judentum*, 39).

the second window facing south and the third facing north toward a street.[98] In the *d* witnesses, BDSlav indicate that the second window faced north toward the street and, in Philonenko's text, the third window faces south. But if we look more carefully at the individual attestations, the third window in *d* is not described in a uniform way. Although prior to this line, MS B seems to indicate that Aseneth's room had three windows (Bu 2:7/Ph 2:12), it does not discuss a third window here.[99] In MS D and MS Slav the third window faces south, but in the Slavonic witnesses, the southern window *also* faces the street.[100] If we break down the evidence even further, more relationships arise: [101]

Slav (estimated translation), from family *d*
And the second (window was facing) <u>north</u> toward the street and the third (was facing) <u>south</u> *toward the street.*

Family *a* (Batiffol 41,18)
καὶ ἡ δευτέρα [θυρὶς] ἦν ἀποβλέπουσα ἐπὶ μεσημβρίαν καὶ ἡ τρίτη ἦν ἀποβλέπουσα εἰς (βορρᾶν) ἐπὶ τὸ ἄμφοδον
And the second (window) was facing <u>south</u> and the third was facing (<u>north</u>) *toward the street.*

Bu 2:7 (family *b*)
καὶ ἡ δευτέρα [θυρὶς] ἦν ἀποβλέπουσα εἰς μεσημβρίαν καὶ ἡ τρίτη ἦν ἀποβλέπουσα εἰς βορρᾶν ἐπὶ τὸ ἄμφοδον τῶν παραπορευομένων[102]
And the second (window) was facing <u>south</u> and the third was facing <u>north</u> *toward the street* <u>*of those passing by*</u>

---

98. From family *b*: Syr, Arm, L2, FW, and L1; also providing this line are Mc and *a* (except that MS A does not mention that the third window faced north; the rest of the *a* witnesses do, however). Both MSS E and G (from *b*) lack 2:7-10 (Burchard, *Joseph und Aseneth*, 81).

99. Both Philonenko's and Burchard's critical editions imply that earlier in the scene, MS B mentions the three windows in Aseneth's room (Philonenko, *Joseph et Aséneth*, 134; Burchard, *Joseph und Aseneth*, 80-81).

100. Burchard, *Joseph und Aseneth*, 81.

101. Burchard, *Joseph und Aseneth*, 80-81.

102. The phrase, ἐπὶ τὸ ἄμφοδον τῶν παραπορευομένων, is attested in some form in Syr, Arm, MSS FW, and L1; and L2 attests to *in (ad) viam publicam*; in other words, a majority of family *b* witnesses attest to the third window facing a public street. The phrase is also attested in Mc (Burchard, *Joseph und Aseneth*, 80-81).

Ngr (family *b*, estimated translation)
And the second (window was facing) <u>north</u> and the third (was facing) <u>south</u>

MS D and MS Slav (family *d*)
And the second (window was facing) <u>north</u> *toward the street* and the third (was facing) <u>south</u> (Slav adds: *toward the street*).

Standhartinger presents the comparison from *Asen.* 2 to support her point about *a/b* changing the story of *d*, but when we look more closely at the witnesses, we are left with a more complicated web of connections. First, I will address the key distinction that Standhartinger presents—the directions that the second and third windows face. Family *a* and most witnesses of *b* could be read as reversing the positions of the windows in MS D and MS Slav (from family *d*), but one set of family *b* witnesses (Ngr) agree with MS D and MS Slav (in both, the second window faces north and the third faces south).[103] More curious to me is the description of the street-facing window in the witnesses here as compared to that window in *Asen.* 10.

In chapter 10, Aseneth is in the process of purging herself of her religious artifacts and affiliations. In families *a* and *d*, Aseneth throws her royal garb through the window "to the poor" (τοῖς πένησιν), breaks her idols into pieces (συνέτριψεν εἰς λεπτά) and gives them to the "poor and needy" (πτωχοῖς καὶ δεομένοις) (Bu 10:11-12/Ph 10:12-13). These three actions are unattested in the *b* witnesses, yet Burchard included them in his reconstruction. Fink has since deleted these references, as will be discussed in the next chapter; for now it is important to note that these readings are shared only by *a* and *d*.[104] Also in chapter 10, the witnesses of *a* and *b* coincide in saying that Aseneth tosses her clothes and sacrifi-

---

103. In the next chapter I will discuss Fink's persuasive argument for contamination between Ngr and *a*, but Fink does not account for this example regarding Ngr and *d* in her textual study (Fink, *Joseph und Aseneth*, 63–71).

104. The phrase, τοῖς πένησι(ν), is attested in MSS AP and family *d* but not in the following: (1) from family *b*: Syr, Arm, L2, FW, L1, G, and E; (2) *c*, and (3) MS Q from family *a*. The phrase, συνέτριψεν αὐτούς [> D] εἰς λεπτά, is attested in AP *d* (and Ngr in 9:2) but not in (1) from *b*: Syr, Arm, L2, FW, L1, G, and E ; (2) *c*, and (3) Q. The phrase, τοῖς [> A B] πτωχοῖς καὶ τοῖς δεομένοις, is attested in AP, B, Slav (τοῖς πτωχοῖς is attested in D and Ngr [9:2]) but not in (1) from *b*: Syr, Arm, L2, FW, L1, G, and E; (2) *c*, and (3) Q (Burchard, *Joseph und Aseneth*, 134–35). Fink removes all three readings from her revision of Burchard's reconstruction (*Joseph und Aseneth*, 113).

cial food through the <u>northern</u> window (Bu 10:11, 13).[105] The modifier, "northern," matches the description of the northern window in Bu 2:7/Ph 2:13, where it faces the street in families *a*, *b*, and *d*.[106] Given that in the *b* witnesses, the northern window overlooks a public street (see inset above), it can be assumed that common people likely received Aseneth's tossed debris, so even though the *b* witnesses lack the phrases τοῖς πένησιν and πτωχοῖς καὶ δεομένοις, such recipients could still be implied. Likewise, although the *d* witnesses do not indicate that Aseneth tosses her items out of the *northern* window in chapter 10 (Ph 10:12–13), since the poor receive these items and in all the *d* witnesses the northern window faces the street (Ph 2:13, and inset above), we can assume that even in the *d* narrative, Aseneth throws things out of her northern window in chapter 10.[107] Returning to Standhartinger's point: It is true that in Bu 2:7/Ph 2:13, *a* and *b* list the windows of Aseneth's room in a different order than what *d* provides, but the above examples from chapter 10 verify that families *a*, *b*, and *d* relay a similar presentation of events. Even though the narratives do not align perfectly, they convey much of the same storyline—namely, that Aseneth throws her belongings through the northern, street-facing window in all the witnesses that attest to this scene. The clarifications of whether or not anyone received Aseneth's tossed items *at best* reflect different choices of narration; some emphasize the northern window, others include the recipients of the tossed items, and some focus on everything. Given the textual similarities between *a* and *d* in chapter 10 (so not just the mention of the recipients but also the description of Aseneth shattering the idols into pieces), it is likely that a common ancestor was copied and/or consulted in the transmission of families *a* and *d*. Whether, though,

---

105. The following *b* witnesses do not attest to 10:11–12: FW and E (Burchard, *Joseph und Aseneth*, 132–36).

106. Even MS B, which portrays two windows instead of three, presents the northern window facing the street. See above as well (Burchard, *Joseph und Aseneth*, 81).

107. I will add here that some witnesses in family *b* mention that Aseneth also threw her idol-remains through the northern window (MSS 436 [L2], L1, and E), and family *c* offers the only other attestation to this particular reference in Bu 2:12/Ph 2:13. What is striking here is that Syr and Arm lack this reference; as we will see in the next chapter, Burchard tends to prioritize Syr/Arm/L2. The Armenian witnesses only mention that Aseneth threw the idols "from her upper room," but Syr may imply that she used the northern window (e.g., she throws the remains out of the same window as in Bu 10:11). Another complication from *b*: in MS W, Aseneth throws her idols through the eastern window (Burchard, *Joseph und Aseneth*, 135).

this ancestor was farther removed from the earliest text than other textual ancestors is far from certain.

One more case in point has to do with the verse that Standhartinger had cited: Bu 2:7/Ph 2:13. If we compare how the witnesses describe the *first* window in this scene (which Standhartinger does not discuss in her example), we discover that *a* and *d* are united with only Syr and Arm (from family *b*) in describing the first window as facing the courtyard (Bu 2:7/Ph 2:13). The rest of the *b* witnesses lack mention of the courtyard here (L2, MSS FW, and L1).[108] As I will discuss further in the next chapter, Burchard and Fink consider Syr, Arm, and L2 to be most valuable in reconstructing the earliest *Aseneth* text. It is interesting that two of these families align only with (supposedly) the latest replications of *Aseneth* (meaning, families *a* and *d*), and all the witnesses in the middle of the transmission period hypothetically deleted the courtyard reference. Adding all the examples that I have noted above about *Aseneth* 2, then, although *b/a* mostly read against *d* in one way (regarding the window-facing directions), one witness group of *d* aligns with families *a* and *b* (Slav attests to the third window overlooking the street), family *d* and one witness group of *b* share a reading (DSlav and Ngr with the directions of the second and third windows), and even *a*, *d*, and two witnesses of *b* (Syr and Arm) read against the other *b* witnesses concerning the courtyard. When looking more closely at the textual evidence, the "*b/a* versus *d*" divide breaks down. As will be discussed in the next chapter, it is also significant that L2 agrees with families *f* (MSS FW and L1) and M*c* in this verse, but not with Syr and Arm.

Although I agree with Burchard and Fink that families *a* and *d* are closely related, I disagree with them that this relationship can defend where the families best lie in the transmission history of *Aseneth*. As Burchard admits, *a* and *c* share several readings in common and present an Atticized style of Greek narration (although seemingly independent in their styles), but at the same time, on several occasions *c* reads with family *b* against *a/d*.[109] In other places in the narrative, *a* preserves indepen-

---

108. Burchard, *Joseph und Aseneth* (2003), 81. Also family M*c* lacks mention of the courtyard. Burchard places the courtyard reference in his reconstruction: καὶ ἦν ἡ μία θυρὶς ἡ πρώτη μεγάλη σφόδρα ἀποβλέπουσα ἐπὶ τὴν αὐλὴν εἰς ἀνατολάς. Fink also retains this reading in her text (*Joseph und Aseneth*, 172).

109. Burchard, *Joseph und Aseneth*, 21–22, 26. Burchard gives the following examples of where *a* and *c* share readings (citations from Burchard's text): 1:2, 5–6; 3:3; 5:5–6; 6:1; 7:5; 8:8; 9:2; 10:2; 11:4, 9, 13; 12:8; 13:11; 14:4; 16:9, 13; 16:16x–17x

dent units found in either *b* or *d*, and *a* lacks some passages that both *b* and *d* share.[110] The most significant example is from the miracle scene with the honeycomb, in which the angelic figure marks the comb with his finger (Bu 16:17–17x/Ph 16:10–12).[111] Discerning whether *b* or *d* is closest in resemblance to *a*, then, will not determine which textual group represents the earliest text of *Aseneth*. There are too many variables in the correspondences among and differences between the witnesses. As I will discuss in the next chapter, Fink has since proposed a more elaborate schema of transmission to resolve some of these complications, but in the end, her hypothesis does not settle how best to understand the production of *a*, *b*, and *d*.

For Standhartinger, the difference of 5138 words between *b* (as represented by Burchard) and *d* (Philonenko's text minus the passages that Standhartinger deletes) cannot be justified simply by scribal error or fatigue or even by epitome.[112] Rather, the *b* version reflects a purposeful adjustment by scribes who were driven by certain ideological preferences. Regarding the textual problem of multiple witnesses, she concludes that

---

(*Joseph und Aseneth*, 22). For where *c* reads with *b* against *a*/*d*, see Burchard, "Zum Stand der Arbeit," 16–20.

110. E.g., *a* and *b* attest to Aseneth's silent prayers: two are offered in Bu 11:1x–18 and one in MS A (53,14–54,17 [Batiffol]), and *a* and *d* attest to the angelic figure's speech in the third-person: e.g., in Ph 15:2 and in MS A (60,22 [Batiffol]) the angel tells Aseneth that God ἤκουσε (εἰσήκουσε: MSS B and A) … (A+: πάντων) τῶν ῥημάτων τῆς ἐξομολογήσεώς σου, but in Bu 15:2 the angel says ἀκήκοα … τῶν ῥημάτων τῆς ἐξομολογήσεώς σου. See also Ph 15:5 and 61,8 (Batiffol) compared with Bu 15:6. Burchard originally argued that *a* and *d* attest to the earliest text in this verse (*Untersuchungen zu Joseph und Aseneth*, 47), but he chose the first-person forms in his reconstruction (e.g., *Joseph und Aseneth*, 187). Kraemer argues that *b* preserves a purposeful alteration in the *Aseneth* tradition that elevated the role of the angelic figure to "divine co-regent" (*When Aseneth Met Joseph*, 60, 120–27).

111. These verses are attested in the following witnesses: (1) from family *b*: Syr, Arm, 435& (L2), L1, and G; and (2) family *d*. The family groups *a* and *c* do not preserve this reading and only attest to some form of the following phrase: ἔθηγε δὲ ὁ ἄγγελος τὸ κηρίον (Burchard, *Joseph und Aseneth*, 215–16).

112. Standhartinger, *Das Frauenbild im Judentum*, 39–40, esp. n. 198. The main reason why *d* should not be considered an epitome of *b* is because *d* incorporates too much of *b*, and *d* does not exclude some literary features that are usually lacking in epitomes (such as speeches). Standhartinger admits, however, that understanding *d* as an epitome would make sense of omissions like 18:3–5.9b–11 and 22:6–8 that are represented in Burchard's text (40 n. 198).

Burchard's text is fairly faithful to family *b*, but she also identifies problematic passages in his reconstruction. She proposes the following portions be treated with caution: the places where Burchard (1) seems to reconstruct the text solely from *a*; (2) draws upon non-Greek witnesses to clarify the Greek of the *b* witnesses; and (3) provides Greek translations of the *b* versions (where he reconstructs the Greek text from mainly the Syriac, Latin, and/or Armenian manuscripts because the Greek witnesses do not attest to those passages or phrases).[113] With these precautions and with the limitations that she had outlined from Philonenko's text in mind, Standhartinger nevertheless concludes that Burchard's reconstruction of *b* and Philonenko's reconstruction of *d* are acceptable representations of two early textual stages of *Aseneth*, and the two reconstructions are helpful tools for observing *Aseneth*'s development.[114]

In response to Standhartinger's argument, Burchard questioned whether his reconstruction represented an expansion and ideological alteration of *d*. Not only does his reconstruction and *d* share too much of sentence- and word-sequences in common, but also in Burchard's opinion, the two should demonstrate more significant differences between parallel sections of the narrative if indeed such purposeful changes were made.[115] So too does Burchard doubt Standhartinger's suggestion that scribal redactors perhaps tried to enhance a destroyed manuscript and, as a result, altered the characterization of Aseneth. If these redactors were restoring the text, then the narrative would have had to have been popular, and if so, how could the redactors know whether audiences would have

---

113. Standhartinger mentioned that the following passages/phrases in Burchard's text are taken from family *a*: 14:9: ὑπολαμπάδος καιομένης; 24:20: καὶ ἐκάθισαν ... πλατεῖα καὶ εὐρύχωρος; and 28:5f. (*Das Frauenbild im Judentum*, 46 n. 216). Fink expands considerably on Standhartinger's critique (*Joseph und Aseneth*, 47, 102–43). Standhartinger referred to the following verses as examples where Burchard relies on textual versions: 5:5; 8:9; 9:2; 11:18; 12:15; 16:19; 17:3; 18:1; 21:7; and 24:19 (*Das Frauenbild im Judentum*, 46 n. 217). Standhartinger referred to the following words/phrases that Burchard translates from the versions into Greek (all Burchard verse citation): 2:8; 5:5; 8:9; 10:17; 12:8; 12:14; 16:10; 16:16; 18:7; 18:9 (three examples); 19:8 (two examples); 19:10; 20:5; 21:4 (two examples); 22:7 (four examples); 22:9; 22:13; 23:8; 23:10 (two examples); 24:17; 26:6; and 29:9 (n. 218). In addition, Standhartinger listed twenty-two times in 21:10–21 where Burchard's reconstruction is taken from translations only (p. 46 n. 218, and pp. 91–92).

114. Standhartinger, *Das Frauenbild im Judentum*, 47.

115. Burchard, *Joseph und Aseneth*, 42.

accepted their so-called different portrayal of Aseneth?[116] Although none of these arguments prove that *d* is abridged, Burchard concludes that the burden of proof lies with those who dispute his theory.[117] For Burchard, the idea of abridgment at a later stage of the transmission process makes more sense than an expansion at a later stage. The earliest manuscript witness (Syriac MS 2071) preserves a long rendition of the narrative, but the earliest manuscript of *d* (MS B) is dated five hundred years later and is found in a collection of hagiographic texts (a genre that thrived during the ninth- and tenth-centuries CE). For Burchard, the popularity of hagiographic collections produces a good reason as to why MS B, then, should be understood as a reduction of the narrative (and thus, perhaps, the *d* family as a whole).[118]

Clearly, our current data offers no sufficient support for some of Burchard arguments. The notion that scribes necessarily were sensitive to whatever impressions readers/listeners had of *Aseneth* (and thus, would have had to produce a portrayal of Aseneth that was acceptable to these audiences) is purely speculative. In addition, his reasonable theory about the abbreviated version of MS B cannot be used to resolve the length of the ancestor of MS D and MS Slav or its relation to Syriac MS 2071. Burchard (and now also Fink) make a convincing case, however, for the close textual relationship between *a* and *d*, and as I will discuss in the next chapter, Fink demonstrates more clearly than Burchard how the ancestor of *ad* likely redacted its exemplar.[119] I agree, then, with Burchard and Fink that *ad* provides secondary readings, in the sense that it demonstrates redactions. But these redactions may reflect contemporaneous scribal activity that not only *a* and *d* witnesses show. As we will see, assigning secondary importance to *a* and *d* does not get us closer to the earliest *Aseneth*.

Standhartinger treads cautiously in her use of the textual reconstructions, and her presentation of the textual evidence confirms the necessity of operating with this skeptical approach. She articulates clearly the limits

---

116. Burchard, *Joseph und Aseneth*, 42. For Standhartinger's suggestion, see *Das Frauenbild im Judentum*, 222–25.

117. Burchard, *Joseph und Aseneth*, 42.

118. Burchard, *Joseph und Aseneth*, 45.

119. Burchard has produced a substantial list of times where *a*/*d* read in common against *b*/*c* ("Zum Stand der Arbeit," 16–24). For Fink, see *Joseph und Aseneth*, 80–98. In these pages, Fink also counters Standhartinger's claim about the placement of *d* in the transmission history.

of Philonenko's work, and she raises important questions about the textual choices Burchard made in his own reconstruction. In particular, her warning about Burchard's inclusion of only *a* attestations was correct, and, as I will explain further in the next chapter, Fink's comprehensive treatment of this critique should have been definitively adopted by all *Aseneth* scholars. With Standhartinger's argument, we also have seen how the textual families *a*, *b*, and *d* indicate a variety of attestations within their respective family groups and/or demonstrate a complex relationship with one or more textual families. At times, the witnesses also narrate the same event in different ways, as demonstrated by Aseneth's casting of her belongings through her northern window in *Asen.* 10. Up to this point, theories about the abridgment or expansion of *Aseneth* betray the assumption that a chronological development of this story's transmission can be established (whereby an earlier telling can be distinguished from a later telling). The diversity in the textual evidence complicates any effort to outline the transmission of this story in such linear terms, and Kraemer's discussion of the witnesses is hindered by the same problems that limit Standhartinger's analysis.

The Revival of Philonenko's Reconstruction: Kraemer's Analysis

Three years after Standhartinger's monograph, Kraemer published her own take on the relationship between Burchard's and Philonenko's texts.[120] She argues that the *b* tradition—what Kraemer referred to as the longer text—brings the *d* tradition (the shorter text) more closely in association with certain biblical paradigms and passages, and the longer text (*b*) clarifies ambiguities in the shorter text (*d*). Kraemer offers compelling evidence of redaction that was influenced by biblical exegesis, but her analysis is too often restricted to just a comparison between the reconstructions. It is clear that manuscripts within each textual family unit exhibit this type of redaction; the fluid nature of how *Aseneth* was transmitted by scribes is not reserved to comparisons between textual families alone. Kraemer also claims, independently of Standhartinger, that the *b* tradition exhibits ideological choices made by scribes to reduce the status of female characters as represented by the *d* tradition. This argument becomes difficult to defend, though, when we examine the individual textual witnesses instead of the reconstructions; there are too many variations in *Aseneth* to identify

---

120. Kraemer, *When Aseneth Met Joseph*.

which text represents the earliest telling. In this section, I will demonstrate how Kraemer's presentation of redactions in *Aseneth* are better applied to comparing individual witnesses instead of family *d* versus family *b*. In particular, I will review Kraemer's analysis of the following passages: Bu 15:12x; Bu 11:1x–18; Bu 18:5–9/Ph 18:3–7; and Bu 15:7/Ph 15:7. In the end, Kraemer proposes ideas that could explain the renditions of *Aseneth* in specific witnesses, but her hypothesis cannot get us to the earliest *Aseneth* text.

Many scholars have identified parallels between *Aseneth* and biblical texts (especially in terms of the LXX/OG), but Kraemer convincingly demonstrates narrative expansions that scribes likely made to correlate biblical passages with *Aseneth*.[121] At times Burchard has noted in his publications when such redaction seems evident in *Aseneth*, but he has not presented this scribal technique in any systematic way.[122] For Kraemer, these expansions are signs of scribal redactions of the shorter text (*d*). A case in point is the presentation of Aseneth's encounter with the angelic figure in chapters 14–17 and its similarities with Judg 13:3–17.[123] The book of Judges portrays an annunciation scene in which an angelic figure visits the wife of Manoah and announces her future conception of Samson, and eventually both Manoah and his wife encounter the angelic figure again. This biblical scene and chapters 14–17 in *Aseneth* share a similar storyline: (1) an angelic figure appears to a female character (Judg 13:3 and Bu 14:3/Ph 14:4); (2) the angelic figure reveals a significant change in the future

---

121. Kraemer, *When Aseneth Met Joseph*, 43 n. 6. For the discussion of the use of the LXX/OG in *Aseneth*, Kraemer cites Burchard, "Joseph and Aseneth," 184; and Philonenko, *Joseph et Aséneth*, passim.

122. An example is Burchard's remarks about the Armenian translation of Bu 18:9 ("Joseph and Aseneth," 232, nn. 18.s., w., and x). This verse appears to use the style and imagery of the Song of Songs to expand upon Aseneth's transformed beauty. Kraemer proposes that this addition emphasizes the bridal aspect of Aseneth's status and in so doing diminishes her angelic position (*When Aseneth Met Joseph*, 71–72), but the bridal and elevated aspects of Aseneth's status are not necessarily mutually exclusive in the narrative. For textual variations of this verse, see Burchard, *Unterweisung in erzählender Form*, 688; Burchard, *Joseph und Aseneth*, 236–38.

123. Burchard also notes that Judg 13 shares similarities with *Asen.* 14–17 but does not provide a detailed discussion ("Joseph and Aseneth," 184). Standhartinger briefly commented on the association of Judg 13 and Burchard's reconstruction in her monograph (*Das Frauenbild im Judentum*, 123–25) and then more extensively in "From Fictional Text to Socio-historical Context," 311–12.

life of the female (Judg 13:3–5 and Bu 15:2–10/Ph 15:2–11); (3) a meal is offered to the angelic figure (Judg 13:15–16 and Bu 15:13–15/Ph 15:13–14; although the angel in the Judges's account refuses the meal); (4) something is consumed by fire (the offerings in Judg 13:19–20 and the honeycomb in Bu 17:3–4/Ph 17:3); and (5) the angelic figure ascends through fire to heaven (Judg 13:20 and Bu 17:8/Ph 17:6).[124]

The pattern of Aseneth's encounter with the angelic figure appears to imitate the encounter in Judg 13, and the longer text (*b*) adds another scene in *Aseneth* that enhances the correspondence between these two accounts.[125] After the angelic figure announces to Aseneth her future status and marriage to Joseph, Aseneth asks the angel his name so that she may praise him, and the angel responds that his name is incomprehensible to humans (Bu 15:12x). In Judg 13:17, Manoah asks the angel his name for reasons similar to Aseneth's, and the angels' responses in each respective passage share resemblances. Compare the following:[126]

> Judges 13:17–18 (Alexandrinus) [A]
> τί ὄνομά σοι, ἵνα ὅταν ἔλθῃ τὸ ῥῆμά σου δοξάσωμέν σε; καὶ εἶπεν αὐτῷ ὁ ἄγγελος κυρίου ἵνα τί τοῦτο ἐρωτᾷς τὸ ὄνομά μου; καὶ αὐτό ἐστιν θαυμαστόν.
> What is your name so that when your word comes, we may glorify you? And the angel of the Lord said to him, "Why do you ask this, my name? Even it alone is wonderful."
>
> Judges 13:17–18 (Vaticanus) [B]
> τί τὸ ὄνομά σοι; ὅτι ἔλθοι τὸ ῥῆμά σου καὶ δοξάσομέν σε. καὶ εἶπεν αὐτῷ ὁ ἄγγελος κυρίου εἰς τί τοῦτο ἐρωτᾷς τὸ ὄνομά μου; καὶ αὐτό ἐστιν θαυμαστόν.
> "What is your name? For may your word come and we will glorify you." And the angel of the Lord said, "Why do you ask this, my name? Even it alone is wonderful."

---

124. Kraemer, *When Aseneth Met Joseph*, 33–34.
125. Kraemer, *When Aseneth Met Joseph*, 63–64.
126. Kraemer provides in her presentation the pericopes from LXX Judges, albeit in transliterated Greek, and most of Bu 15.12x, albeit some of it in transliterated form (*When Aseneth Met Joseph*, 62–63, 85 n. 42.).

1. The Reconstructed Texts of *Aseneth*: Standhartinger and Kraemer

Bu 15:12x

<u>τί ἐστι τὸ ὄνομά σου</u> κύριε ἀνάγγειλόν μοι ἵνα ὑμνήσω καὶ <u>δοξάσω σε</u> εἰς τὸν αἰῶνα χρόνον. καὶ εἶπεν αὐτῇ ὁ ἄνθρωπος· <u>ἵνα τί τοῦτο ζητεῖς τὸ ὄνομά μου Ἀσενέθ</u>; τὸ ἐμὸν ὄνομα ἐν τοῖς οὐρανοῖς ἐστιν ἐν τῇ βίβλῳ τοῦ ὑψίστου γεγραμμένον τῷ δακτυλῳ τοῦ θεοῦ <ἐν ἀρχῇ τῆς βίβλου> πρὸ πάντων ὅτι ἐγὼ ἄρχων εἰμὶ τοῦ οἴκου τοῦ ὑψίστου. καὶ πάντα τὰ ὀνόματα τὰ γεγραμμένα ἐν τῇ βίβλῳ τοῦ ὑψίστου ἄρρητά ἐστι καὶ ἀνθρώπῳ οὔτε εἰπεῖν οὔτε ἀκοῦσαι ἐν τῷ κόσμῳ τούτῳ ἐγκεχώρηται <u>ὅτι μεγάλα ἐστί τὰ ὀνόματα ἐκεῖνα καὶ θαυμαστὰ καὶ ἐπαινετὰ σφόδρα</u>.

"<u>What is your name</u>, lord? Tell me so that I may sing in praise (of you) and <u>glorify you</u> forever." And the man said to her, "<u>Why do you seek this, my name, Aseneth?</u> My name in the heavens is in the book of the Most High, written by the finger of God <in the beginning of the book> before all (other names) because I am *archōn* of the house of the Most High. And all the names written in the book of the Most High are unspeakable, and it is not allowed for a person either to speak or to hear (the names) in this world <u>because those names are exceedingly great, wonderful, and praiseworthy</u>."

These passages correspond in the following places: (1) the human character's question, "What is your name?" (τί [τὸ] ὄνομά σοι; or τί ἐστι τὸ ὄνομά σου); (2) the expressed motivation to "glorify" (δοξάζω) the name of the angel; (3) the angel's query about why the recipient wishes to know his name; and (4) the reason that the angel's name is too "wonderful" (θαυμαστός), supposedly, for the recipient to hear. It is conceivable that Bu 15:12x represents a redaction by scribes to further align Aseneth's encounter with the angel with the scene in Judg 13. As Kraemer maintains, it seems more difficult to argue why a scribe would delete this scene (given the other references to Judg 13) than it is to suggest that this verse was added later as a result of the perceived association between *Aseneth* and Judg 13.[127]

---

127. Kraemer, *When Aseneth Met Joseph*, 80. Standhartinger sees Bu 15:12x as redundant since the angelic messenger already had introduced himself to Aseneth in Bu14:8/Ph 14:7 (*Das Fraeunbild im Judentum*, 222). For Burchard's rebuttal, see "Zum Stand der Arbeit," 19 n. 86. Fink considers the lack of 15:12x in *ad* to indicate that its exemplar shows proof of a later document of this narrative's reception history. She

Nevertheless, this example also betrays the limit of Kraemer's investigation. Her primary argument as to why 15:12x is modeled after Judg 13 relies on the literal correspondence between Burchard's reconstruction and the book of Judges. The longer text (Bu 15:12x), then, indicates an expansion of the scene that correlates it more with Judg 13, but the individual textual witnesses reveal a variation of scribal activity. Longer *texts*—not just manuscripts from family *b*—attest to these expansions, and none of the *b* witnesses provide all of the correspondences listed in the previous paragraph. The question, "What is your name?," is attested well in both the *b* and *c* families, and the motivation to "glorify" is provided in *c* witnesses and most but not all of the *b* witnesses.[128] From family *b*, the Greek verb δοξάζω only appears in MS G and MS 671 (Ngr); MS L1 and MS L2 seem to attest to δοξάζω (L1 provides *glorificem* and L2 [except for MS 445 of group 435&] provides *honorificem*); and perhaps the Armenian translated the same verb (an equivalent of *honorificem*, according to Burchard).[129] The other *b* witnesses that provide some form of 15:12x do not attest to δοξάζω (MS E) or they offer something else (MSS FW read εὐλογήσω).[130] As for the angel's question, "Why do you ask/seek this, my name?," only MS G and MSS 435& (L2) of family *b* attest to this question; in fact Burchard adopts the Greek sentence verbatim from MS G.[131]

---

proposes that the differentiation between the angel's unpronounceable name and his pronounceable title was no longer considered relevant to the Christian scribes of this exemplar. (*Joseph und Aseneth*, 97).

128. The following witnesses provide an inquiry about the angel's name: (1) from former family *b*: Arm, L2 (although MS 436 differs from MSS 435&), MSS FW, L1, MS G, and MS E; and (2) *c*. Family *c* attests to δοξάζω as do also (explained below) some from family *b*. The entire verse of 15.12x is lost or unreadable in the Syriac (Burchard, *Joseph und Aseneth*, 197; Fink, *Joseph und Aseneth*, 297).

129. Burchard, *Untersuchungen zu Joseph und Aseneth*, 68; and Burchard, *Joseph und Aseneth*, 197. See also Fink, *Joseph und Aseneth*, 297, which provides a critical edition of MSS 436 and 435& of L2. Burchard's critical edition (*Joseph und Aseneth*, 197) implies that 435& read *glorificem* (similar to L1 but different than the reading in MS 436), but Burchard does not make this case in *Untersuchungen zu Joseph und Aseneth* and Finks's presentation negates that implication.

130. Burchard, *Joseph und Aseneth*, 197.

131. Burchard, *Untersuchungen zu Joseph und Aseneth*, 69; and Burchard, *Joseph und Aseneth*, 197–99. Manuscripts 435& of L2 seems to conflate τὸ ὄνομα μου in this phrase with τὸ ἐμὸν ὄνομα that immediately follows (τὸ ἐμὸν ὄνομα ἐν τοῖς οὐρανοῖς ἐστιν). Fink provides the following for the ending 15:12x in 435&, beginning from "Why do you ask my name?": *Si nomen meum queries,/in celis scriptum est/in prin-*

Finally, θαυμαστός (or its equivalent) is attested in (1) Arm, MS 436 (L2), MS F, and possibly L1 (which reads *mira*) from *b*; and (2) all the *c* witnesses. Of these manuscripts, all but L1 provide the triadic phrase, "very great, wonderful, and praiseworthy;" L1 attests to "very great and wonderful" (*quoniam magna sunt et mira valde*). Looking more closely at the *b* witnesses, the remainder of the manuscripts from L2 (435&) present a couplet but only MS 445 and MS 446 make sense (*valde celanda sunt et magna* and *magna sunt et celanda valde*, respectively; "very great and hidden").[132] Finally, MS W, MS G, and MS E do not attest to any part of the closing triadic phrase of Bu 15:12x.[133] In summary, of the literary associations between Bu 15:12x and LXX Judg 13 provided above, numbers 1, 2, and 4 (the question, "What is your name?" and the supposed equivalents of δοξάζω and θαυμάστος) appear from family *b* in only L1, MS 436 (L2), and perhaps in Arm, but we are left to guess what the Greek *Vorlagen* for these translations displayed. Among the Greek witnesses of *Aseneth*, only family *c* (not *b*) preserves all three of these elements (nos. 1, 2, and 4).

---

cipio libri primi,/quia princeps sum domus dei altissimi (*Joseph und Aseneth*, 297). Fink cautiously retains the Greek sentence, ἵνα τί τοῦτο ζητεῖς τὸ ὄνομά μου Ἀσενέθ, in her revision of Bu 15:12x, mostly because she surmises that MSS G and 435& produced these readings independent of each other (149–50). Her argument appears to assume that her stemma of the textual transmission is correct, and therefore, given that L2 and MS G descend from different majuscules (according to her stemma), it is likely that the question was in the earliest text (and following this logic, all the other witnesses discarded the line). We will return to this point in the next chapter. Kraemer also surmises that the question, "Why do you ask this, my name?," links Bu 15:12x with Gen 32:27–30 in which Jacob encounters the angel. In the Genesis scene, Jacob persists in asking the angel his name and the angel inevitably replies, "Why do you ask this, my name?" (ἵνα τί τοῦτο ἐρωτᾷς τὸ ὄνομά μου; [32:30]) (*When Aseneth Met Joseph*, 63). Also, the renaming scene of Jacob and the renaming scene concerning Aseneth share similar language. Compare οὐ κληθήσεται ἔτι τὸ ὄνομά σου Ιακωβ, ἀλλὰ Ισραηλ ἔσται τὸ ὄνομά σου (Gen. 32:29) and καὶ οὐκέτι κληθήσει Ἀσενέθ, ἀλλ' ἔσται τὸ ὄνομά σου πόλις καταφυγῆς (Bu 15:7) (Kraemer, *When Aseneth Met Joseph*, 85 n. 43). Since MSS G and 435& (L2) also attest to Aseneth's question, "What is your name?," as well as Aseneth's motivation to "glorify" the angel (δοξάζω), it seems more likely that Judg 13, and not Gen 32, inspired the additions to 15:12x in these witnesses.

132. The other manuscripts of L2 read *magna sunt et claudenda nimis*. Burchard suggests that *claudenda* was meant to read *laudanda*; in MS 455, another hand corrected *claudenda* to read *celanda* (*Untersuchungen zu Joseph und Aseneth*, 72; and Burchard, *Joseph und Aseneth*, 199). See also, Fink, *Joseph und Aseneth*, 298.

133. Burchard, *Joseph und Aseneth*, 199.

With the remaining *b* witnesses, MS G just attests to numbers 1–3 ("What is your name?," δοξάζω, and the angel's query); MSS 435& (L2) provide numbers 1–3 and recount the greatness of the angel's name (albeit, not in terms of θαυμαστός); MS F provides numbers 1 and 4 (and reads εὐλογήσω for number 2); MS W provides number 1 plus εὐλογήσω for number 2; and MS E just offers Aseneth's initial question to the angel (no. 1).

So Kraemer's assessment needs to be qualified: based on family *c* and L1 (with perhaps Arm and 436 [L2]) from *b*, one trajectory in the transmission of *Aseneth* reveals a possible attempt to associate the encounter between Aseneth and an angel more closely with the encounter between Manoah and his wife and an angel in the book of Judges. Manuscripts G and 435& (L2) from *b* demonstrate other ways that Aseneth's encounter with the angel was further connected with Judg 13. Perhaps MS F was produced with this allusion in mind, but its choice of εὐλογήσω instead of δοξάζω weakens the link between its version of 15:12x and Judg 13, and MS E and MS W are least convincing in demonstrating a close connection between *Asen.* 15 and LXX Judg 13. When we look at the textual evidence in this way, we can identify distinctions in presentation, but the argument that the longer text (Burchard's reconstruction) lengthened the shorter text (Philonenko's reconstruction) is compromised. One may still argue that textual witnesses in *b* and *c* lengthened exemplars of *d*, but the variations displayed among the witnesses may simply show different renditions of the *Aseneth* story. A good example of this point comes from Burchard's reconstruction of 11:1x–18.

In this scene, Aseneth prays to God after seven days of repentance and solitude. In Philonenko's text, Aseneth offers one prayer that she utters aloud (12:1–13.12/Bu 11:19–13:15), but preceding this prayer, Burchard's text has two additional prayers that Aseneth speaks "in her heart" (ἐν τῇ καρδίᾳ αὐτῆς, 11:3–18). Kraemer surmises that Bu 11:1x–18 resulted from a scribe's reflection upon Aseneth's words in Bu 12:5/Ph 12:6: οὐκ εἰμὶ ἀξία ἀνοῖξαι τὸ στόμα μου πρὸς σέ ("I am not worthy to open my mouth to you"). The two prayers in the longer text set up how Aseneth could dare to speak aloud; she prayed silently, confessing her sins and praying to be able to address God aloud.[134] Certainly Bu 11:1x–18 displays Aseneth's deliberation over whether or not she should open her mouth, and it is plausible that Bu 12:5/Ph 12:6 functioned as a catalyst for this expan-

---

134. Kraemer, *When Aseneth Met Joseph*, 54.

sion. Yet once again the explanation for chapter 11 needs to be qualified. According to Burchard's apparatus, all manuscripts that preserve chapters 10–13 of *Aseneth*, except for the *d* tradition, attest to some form of 11:1x–14 in Burchard's reconstruction, but not all attest to the same portions of this chapter.[135] Most notably from family *b*, witnesses Syr, Arm, and MS G attest more or less to Bu 11:1x–18 in its entirety (as does also family *c*); MS 436 (L2) only attests to Bu 11:15–18, and the following manuscripts omit Bu 11:15–18: MS FW, MS Ngr, MS L1, and MS E (as well as family *a*).[136] If we look more closely at Bu 11:15–18, more complexities emerge. Part of verse 18 of Burchard's text (the longer text) reads as follows:

καὶ εἰ θυμῷ κύριος πατάξει με αὐτὸς πάλιν ἰάσεταί με καὶ ἐάν παιδεύσῃ με ἐν ταῖς μάστιξιν αὐτοῦ αὐτὸς ἐπιβλέψει ἐπ' ἐμοὶ πάλιν ἐν τῷ ἐλέει αὐτοῦ καὶ ἐάν θυμωθῇ ἐν ταῖς ἁμαρτίαις μου πάλιν διαλλαγήσεταί μοι καὶ ἀφήσει μοι πᾶσαν ἁμαρτίαν.

And if the Lord strikes me in anger, He in turn will heal me. If He disciplines me with His whips, He in turn will look upon me in His mercy, and if He is angry because of my sins, He in turn will be reconciled with me and He will pardon me (of) every sin.

Of the Greek witnesses, only family *c* appears to attest to this sentence; no Greek witnesses of former *b* provide this line. Witnesses Arm (of family *b*) and *c* appear to share the most in common, but Arm does not appear to reflect a word-for-word translation of a Greek exemplar that was similar to that of *c*.[137] Latin MS 436 (L2 of family *b*) comes close to Arm and

---

135. Burchard, *Joseph und Aseneth*, 141–49. See also, Burchard, "Joseph and Aseneth," 217 n. 11b.

136. Burchard, *Joseph und Aseneth*, 141–49.

137. Burchard provides the following translation of the Armenian attestation (it is unclear which Armenian manuscripts actually attest to this line): "und wenn (er) zürnend schlägt mich, ist (er) fähig, wieder (zu) heilen mich; und wenn (er) zurechtweist mich (durch) Martern, ist (er) fähig, doppelt (zu) trösten mich, und im Zurechtweisen wird (er) erneuern mich (durch) Barmherzigkeit seine; und wenn (er) zürnt wegen Sünden meine, wird (er) versöhnen sich mit mir und wird vergeben mir alle Sünden meine." (*Joseph und Aseneth*, 153). The greatest differences between *c* and Arm are: (1) ἐπιβλέψει ἐπ' ἐμοί in *c* and "(zu) trösten mich" in Arm; and (2) Arm has an extended phrase—"im Zurechtweisen wird (er) erneuern mich (durch) Barmherzigkeit seine"—that does not appear fully in *c*. Family *c* only refers to God's compassion as a part of "looking upon" Aseneth (ἐπιβλέπω, above).

c, but it shares a similar line with Arm that *c* lacks (cf. *ipse refovebit me misericordia sua* in MS 436 and "wird [er] erneuern mich [durch] Barmherzigkeit seine" in Arm). The Syriac (of family *b*) has traces of the above portion of Burchard's 11:18, and although the Latin MSS 435& (L2) do not attest to 11:15–18, they provide a resemblance of the first two parts of the above sentence from 11:18 in their rendition of 11:13 (cf. καὶ εἰ θυμῷ κύριος πατάξει με αὐτὸς πάλιν ἰάσεταί με καὶ ἐὰν παιδεύσῃ με ἐν ταῖς μάστιξιν αὐτοῦ αὐτὸς ἐπιβλέψει ἐπ' ἐμοὶ πάλιν ἐν τῷ ἐλέει αὐτοῦ and *si iratus michi fuerit dominus ipse remediatur michi. et si castigaverit me in verberibus suis ipse revocabit me in misericordiam suam*).[138] In summary, then, not only does the textual evidence suggest that one trajectory of the tradition provides one silent prayer (11:1x–14 or 11:15–18) and another trajectory presents two silent prayers (11:1x–18), but also few of these prayers look exactly the same. Since family *d* lacks these soliloquies, it represents a trajectory in the tradition that maintained a more concise account of Aseneth's deliberation, but there are too many variables in all the witnesses to discern one decisive path of redaction. Our witnesses demonstrate a variety of expressions of how Aseneth ponders her predicament, but these witnesses do not simply reflect a redaction that was based on a response to Ph 12:6 in the *d* family alone.

The seeming expansions of *Aseneth* that Kraemer identifies, admittedly could have been motivated by scribes fleshing out biblical allusions or even tweaking the characterization of Aseneth. This argument is easier to make, however, when one just looks at two texts (the two reconstructions). Our examples from chapters 15 and 11 above illustrate that the textual witnesses—even those outside of families *b* and *d*—reflect so many variations in the telling of *Aseneth* that we need to raise the question whether we can discern the path of redaction. As I will discuss in the next chapter, Fink provides an extensive attempt to answer this question, but for now I will simply state that the witnesses of *b* and *d* ultimately fail to support Kraemer's argument that the longer text is a redaction of the shorter text. This can most persuasively be shown in places where Kraemer claims that the

---

138. Burchard provides the following for the Syriac: *et si irascetur mihi et castigabit me, Dominus est, et ipse posside(bi?)t me; et si rursus percutiet me ipse sanabit me* (*Joseph und Aseneth*, 152). See also Fink, *Joseph und Aseneth*, 283–85. In addition, ch. 11, v. 18 in MS 436 from L2 shares similarities with MSS 435& in 11:13. Part of MS 436 reads: *Si enim iratus michi fuerit deus, ipse remediabit me et castigabit me in verbis suis, ipse refovebit me misericordia sua* (Fink, *Joseph und Aseneth*, 284).

longer text diminishes the characterization of the Aseneth as portrayed in the shorter text.

One example is the comparison between Ph 18:3–7 and Bu 18:5–9, where Kraemer contends that the shorter text associates Aseneth with Moses but the longer text weakens this correlation. In chapter 18 of both reconstructions, Aseneth prepares for Joseph's second arrival by clothing herself in her best garments, "which had the appearance of lightning" (Bu 18:5/Ph 18:3), adorning herself with her best jewelry, and covering her head with a veil (θέριστρον). She then requests a bowl of fresh spring water, and the narrator describes her face as shining "like the sun" and her eyes "like a morning/rising star" (Bu 18:8–9/Ph 18:7). The longer text adds the following to this scene: (1) the description of Aseneth's special robe as a wedding garment and her veil as that of a bride (Bu 18:5–6); (2) the motivation for Aseneth's request for the water (in order to wash her face) (Bu 18:9); and (3) the extended description of Aseneth's beauty after she receives the bowl (Bu 18:9).[139] Kraemer also mentions the longer text's addition of a servant (τροφεύς in Burchard's reconstruction) who, out of concern for Aseneth, initially calls attention to her ash-covered appearance (Bu 18:3–4). The servant's comments remind Aseneth that she must alter her physical appearance in order to look appealing to Joseph, and it is for this reason she requests the bowl of water (point 2 above).[140] Given these alterations, Kraemer suggests that the scribe(s) of the longer text may have purposefully accentuated the bridal imagery, which in and of itself "mutes the mystical angelic motifs" that the shorter text uses to portray Aseneth.[141]

---

139. Kraemer, *When Aseneth Met Joseph*, 70–72.
140. Kraemer, *When Aseneth Met Joseph*, 69–71.
141. Quotation from Kraemer, *When Aseneth Met Joseph*, 72. Kraemer partially supports the claim of accentuated bridal imagery by her interpretation of the Song of Songs. The extended description of Aseneth's beauty in Bu 18:9 imitates the language between the protagonists of the Song of Songs. Kraemer assumes that the Song of Songs is about marriage and *Aseneth*'s reference to this biblical text here possibly "constitutes an intentional further recasting of Aseneth in the person of the beloved bride" (*When Aseneth Met Joseph*, 72). Although there is ample evidence that the Song of Songs was interpreted in later periods by both Christian and Jewish communities as a metaphor of marriage between God and believers, it is not necessarily evident that the application of Song of Songs imagery in 18:9 was intended to emphasize Aseneth's and Joseph's *marriage*. At the literal level, the Song of Songs primarily expresses the physical attraction and love between a man and a woman; little is mentioned about marriage in the text itself. It is equally possible that this Songs-like enhancement in ch. 18 was intended to

In particular, Kraemer interprets the longer text's modification of the veil's usage as a significant alteration of the shorter text:

> Taken together with the garment of light, these scenes [adorning herself in jewelry, covering her head with a veil, and seeing her face reflecting off the water like the sun] in the shorter version affirm Aseneth's angelic transformation. It may also allude to the transformation of Moses in Exodus 34.29–34, which says that when Moses came down from Sinai, he did not know that his face shone because he had been talking to God. After this experience, Moses veils his face before the Israelites except when he goes to speak with God. This lends the veiling of Aseneth an interpretation alternative to the view that it reflects her status as a respectable woman. In subsequent Jewish mystical traditions, Moses' face was believed to shine with the reflection of God's glory. Aseneth's veiling may be analogous to that of Moses: just as Moses spoke with God face to face and beheld an aspect of God, so Aseneth has conversed with God, or at least God's manifestation in the form of the angel. Therefore, like Moses, her face shines and requires a veil to protect others from the brilliance of her face. If so, the reading of the longer text, which makes her veil unambiguously that of a bride, effectively, and perhaps intentionally, mutes the association of Aseneth with Moses.[142]

Although Kraemer presents this suggestion tentatively ("it may also allude to"), she returns to the idea that Aseneth is a female Moses of sorts. When discussing Aseneth's transformation, Kraemer suggests that Aseneth's encounter with the angelic figure is akin to Moses's encounter with God at Sinai. Just as Moses ascended Mount Sinai and God descended to meet him, Aseneth ascends to her upper room, which she transforms into a sacred place, and the angelic figure descends to her.[143]

Although ancient audiences could have interpreted the text in the way that Kraemer proposes, there are other, equally viable ways they could have understood this scene. As Kraemer admits, a significant part of Aseneth's

---

add to the sexual quality of the story and not necessarily to emphasize Aseneth's status as a bride. Kraemer does not explain why the bridal imagery and the angelic motifs are mutually exclusive. Her discussion implies that bridal imagery expresses the restriction of women and their societal roles whereas angelic motifs indicate the empowerment of women (see *When Aseneth Met Joseph*, 191–221).

142. Kraemer, *When Aseneth Met Joseph*, 72–73.
143. Kraemer, *When Aseneth Met Joseph*, 116.

ordained purpose is to marry Joseph.[144] The angelic figure's primary message includes the proclamation that Aseneth will be Joseph's bride and Joseph will be her groom (Bu 15:6/Ph 15:5). The angelic figure also orders Aseneth to put on a wedding garment (στολὴ γάμου) and to "adorn yourself like a bride" (κατακόσμησον σεαυτὴν ὡς νύμφην) (Bu/Ph 15:10).[145] Kraemer argues that in chapter 15, the longer text "expands on the bridal imagery, calling Aseneth's ornaments bridal as well and exhorting her to dress not merely as a bride, as in the short text, but as a good bride (νύμφη ἀγαθή)."[146] Although this observation correctly distinguishes between the reconstructions, the individual witnesses exhibit some freedom in describing Aseneth's garb in chapter 15, and all that preserve this scene (except for the Slavonic version) clearly imply that she should prepare to marry Joseph.[147] In chapter 18, then, the emphasis on Aseneth's clothing as bridal may simply be a reminder to the audience that Aseneth is following through with the angelic figure's command.[148] Even the Slavonic version (from the *d* family) preserves this purpose of Aseneth's actions in chap-

---

144. Kraemer, *When Aseneth Met Joseph*, 30.

145. In a footnote discussing ch. 15, Kraemer stated: "Interestingly, though, στόλην τοῦ γάμου is absent in A (Batiffol, 'Livre') and in the Syriac at 15:10, and this entire episode is absent in L1; according to Burchard, 'Joseph and Aseneth,' it is present in L2" (*When Aseneth Met Joseph*, 86 n. 67). This statement needs correction. First, Batiffol's representation of MS A lacks στολὴ γάμου in ch. 18 (Batiffol: 67,20) but attests to this phrase in ch. 15 (Batiffol: 62,3). Also, as will be discussed shortly, MS A complicates Kraemer's understanding of the motivations behind the longer text in ch. 18. Second, the Syriac lacks 15:10 because 13:15–16:7 *are lost*; we can say nothing conclusive about the *Aseneth* tradition represented by the Syriac manuscript with regard to these chapters. Third, according to Burchard's critical edition, L1 attests to the phrase *stolam nuptialem*, L2 attests to *vestem nuptialem*, and in general, some form of στολὴ γάμου is represented in all the manuscript families (also from family *b*: Arm, FW, G, and E; and from *a* [MSS AP], *c*, and *d* [MSS BD]). The following witnesses attest to some form of the phrase κατακόσμησον σεαυτὴν ὡς νύμφην: (1) from *b*: Arm, L2, FW, L1, and G; (2) *a*; (3) *c*; (4) MSS B and D from *d*. Manuscript E (also from *b*) also refers to Aseneth dressing like a bride (but does not attest to κατακόσμησον or an equivalent verb) (Burchard, *Joseph und Aseneth*, 195).

146. Kraemer, *When Aseneth Met Joseph*, 86.

147. For the freedom in describing Aseneth's garb, see Burchard, *Joseph und Aseneth*, 195. Regarding the witnesses of family *b*, ἀγαθή is not attested in 435& (L2) and L1; MS G provides καλῇ instead; and the Syriac is missing leaves in this portion of the narrative. Family *a* (and *c*) attests to ἀγαθή, but family *d* does not (Burchard, *Joseph und Aseneth*, 195).

148. Kraemer offered a similar solution for the reason why the longer text has

ter 18. Although it omits Bu 15:7–12x/Ph 15:6–13 (from καταφυγῆς ... αἰῶνα), in chapter 18, the Slavonic version narrates that Aseneth "brought out her wedding-raiment, and decked herself like a bride for the marriage-chamber."[149] It is also interesting to note that MS A (the primary witness of the *a* family) has many of the features displayed in the longer text (i.e., the scene with a head servant [ὁ ἐπὶ τῆς οἰκίας αὐτῆς] and the expanded reflection upon Aseneth's physical appearance), but lacks the emphasis of her garb as bridal.[150] At the very least, MS A demonstrates that the servant passage and the description of Aseneth's beauty are not necessarily associated with portraying Aseneth as a bride (as Kraemer claimed). Clearly the textual evidence preserves different descriptions of Aseneth as she prepared to meet Joseph a second time. Given these concerns, the correspondence Kraemer identifies between Aseneth and Moses, especially in terms of her use of a "veil" (θέριστρον in the Greek witnesses) seems even less apparent. There is no explicit literal connection between *Aseneth* and LXX Exod 34 (e.g., Moses puts on a κάλυμμα and not a θέριστρον), and it is not evident how highlighting Aseneth's relationship with Joseph (by using explicit bridal language or by alluding to the love expressed in the Song of Songs) inevitably diminishes her status in the narrative.

In this case, the textual evidence fails to indicate the motive that Kraemer proposes. According to the storyline of *Aseneth*, the angelic figure assures Aseneth that she will marry Joseph (ch. 15), and so the description of Aseneth's bridal appearance in chapter 18 is not surprising. The depiction of Aseneth as a bride is attested in both the *d* and *b* families (from which the shorter and longer texts supposedly derive), and Aseneth's veiled head in Ph 18:6 does not allude clearly to Moses in LXX Exod 34. Finally, the portrayal of Aseneth as a bride or as physically beautiful does

---

"And Aseneth remembered the figure and his commandment" in Bu 18:5b (*When Aseneth Met Joseph*, 70).

149. For the omission, see Burchard, *Joseph und Aseneth*, 191. The translation is the one provided by Brooks. According to him, this verse is all the Slavonic reads for Bu 18:5/Ph 18:3 (beginning at "she brought out her," ἐξήνεγκε) to Bu 19:1/Ph 19:1a (ending at "'Joseph stands/is before the doors of our courtyard'") (E. W. Brooks, *Joseph and Aseneth*, TED 2 [London: SPCK, 1918], 56 n. 1). According to Burchard, from 18:5 (ὡς ἀστραπήν) to 20:2 (as far as οἰκίαν αὐτῆς), the Slavonic (translated into German) reads "und schmückte sich wie (eine) Braut in (dem) Gemach. Herzukam aber Iosif" (*Joseph und Aseneth*, 233).

150. Batiffol 67, 8–18 and 67, 20. See also Burchard, *Joseph und Aseneth*, 231–38.

1. The Reconstructed Texts of *Aseneth*: Standhartinger and Kraemer   69

not necessarily reduce her status in the story given her role at the end of the narrative.

Some of Kraemer's identified biblical allusions need clarification or are more difficult to defend after viewing the individual textual witnesses.[151] Her dependence upon the textual reconstructions undermines her fundamental thesis about the transmission history of *Aseneth* (*d* as earliest from which *b* descends), and this point is best demonstrated by her exegesis of Bu 15:7b/Ph 15:7. According to Kraemer, the portrayal of Metanoia in the two reconstructions represents a shift in female characterization. She displays the two traditions as follows, with the longer text's additions in

---

151. Two examples that influence Kraemer's argument for the provenance of *Aseneth* are (1) Bu 11:3,15 and LXX Ps 29:12–13; and (2) Bu 16:15 and LXX Gen 2–3. Building upon her assessment that ch. 11 explains Aseneth's comment in Bu 12:5/Ph 12:6 ("I am not worthy to open my mouth before you"), Kraemer suggested that ch. 11 may have used the form of a psalm like Ps 29 to construct Aseneth's prayer. "A passage such as LXX/OG Psalm 29.12–13 might well have provided the skeletal framework for this section: 'You have turned my mourning into dancing; you have taken off my sackcloth and clothed me with joy, so that my soul may praise you and not be silent'" (*When Aseneth Met Joseph*, 54). As discussed above, Kraemer presented a plausible reason for why Aseneth prays "in her heart" in some manuscripts because the phrase from 12:5/12:6 appears to be well attested. Although it is conceivable that passages like Ps 29 fed the imagination of scribes transmitting *Aseneth*, it is difficult to defend the likelihood of scribes associating Ps 29 with Aseneth praying silently. Kraemer referred to this suggested association again in her summary of how the longer text alters the presentation of Aseneth (she mistakenly refers to vv. 11–12 of Ps 29, but she provides vv. 12–13 of LXX/OG Ps 29 in her notations) (*When Aseneth Met Joseph*, 207). Referring to Bu 16:15 ([and the angel] εἶπεν αὐτῇ φάγε καὶ ἔφαγεν), Kraemer stated, "The seemingly small addition of the angel's injunction to Aseneth to eat allows the story to be read now as an inversion of Genesis 2–3. There, of course, a woman eats the fruit of mortality and shares it with her husband. Here a masculine figure (a double of Aseneth's future husband, Joseph) eats the food of immortality and then gives some to the woman. Not only does the angel give this transformative food to Aseneth, but also he explicitly tells her to eat it. In Genesis 3.12, Adam says only that Eve gave him the fruit and he ate it. But in Genesis 3.17, God says to Adam, 'You have listened to the voice of your wife,' implying that Eve actually spoke to Adam. Thus this small detail reverses the biblical account with careful precision" (*When Aseneth Met Joseph*, 65). It becomes clear in Kraemer's discussion that she believed this interpretation is intended in the longer text (*When Aseneth Met Joseph*, 70, 197, 208–9, 220 n. 60, 263, 266, 269). It is possible that ancient audiences interpreted this passage in this way, but the exegetical connection is far from obvious; Kraemer's argument is undermined by her dependence upon it.

bold and, when different than the longer text, the shorter text's presentation in parentheses:[152]

> For Metanoia/Repentance is **in the heavens, an exceedingly beautiful and good** a daughter of the Most High, and she appeals to the Most High on your behalf every hour, and on behalf of all those who repent **in the name of the Most High God**, because he is the father of Metanoia and she is the (mother) **guardian** of virgins, and **loves you very much and** at every hour she appeals to (him) **the most High** for those who repent, for she has prepared (a heavenly bridal chamber for those who love her) **for all those who repent a place of rest in the heavens and she will renew all those who repent** and she will serve them for eternal time.
>
> And Metanoia is a very beautiful virgin, pure **and laughing always** and holy and gentle, and God the Most High **Father** loves her and all the angels stand in awe of her. **And I, too, love her exceedingly, because she is also my sister. And because she loves you virgins, I love you too.**

Kraemer contends that the longer text shifts the "more gender-specific imagery" of Metanoia as "mother" and as one "who prepares her daughter's bridal chamber," to "a more inclusive image of the overseer [ἐπίσκοπος] who prepares a place of rest."[153] Along with more explicitly associating Metanoia with Wisdom, the longer text relegates the position of Metanoia in terms of her relation to God and to the angelic figure.[154] In the shorter text, Metanoia is an active agent whom the angels revere; in the longer text, Metanoia's extraordinary status (as daughter of God) is diminished by the "narrator's voice asserting a causal relationship between her attributes and divine response" and by the angelic figure asserting his identity in relationship to Metanoia and God.[155] This alteration in the longer text,

---

152. Kraemer, *When Aseneth Met Joseph*, 61.

153. Kraemer, *When Aseneth Met Joseph*, 61.

154. Kraemer suggested the following literary correspondences: (1) Metanoia's dwelling in the heavens and Wis Sol 9:10, (2) Metanoia preparing a place of rest and Wis 8:16 [and one could add Sir 6:28], and (3) Metanoia's laughter and Prov 8:30 (*When Aseneth Met Joseph*, 61).

155. Quotation from Kraemer, *When Aseneth Met Joseph*, 62. Kraemer seems to suggest that in the shorter text, this pericope solely introduced the qualities of Metanoia, but in the longer text, the angelic figure asserts his identity into his portrayal of Metanoia. The third-person description changes to a first-person address, "And I, too, love her exceedingly." Furthermore, Kraemer identified in several places (like Ph 15.2–5/Bu 15:4–6) where, in the shorter text, the angelic figure acts as a messenger of

"offers a diminished portrait of Metanoia more reliant on ancient constructions of the proper woman."[156] Instead of being identified in terms of her active traits, she is identified in terms of her relationship with male figures and "she is loved by [God and the angelic figure] not for her role in the salvation of the repentant but for her qualities of beauty, chastity, good disposition, and meekness."[157]

A few qualifications can be made about this reading of the two reconstructions. First, Kraemer identifies the recipients of the bridal chamber as female (daughters), but they are not specifically distinguished as female in the Greek (τοῖς ἀγαπῶσιν αὐτήν, "those who love her [Metanoia]"), according to Philonenko's reconstruction).[158] The text could also imply that Metanoia prepares men's bridal chambers (see more below). Second, Kraemer did not clarify how the "narrator's voice" in the longer text exhibits a "causal relationship" between Metanoia's attributes and God's response and thus diminishes the portrayal of Metanoia. Perhaps she was suggesting that the additional reminders of "the God Most High" in the longer text draw more attention to the source of Metanoia's abilities and detracts from focusing on the extraordinary nature of Metanoia herself. To Kraemer, the longer text's emphasis on Metanoia's inactive characteristics had a "domesticating" effect on the portrayal of Metanoia, but the shorter *and* longer texts portray Metanoia with these attributes (beautiful, chaste, gentle). Kraemer also did not address how the title of ἐπίσκοπος in the longer text diminishes Metanoia's status.[159] As Kraemer noted elsewhere in her discussion, this title is also used to describe Pentephres (21:11 of the longer text), and so its application to Metanoia's status may imply her active role.[160]

God (speaking of God's power in the third-person), but in the longer text, Kraemer argued, the angelic figure serves as a "divine co-regent" (speaking of God's power in the first-person) (*When Aseneth Met Joseph*, 60, 120–27). In 15:8 of the longer text, the angelic figure adds that he loves Metanoia "too" (e.g., just as God loves her, so does the angel) and he places himself alongside Metanoia by identifying himself as her brother.

156. Kraemer, *When Aseneth Met Joseph*, 208.
157. Kraemer, *When Aseneth Met Joseph*, 208.
158. Kraemer also alluded to Anna in Tobit and the Seila's mother in Pseudo-Philo as other examples where mothers prepared their daughters' bridal chambers (*When Aseneth Met Joseph*, 84 n. 36).
159. Kraemer, *When Aseneth Met Joseph*, 61–62, 208.
160. For the title also being used of Pentephres, see Kraemer, *When Aseneth Met Joseph*, 84 n. 35.

These comments aside, the textual evidence for this pericope raises a more pressing concern when addressing Kraemer's analysis. There are irreconcilable differences attested in the textual witnesses with regard to this scene, and especially since the *d* family *alone* displays significant variations, it is difficult to ascertain any general pattern in the transmission of this passage. To demonstrate this point, below is Philonenko's reconstruction of 15:7 and what the *d* manuscripts exhibit individually (Slav lacks Ph 15:6–13).[161]

Ph 15:7	B	D
Διότι ἡ μετάνοιά ἐστι θυγάτηρ τοῦ ὑψίστου καὶ αὐτὴ παρακαλεῖ τὸν ὕψιστον ὑπὲρ σοῦ πᾶσαν ὥραν καὶ ὑπὲρ πάντων τῶν μετανοούντων,	διότι ἡ μετάνοιά ἐστι θυγάτηρ τοῦ ὑψίστου καὶ αὐτὴ παρακαλεῖ τὸν θεὸν τὸν ὕψιστον ὑπὲρ τῶν μετανοόντων	διότι ἡ μετάνοιά ἐστι θυγάτηρ τοῦ ὑψίστου καὶ αὐτὴ παρακαλεῖ τὸν ὕψιστον ὑπὲρ σοῦ πᾶσαν ὥραν
ἐπειδὴ πατήρ ἐστι τῆς μετανοίας καὶ αὕτη ἐστὶ μήτηρ παρθένων καὶ πᾶσαν ὥραν περὶ τῶν μετανοούντων ἐρωτᾷ αὐτὸν διότι τοῖς ἀγαπῶσιν αὐτὴν ἡτοίμασε νυμφῶνα οὐράνιον, καὶ αὕτη διακονήσει αὐτοῖς εἰς τὸν αἰῶνα χρόνον.	ἐπειδὴ πατήρ ἐστι τῆς μετανοίας καὶ τοῖς ἀγαπῶσιν αὐτὸν ἡτοίμασεν εἰς νυμφῶνα οὐράνιον καὶ αὕτη διακονήσει αὐτοῖς εἰς τὸν αἰῶνα χρόνον.	διότι αὕτη ἐστὶ μήτηρ παρθένων καὶ πᾶσαν ὥραν περὶ τῶν μετανοόντων ἐρωτᾷ αὐτὸν διότι τοῖς ἀγαπῶσιν αὐτὴν ἡτοίμασε νυμφῶνα οὐράνιον καὶ αὕτη διακονήσει αὐτοῖς εἰς τὸν αἰῶνα χρόνον.

---

161. The gap in the Slavonic witnesses not only includes the explication about Metanoia but also the detailed description about the significance of Aseneth's new name and the proclamation that she is destined to marry Joseph. The content in the chart is taken from Philonenko's apparatus, and Burchard's detailed discussion in *Untersuchungen zu Joseph und Asenath*, 55–67; and in *Joseph und Aseneth*, 190–93. Standhartinger also noted the difficulties of Philonenko's reconstruction of this verse (*Das Frauenbild im Judentum*, 45 n. 210).

The *d* witnesses that attest to 15:7 vary in the following ways: MS B appears to focus more on God than on Metanoia. A bridal chamber is prepared for those who love *him* (αὐτόν), and given the ambiguity of B's passage, it may be *God* who prepares the bridal chamber.[162] Only MS D expresses Metanoia as a mother and emphasizes that a bridal chamber is arranged for those who love *her* (αὐτήν). Furthermore, it could be argued that MS B emphasizes God as the active agent (Metanoia appeals to God on behalf of the repentant "since he is [the] father of Metanoia"), whereas MS D accentuates Metanoia as the primary agent (she appeals to God "because she is [the] mother of *parthenoi*"). Burchard warns that 15:7–8 (of both reconstructions) are problematic, and he published a full apparatus of the textual evidence in his first monograph on *Aseneth* that exposes the complexity of how this verse was preserved and transmitted.[163] Only *one b* witness refers to God as the father of Metanoia in this verse (MS G reads πρὸς πατρὸς αὐτῆς). Family *c* also attests to πατρὸς αὐτῆς, and only family *a* and MS B (of the *d* family) attest to: ἐπειδὴ πατήρ ἐστι τῆς μετανοίας, which is what Burchard provides in his reconstruction (Kraemer's "longer text"). The Syriac folios are missing for this chapter, but the rest of the *b* witnesses (Arm, L2, FW, L1, and E) and of *d* (D and Slav) lack reference to God as Metanoia's father.[164] Another poignant example: although no other witnesses attest to the maternal image of Metanoia in the exact same place as it is in MS D, the Latin MS 436 (from L2 of family *b*) presents a lengthy addition elsewhere in this verse that portrays Metanoia as a mother.[165] It is impossible to discern the earliest form of this passage, especially with regard to Metanoia's particular relationship with God and humans.

---

162. One could supply the analogue from midrashim in which the king builds a bridal chamber for his son. See, e.g., Lam. Rab. 4.11.

163. "This is one of the most badly damaged passages of this book, especially in the second half of vs. 7." (Burchard, "Joseph and Aseneth," 226 n. k. For the apparatus, see Burchard, *Untersuchungen zu Joseph und Aseneth*, 55–67.

164. Burchard, *Joseph und Aseneth*, 192. Fink revises Burchard's text to reflect the reading from G and family *c*, and she maintains that the attestation in MS B is a contamination from the ancestor of MS A (*Joseph und Aseneth*, 55, 119).

165. This addition is located after the mention of the "prepared place" (in BD it is a bridal chamber, for 436 it is a place of rest). Also in MS 436, although Metanoia is called the mother of all those who repent, God is called the father of virginity (*et sicut dominus pater est virginitatis ita penitentia mater est omnium penitentium*) (Burchard, *Joseph und Aseneth*, 193; Fink, *Joseph und Aseneth*, 295–96).

Overall in her monograph, Kraemer convincingly demonstrates that some of the differences between the longer and shorter texts reflect redactions, especially in terms of literary expansions that associate *Aseneth* more closely with septuagintal passages. Nevertheless, as we have seen, redaction occurred with most of the manuscripts, not just between manuscript families. Even the *b* family shows signs of multiple kinds of tellings within its manuscript group, as demonstrated with the examples of Bu 11:1x–18 and Bu 15:12x. How Kraemer interpreted *Asen.* 18 and 15 in the shorter and longer texts also reveals the shortcomings of using the two reconstructions to propose purposeful choices made in the transmission of this narrative. When examining individual witnesses, we found variants of *Asen.* 18 and 15 within the *d* family alone (where the Slavonic emphasizes Aseneth as a bride in ch. 18, and MS B highlights the agency of God in ch. 15). Distinct ideological readings that Kraemer only assigned to the longer text turned out to exist in witnesses of the shorter text as well. This evidence undermines the argument that family *b* reveals purposeful redactions of the *d* family. Furthermore, given the variants across manuscript families, it is less certain that a shorter text is necessarily the earliest or that we can plot out the chronological order in which exemplars were produced. It is equally likely that several renditions of *Aseneth* existed at any given time, some shorter and others longer.

The Limitations of Comparing the Reconstructed Texts of *Aseneth*

As we have seen, the manuscript evidence exhibits more variety than what the reconstructions suggest; redaction seems to have occurred within textual families (such as in chs. 11 and 15), and some indications of redaction are best understood as different approaches to narrating the same scene (e.g., regarding the window scene in ch. 10 and Aseneth's preparation in ch. 18). When viewing the witnesses independently, then, it becomes more difficult to identify specific, ideologically based alterations to the narrative. Scholarly dependence upon these reconstructions, though, produces even more fundamental problems. Standhartinger's and Kraemer's theses presume that Burchard's and Philonenko's reconstructions represent textual snapshots in the earlier stages of the transmission of *Aseneth*. Such analysis implies (whether intentional or not) a linear trajectory of influence whereby scribes copied and redacted one text to produce the other, but neither reconstructed text actually exists in the evidence. It is more precise to say that some witnesses seem to exhibit scribal redactions of the narrative, and many of these choices could have been made independently by several scribes (such as the biblical expansions noted by Kraemer). The assumed chronological order of the two reconstructions (whereby one represents the earliest text) also detracts from the idea that several different narrations of *Aseneth* could have existed at the same time, even during its earliest stages of existence. To depend on either reconstruction alone disregards the individual adaptations and differences between manuscripts and manuscript families, and acknowledging this multiplicity may be the key to understanding the transmission of *Aseneth*. I will note, however, that Standhartinger and Kraemer produced their analyses before the publication of Burchard's 2003 critical edition. I can attest to the difficulty in tracking down and viewing the individual witnesses, and so Standhartinger and Kraemer worked with what was available and they produced very compelling arguments. My criticism rests more on scholars post-2003 who continue to rely on the notion of a shorter or longer text, who continue to rely on Standhartinger's and Kraemer's models. The evidence is significantly more visible now, and we need to think differently about *Aseneth*.

Although Burchard modified his assessment of the transmission history of *Aseneth*, in the end he maintains the same foundational premise that the witnesses are best construed in a linear, sequential order. For him, his reconstruction best represents the earliest retrievable text of *Aseneth*, and the textual families represent general stages in the transmission process (whereby *a*/*d* are latest). Fink has made significant improvements to Burchard's text, but she, too, relies heavily on a linear schema of textual transmission. It is to the recent proposals of Burchard and Fink we now turn.

2

The Reconstructed Texts of *Aseneth* and Their Limitations: The Texts of Burchard and Fink

In his 1987 article, "The Present State of Research," Burchard expressed his reservations about the configuration of family *b* as follows:

> The trouble with this text [Burchard's reconstruction] is that in piecing it together I have come to realize that the existence of β [the hypothetical archetype of the *b* family] is far from being proven. **b** is a very variegated group in which several subgroups are discernible. My conclusion that they form a family with a common ancestor may have been precipitated by the discovery that they do not belong to either **a**, **c**, or **d**, but that is not enough. Further research into **b** is in order.... Attention ought to focus on the three-some, Syriac, Armenian and Latin II. They have much in common and their readings are sometimes superior to their rivals on internal grounds, the Greek evidence included....
>
> That leaves us with a problem which exists no matter how the textual history of JosAs [*Joseph and Aseneth*] (and that of most other Pseudepigrapha, too) is conceived, but is aggravated if the Syriac, Armenian, and Latin II are major witnesses to its oldest form. Our Greek manuscripts are Middle or even Late Byzantine. Whatever variant is judged to be original, how can we be sure about the original Greek wording? If **b** readings are preferred the case is particularly difficult because the oldest Greek manuscript is 15th century. And what if a good reading from the older versions is not represented among the Greek **b** manuscripts but only by $\alpha\delta$ or ζ [the hypothetical archetypes of (1) one common source of the families *a* and *d* (thus *ad*), and (2) family *c*, respectively], not to mention the need of retranslation if readings from the version are not found in Greek at all? Fortunately many of these problems will not affect a translation.[1]

---

1. Burchard, "Present State of Research," 34, emphasis original.

In the same article, Burchard also acknowledges that archetypes β, αδ, and ζ developed more independently than he had once presumed, "so I think that the idea that [they] evolved in a straight line has to be abandoned altogether."[2]

The questions that Burchard posed here led him to review his transmission history of *Aseneth*. In his 2003 critical edition, Burchard abandoned the Greek sigla α, β, ζ, δ, γ, φ (the latter two had signified the ancestors of [1] MSS G and Ngr, and [2] MSS F, W, and Romanian, respectively), and MS ω (which had signified the *Urschrift*), and he argued for a more complicated chronology of transmission.[3] As I mentioned in chapter 1, Burchard made the following adjustments to his classification of the witnesses: (1) family *b* has dissolved into family *f* (consisting of FWRum, GNgr, and L1) and several individual manuscript categories (Syr, Arm, L2, and E); and (2) family *c* includes the palimpsest Rehdinger 26 (referred to as "M"), which changes our understanding of this manuscript group.[4] Palimpsest M likely preserved chapters 1–29 (compared to MSS H, J, and K of family *c* that end at 16:17y in Hellenistic Greek), and it adds to the connection between family *c* on the one hand, and Syr, Arm, and L2 on the other, although *c* and *a* also share many readings in common.[5] Despite these alterations, Burchard's reconstruction remains much intact, and in spite of his call to the contrary, his history of this narrative's transmission implies more of a straight, genealogical line than what the manuscripts demonstrate. As we will see, Fink's position is hindered by similar issues.

This chapter reveals problems inherent in Burchard's and Fink's proposals about the transmission history of *Aseneth*, which are based on the idea that all witnesses but the Syriac descend from two, independent majuscules/minuscules. The variegated nature of the evidence (even beyond

---

2. Burchard, "Present State of Research," 34.
3. Burchard, *Joseph und Aseneth*, 11.
4. Burchard, *Joseph und Aseneth*, 16–22; Burchard, "Ein neuer Versuch," 239–43.
5. Burchard, *Joseph und Aseneth*, 20–22. As Burfeind identified, 19:10 in M is the only Greek text to preserve the phrase τῷ νεύματι τῶν ὀφθαλμῶν αὐτοῦ, which is otherwise only preserved in translation in Syr, Arm, and L2 ("Der Text von *Joseph und Aseneth*," 52–53; and Burchard, *Joseph und Aseneth*, 22). The manuscript is difficult to read, but it appears that M supports the relationship of family *c* siding more often with the previously categorized *b* manuscripts against families *a* and *d*. Burchard lists as examples the following shared readings between *c* and *a*: 1:2, 5–6; 3:3; 5:5–6; 6:1; 7:5; 8:8; 9:2; 10:2; 11:4, 9, 13; 12:8; 13:11; 14:4; 16:9, 13; 16:16x–17x (*Joseph und Aseneth*, 22).

2. The Reconstructed Texts of *Aseneth*: Burchard and Fink

the former *b* family group) cannot just be explained by two majuscules (or minuscules), nor does it reflect a discernable stemma or chronological classification of the witnesses. Fink improves Burchard's reconstructed text, and even though she exposes how varied the *Aseneth* witnesses can be when they describe a common scene, she ultimately prioritizes readings that support the two-majuscule/minuscule hypothesis. I will close the chapter by identifying the limitations of Burchard's and Fink's contributions and by indicating the purpose of the next chapter where I propose the value of discussing a *fabula* of *Aseneth*. For clarity, I provide again table 1.1 of Burchard's classifications; in this chapter and in the remainder of the monograph, I will refer to Burchard's 2003 classification of the textual witnesses.

Table 1.1. Burchard's classification of the textual evidence of *Aseneth*

Pre-2003 Critical Edition Classifications	2003 Critical Edition Classifications
Family *b* =	Syr
Syr	Arm
Arm	L2
L2	Family *f* = FW, G, Ngr, and L1
FW, G, and Ngr (Greek)	E
L1	
E (Greek)	
Family *c* = HJK (Greek)	Family M*c* = HJK and palimpsest M (Greek)
Family *a* = A, CR, O, PQ (Greek)	Family *a* = A, CR, O, PQ
Family *d* = BD (Greek) and Slav	Family *d* = BD and Slav

Transmission History of the *Aseneth* Witnesses: Burchard's and Fink's Assessments

Burchard posits that either (1) all the manuscripts descend from an archetype that dates to the fifth or sixth century CE and also contains a homily on Joseph (which Burchard calls Life of Joseph or LJos), or (2) the Syriac descended from one exemplar dating to the fifth or sixth century CE, and the rest of the manuscripts (except for the Ethiopic) descended from another exemplar (fifth or sixth century CE) that contained LJos (or the

LJos-JosAs archetype).⁶ Either way, from either hypothetical LJos-JosAs archetype stated above, Burchard proposes that two independent Greek majuscules were transliterated into two separate minuscules sometime during the ninth to tenth centuries CE. The Armenian and L2 translations descend from one minuscule, and the remaining manuscripts (*f*, E, Mc, *a*, and *d*) descend from the other.⁷ Of these witnesses, Burchard identifies Arm and L2 as highest in textual value for reconstructing the *Urschrift* of *Aseneth* because Arm, L2, and Syr share readings against the rest of the manuscripts.⁸ As outlined in the beginning of the last chapter, family *f* preserves the next significant set of witnesses for Burchard, followed by E, Mc, *a*, and *d*, in that order of importance.

Fink modifies Burchard's theory of transmission by presenting a more detailed stemma and by revising Burchard's reconstruction (fig. 2.1). Fink posits that the archetype of all our witnesses (ω') had LJos attached (although the exemplar of the archetype did not), and the tradition divided into two branches from that archetype. One branch of the tradition produced the exemplar (designated as "ε") of (1) the *Vorlage* of Syr (Syr^{Gr}), and (2) a single minuscule (designated as *M1*) from which both *Vorlagen* of Arm and L2 (Arm^{Gr} and L2^{Gr}) descend. The other branch produced a single minuscule (*M2*) that produced MS E and an exemplar (η) from which all the rest of the witnesses descend. Fink argues for a very linear development of these latter witnesses; the exemplar of the *f* witnesses (Ahn *f*) developed first from exemplar η, then came the exemplar of Mc (designated as "θ") descended from η, then lastly, one exemplar of both *a* and *d* (designated as "Ahn *ad* [ι]"), descended from θ and produced the two family groups *a* and *d*. Fink's stemma includes more stages in the transmission process than what Burchard suggests, and her more complicated picture helps to make sense of some of the evidence.

---

6. Burchard, *Joseph und Aseneth*, 30–33. As evident from canonical lists and literary references to *Aseneth* in Ethiopic literature, there was an Ethiopic translation. Burchard provides a list of the most useful references to the Ethiopic for conducting text-critical work ("Der jüdische Asenethroman," 608–13), but it is impossible to ascertain the placement of the Ethiopic version in the transmission history (Burchard, *Joseph und Aseneth*, 30).

7. Burchard, *Joseph und Aseneth*, 26–28.

8. See Burchard, *Joseph und Aseneth*, appendix 5.3, pp. 368–69. See also Fink, *Joseph und Aseneth*, 18–22.

2. The Reconstructed Texts of *Aseneth*: Burchard and Fink

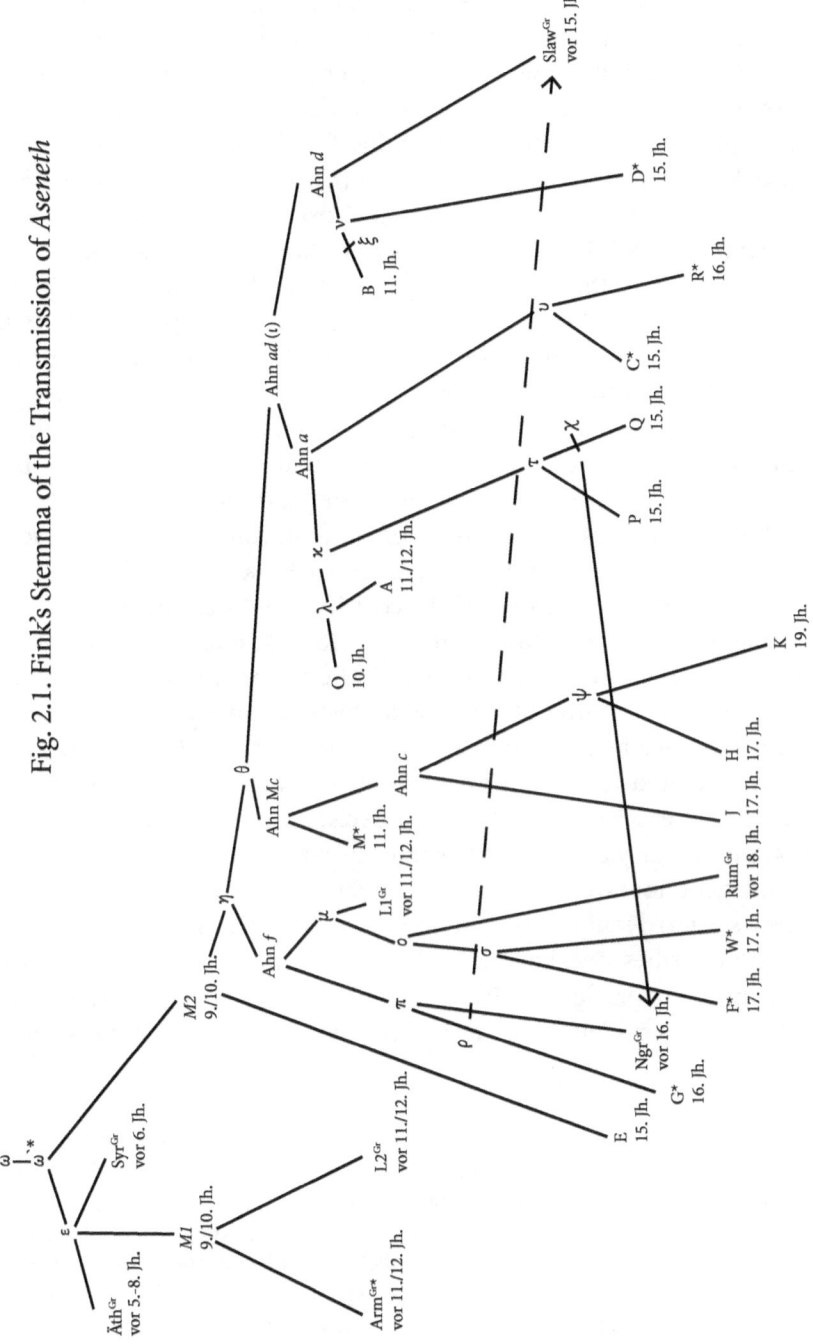

Fig. 2.1. Fink's Stemma of the Transmission of *Aseneth*

Fink's work significantly contributes to the text-critical study of *Aseneth*. First, she identifies at least 270 contaminated readings, which demonstrate the fluidity in the transmission of this story. She proposes four particular points of contamination in her stemma: (1) the exemplar of M and c (Ahn Mc) was used in the production of the exemplar of family *a* witnesses (Ahn *a*); (2) the exemplar of MS A (Vorfahr A, or λ) of family *a* was used to produce the exemplar of MS B (Vorfahr B, or ξ) of family *d*; (3) the exemplar of MS G (Vorfahr G, or ρ) of family *f* was used to produce the *Vorlage* of Slav (Slav^{Gr}) of family *d*; and (4) the exemplar of Q (from family *a*, and designated as Vorfahr Q or χ) was used to produce the Classical Greek version of Ngr (Ngr^{Gr}) of family *f*. Fink contends that these contaminations occurred in chronological order (where Ahn *a* used Ahn Mc before Vorfahr B used Vorfahr A, and so on) during the medieval production of the manuscripts when scribes could consult another copy of the story. Second, Fink advocates for greater textual value of MS E; even though E paraphrases or is abridged often, Fink contends that it preserves readings that are close to the archetype. Third, Fink provides her decipherment of palimpsest M (16:13–29:9, according to Burchard's versification) and a parallel, annotated presentation of MSS 436 and 435& (both of L2). Making these texts available is immensely helpful in improving our understanding of this narrative's transmission history. Finally, in Fink's revision of Burchard's reconstruction, she deletes words/phrases that she concludes are contaminated readings or are only from Ahn *ad* or Ahn *a*, and she presents her reasons for each textual decision. In addition, she lists and offers commentary on all readings that she admits are debatable.[9]

Fink's monograph considerably enhances our understanding of the witnesses. Her detailed presentation of textual contaminations demonstrate how scribes tweaked and fiddled with the *Aseneth* story, and her transcriptions of particular witnesses show how varied each narrative could be. Despite this evidence, however, Fink adapts Burchard's reconstruction

---

9. Fink, *Joseph und Aseneth*. Fink's presentation of the stemma is provided on pp. 14–101; her extensive discussion of the contaminated readings on pp. 48–71; a list and her commentary on the deleted readings on pp. 102–43; and a list and commentary on the questionable readings on pp. 143–61. Her transcription of palimpsest M is on pp. 32–44, and her transcription of the parallel texts of L2 are found on pp. 259–325. For a helpful summary of Fink's work, see her synopses in Fink, "Textkritische Situation," in Reinmuth, *Joseph und Aseneth*, 33–44; and Fink, "Anhang: Erläuterung zum Stemma," 45–53.

according to Burchard's two-majuscule/two-minuscule hypothesis, and as a result, there are times when she favors her hypothesized stemma over and against irreconcilable textual attestations. In this section, I will highlight complications in Burchard's hypothesis, in particular discussing the evidence of Bu 10:2 and Bu 18:9, and I will address the limitations of his and Fink's approaches with the manuscript evidence. Notwithstanding Burchard's caution about creating any sequential classification of the witnesses, Burchard's proposed transmission history of *Aseneth* presents an orderly path of production that the witnesses do not clearly demonstrate. The manuscripts reflect different kinds of usages that likely influenced how *Aseneth* was transmitted, and Burchard's reliance on *Aseneth*'s association with the Life of Joseph to construct his transmission history is premature. Likewise, Fink's extension of Burchard's proposal does not convincingly defend her stemma, and in fact, many of her observations further prove my point. Given the variegated evidence of the *Aseneth* witnesses, a linear and chronological stemma for *Aseneth*'s transmission is unattainable, and reconstructions of *Aseneth* should be treated with caution.

Burchard's transmission history relies upon his theory that all the witnesses, except for the Syriac, descend from two majuscules, and Fink assumes the same. Beginning in the ninth century, Greek textual transmission began to shift from the majuscule to the minuscule script, and by the end of the tenth century, minuscules became the norm.[10] Given that one Syriac witness (MS 2071) dates to the seventh century and that *Aseneth* was probably composed in Greek, there was likely at least one Greek majuscule of the narrative that was then transliterated into minuscule by the tenth century. In Byzantine studies, it can often be assumed that every majuscule text was transliterated into minuscule only once, and after that point the minuscule copy became the exemplar.[11] L. D. Reynolds and N. G. Wilson explain this principle as follows:

---

10. N. G. Wilson, *Scholars of Byzantium* (Baltimore: Johns Hopkins University Press, 1983), 66–67; L. D. Reynolds and N. G. Wilson, *Scribes and Scholars: A Guide to the Transmission of Greek and Latin Literature* (New York: Oxford University Press, 1991), 58–60.

11. Reynolds and Wilson, *Scribes and Scholars*, 60; Wilson, *Scholars of Byzantium*, 67. On this matter, Burchard refers to Alphonse Dain (*Les manuscrits*, Collection d'Etudes Anciennes [Paris: Les Belles Lettres, 1964], 130) (Burchard, *Joseph und Aseneth*, 26). Fink states that more transliterations of a majuscule text occur only when the evidence has been disseminated more broadly and is dated further apart (Fink, *Joseph und Aseneth*, 22).

The theory has a certain a priori justification on two grounds, since the task of transliteration from a script that was becoming less and less familiar would not be willingly undertaken more often than was absolutely necessary, and there is at least some likelihood that after the destruction of the previous centuries many texts survived in one copy only.[12]

Burchard applies this general rule to his hypothesis about the transmission of *Aseneth*. His analysis assumes that few majuscules of *Aseneth* survived by the ninth century, and he concludes that each witness category (meaning, Arm, L2, *f*, E, Mc, *a*, and *d*) could not have descended from distinct transliterated minuscules.[13] Instead, he proposes that two majuscules survived up to the ninth century and that, from their respective minuscule copies, the remaining witnesses (except for the Syriac) were produced. Fink qualifies her position more, by acknowledging cases where more transliterations per majuscule were performed, but she too concludes that all the witnesses except for the Syriac descend from two minuscules, transliterated from only two majuscules.[14] The two-majuscule theory is primarily supported by one verse (Bu 10:2) in which Arm, Syr, and MS 436 (from L2) provide a reading that is distinct from the rest of the manuscripts. Burchard admits that more examples are necessary to defend this hypothesis, and he tentatively suggests Bu 22:5 where Syr, Arm, and MS 436 (L2) read the translated equivalent of καὶ ἦλθον Ἰωσὴφ καὶ Ἀσενέθ and other witnesses read some form of καὶ ἦλθεν Ἰωσὴφ καὶ Ἀσενέθ.[15] This example, however, can be explained by Greek grammatical tendencies that are found in the Septuagint. In Hebrew prose, oftentimes third-person singular verbs are used with plural subjects.[16] It is very possible that more than one scribe who was

---

12. Reynolds and Wilson, *Scribes and Scholars*, 60.
13. Burchard, *Joseph und Aseneth*, 26.
14. Fink, "Textkritische Situation," 43.
15. The other witnesses are: MSS FW, L1, G, *d*, and *a*; palimpsest M is unreadable; MS E paraphrases; and the line is absent in MSS 435& [L2] because it ends at 21:9 (Burchard, *Joseph und Aseneth*, 27).
16. In the MT, this is especially the case with prepositive verbs (i.e., when the verb precedes the plural subject). Paul Joüon mentions that according to Menahem Moreshet, the number of times that plural subjects appear with singular verbs in the prepositive position is six times to one in the MT (*Leshonenu* 31 [1967]: 253, as cited in Joüon, *A Grammar of Biblical Hebrew*, trans. and rev. T. Muraoka, SubBi 14 [Rome: Pontifical Biblical Istitute, 1991], 2:556). E.g., Gen 33:7 reads ותגש גם-לאה

familiar with septuagintal Greek switched the grammatical number of the verb, so this example does not necessitate that MSS FW, G, L1, *d*, and *a* descended from one minuscule. Likewise, more than one scribe may have preferred the plural verb, and so Arm and MS 436 may not descend from another particular minuscule. Burchard's example from Bu 10:2, however, deserves consideration.

Burchard proposes the following as the earliest form of a line in Bu 10:2 (Ph 10:3), and Fink adapts Burchard's reconstructed text to include the line below:[17]

καὶ ἀνέστη Ἀσενὲθ ἀπὸ τῆς κλίνης αὐτῆς καὶ κατέβη ἡσύχως τὴν κλίμακα ἐκ τοῦ ὑπερῴου καὶ ἦλθεν εἰς τὸν μυλῶνα καὶ ἡ μυλωρὸς ἐκάθευδε μετὰ τῶν τέκνων αὐτῆς.
And Aseneth rose from her bed and quietly descended the staircase from the upper story, and she came to <u>the mill house</u>, and <u>the female miller</u> was sleeping with her children.

The attestations of "mill house" and "female miller" are in a few witnesses, but for comparison, all attestations of the line "and she came … with her children" are provided below:[18]

Syr: *et in pistrinum pervenit et molitrices* [*meaning: female millers*] *earumque liberi dormiebant*[19]
Arm: and she came to the mill house and the miller slept with (the miller's) children[20]

וילדיה וישתחון, and LXX Gen provides: καὶ προσήγγισεν Λεια καὶ τὰ τέκνα αὐτῆς καὶ προσεκύνησαν. Joüon also cites Num 12:1; Gen 24:61; 31:14, all of which have singular verbal forms for their respective plural subjects in the LXX (556).

17. Burchard, *Joseph und Aseneth*, 26–27; Fink, *Joseph und Aseneth*, 111, 176.

18. Burchard, *Joseph und Aseneth*, 127. Manuscript G lacks this verse, and the verse is unreadable in palimpsest M.

19. The Latin translation is taken from Brooks (*Historia ecclesiastica Zachariae Rhetori*, 21). The female noun *molitrix* for "female miller" appears to be unattested in Classical Latin.

20. Burchard provides in German the following for the Armenian (English in parentheses is what the apparatus implies about the Armenian attestations): "(and she entered) nahe zu der Mühle und der Müller (die Müllerin?) schlief (with her children)" (*Joseph und Aseneth*, 127).

435& (L2): *Veniens ad moldendinum*[21]
436 (L2): *et venit in molinam, ubi molendaria molebat cum filiis suis*[22]

F and W: καὶ ἦλθεν εἰς τὸν πυλῶνα καὶ ἡ πυλωρὸς ἐκάθευδε μετὰ τῶν τέκνων αὐτῆς

L1: (and she came) *ad portam et portarius dormiebat (cum pueris suis)*[23]

E: καὶ ἦλθεν εἰς τὸν πυλῶνα καὶ ἡ πυλωρὸς ἐκάθευδε

c: ἐλθοῦσα οὖν πρὸς τὸν πυλῶνα εὗρε τὴν πυλωρὸν καθεύδουσαν μετὰ τῶν τέκνων αὐτῆς

a: καὶ ἐλθοῦσα παρὰ τὸν πυλῶνα εὗρε τὴν θυρωρὸν καθεύδουσαν μετὰ τῶν τέκνων αὐτῆς (Q lacks μετὰ ... αὐτῆς)

d: παρὰ (Slav: πρὸς) τὸν πυλῶνα (D adds: αὐτῆς) καὶ εὗρε τὴν θυρωρὸν καθεύδουσαν μετὰ τῶν τέκνων αὐτῆς

The following witnesses attest to a "mill house": Syr, Arm, and L2 (both 436 and 435&); Syr and 436 (L2) clearly refer to a "female miller," and although Arm provides "miller," it is unclear whether a female is meant since there is no grammatical gender in the Armenian language. Several other witnesses provide τὸν πυλῶνα (gateway or doorway) instead of "mill house" and ἡ πυλωρός (female gatekeeper or doorkeeper) instead of "(female) miller." Families *a* and *d* attest to ἡ θυρωρός instead of ἡ πυλωρός, and the witness group L1 attests to *portarius*, which could be a translation of either πυλωρός or θυρωρός, but it nonetheless makes the watcher male and not female.

According to Burchard, μυλών (mill house) and ἡ μυλωρός (female miller) make the most sense in the context of the story.[24] In chapter 10, Aseneth descends from the upper story to gather ashes that she will use during her days of repentance. In contrast to the other witnesses, Arm, MS 436 (from L2), MS F and MS W (the latter two witnesses from family

---

21. Fink, *Joseph und Aseneth*, 259–325.
22. Fink, *Joseph und Aseneth*, 259–325.
23. The Latin in parentheses is provided by Batiffol's published text of L1 (MSS 421 and 431) ("Liber de Aseneth," in *Le Livre de la Prière d'Asenath*, 97). See also, Burchard, *Joseph und Aseneth*, 127.
24. The presentation of Burchard's argument in this paragraph is taken from "Zum Stand der Arbeit," 22; and Burchard, *Joseph und Aseneth*, 26–27; 127.

f) report that Aseneth gathers the ashes from a hearth, and based on this attestation, Burchard surmises that the original majuscules had the servant near a hearth.[25] For Burchard, that Aseneth would enter through a gateway (πυλών; attested in MSS FW) is less convincing than a "mill house" (μυλών; the equivalent attested in Arm and L2 [436 and 435&]), because in chapter 2, πυλών signifies a gate to a courtyard and there would not be a fire near a courtyard gate. Since also in chapter 2, eighteen men, not women, guard the πυλών, Burchard also questions the attestation of a female gatekeeper (ἡ πυλωρός; in MSS FW). Some sort of hearth as the location where Aseneth collected ashes also would fit better with a mill house (μυλών) than with a gateway, and so, a female miller (ἡ μυλωρός or even μυλωθρός; the equivalent attested in MS 436 [of L2] and perhaps in Arm) sleeping near a hearth makes more sense than a gate- or doorkeeper doing so.

In response to Burchard's theory, Standhartinger points out that the feminine form of μυλωρός is not attested in Greek, which is likely why Burchard tentatively suggests μυλωθρός.[26] Fink mentions that ἡ μυλωθρός is attested in Greek dictionaries but, as discussed below, I can only detect the word three times in two sources. If indeed the earliest text read "female miller," Standhartinger suggests it would have read ἡ μυλωθρίς, but even as Fink admits, it becomes more difficult to argue for scribal confusion when we have to account for the misreading of μ and the deletion of θ (from μυλωθρίς or μυλωθρός to πυλωρός).[27] Fink concludes that even though ἡ μυλωρός may be a *hapax legomenon*, this Greek word is what the *Vorlagen* of Syr, Arm, and L2 likely read. There is a series of Greek nouns that end in -ος and indicate gender only by modifiers, so ἡ μυλωρός is not inconceivable. Fink also seems to say that since, in her opinion, the exemplar (ε) of Syr, Arm, and L2 clearly had a "female miller," ἡ μυλωρός is the best guess for what the archetype (ω') had.[28]

According to Burchard and Fink, then, ἡ μυλωρός was originally in the Greek majuscules of *Aseneth*, and the minuscule copy from which Arm

---

25. Syr, 435& (from L2), L1, E, *c*, *a*, and *d* all indicate that Aseneth gathers ashes but do not state from where exactly. G has gaps in this section (*Joseph und Aseneth*, 127).

26. Angela Standhartinger, review of *Joseph und Aseneth*, by Christoph Burchard, *JSP* 15 (2006): 152.

27. Standhartinger, review of *Joseph und Aseneth*, 152; Fink, *Joseph und Aseneth*, 23–24.

28. Fink, *Joseph und Aseneth*, 24–25.

and L2 derive transliterated the uncial M correctly (thus, M → μ). Since in later majuscules, M and Π in uncial script looked similar, the minuscule copy from which the rest of the manuscripts descend mistakenly read the uncial M as Π (transliterating M → π), or the minuscule descended from a miscopied majuscule that provided the letter Π instead of M (copying M as Π).²⁹ So, one minuscule copy read μυλών and μυλωρός, and the other read πυλών and πυλωρός. Later in the transmission of *Aseneth*, πυλωρός was changed to θυρωρός for contextual reasons because the minuscule letter θ was not easily confused with the letter π. Fink surmises that the scribe of Ahn *ad* made this change to avoid the repetition of the root (πυλών/πυλωρός).³⁰ Therefore, only two majuscules were transliterated into two minuscules from which all but the Syriac witnesses descend. Arm and L2 descend from one majuscule that was similar to the *Vorlage* of the Syriac witnesses (with μυλών and μυλωρός), and the rest of the manuscripts descend from a minuscule that was either transliterated incorrectly or its majuscule bore a scribal error (that read πυλών and πυλωρός).

Here we appear to have two patterns in the transmission of the narrative, and Burchard's suggestion that the letter M was misread as Π helps to explain this difference. But it is equally the case that the letter Π was misread as M. Syr, Arm, and L2 (436), then, could preserve a *misreading* of πυλωρός and πυλών, and if it is true that in the majuscule script Π and M were often confused, could not more than one scribe have made this error? Another complication is the discrepancy of Greek attestations of μυλωρός in ancient literature as compared to the frequency of πυλωρός and even θυρωρός (doorkeeper, attested in *a* and *d*). According to the Thesaurus Linguae Graecae (TLG), μυλωρός appears four times in its collection of Greek literature, two of which are in grammatical works that provide examples of words ending in -ωρός, and interestingly they list the sequence πυλωρός, θυρωρός, and μυλωρός as examples.³¹ The more common cognate μυλωθρός appears thirty-two times and is attested from the fourth century BCE up to the fifteenth century CE.³² As pointed out by Standhartinger, the femi-

---

29. Burchard cites Dain, *Les manuscrits*, 131 (*Joseph und Aseneth*, 27).

30. Fink, *Joseph und Aseneth*, 25.

31. Two attestations come from Aesop's *Fabulae Aphthonii rhetoris* (sixth century BCE; 13:6, 9). The two grammatical works are *De prosodia catholica* by Aeilius Herodianus and Pseudo-Herodianus (second century CE; 3.1:200, line 33) and *Canones sive De Orthographia* by Theognostus (ninth century CE; §395, line 2).

32. TLG lemma search under all forms of μυλωθρός.

nine noun ἡ μυλωρός is unattested in Greek, but ἡ μυλωθρός is attested as a synonym of ἀλετρίς in Heschyius's *Lexicon* and then twice in the Suda (tenth century CE).[33] Compared to μυλωρός/μυλωθρός, however, πυλωρός and θυρωρός are far more common in Greek literature (attested 433x and 386x, respectively). When these terms show up together, they often refer to guarding positions, seemingly used as synonyms (so either could be read as "gatekeeper" or "doorkeeper") or signifying specific guarding duties (e.g., πυλωρός watch over ἡ πύλη, θυρωρός over ἡ θύρη).[34] Unlike μυλωρός/μυλωθρός, the words πυλωρός and θυρωρός also are attested in Septuagint texts (thirty times and ten times, respectively). The former (πυλωρός) usually means "gatekeeper" (except for 1 Chr 15:23 where it signifies the doorkeeper of the ark), and the latter (θυρωρός) usually refers to guards of a gate (πύλη) (of the Jerusalem temple [1 Esd 1, 1:15; 7:9; Ezek 44:11] or of a city [2 Kgs 7:11]).[35] In New Testament texts, θυρωρός is attested four times, two of which refer to a female gatekeeper (ἡ θυρωρός) who guards a courtyard (θύρα) (John 18:16–17), and in the Testament of Job, ἡ θυρωρός refers to the female doorkeeper of Job's home (6:5–6; 7:1, 5).[36] I will also add that two papyri from Hellenistic Egypt also mention female guards; the wife of Malephis was a temple guardian (ἡ θυρωρός) who was murdered during a robbery, and an unnamed female doorkeeper (ἡ θυρωρός) is accused of beating up the sender of another document (BGU IV 1061 and BGU VIII 1881, respectively, both dated to the first century BCE).

Given this evidence, there are several scenarios that could have produced what the *Aseneth* manuscripts provide for Bu 10:2/Ph 10:3. Just as likely as what Burchard and Fink suggest, the Syr, Arm, and L2 witnesses

---

33. Heschyius's *Lexicon (A–O)*, alphabetic letter *alpha*, entry 2894; the Suda, alphabetic letter *alpha*, entry 1146 and *epsilon iota*, entry 66 (where references to ἀλετρίς in Callimachus's *Hecate* are explained by ἡ μυλωρός).

34. The two words appear within three lines of each other thirteen times, beginning with texts from the first century CE (TLG). In *Pratum spirituale* by Joannes Moschus (sixth to seventh centuries CE), the terms appear to be interchangeable (143:3005), and the example of the specific designations of the words is from *De pronominibus* by Apollonios Dyscolus (second century CE; pt. 2, 1.1:56).

35. The only exception to the meaning of θυρωρός is in 2 Sam 4:6 where it refers to a porter of a household.

36. The other two New Testament attestations are from Mark 13:34, which refers to the doorkeeper of a household, and John 10:3, the gatekeeper for sheep. Another female doorkeeper shows up in Euripides's play, *Iphigeneia at Tauris*, where Iphigenia is called ἡ πυλωρός of the temple of Artemis (line 1153).

may have depended on a misreading of πυλών and πυλωρός, providing a translation of μυλών and μυλωρός (or even μυλωθρός) instead. One connotation of the word πυλωρός in late antiquity may have been a factor in this alteration. In the Constitutiones Apostolorum (fourth century CE), πυλωρός specifically is a male position appointed by the bishop, and this position shared responsibilities and benefits in common with singers.[37] The Syriac, Armenian, and L2 witnesses may descend from one or more majuscules produced by scribes who knew the ecclesial role of πυλωρός and concluded that, since M and Π are often confused, μυλωρός made more sense than πυλωρός.

Furthermore, the attestation of ἡ θυρωρός in *a* and *d* also may not represent a later stage in the transmission process. Given the usage of the term in Hellenistic papyri and Hellenistic Jewish/Judean texts that became Christian texts, the seeming correction of θυρωρός could have been made at the majuscule or early minuscule stages. The fact that, in *a* and *d*, a θυρωρός guards a πυλών is also not unusual when we see how the word is used in septuagintal texts (see 1 Esd 1:15; 7:9; Ezek 44:11; and 2 Kgs 7:11 above). The manuscripts of L1, then, do not definitely attest to πυλωρός, as Burchard assumes, because *portarius* could be a translation of either πυλωρός or θυρωρός.[38] Second Kings 7:11 in the Vulgate, for example, provides *portarius* for θυρωρός. Burchard may have suggested that θυρωρός is a late addition because *c*, *a*, and *d* share similar phrasing against the other manuscripts; when Aseneth approaches the πυλών, these witnesses read the following: εὗρε τὴν [πυλωρὸν: *c*; θυρωρὸν: *a d*] καθεύδουσαν (as compared to the phrase in MSS E and FW: ἡ πυλωρὸς ἐκάθευδε).[39] Fink argues that these grammatical similarities suggest the chronological order of transmission from the exemplar of Mc (θ) to the exemplar Ahn *ad*.[40] Maybe *a* and *d* demonstrate a redaction of πυλωρός (by their shared ancestor even), but it is equally likely that *c* demonstrates a redaction of θυρωρός so as to make πυλωρός more symmetrically tied with πυλών.

As I mentioned earlier, Burchard's rendering of the production of Bu 10:2 also depends on the existence of a fireplace in the scene, but Aseneth fetches ashes "from the hearth" in few witnesses (Arm, MS 436 of L2,

---

37. Apos. Con. 2.26.23; 2.28.15; 2.57.40; 3.11.2, 7; 6.17.7.
38. Burchard, *Joseph und Aseneth*, 26, 127.
39. Burchard, *Joseph und Aseneth*, 26, 127.
40. Fink, *Joseph und Aseneth*, 25.

and MSS F and W of family *f*).⁴¹ Because this reading is in each so-called majuscule group (Arm and MS 436, on one side; MSS F and W, on the other), Burchard seems to assume that "from the hearth" was in the earliest retrievable text (Fink's ω', at the least). He also indicates that with the description of the hearth, these witnesses provide a more complete scenario, and thus their reading is more reliable.⁴² It is not clear, however, why all the other witnesses (or their exemplars) would have deleted "from the hearth." The other witnesses that attest to Bu 10:2 only mention that Aseneth retrieved "ashes" (τέφρα or its equivalent), so the phrase "from the hearth" may have been added to the narrative to describe the scene in more detail.⁴³ In fact, if we compare in the witnesses who (or what) Aseneth passes beyond her stairway, we can see that the variegated evidence becomes even more muddled. Below is the list of attestations again, but arranged this time between witnesses that mention a "hearth" later in the verse and those that do not:

Witnesses that mention a "hearth" in the scene
Arm: and she came to the mill house and the miller slept with (the miller's) children
436 (L2): *et venit in molinam, ubi molendaria molebat cum filiis suis*
FW (*f*): καὶ ἦλθεν εἰς τὸν πυλῶνα καὶ ἡ πυλωρὸς ἐκάθευδε μετὰ τῶν τέκνων αὐτῆς

Remaining witnesses that attest to this verse, all without a "hearth" in the scene
Syr: *et in pistrinum pervenit et molitrices* [meaning: female millers] *earumque liberi dormiebant*
435& (L2): *Veniens ad moldendinum*
L1: (and she came) *ad portam et portarius dormiebat* (with her children)⁴⁴

---

41. Manuscript 436 reads *cinere de foco*, and according to Burchard, Arm reads something similar. Manuscripts F and W have: ἐκ τῆς τέφρας τῆς ἱστίας (Burchard amends the text to ἑστίας, but he admits that the phrase is uncertain; *Joseph und Aseneth*, 127).

42. Burchard, "Zum Stand der Arbeit," 22 n. 97.

43. Burchard, *Joseph und Aseneth*, 127.

44. The English translation in parentheses indicates what Burchard's annotations imply in his critical edition (*Joseph und Aseneth*, 127).

E: καὶ ἦλθεν εἰς τὸν πυλῶνα καὶ ἡ πυλωρὸς ἐκάθευδε
c: ἐλθοῦσα οὖν πρὸς τὸν πυλῶνα εὗρε τὴν πυλωρὸν καθεύδουσαν μετὰ τῶν τέκνων αὐτῆς
a: καὶ ἐλθοῦσα παρὰ τὸν πυλῶνα εὗρε τὴν θυρωρὸν καθεύδουσαν μετὰ τῶν τέκνων αὐτῆς (Q lacks μετὰ … αὐτῆς)
d: παρὰ (Slav: πρὸς) τὸν πυλῶνα (D adds: αὐτῆς) καὶ εὗρε τὴν θυρωρὸν καθεύδουσαν μετὰ τῶν τέκνων αὐτῆς

Burchard contends that Arm, L2, and Syr preserve the earliest reading, but these witnesses are not uniform. The Syriac witnesses portray a group of female millers sleeping with their children, MSS 435& of L2 simply mention a mill-house, and MS 436 of L2 displays the servant near a "hearth" grinding grain with her children instead of sleeping.[45] The Armenian also has the miller (the gender unspecified) near a hearth, but the miller sleeps with her/his children; it shares the most in common with MSS FW, albeit that the latter has a gatekeeper at a gate and not a miller in a mill house. I will add another complication: in the very next line of Burchard's and Fink's text (Bu/F 10:2), Aseneth takes down a skin curtain from a window (ἐκ τῆς θυρίδος), but in Arm, MS 436 of L2, MS E, and families *a* and *d* she pulls the curtain from a *doorway* (ἐκ τῆς θύρας, or its equivalent).[46] The Syriac, MSS FW and L1 (both of family *f*), and family *c* attest to the window, and if we now collect together the evidence for the mill imagery, hearth, and window in Bu 10:2, *no witness* matches that set of criteria.

Let us now apply the evidence to Fink's stemma (see fig. 2.1).[47] For Burchard's basic theory about the transmission of Bu 10:2 to work, we have to conclude the following: (1) the *Vorlage* of Syr (Syr[Gr]) and the majuscule that produced the *Vorlagen* of Arm (Arm[Gr]) and L2 (L2[Gr]) descend from an exemplar that had a hearth and mill-house/miller (and perhaps also a window). The Syriac witnesses show scribal deletion of the hearth (not to mention the increase of millers) but had the curtain in a window; the Arm/L2 majuscule attested to the curtain in a doorway; and MSS 435& of L2 deleted the hearth and miller; and (2) the rest of the witnesses descend

---

45. Fink suggests that the scribe of MS 436 either accidentally or purposefully changed *dormiebat* to *molebat*, creating a wordplay with *molendaria* (*Joseph und Aseneth*, 249).

46. Burchard, *Joseph und Aseneth*, 127. MS 436 has "*de ostio*" (Fink, *Joseph und Aseneth*, 278).

47. Fink, *Joseph und Aseneth*, 17.

from a majuscule that had a hearth and gate/gatekeeper. Either this majuscule had a window and MS E and the exemplar of families *ad* (Ahn *ad*) changed it to a doorway, or the majuscule had a doorway, which the exemplars for MSS FW and L1 (μ) and family *c* (θ) changed to a window. Independent from each other, MSS E, L1 of family *f*, and exemplars of *c* and *ad* also all deleted the hearth from the scene (since MSS F and W kept it). So, the scribes of these manuscripts deleted a phrase that further explained the location of Aseneth's ashes. The scribe of *ad* then changed the term for gatekeeper from πυλωρός to θυρωρός.

Some of these guesses may be correct, but why would so many unrelated manuscripts delete Aseneth's retrieval of ashes "from a hearth" instead of a few manuscripts adding it? Also, although families *c*, *a*, and *d* appear closely related in some ways, as do MSS F,W, and E, these affinities do not clearly determine which reading is late and which is early. As suggested above, the scribe of Ahn *c*, influenced by biblical phrases, could have changed θυρωρός to πυλωρός, and the *Vorlage* of L1 may have read θυρωρός. What is clear is that scribes found this verse to be an unusual scene that needed clarification, which seems to be the best explanation for why the curtain hangs in either a "window" or a "doorway." Burchard's transliteration theory explains how scribes may have fixed the text but does not convincingly show which reading was the earliest or that only two majuscules were transliterated. So too, perhaps there was a hearth in the earliest text of *Aseneth*, but its deletion in so many unrelated witnesses is problematic when the inclusion of a "hearth" better explains the scene.

In defending Burchard's two-majuscule theory, Fink focuses on demonstrating how the manuscript evidence descends from at least two minuscules which she labels as *M1* and *M2* in her stemma (see fig. 2.1). She relies on one line in Bu/F 18:9, which I provide below; first Burchard's and Fink's reconstruction is presented, and then the individual attestations.[48] Given the odd variations in the witnesses, I provide rough translations for each attestation.

Burchard's and Fink's texts: καὶ αἱ <παρειαὶ> [F: παρεια<ὶ>] αὐτῆς ὡς ἄρουραι τοῦ ὑψίστου καὶ ἐν <ταῖς παρειαῖς> ἐρυθρὸς [F: ἐρυθρό<τη>ς] ὡς αἷμα υἱοῦ ἀνθρώπου

---

48. Burchard, *Joseph und Aseneth*, 237.

And her <cheeks> were like fields of the Most High, and (the) red (color) on <her cheeks> was like blood of a son of man

Arm: And her gait (of steps? of feet?) was like straight and beautiful furrows, and her red cheeks were like parts (of a) pomegranate[49]

F: καὶ αἱ πορίαι αὐτῆς ὡς ἀροῦραι τοῦ ὑψίστου καὶ ἐν πορίαις ἐρυθρὸς ὡς αἷμα υἱοῦ ἀνθρώπου

and her gait [reading πορεῖαι] was like fields of the Most High and red in gaits (?) like blood of a son of man

W: καὶ αἱ πορίαι αὐτῆς ὡς ἀροῦραι τοῦ ὑψίστου

and her gait [reading πορεῖαι] was like fields of the Most High

436 (L2): *gene eius tamquam rubor sanguinis filii hominis*

her cheeks [reading *genae*] were as red of (the) blood of a son of man

Syr: *et maxillas suas ut arva Altissimi et super eis ruborem ut sanguinis hominis*

And her jawbones were like fields of the Most High and (the) redness upon them was like human blood

AP (a): καὶ τὰς παρειὰς αὐτῆς (> A) ὡς τὰ ἄστρα τοῦ (τὰ ἄστρα τοῦ: ἄστρον A) οὐρανοῦ

And her cheeks were like the stars (or: star) of heaven

Burchard had proposed that in Arm and MSS FW, the letter α was misread or misheard as ο in the Greek exemplars of these respective witnesses to produce πορίαι (meaning: πορεῖαι) for παρειαί.[50] As Fink also explains, the exemplars would have been minuscules, since the confusion between α and ο in minuscules was far greater than between A and O in majuscules. This would mean that the Greek *Vorlage* of Arm (Arm^Gr) was a minuscule bearing the error of πορεῖαι, but the transliterated minuscule *M1* had the correct reading (παρειαί) since L2 does not show this error. As for the attestation of πορίαι in MSS FW, the exemplar of these bore the misreading, but exemplar η (from which Ahn *f*, Mc, *a* and *d* descend) did not because family *a* attests to the correct reading, παρειαί (see fig. 2.1). In other words, minuscule *M2* also had the correct reading of παρειαί. Furthermore, the misreadings of πορεῖαι occurred independent of one another, since MS F

---

49. Burchard provides the following in the apparatus: "und (der) Gang ([die] Schritte?, + [der] Füsse?) ihrer wie Furchen glatte und schöne und (die) Backen ihre rot wie Teile (eines) Granatapfels" (*Joseph und Aseneth*, 237).

50. Burchard, "Ein neuer Versuch," 243 n. 22.

2. The Reconstructed Texts of *Aseneth*: Burchard and Fink 95

continues the misreading in the second part of the line (continuing with πορίαις) when the Armenian reveals the correct reading ("cheeks" for παρειαί).[51] Fink provides this example from Bu 18:9 to bolster the claim that all the witnesses descend from two majuscules that were transliterated into just two minuscules, but this example actually creates more problems than it solves.

I agree with Burchard and Fink that πορίαι is likely a miscopying of παρειαί at the minuscule stage, but I am not convinced by the chronological map of transmission that Fink depicts. Arm may demonstrate a rough equivalent to ἀροῦραι τοῦ ὑψίστου in MSS FW ("straight and beautiful furrows"), but this is far from certain, and in the second clause, MS F uses the analogy "red like human blood" while Arm refers to the redness of a pomegranate. Although MS 436 (the only witness of L2 that attests to this line) likely refers to cheeks (*genae*) and is linguistically very similar to the second clause in MS F (cf. ἐρυθρὸς ὣς αἷμα υἱοῦ ἀνθρώπου and *rubor sanguinis filii hominis*), it is misleading to say that L2 does not preserve the mistake of πορίαι that Arm and MSS FW share. Manuscript 436 does not have any reference to this part of the line; there is no mention of a "gait" in "furrows/fields."[52] Fink suggests that due to haplography, the scribe skipped the first part of this line, which could be true but not definitively so.[53] Given the abbreviated renditions of this line in other witnesses, MS 436 may just offer one of several ways that scribes transmitted this line. The Syriac shares the most in common with MSS FW, especially if we consider the likely transmission error of miscopying παρειαί; the Syriac lacks the phrase "son of a man," but it compares her jawbones to "fields of the Most High" and to the redness of human blood. The only other witnesses that attest to this line in Bu 18:9 are MSS A and P from family *a*, but Aseneth's cheeks are likened to stars, not to a field of the Most High, the redness of blood or a pomegranate.

Fink focuses on the miscopying of παρειαί to delineate the path of transmission of the manuscript evidence, but her argument depends more on her stemma than on the details of this line. I agree with her assessment (and Burchard's) that παρειαί was likely in the earliest rendering of the line (it makes far more sense than πορεῖαι in the context of the passage), but this does not necessitate that just two minuscules of *Aseneth* existed

---

51. Fink, *Joseph und Aseneth*, 25–26.
52. Fink, *Joseph und Aseneth*, 308.
53. Fink, *Joseph und Aseneth*, 228.

or that the witnesses should be grouped in the way that Fink proposes. Manuscript F (*f*) provides a reading in common with the Syriac, Arm provides a loose paraphrase of that rendition, and MS 436 (L2) and MS W (*f*) repeat different parts of the MS F/Syriac line. Manuscripts F and W may be related to Arm and L2 and/or to Syr more than what Fink's stemma suggests (and the "hearth" connection of MSS FW, Arm, and L2 above echo this point). Manuscripts A and P possibly exhibit a redaction of ἄρουραι τοῦ ὑψίστου, but this too is far from certain.[54] In fact, as Burchard warns, the entire scene describing Aseneth's appearance in Bu 18:9 is extremely varied among the witnesses.[55] Too many scribes fiddled with chapter 18 for us to discover the *Urschrift* of *Aseneth*, as several witnesses do not even convey portions of Burchard's 18:9–11.[56] Most interestingly, although Fink's argument about Bu 18:9 depends on scribes of Arm[Gr] and MSS FW miscopying their respective exemplars *independently* from one another, Fink does not consider that similar, independent miscopying occurred in the transmission of Bu 10:2 (in the misreading of μυλών/μυλωρός or πυλών/πυλωρός). With the latter example, Fink and Burchard entertain the idea of independent yet similar scribal decisions but only when the decisions support their stemmata, such as when Burchard claims that

---

54. In Fink's decipherment of palimpsest M, she suggests that the text reads ουρανου before the description of "lips" (τα δε χειλη), which in Burchard's reconstruction immediately follows the description of Aseneth's cheeks (Fink, *Joseph und Aseneth*, 40). For "heaven" Fink indicates that "νου" is clearly discernible, but since she does not refer to M in her argument, it appears that this reading is not reliable enough to use. But if Fink's reading is correct, then M may have shared the same reading as *a* ("stars of heaven"). It is true that Fink could adjust her hypothesis by moving up her stemma, placing the redaction at the θ exemplar instead of Ahn *ad*, for example, but my point is that overall the variables of attestations are too high to settle on a particular trajectory of transmission.

55. "18,9 ist zerschrieben und lückenhaft überliefert, besonders die Beschreibung von Aseneths Aussehen" (Burchard, *Joseph und Aseneth*, 236).

56. In place of Bu 18:9 τὸ πρόσωπον αὐτῆς καί–18:10, MS E reads, καὶ ἵστατο συν ταῖς παρθένοις προσδεχόμεναι τὴν Ἰωσὴφ παρουσίαν. As for witnesses from family *f*, Bu 18:9 καὶ οἱ ὀφθαλμοί–18:10 does not appear in MS G; MS 671 (Ngr) provides a different line (βλέπει ὅτι τὸ κάλλος ἦτον ὡς καὶ τὸ πρῶτον λαμπρώτατον), and L1 lacks any of Bu 18:2–19:1. Family group Mc only has palimpsest M referring to ch. 18 (since the reliable portion of *c* ends in ch. 16), and it seems to be similar to *a* in using the word "heaven," but it also shares similarities with Syr, Arm, and L2 (such as in the description of Aseneth's teeth like warriors drawn up for battle). Finally, family *d* lacks much of Bu 18:6–11 (Burchard, *Joseph und Aseneth*, 235–39).

multiple exemplars deleted the "hearth" when the initial two majuscules attested to it. If we accept that similar scribal emendations were made to several witnesses, however, our evidence may reflect more scribal involvement than what a two-majuscule/minuscule theory allows. The witnesses may descend from several majuscules, and at least, they indicate that the transliteration stage from majuscule to minuscule or the transmission of minuscules alone was a more complicated process. In the end, we cannot identify well whether the witnesses demonstrate scribal changes that occurred in a sequential way in the transmission process or that happened contemporaneously with each other.

There is no evidence to prove that only two majuscules of *Aseneth* survived up to the ninth century CE.[57] It turns out that textual transmission during the Byzantine period did not neatly reflect the generally applied principle of "one majuscule for every one minuscule." Not all of the manuscript evidence can be explained with this theory; sometimes there appears to have been more than one majuscule of a text that was transliterated during the ninth and tenth centuries.[58] Once the minuscule script had been established among scribes, it was likely that majuscule texts were ignored and only their respective minuscule copies were followed, but this shift took time. Wilson explains the process as follows:

> Copying from them (books in majuscule) in the new script is often stated to have been a difficult process that scribes would not have wished to undertake on more than one occasion, and it has been suggested that as a rule only one manuscript served as the basis from which all subsequent minuscule copies were made. In fact, however, copying was only likely to become difficult when the new script was so well established as a standard that the average reader began to find the old capital letters less easy. But until that point was reached one capital letter script was much the same as another, and indeed initially it will have been easier to work with the traditional script than the new one.[59]

It is possible that, in the beginning stages of the majuscule-minuscule transfer, more than two majuscule copies of *Aseneth* existed before the

---

57. Standhartinger also argues this point (review of *Joseph und Aseneth*, 152).
58. Reynolds and Wilson, *Scribes and Scholars*, 60–61. Reynolds and Wilson provide the explicit example of MS Vienna, supp. gr. 39 in the Plato tradition that differs significantly in errors compared to the rest of the witnesses.
59. Wilson, *Scholars of Byzantium*, 67.

dominant transition to the minuscule script occurred. Even if a textual tradition appears to have descended from a single archetype, this may not be because only one majuscule had survived; rather, one particular majuscule may have been housed in a location that was convenient to scribes, thus making that majuscule dominant.[60] A completely different matter occurred with texts that were used in educational curricula. There is evidence of contamination whereby one copy was compared with others, indicating that perhaps two or more transliterations were made of particular texts or that variant readings were added to the margins of one minuscule that was housed in a central location for easy access.[61] Burchard admits that scribal transliteration of *Aseneth* could have involved more than one majuscule whereby the scribe revised or amended the text based on other majuscule copies.[62] In the case of Homeric literature, it was likely that more than two majuscules were transliterated into minuscules, and Burchard at one point considered three transliterations of *Aseneth* instead of two, but for unexplained reasons he omits this idea in the introduction of his critical edition.[63]

Certainly, as far as we know, *Aseneth* did not have the appeal of Homer from the ninth century onward, but this narrative was used in a variety of ways, and it is conceivable that some copies were centrally located for several scribes to study and other copies were circulated through private hands. In the Armenian witnesses, *Aseneth* is placed within Christian

---

60. Wilson, *Scholars of Byzantium*, 67.
61. Reynolds and Wilson, *Scribes and Scholars*, 61.
62. Burchard, *Joseph und Aseneth*, 27.
63. For Homer, see Margalit Finkelberg, "Regional Texts and the Circulation of Books: The Case of Homer," *GRBS* 46 (2006): 247. Michael Haslam proposes that at least four majuscules of the *Iliad* (possibly dated to the sixth or seventh centuries) were transliterated into minuscules ("Homeric Papyri and the Transmission of the Text," in *A New Companion to Homer*, ed. Ian Morris and Barry Powell, Mnemosyne Supplementum 163 [Leiden: Brill, 1997], 92–93). Haslam also mentions that medieval Demosthenic literature descended from four majuscules (93). Burchard posits that Arm and L2 each descended from independent minuscules because although they attest to the same phrases in Bu 10:2, they differ in the last phrase of Bu 2:11. Arm appears to have read ὀπώρα ἦν θερισμοῦ, but 436 (L2) reads ὥρα γὰρ ἦν θερισμοῦ (as also the following witnesses: L1 *c d a*; FW read ὥρα θερισμοῦ) (Burchard, *Joseph und Aseneth*, 84). Burchard suggests that Arm translated a Greek minuscule that had mistransliterated ὅτι ὥρα (which is akin to διότι ὥρα and shows up in Bu 3:5 and 24:15) for ὀπώρα because in majuscule script ΤΙ and Π were easily confused ("Character and Origin," 87–88).

Bibles (most of the manuscripts in Armenian subfamilies *b*, *c*, and *e*), in four groups of miscellanies (Arm subfamilies *a*, *d*, *g*, and *h*), and in a one volume library (Arm subfamily *f*) containing the sequence: New Testament with pseudepigrapha, the Old Testament with pseudepigrapha, and several philosophical and theological works (some of which are by Philo).[64] One Syriac witness (MS 2071) is located within a chronicle attributed to Pseudo-Zacharias; Greek MSS A and O of family *a* are a part of menologia; Greek MS B of family *d* is in a hagiographical collection; and Greek MSS G and Ngr of family *f* include a series of miniatures that illustrate the narrative.[65] The transmission of *Aseneth*, at the least, appears to have been for instructional or liturgical purposes on some occasions and at other times for private consumption.

The perceived benefits of *Aseneth* likely influenced how it was transmitted; either for ecclesiastical or private use, scribes may have altered or expanded certain portions based on their assumptions about the narrative's value or even to resolve problems that their exemplars posed. Two of Burchard's most valued manuscript groups (435& [L2] and Arm) do not provide a full account of the second half of *Aseneth* (as represented by Burchard's reconstruction). Manuscripts 435& (L2) end at 21:9 and exhibit several smaller gaps (most notably 11:15–18), and of the two Armenian groups of witnesses, one consists of MS 332 (Arm[f]) and ends at Bu 28:13, and the remainder of the witnesses (subfamilies *a–e*, *g*, and *h*) all substitute Bu 25:3–27:11 with a pastiche of passages from these omitted chapters.[66] Burchard surmises that the latter Armenian witnesses demonstrated a scribal interest to shorten the text by, for example, diminishing the bloodshed exercised on account of Aseneth rather than repairing a damaged manuscript.[67] The next best witnesses according to Burchard (family *f*), exhibit a range of alterations as well. Greek MSS F and W provide expansions between 7:6–7; 21:9–22:1; and after 29:9 (and the last two are of significant length), Greek MS G substitutes 2:6–10:1 with a short paraphrase of these chapters, and

---

64. Burchard, "Character and Origin," 76; Burchard, *Joseph und Aseneth*, 12–13. Burchard classified the Armenian witnesses into eight subgroups that he identified as Armenian families *a* through *f*.

65. Burchard, *Joseph und Aseneth*, 17–18, 22–25, 28–30.

66. Burchard, *Joseph und Aseneth*, 16 and 13, respectively. Witnesses in Arm[c] and Arm[g] end that narrative even sooner than 27:11 (Burchard, "Character and Origin," 80 n. 17).

67. Burchard, *Joseph und Aseneth*, 13.

Latin MSS L1 substitute 26:6–29:4 with a heavily abridged and jumbled text that reveals several large gaps in the narrative.[68] The Greek family c (MSS H, J, and K) is based on an exemplar that ended the narrative in chapter 16, and since palimpsest M (in the new family Mc) indicates that c descended from a *Aseneth* narrative that contained chapters 1–29, it appears that family c represents an abridged version of the story.[69] Manuscript J ends at 16:10, but MS H and MS K end at 16:17y in Hellenistic Greek and then continue the narrative up to 21:9 in Modern Greek. The modern portion, however, is entirely different from chapters 16–21 in the other manuscripts. As we have also seen, many of the observations that both Standhartinger and Kraemer present in their textual comparisons between Burchard's and Philonenko's reconstructions indicate scribal emendations to particular manuscripts. Whereas the Byzantine text type of the Greek New Testament dominated transmission from the sixth/seventh to the fifteenth centuries, the Greek transmission of *Aseneth* appears to have been more various (at least from the Byzantine period onward and perhaps even earlier), and the transmission of the translations appears to have been just as fluid.[70] This narrative bypassed the scribal desire for a fixed tradition, which makes it harder to think in clear genealogical terms when it comes to the transmission history of this narrative.

Burchard's hypothesis is driven by another feature, namely, the narrative that he calls the Life of Joseph, which appears before *Aseneth* in many Armenian and Greek witnesses.[71] This homily, entitled in most

---

68. for MSS F and W, see Burchard, *Joseph und Aseneth*, 346–51. For MS G, see Burchard, *Joseph und Aseneth*, 345–46. For L1, see Burchard, *Joseph und Aseneth*, 18–19; and full list of gaps provided in Burchard, "Ein neuer Versuch," 240.

69. Burchard, *Joseph und Aseneth*, 20–21, 349–51.

70. For the Byzantine text type dominating the New Testament transmission, see Bruce M. Metzger, *A Textual Commentary on the Greek New Testament*, 2nd ed. (London: United Bible Societies, 1994), 7.

71. This homily has not been studied very extensively. The Life of Joseph that apparently MS D provides was published by Edward Thwaites (Τὰ τοῦ ὁσίου πατρὸς Ἐφραὶμ τοῦ Σύρου πρὸς τὴν Ἑλλάδα μεταβληθέντα [The translated works of the holy father Ephraim the Syrian into Greek], Oxford, 1709), and Josephus S. Assemanus produced a Latin translation of a Greek text in *Sancti patris nostri Epharem Syri Opera Omnia quae extant Graece, Syriace, Latine* (Rome, 1743), 2:21–41. According to Burchard, the oldest witness consists of partially published papyrus fragments dated to the sixth/seventh centuries CE (Paris, Bibliothèque Nationale, Suppl. Gr. 1379) (Burchard, *Joseph und Aseneth*, 31).

Greek manuscripts as λόγος εἰς τὸν πάγκαλον Ἰωσήφ, is a pseudepigraphic work attributed to Ephraem of Syria, and it consists of a short portion that offers parallels between Joseph of Genesis and Jesus in the Gospels (presenting Joseph as the true typos of the son of God), followed by a longer portion that attests to the virtues of Joseph as presented in Genesis and other sources.[72] As I stated at the start of this chapter, Burchard posits that this coupling of Life of Joseph (LJos) and *Aseneth* (JosAs) occurred very early on. By the fifth century, Burchard maintains, there were either two exemplars (one from which the supposed two majuscules were produced and the other from which the Syriac descends) or one exemplar (from which the two majuscules and Syriac descend); in either case, at least one exemplar displayed the sequence of Life of Joseph followed by *Aseneth* (or as Burchard refers to it, LJos-JosAs). Fink modifies Burchard's theory and suggests that the archetype of all the witnesses had LJos attached (although its exemplar did not); one branch of the archetype (indicated by ε) was the exemplar for Syr^{Gr} and the minuscule that produced Arm^{Gr} and L2^{Gr}, and the other branch produced the minuscule from which the rest of the witnesses descend (see fig. 2.1).[73] No Syriac witness provides this coupling, but the witnesses that seem to display the coupling are well-represented among the different manuscript categories. The sequence of LJos-JosAs apparently occurs in many Armenian witnesses (discussed further below); family *f* (in MSS F, W, G, and Ngr, of which the latter two also provide miniatures to both narratives); in palimpsest M of family Mc; MSS C and R of family *a*; and MS D of family *d*.[74]

It is intriguing that this coupling is widespread, but what is left to examine is what each witness of LJos looks like. For example, are there differences between the witnesses like those of *Aseneth*? If there are differences, how does each witness relate to its particular presentation of *Aseneth*? Manuscripts C and R of family *a* preserve only a part of *Aseneth*; MS C breaks off at 10:5 and R breaks off at 5:1. Could scribes of these manuscripts have understood these renditions of *Aseneth* simply as

---

72. Burchard, *Joseph und Aseneth*, 30–31. Burchard argues that this piece is one of many Greek Ephraem-Pseudepigrapha produced during the fifth to sixth centuries (31). Vikan dates the piece to the same time period, although he leaves open the idea that it was originally composed by Ephraem in Syriac ("Illuminated Manuscripts," 23).

73. Fink, *Joseph und Aseneth*, 17.

74. Burchard, *Joseph und Aseneth*, 30–31; Burchard, "Der jüdische Asenethroman," 560–61. Fink, *Joseph und Aseneth*, 14–16.

additional stories about Joseph (and not be about Aseneth in particular)? Likewise, MSS G and Ngr also appear to concentrate on the Life of Joseph rather than on *Aseneth*. Manuscript G has sixty-three miniatures to the Life of Joseph and seventeen to *Aseneth*; MS 661 (of Ngr) has twenty-one miniatures to the Life of Joseph and three to *Aseneth*; and MS 671 (of Ngr) has twenty-eight miniatures to the Life of Joseph and nineteen to *Aseneth*.[75] Especially when we look at MS G, which provides a short paraphrase to 2:6–10:1 (a part of the story that many scholars consider essential for understanding the plot), what is the overall impression that the coupling provides in this witness?[76] Manuscript 671 concludes its telling of *Aseneth* by narrating how ἡ πάγκαλη Ἀσενέθ and ὁ πάγκαλος Ἰωσήφ rejoiced at the years of Joseph's rule, and then it ends with a doxology to the Trinity.[77] This seems to indicate that in MS 671, *Aseneth* is meant to be an extension of a narrative about Joseph. If so, how exactly does the manuscript tell the *Aseneth* story to fit its telling of the Life of Joseph? So too, given that MSS F and W provide expansions to *Aseneth*, do these particular narrations of *Aseneth* relate to their respective narrations of the Life of Joseph? Palimpsest M offers only a little to this discussion. The beginning of *Aseneth* on folio 79v follows the conclusion of LJos, and although other folios of LJos have been detected in the palimpsest, LJos as a literary unit in this witness has yet to be studied.[78] The evidence for LJos, then, may better explain why *Aseneth* was copied but may not help us get at the earliest *Aseneth* text.

The issue becomes even more complex when we look at the Armenian evidence. Of the fifty manuscripts thus identified by Burchard, seven manuscripts present the triplet of LJos-JosAs-Testament of the Twelve Patriarchs (referred to as "TestXII" hereafter), three manuscripts provide the triplet TestXII-LJos-JosAs; fourteen provide the coupling TestXII-JosAs (no LJos), and one displays the LJos-JosAs coupling and TestXII lies earlier on in the manuscript (MS 3715, Erevan 349).[79] Half of the

---

75. Burchard, "Der jüdische Asenethroman," 630.

76. For 2:6–10:1 as central to the plot, see, e.g., Jill Hicks-Keeton, whose primary thesis of the "life-giving" God is centered on ch. 8 (*Arguing with Aseneth*).

77. Burchard, *Joseph und Aseneth*, 358.

78. Burfeind, "Der Text von *Joseph und Aseneth*," 46; and Fink, *Joseph und Aseneth*, 34–35.

79. The triplet of LJos-JosAs-TestXII: (1) from Burchard's category Arm[a]: MS 331, Oxford, and MS 341, Vienna 126; (2) MS 352, Venice 679 from Arm[d]; and (3) the fol-

known Armenian manuscripts, then, provide some kind of coupling with *Aseneth*, but it is more involved than what the Greek witnesses display. Most of these twenty-five Armenian manuscripts provide the couplets or triplets in a Bible, and they are represented across Armenian textual family lines (at least in terms of how Burchard has classified them).[80] This commonality may point to a common *Vorlage* with a certain coupling (or tripling), but it could also simply indicate scribal interests in aligning certain stories about Joseph and the patriarchs and incorporating them into Armenian Bibles.[81] Although the council of Partaw produced a canonical list of books in 768 CE, the list does not seem to have been binding, which helps to understand the great diversity among Armenian Bibles.[82] Our evidence for the inclusion of LJos, TextXII, or *Aseneth* in

---

lowing from Arm[e]: MS 379, Erevan 347; MS 3718, Jerusalem 1934; MS 3720, Malibu. Burchard lists a possible fourth manuscript (Erevan 5809) from this *e* group that may also provide the triplet LJos-JosAs-TestXII, but it is not clear whether he has personally viewed it ("Neues von Joseph und Aseneth auf Armenisch," in *Gesammelte Studien zu Joseph und Aseneth*, SVTP 13 [Leiden: Brill, 1996], 143). The manuscripts that provide the triplet TestXII-LJos-JosAs: all from family Arm[e]: MS 333, Jerusalem 1925 [Erznka Bible]; MS 363, Erevan 354; and MS 3714, Erevan 2587. The manuscripts that provide TextXII-JosAs: (1) eight from family Arm[b]: MS 362, Rome, Cas.; MS 372, Rome, Vatican; MS 3710, Erevan 188; MS 3717, Jerusalm 1927; MS 371, London; MS 377, Erevan 205; not numbered by Burchard because not viewed by him, Jerusalem 1929; and MS 384, Erevan 669; (2) four from family Arm[c]: MS 342, Erevan 346; MS 351, Venice 280; MS 353, Kayseri; and (unseen by Burchard), Jerusalem 2558; (3) one from family Arm[d]: MS 354, Vienna 705; and (4) one from family Arm[e]: MS 3713, Erevan 2126. The sequence TestXII-JosAs also appears in MS 332, Erevan 1500, the only manuscript in Arm[f] and the most complete and reliable Armenian witness. Burchard doubts, however, that the sequence was produced from one *Vorlage*; based on his evaluation of each story in MS 332, he suggests that the thirteenth century scholar Mechitar of Ayrivankʿ (who produced MS 332) placed the two narratives in this sequence because of the canonical list he had copied from that of John Sarkavag (eleventh century CE) (Burchard, "Character and Origin," 77–78, 82–84; Burchard, "Zur armenischen Übersetzung von Joseph und Aseneth," *Revue des Études Arméniennes* 17 [1983]: 215–16; Burchard, *Joseph und Aseneth*, 3–6). See also Michael E. Stone, "Armenian Canon Lists III: The Lists of Mechitar of AYRIVANKʿ (c. 1285 C.E.)," *HTR* 69 (1976): 289–300.

80. See list in Burchard, "Zur armenischen Übersetzung," 215–16.

81. See Burchard's discussion on the matter, "Character and Origin," 82–88, and S. Peter Cowe, "A Typology of Armenian Biblical Manuscripts," *Revue des Études Arméniennes* 18 (1984): 61–62.

82. Michael E. Stone, "Armenian Canon Lists I: The Council of Partaw (768 C.E.)," *HTR* 66 (1973): 479–86; Cowe, "Typology of Armenian," 61; and Cowe, "The

Bibles appears later in Armenian scholarship, first attested in canonical lists (as early as the eleventh century) and later in our manuscripts mentioned above (most of which are from the seventeenth century).[83] Until more careful textual comparison is made with regard to how each Armenian telling of *Aseneth* relates (or not) to its alignment with LJos or TestXII, it is difficult to propose a particular trajectory of the textual transmission of *Aseneth*.

The coupling of LJos-JosAs (and the various coupling or tripling of LJos, JosAs, and TestXII in Armenian manuscripts) may provide more information about the cultural context of the scribes who produced our manuscript evidence than it indicates anything (if at all) about the chronological production of our *Aseneth* witnesses. If LJos was attached to *Aseneth* early on, why is it missing in the Syriac and the L2 manuscripts? Manuscript E, L1 and Slavonic witnesses, and the more reliable manuscripts of family *a* (especially MS A) do not refer to LJos either. Especially given, as Fink argues, the contamination between the ancestors of *Mc* and family *a* or between the ancestor of MS G and the Greek *Vorlage* of the Slavic witnesses, why would LJos be deleted in *a* and Slav? Burchard and Fink do not address these questions. Given the popularity of Joseph in late antiquity, the LJos-JosAs coupling makes sense, but the causes for the coupling may be varied. Standhartinger has also raised the combined point that LJos is a composite work that borrowed from several sources and what Burchard refers to as Life of Joseph may not be as uniform as his discussion suggests. This work is also referred to as *In pulcherrimum Ioseph* or, in Armenian, *On the Seven Vahangs of Joseph*, and it is preserved in manuscripts beyond our *Aseneth* witnesses (in Greek, Latin, Armenian, Coptic, Georgian, Slavonic, and Arabic). There has not been sufficient examination of how common these witnesses are in their composite presentations on Joseph, and so it is premature to incorporate the so-called LJos into a transmission history of *Aseneth*.[84]

Bible in Armenia," in *The Bible from 600–1450*, vol. 2 of *The New Cambridge History of the Bible*, ed. Richard Marsden and E. Ann Matter (Cambridge: Cambridge University Press, 2012), 157. It is uncertain, however, whether this list was intended for official use in the Armenian church (Stone, "Armenian Canon Lists I," 486; and Cowe, "Typology of Armenian," 61).

83. Stone, "Armenian Canon Lists III"; Cowe, "Typology of Armenian"; and Burchard, "Der jüdische Asenethroman," 581–88.

84. Standhartinger, "Recent Scholarship," 356–58.

In summary, Burchard's and Fink's rationale for their reconstructions is based on the idea that most of the witnesses descend from just two majuscules/minuscules. Their theory is based on Bu 10:2, and for Fink, also on Bu 18:9, but I have shown how there are other ways to understand the variations in the manuscripts that attest to these verses. What I will continue to demonstrate in this chapter and the next is that there is no simple way to delineate the evolution of *Aseneth*'s transmission. It is also premature to incorporate the so-called Life of Joseph into the discussion given the unexamined variables associated with that tradition. I will close this chapter by discussing Burchard's reconstructed text, Fink's adaptations of it, and the unresolved problems that persist with both reconstructions. Fink's corrections improve Burchard's text in the sense that she produces a text that is better aligned with his stated principles, but her text too often relies upon the logic of her stemma in spite of the evidence.

The Limitations of Fink's Reconstructed Text and the Inherent Flaws of Burchard's Reconstructed Text

Burchard's and Fink's proposed transmission histories are problematic. They rely on neat, genealogical lines that are not clearly demonstrated in the evidence; and despite their assessment of the witnesses, their respective reconstructions betray that the two-majuscule/minuscule theory does not resolve all the challenges posed by the evidence. There are also times when Burchard and Fink appear to choose readings for subjective, aesthetic reasons, and my critique rests mostly on Fink's reconstruction since her adaptation attempts to correct Burchard's text. Fink appears to promote certain readings so as to match her hypothesized stemma (Bu/F 8:5; 15:5; and 2:7), or she seems to choose readings based on aesthetic reasons over and against what the evidence suggests (Bu/F 10:11; 3:1; and 7:4). Since Fink works off of Burchard's work, I will begin presenting Burchard's articulation of how he produced his text, the corrections Fink made to Burchard's reconstruction, and then I will conclude with my critique of both Burchard's and Fink's textual decisions. In the end, their dependence upon their transmission histories prevent them from taking more seriously the variations preserved in the witnesses.

As we have seen, Burchard maintains that Syr, Arm, and L2, especially when these witnesses agree, are the best attestations to the earliest, retrievable text of *Aseneth*, and family *f* (FWRum, GNgr, L1) and MS E are the next important witnesses; I will call this list of manuscripts Burchard's "primary witnesses." In producing his text, if the primary witnesses are divided in their readings and the other witnesses (i.e., Mc, *a*, or *d*) favor one of those readings, then Burchard used the other witnesses to override what the minority reading of the primary witnesses provide. If the primary witnesses exhibit a broad scope of attestations, however, he supposedly chose the fullest reading among the primary witnesses even if the shorter reading was preserved in the remaining witnesses. Finally, Burchard chose lengthier passages from families *a*, *d*, and/or *c*, even when they are not preserved in the primary witnesses, because he considered these kinds of surpluses likely to descend from the earliest text.[85] To be fair, Burchard proposed his two-majuscule theory decades after the creation of his reconstructed text, so his reliance on these surpluses, for example, was motivated by reasons other than the two-majuscule theory. Burchard also suggests in the notations of his critical edition (2003) that some of these surpluses should be deleted from his text.[86] Burchard's two-majuscule theory evolved from his close analysis of the textual evidence and his work on the reconstructed text. Over time he became convinced that Syr, Arm, and L2 were closely aligned on one side and *f* and E on the other (with Mc defying neat placement in either group), and Bu 10:2 appeared to confirm how he was categorizing the evidence.

Burchard's application of his principles, however, sometimes produced questionable results in his reconstructed text. Fink has convincingly demonstrated, for example, that the surpluses from families *a* and *d* should not be included in the reconstruction, and she deletes them from her adapted text.[87] One case in point is Bu 10:11–12/Ph 10:12–13, in which only families *a* and *d* relate that Aseneth threw her royal garb through the window "to the poor" (τοῖς πένησιν), broke her idols into pieces (συνέτριψεν εἰς λεπτά), and gave them to the "poor and needy" (πτωχοῖς καὶ δεομένοις). As discussed in chapter 1, these clarifications seem to be tied to a common ancestor of *ad*, and Fink deletes them from her text for this reason. In Burchard's critical edition, he also recommends that the τοῖς πένησιν and πτωχοῖς καὶ δεομένοις be removed from his text, although he retains συνέτριψεν εἰς λεπτά for unexplained reasons.[88] Burchard admits that further examination

---

85. Burchard, *Joseph und Aseneth*, 37–38.
86. Burchard, *Joseph und Aseneth*, 48.
87. For a thorough discussion, see Fink, *Joseph und Aseneth*, 80–95, 102–43.
88. Burchard, *Joseph und Aseneth*, 375.

2. The Reconstructed Texts of *Aseneth*: Burchard and Fink   107

is required for the times that he chose attestations shared by only families *a* and *d* or exhibited only by *a*, and Fink's work responds to this call.[89]

Yet even some of Fink's modifications do not resolve the problems of Burchard's reconstruction, and there are times when she appears to prioritize her stemma over deleting sole attestations from *a* or from Ahn *a*/*d*. Let us examine Bu 8:5 as an example. In chapter 8, Aseneth meets Joseph for the first time, and Burchard's reconstruction provides the following:

καὶ ὡς προσῆλθεν Ἀσενέθ φιλῆσαι τὸν Ἰωσὴφ ἐξέτεινεν Ἰωσὴφ τὴν χεῖρα αὐτοῦ τὴν δεξιὰν καὶ ἔθηκε πρὸς τὸ στῆθος αὐτῆς <u>ἀνάμεσον τῶν δύο μασθῶν αὐτῆς καὶ ἦσαν οἱ μασθοὶ αὐτῆς ἤδη ἑστῶτες ὥσπερ μῆλα ὡραῖα</u>.[90]

And as Aseneth came forward to kiss Joseph, Joseph stretched out his right hand and placed it toward her chest <u>between her two breasts, and her breasts now</u> <u>were standing up like ripe apples</u>.

None of Burchard's primary witnesses provide the entire underlined portion of this verse. Arm, 435& (L2), *c*, and *d* provide none of it; MSS FW (family *f*) provide a completely different scene by instead reading, καὶ ἠσπάσαντο ἀλλήλους; and MS G (family *f*) lacks 8:5 all together. The witnesses Syr, 436 (L2), L1 (from family *f*), E, and *a* share in some fashion the content and expression of ἀνάμεσον τῶν δύο μασθῶν αὐτῆς καὶ ἦσαν οἱ μασθοὶ αὐτῆς ἤδη ἑστῶτες. The full readings for the underlined portion are as follows:[91]

Syr: *inter duas mamillas eius incipientes*
436 (L2): *inter duas mammillas et mammille errant recte*[92]
L1: (between two breasts) *et mamille eius prominebant foras*[93]

---

89. Burchard, *Joseph und Aseneth*, 48. Burchard provides the examples of Bu 2:9; 25:7 end–8; and 26:6 for *ad* attestations that are incorporated into his reconstruction and Bu 24:20 for an attestation only from *a*.

90. Burchard, *Joseph und Aseneth*, 115–16. All attestations of this verse that are presented in this paragraph are taken from the notes on the same pages in Burchard's critical edition.

91. Burchard, *Joseph und Aseneth*, 116; Fink, *Joseph und Aseneth*, 273; Brooks, *Historia ecclesiastica Zachariae Rhetori*, 20.

92. Fink corrects the text that Burchard provides (*inter duas mammellas et mamelle errant recte*) (Fink, *Joseph und Aseneth*, 273).

93. Batiffol provides the following from his text based primarily on MSS 421 and

E: ἀνάμεσον τῶν δύο μαζῶν αὐτῆς καὶ εἶσαν ἤδει παρεστῶτες
A: ἀνάμεσον τῶν δύο μασθῶν αυτῆς καὶ ἦσαν οἱ μασθοὶ αὐτῆς ἤδη ἐστῶτες ὥσπερ μῆλα ὡραῖα
P: ἀνάμεσον τῶν δύο μασθῶν αὐτῆς καὶ ἦσαν οἱ μασθοὶ αὐτῆς ἤδη ἐστῶτες ὥσπερ μῆλα ὡραῖα ἐν τῶ στήθη αὐτης
Q: ἀνάμεσον τῶν δύο μασθῶν καὶ ἤδη ἦσαν ὡς δύο μῆλα ὡραῖα

As we can see, the phrase, ὥσπερ μῆλα ὡραῖα ("like ripe apples"), is only attested in MSS A and P (from family *a*). Here is a case where Burchard includes a surplus from family *a* simply because it provides a longer description of the scene, and for this reason Fink deletes ὥσπερ μῆλα ὡραῖα from her text. All the witnesses that provide this scene (except MSS F and W) relay that Joseph physically stopped Aseneth's approach with his hand to her chest, and it is likely that this image solicited further description of Aseneth's breasts. Burchard argues that the underlined portion above does not express Aseneth's sexual arousal but rather underscores that she was an alien woman (and not a child) who threatened Joseph.[94] His reading would make this phrase more connected to the plot (since the scene immediately follows Joseph's identification of Aseneth as a foreign woman [Bu 7:2–6/ Ph 7:1–7]) and thus may be another reason why Burchard incorporated it.[95] If the phrase was original, some scribes may have deleted the extended commentary; according to Burchard, MS G in general eliminates the erotic element of *Aseneth*, and G lacks this particular scene.[96]

On the other hand, some scribes could have extended the gaze of the reader by describing Aseneth's appearance in more detail. The witnesses of family *a* appear to have provided the most extensive descriptions, but Syr, MS 436 (L2), L1 (*f*), and MS E seem to elaborate about Aseneth's breasts in different, albeit similar, ways. For unexplained reasons, Fink retains most of what MS A and MS P provide (and which Burchard also uses in his text): ἀνάμεσον τῶν δύο μασθῶν αὐτῆς καὶ ἦσαν οἱ μασθοὶ αὐτῆς

---

431 (Burchard's classification) from L1: *medio duarum mamillarum et mamille eius prominebant foras* (*Le Livre de la Prière d'Asenath*, 96).

94. Burchard, *Joseph und Aseneth*, 43.

95. Kraemer suggests that the underlined portion here was a scribal addition that aligned this scene more closely with biblical allusions to female beauty (such as in the Song 7:8) (*When Aseneth Met Joseph*, 51).

96. Burchard, *Joseph und Aseneth*, 17–18.

2. The Reconstructed Texts of *Aseneth*: Burchard and Fink

ἤδη ἑστῶτες.⁹⁷ Even though Fink argues against the reliance on families *a* and *d* in reconstructing the text, she retains this particular line because of her stemma (see fig. 2.1). It appears that Fink assumes that MS 436 (L2) reflects a minuscule that had a similar reading as the minuscule that produced MS E, L1 (*f*), and MS A and MS P (*a*). In other words, supposedly *M1* and *M2* both had what Fink proposes, and all the other witnesses deleted or altered the story in this passage. It is not clear, though, why the Greek rendering of MSS A and P is used, particularly with regard to the particle ἤδη, which is not reflected in the Latin texts. What is more, Syriac's rendition at the very least suggests that scribes may have taken poetic license in helping the reader/listener visualize this scene (whereby *incipientes* does not equate with any other rendition of this line). All the witnesses that attest to this scene show distinct ways in which Aseneth is described; the overall sense is common but not the detailed wording of the verse. Fink's critique of Burchard's use of surpluses from *a* (or Ahn *ad*) needs to be qualified by the fact that she relies on attestations from *a* or Ahn *ad* when they best suit her stemma.

Another example where Fink prioritizes her stemma over the evidence is in Bu 15:5/Ph 15:4, when the angelic messenger blesses Aseneth. As discussed in the previous chapter, Standhartinger challenged Philonenko's inclusion from non-*d* witnesses to produce a triadic blessing in this verse (ἀνακαινισθήσῃ καὶ ἀναπλασθήσῃ καὶ ἀναζωοποιηθήσῃ), but Burchard's and Fink's inclusion of the same phrase also can be questioned. I provide below the blessing in Burchard's and Fink's reconstruction and then in the individual witnesses:⁹⁸

> **Bu/F:** (ἰδοὺ δὴ ἀπὸ τῆς σήμερον) ἀνακαινισθήσῃ καὶ ἀναπλασθήσῃ καὶ ἀναζωοποιηθήσῃ
> (See, now, from today,) you shall be renewed, refashioned, and revived
>
> **MS 436 (L2):** *vocaberis et reformaberis et revivificaberis*
> **Arm^a and Arm^d:** ἀνακαινισθήσῃ καὶ ἀναπλασθήσῃ (its equivalent in Armenian)
> **Arm^bcef:** ἀνακαινισθήσῃ καὶ ἀναζωοποιηθήσῃ (its equivalent in Armenian)

---

97. Fink, *Joseph und Aseneth*, 175.
98. Burchard, *Joseph und Aseneth*, 189; Fink, *Joseph und Aseneth*, 295.

MS E: ἀνακαινισθήσῃ
MSS F and W: ἀνακαινισθήσῃ καὶ ζωοποιηθήσῃ [W: ζωοποιῆσει]
MS G: ἀνακαινισθήσῃ
MS 671 (Ngr): ἀνακαινισθήσῃ καὶ ζωοποιηθήσῃ
L1: *renovata es et vivificata es*
Family *c*: ἀνακαινισθήσῃ καὶ ἀναπλασθήσῃ
MSS A and P (family *a*): ἀνακαινισθήσῃ καὶ ἀναπλασθήσῃ καὶ ἀναζωοποιηθήσῃ
MSS B, D, and Slav (family *d*): ἀνακαινισθήσῃ καὶ ἀναζωοποιηθήσῃ [D: ζωοποιηθήσῃ]

Only MS A and MS P definitely provide the threefold blessing, ἀνακαινισθήσῃ καὶ ἀναπλασθήσῃ καὶ ἀναζωοποιηθήσῃ. It is possible that the Latin MS 436 (from L2) translated the same Greek blessing, which is probably why Burchard and Fink include the triadic blessing in their respective texts. Manuscript 436 provides the equivalent of the latter two Greek words (ἀναπλασθήσῃ καὶ ἀναζωοποιηθήσῃ), and even though it reads *vocaberis* for the corresponding verb ἀνακαινισθησῃ, Burchard proposes that it originally had *renovaberis* or *novaberis* and Fink suggests *novaberis*.[99] Burchard also proposes that the Armenian version originally had the threefold blessing, but none of the Armenian witnesses provide such an example. In fact, a twofold blessing is most common across all witness groups. Family *c* and two manuscript families of Arm (Arm[a] and Arm[d]) read ἀνακαινισθήσῃ καὶ ἀναπλασθήσῃ (or its equivalent); MSS F, W, 671 (from Ngr) (all from family *f*), the other four manuscript families of Arm (Arm[bcef]), and the *d* witnesses all have some form of ἀνακαινισθήσῃ καὶ ἀναζωοποιηθήσῃ (or ζωοποιηθήσῃ [F D (671)] or ζωοποιῆσει [W]); and L1 (from family *f*) provides a similar twofold blessing: *renovata es et vivificata es*. Manuscripts E and G (the latter from family *f*) just read ἀνακαινισθήσῃ; the phrase is all together lacking in MSS 435& (from L2) and Q (from family *a*); and the Syriac folios attesting to Bu 13:15–16:7 are lost.[100]

Fink appears to retain the attestation of MSS AP because to her it seems to pair well with MS 436 (L2), thereby confirming her suspicions that *M1* and *M2* had the triadic blessing of ἀνακαινισθήσῃ καὶ ἀναπλασθήσῃ καὶ ἀναζωοποιηθήσῃ. This would mean, then, that scribes more often deleted a

---

99. Burchard, *Joseph und Aseneth*, 189; Fink, *Joseph und Aseneth*, 295.
100. Burchard, *Joseph und Aseneth*, 189.

third blessing than they added a third one (or even added a second and third one). In addition, Fink would have to claim that the Armenian originally had three blessings, and through transmission, scribes mixed and matched two different couplets. I find it intriguing that the two different blessings in the Armenian are shared with other witnesses (*c* on the one hand, and MSS FW, L1, and *d* on the other), but their similarities may not descend from the particular two majuscules/minuscules that Burchard and Fink posit. According to Burchard, Mc shares many affinities with Syr/Arm/L2, so could Arm^a and Arm^d descend from something shared by *c*? Likewise, we saw that in Bu 18:9, MS F and MS W share similarities with Arm, so could Arm^{bcef} share a common reading with that of family *f*? Since we are unable to verify what the Syriac had, I am not sure how much more we can definitively say about the beginnings of Bu 15:5. Once again, scribal variety seems to be dominant in the transmission of the verse; the sense is clear that Aseneth receives a blessing of renewal, but the details are not uniform.

The example of Bu 15:5 also reveals another limitation in the two-majuscule/minuscule argument, which is important to raise given Burchard's prioritization of Arm and L2 and given how Fink deals with these witness groups when they disagree. As we have seen above with the triadic or dual blessings, the Armenian is more closely tied with the rest of the witnesses than with L2. Although the best detection of shared textual descent is to identify common mistakes (so Burchard's theory about Bu 10:2 and the transmission of μυλών/μυλωρός and πυλών/πυλωρός), the disagreements between Arm and L2 indicate that the transmission process was more complicated than what Burchard or Fink propose. Other examples include passages that I discussed in chapter 1: (1) Bu 2:7, where Arm, Syr, *a*, and *d* modify that the eastern window faces ἐπὶ τήν αὐλήν (or its linguistic equivalent), and L2, FW, and L1 (from *f*), and Mc do not; (2) Bu 11:1x–18 in which Arm is more closely aligned with MS G (from family *f*) and family *c* than with L2; (3) Bu 15:7, in which similar divisions between Arm and L2 occur in several places (including the fact that MSS 436 [L2] and D [from family *d*] are the only witnesses to attest to Repentance as a "mother"); and (4) Bu 15:12x, in which MS 436 (L2) and G share, against all other witnesses including Arm, the question, "Why do you seek this, my name, Aseneth?"[101] Fink's reconstructed text does not differ from

---

101. In the previous chapter, see my review of Standhartinger's analysis regarding Bu 2:7 and my review of Kraemer's analysis for Bu 11:1x–18; Bu 15:7/Ph 15:7; and Bu 15:12x.

Burchard's in these verses, and so she retains Burchard's choices of siding either with Arm or L2 in these cases. When Arm and L2 disagree, and even more noteworthy, when Arm sides with some supposed *M2* descendants and L2 sides with other supposed *M2* descendants, the only way to save the stemma is to argue for one side and claim that the other side deleted or changed the text. So, for example, since Arm and the ancestor of *ad* attest to ἐπὶ τὴν αὐλήν in Bu 2:7, Fink's stemma could imply that *M1* and *M2* provided the phrase only if we assume that the scribes producing L2, FW, L1, and M*c* (or their respective exemplars) all deleted it. It is equally likely, however, that more than one scribe added the courtyard reference in Bu 2:7 so as to connect that window with the one Aseneth looks through when she watches Joseph enter the household courtyard (*Asen.* 5).[102] It is at times like this where Fink's analysis treats family *a* or its predecessor Ahn *ad* as one scale of a balance. The assumption is that if *a* or *ad* arguably attest to a reading, and Arm or L2 do as well, then that reading goes back to the earliest text. Fink may be correct with some of her textual decisions, but the manuscripts defy such a tidy formula and some of Fink's choices seem forced.

One example can be found in Bu/F 10:11, when Aseneth is changing into mourning attire. Both Burchard and Fink provide that, among other things, Aseneth removes "her choice robe" (τὴν στολὴν αὐτῆς τὴν ἐκλεκτήν). This phrase is only attested in families *a* and *d*, and although Fink admits that her reading is questionable, she nevertheless keeps it in the text.[103] Manuscript 436 (L2) indicates that Aseneth's robe is valuable, but its attestation is not equivalent to the Greek (*sericam et aurem*). Although other witnesses mention a garment (L1 [*f*] and *c* refer to ἱμάτια), other manuscripts provide comprehensive terms for what Aseneth removes. The Syriac simply refers to "everything" (*ea cuncta*); the Armenian has "all the

---

102. As far as I can tell, in Bu/F 5:2, Aseneth watches through her "eastern window" in all the manuscript categories but MS E and perhaps Arm (but see below). I have detected the reference in the following witnesses: Syr, L2, *f* (MSS FW and L1), M*c*, *a*, and *d* (Brooks, *Historia ecclesiastica Zachariae Rhetori*, 18; Fink, *Joseph und Aseneth*, 268; Batiffol, *Le Livre de la Prière d'Asenath*, 45 and 93; Wright, "After Antiquity," 2:33). Since in Burchard's critical edition he notes the variants for "window" (which Arm supplies) but not for "eastern," it is possible that Arm also attests to the window facing east. The fact that Burchard provides no list of variants for κατὰ ἀνατολάς leads me to believe that, in his mind, there were no variants of value to list. To Burchard, it would not be worth mentioning if only MS E lacked the reference (*Joseph und Aseneth*, 99).

103. Fink, *Joseph und Aseneth*, 147.

jewelry/adornment" ("den Schmuck allen"); MSS 435& (L2) summarize with a similar line (*omnem ornatum*); and MS G (*f*) provides "all the golden items" (πάντα τα χρυσά) (MSS FW [*f*] and E lack 10:11).[104] Working within the logic of the two-majuscule/minuscule theory, and even using *ad* as one scale of the balance, it is not clear why the phrase "her choice robe" trumps the other readings. At times, then, Burchard's and Fink's textual decisions seem to be made for aesthetic reasons, even if the evidence or the two majuscule/minuscule theory does not substantiate those textual choices.

Let us examine two more cases where textual decisions seem to be based on stylistic reasons. The first example is Bu/F 3:1, when the narrator refers to Joseph coming to Heliopolis to gather the grain of abundance.[105] Burchard suggests that the text should include the phrase, "of the seven years," after "grain," which Fink adds to her text (ἦν συνάγων τὸν σῖτον <τῶν ἑπτὰ ἐτῶν> τῆς εὐθηνίας). Burchard contends that the phrase, "of the seven years," is suitable to the style of *Aseneth*, and he seems to be convinced of its early status because, as he explains, it is attested in the Syriac and somewhat in the Armenian. Both Burchard and Fink indicate that the Armenian's attestation, "the grain of the fullness of the years," is related to what the Syriac provides (*frumentum annorum septem ubertatis*), and it is possible that the Armenian displays only a deletion of the word, "seven" (translating τὸν σῖτον τῆς εὐθηνίας <τῶν ἐτῶν>, for example). The only L2 witness to attest to 3:1, MS 436, does not provide the phrase, but Fink explains that "of the seven years" was likely removed since it did not make sense with what 436 provides ("abundance of fruit/produce" instead of grain; *et erat colligens habundantiam frugum*). Since the beginning of 3:1 also mentions the seven years of abundance (καὶ ἐγένετο ἐν τῷ πρώτῳ ἔτει ἐτῶν τῆς εὐθηνίας [Bu/F]), Fink surmises that the other textual witnesses left out the second mention of "the seven years," as most of them tend to shorten the text (Fink refers to MS E and families *c*, *a*, and *d*; family *f* also lacks the second phrase). I do not find Burchard's or Fink's arguments here convincing. Most of the witnesses try to convey the narrative timeframe of the book of Genesis (during the years of prosperity), but the phrase, "of (the) seven years," can only be confidently associated with the Syriac witnesses. Below is a list of all the attestations that exist of the clause in question:

---

104. Burchard, *Joseph und Aseneth*, 133.
105. The information in this paragraph is taken from Burchard, *Joseph und Aseneth*, 85; and Fink, *Joseph und Aseneth*, 105 and 263.

Syr: *et is colligebat ac coacervabat frumentum annorum septem ubertatis*
Arm: "und sammelte den Weizen (der) Fülle der Jahre"
436 (L2): *et erat colligens habundantiam frugum loci illius*
FW and L1 (*f*): καὶ ἦν συνάγων τὸν σῖτον τῆς εὐθηνίας (L1: + *illius*)
E: συνάγων τὸν σῖτον
***c*:** καὶ ἦν συνάγων τὸν σῖτον ἐν τῇ πόλει ἐκείνῃ τῆς εὐθηνίας
***a*:** συνάγων τὸν σῖτον τῆς χώρας ἐκείνης (τ.χ.ἐ. = Q has ἡλίου πόλεως)
B and Slavonic (*d*): καὶ ἦν συνάγων τὸν σῖτον τῆς χώρας ἐκείνης

The narrative is clearly set within the timeframe of Joseph's harvest collection, and most witnesses try to associate this line with the Genesis account (the time "of abundance," τῆς εὐθηνίας) or with the beginning of the *Aseneth* storyline (where Joseph collects the grain "of that land," τῆς χώρας ἐκείνης [Bu 1:1]). Burchard's and Fink's proposals depend on the idea that *M1* and *M2* both deleted the reference of "seven years" (following the two-majuscule/minuscule theory) or that several witnesses on both sides of the *M1–M2* balance independently removed the phrase from their respective texts. In other words, scribes deleted a phrase that aligned *Aseneth* with the Genesis narrative. It seems easiest to say that the Syriac demonstrates one of several ways that chapter 3 was introduced, which is clear in that Arm and L2 do not align perfectly. Within the logic of Fink's stemma, it is not definitive what *M1* read in this line. The retention of "τῶν ἑπτὰ ἐτῶν" in the reconstructed texts appears, then, to be for aesthetic reasons only.

My second example of a stylistic choice is Bu 7:4, and here we have a case in which Burchard and Fink seem to assume that ultimately the longer line preserves the earlier line, even if it does not easily fit into their stemmata. In *Asen.* 7, the narrator describes how Joseph had fended off women in the past, and in this verse, we hear Joseph's inner thoughts about his motivation for his chastity. Below is the entire quote from Burchard's and Fink's reconstruction of 7:4:[106]

οὐχ [F: οὐ μὴ] ἁμαρτήσω ἐνώπιον κυρίου τοῦ θεοῦ τοῦ πατρός μου Ἰσραὴλ οὐδὲ κατὰ πρόσωπον τοῦ πατρός μου Ἰακώβ
I will not sin before the Lord, the God of my father, Israel, nor in the face of my father Jacob.

---

106. Burchard, *Joseph und Aseneth*, 110; Fink, *Joseph und Aseneth*, 174.

2. The Reconstructed Texts of *Aseneth*: Burchard and Fink 115

When examining the witnesses, Fink's decision to retain the last clause, "nor in the face of my father Jacob," is unclear. Below are what the witnesses provide for "God of my father … my father Jacob" in Bu/F 7:4:[107]

Syr: *domino deo patris mei Israel*
Arm: "(dem) Herrn dem Erlöser Israels"
L2: *domino deo patris mei Israel*
E: κυρίου τοῦ θεοῦ μου
W (*f*): κυρίου τοῦ θεοῦ τοῦ πατρός μου Ἰσραὴλ οὐδὲ κατὰ πρόσωπον τοῦ πατρός μου Ἰακώβ
L1 (*f*): *dei patris mei Israel, neque iniquitatem faciam ante faciem dei patris mei Iacob*
J (*c*): κυρίου τοῦ θεοῦ τοῦ πατρός μου Ἰσραὴλ οὐδὲ κατὰ πρόσωπον τοῦ θεοῦ τοῦ πατρός μου Ἰακώβ
H and K (*c*): κυρίου τοῦ θεοῦ τοῦ πατρός μου Ἰακώβ
a: κυρίου τοῦ θεοῦ καὶ τοῦ προσώπου τοῦ πατρός μου Ἰσραὴλ
d: τοῦ θεοῦ Ἰσραὴλ

None of the witnesses from Syr or those that descend supposedly from *M1* (so not Arm or L2) provide the clause, "nor in the face of my father Jacob," and neither do MS E and family *d* (from the *M2* side). Only MS W from family *f* provides οὐδὲ κατὰ πρόσωπον τοῦ πατρός μου Ἰακώβ, the Greek clause in Burchard's and Fink's texts. Fink's decision, then, implies that she assumes the following (see fig. 2.1): (1) MS W reflects *M2*; (2) MS E deleted the clause (οὐδὲ κατὰ πρόσωπον τοῦ πατρός μου Ἰακώβ); (3) either ancestor η added τοῦ θεοῦ before τοῦ πατρός μου Ἰακώβ (explaining why L1 and *c* have it) and MS W deleted it, or L1 and *c* added the phrase independent of one another; (4) the predecessor of *a* (Ahn *a* or Ahn *ad*) either deleted τοῦ θεοῦ or never had it (corresponding to the respective scenarios of #3 above), altered the syntax of the sentence (changing οὐδέ to καί) and changed Ἰακώβ to Ἰσραὴλ; and (5) Ahn *d* abbreviated the phrase in *a*. We are also to assume that the Syriac and *M1* (or Arm^Gr and L2^Gr separately) deleted the phrase, οὐδὲ κατὰ πρόσωπον τοῦ πατρός μου Ἰακώβ. It is curious to me why Fink (and Burchard) did not simply pro-

---

107. Greek in parentheses indicates that the witness seems to provide but Burchard is not more forthcoming on the details (Burchard, *Joseph und Aseneth*, 110; Fink, *Joseph und Aseneth*, 271; Batiffol, *Le Livre de la Prière d'Aseneth*, 95; Brooks, *Historia ecclesiastica Zachariae Rhetori*, 19).

vide, "the God of my father, Israel," a phrase well-attested on both sides of Fink's stemma. Instead, both Burchard and Fink appear to be interested in the longer line. Within the logic of Burchard's two-majuscule theory and Fink's stemma, their desire for the fuller reading does not work in this case.

My main critique of Burchard's and Fink's reconstructions is that too many times the manuscript evidence is constrained by overarching hypotheses about how *Aseneth* was transmitted (the two-majuscule/minuscule hypothesis). Fink correctly deletes Burchard's surpluses from families *a* and *d* that he had supposed were earliest readings (such as in her adaptation of Bu 10:11), but her reliance on the same textual families to even the balance of *M1* and *M2* depends too often upon the idea that scribes altered portions of their texts only when those supposed changes support her stemma. As I have discussed above, the witnesses reveal a variety of scribal choices that make it difficult to posit a linear, sequential path of transmission. For example, the triadic blessing in Bu/F 15:5 may not have been the earliest rendering or may have been one of a set of renderings that scribes transmitted. Just like Burchard who erred by including emendations of *a* and *d* in his text, Fink retains readings that do not fit her stemma but seemingly are kept for aesthetic reasons (Bu/F 10:11; 3:1; and 7:4). In the end, constructing the earliest *Aseneth* text is out of reach because the evidence will not fit neatly in any stemma.

Burchard, and now Fink, have advanced our understanding considerably of the textual evidence for *Aseneth*, yet their products are hindered by the limits of the project itself. For textual evidence such as what *Aseneth* yields, with its tweaking, expanding, or shrinking of phrases and descriptions, it is impossible to produce the earliest text. We are left with either forgoing a fixed, reconstructed text (as I will in the next chapter), or we are left to manipulate the text to fit a certain transmission theory. A salient example of such tinkering is in Fink's adaptation of Bu 1:6, where the narrator describes the activity of the high-ranking men in response to the widespread report of Aseneth's beauty. Burchard's text (Bu 1:6) reads that the men ἐμνηστεύοντο αὐτήν ("were attempting to court her"), which is attested in some form in Arm, L2, Mc, *a*, and *d*. There is, however, another dominant reading that is preserved in Syr, *f* (FW, L1, and G), and E: ὕμνουν αὐτήν ("they were praising her [in song]").[108] In the context of the story,

---

108. Burchard, *Joseph und Aseneth*, 73.

ὕμνουν is the *lectio difficilior*, which typically is assumed to indicate the more original reading, and Fink suggests the possibility that the ancestor of Arm, L2, *and* the hypothetical ancestor θ (the ancestor of Mc, *a*, and *d*) changed "praise" to "court" independently from each other. Fink settles, however, on the idea that both readings existed at the initial stages of transmission, and over the course of hand-copying, one of the two was deleted by scribes. Fink's text, then, provides ὕμνουν <καὶ> ἐμνηστεύοντο.[109] Fink's solution is ingenious; it fits the two-majuscule/minuscule theory well. Yet, I question the reliance on the idea that the scribes of *Aseneth* were mostly deleting parts of what otherwise was a fairly comprehensive text; the evidence, rather, seems to indicate that two dominant readings occurred in narrating how men expressed their feelings for Aseneth.

A New Path to the Earliest *Aseneth*

There is no doubt that Burchard's reconstruction has provided a valuable service to the study of *Aseneth*, and his careful text-critical study of all the witnesses continues to be extraordinary.[110] Fink's contribution considerably improves our study of the witnesses, and her presentation of the evidence is formidable. No decent examination of *Aseneth* can ignore her work. Scholarly dependence upon either Burchard's or Fink's reconstruction, however, can diminish an awareness of the diversity that exists among the witnesses and thus obscure our understanding about how this story was transmitted. As I discussed in the last chapter, the same issues occur when we simply compare the reconstructions of Burchard and Philonenko. Interestingly, the differences in narration between the manuscripts oftentimes do not change the general plot of the story, so these differences may reveal scribal flexibility in the transmission process of a common story. Such flexibility, though, complicates identifying the earliest text or even a cogent genealogy of the manuscripts, and even Burchard's primary witnesses seem to betray redactions that hide what their exemplars displayed. Some of the choices that Burchard and Fink make for their reconstructions conceal such complexities of transmission, but if it is presumed that their choices represent the earliest retrievable text, then their reconstructions certainly affect how *Aseneth* is discussed in

---

109. Fink, *Joseph und Aseneth*, 103.
110. As evident with his edition of the Armenian, *Minor Edition*.

scholarship. Here is the crux of the matter: Academics build their theses about the social environment or author of *Aseneth* by assuming that the reconstructed text *is* the earliest rendering of the story, but this reliance can produce a house of cards.

One case in point is the description of the bees in chapter 16. After Aseneth consumes a portion of the honeycomb, unusual bees rise out of it. Burchard's reconstruction of 16:18 describes their appearance as follows, and the individual attestations of the underlined portions are provided for comparison:[111]

> καὶ ἦσαν αἱ μέλισσαι λευκαὶ ὡσεὶ χιὼν καὶ τὰ πτερὰ αὐτῶν <u>ὡς πορφύρα καὶ ὡς ὑάκινθος καὶ ὡς κόκκος καὶ ὡς βύσσινα ἱμάτια <χρυσο ὑφῆ> καὶ διαδήματα χρυσᾶ ἐπὶ τὰς κεφαλὰς αὐτῶν</u>
> And the bees were white as snow, and their wings were <u>like purple, violet, scarlet, and fine linen cloths <interwoven with gold>, and gold diadems were on their heads</u>.

Individual attestations of this line:

> **Syr:** *ut color purpurae et hyacinthorum et cocci et byssi auro texti et coronoa aurea in capite uniuscuiusque earum*
> **Arm:** like purple and very long, and like red crimson and several like embroidered fine linen (cloths) (and gold diadems were on their heads [only in MS 332: + of each])[112]
> **435& (L2):** *quasi purpura iacinctina aut serica vestimenta contexta auro mundo. habebant circa capita sua dyademata aurea*[113]
> **F (f):** ὡς πορφ[+ gap of about ten letters]θοι καὶ ὡς βύσσινα ἱμάτια χρ[+ gap of about five letters] καὶ διαδήματα χρύσαια ἐπὶ τὰς κεφαλὰς αὐτῶν

---

111. Burchard, *Joseph und Aseneth*, 219.

112. Burchard translates the Armenian as follows: "wie purpurne und sehr-lange und wie rote karminene und (die) einiger wie Byssus(gewänder) bestickte." His critical apparatus implies that Arm provides "and gold diadems on their heads," where the Armenian is equivalent to καὶ διαδήματα χρυσᾶ ἐπὶ τὰς κεφαλὰς αὐτῶν (*Joseph und Aseneth*, 219).

113. Burchard provides *et habebant circa capita sua dyademata aurea*, but Fink notes that *et habebant* is only attested in MS 445 of 435&. I provide here Fink's rendition of 435& (Burchard, *Joseph und Aseneth*, 219; Fink, *Joseph und Aseneth*, 303).

2. The Reconstructed Texts of *Aseneth*: Burchard and Fink 119

G (*f*): πορφύρα καὶ ὡς ὑάκινθος καὶ ὡς κόκκος καὶ ὥσπερ διαδήματα χρυσᾶ ἦσαν ἐπὶ τὰς κεφαλὰς αὐτῶν τῶν μελισσῶν
L1 (*f*): *purpuree ut iacinctus*
671 (Ngr of *f*): (something akin to this phrase: καὶ διαδήματα χρυσᾶ ἐπὶ τὰς κεφαλὰς αὐτῶν)[114]
A (*a*): ὡς πορφύρα καὶ ὑάκινθος καὶ ὡς κόκκος
PQ (*a*): ὡς πορφύρα (Q: πορφύραν) καὶ ὑάκινθος
B (*d*): ὡς πορφύρα καὶ ὡς ὑάκινθος καὶ ὡσει νήματα χρυσοῦ καὶ ἦσαν διαδήματα χρυσᾶ ἐπὶ τὰς κεφαλὰς αὐτῶν
D (*d*): ὡς πορφύρα καὶ ὡς ὑάκινθος καὶ εἰσι διαδήματα χρυσᾶ ἐπὶ τὰς κεφαλὰς αὐτῶν
Slavonic (*d*): like purple and like violet and on their heads like gold

No Greek witness provides what Burchard produces in his reconstruction. He appears to retrieve his rendition from the Syriac, but the Syriac is the only witness that provides the entire costume of colors and cloths. Burchard translates the first half of the Armenian version with a question mark, which implies uncertainty in what he provides (from "like purple … linen [cloths]). The Armenian witnesses then appear to coincide with MSS F, G, Ngr (all from *f*), B, and D (both from *d*), reading the equivalent of καὶ διαδήματα χρυσᾶ ἐπὶ τὰς κεφαλὰς αὐτῶν. Burchard does not offer any indication if or in what ways the Armenian witnesses may differ in comparison, though. From L2, only MSS 435& attest to this scene, and they lack the mention of scarlet. From family *f*, MS F appears to lack scarlet (κόκκος), MS G lacks byssus cloth, and L1 leaves out scarlet, byssus, and the diadems. Family *a* only mentions the colors of the bees' wings, and only MS A lists all three colors in family *a*. Finally, MS B and MS D do not mention scarlet, and the Slavonic witnesses mention nothing about scarlet or byssus cloth. Manuscript E lacks this line, and although palimpsest M provides this scene, this line is too indecipherable to include in the discussion.[115] Fink retains Burchard's reconstructed line

---

114. Burchard places "671" in parentheses in his critical apparatus, which implies that the wording in 671 is very similar to this attestation but not exactly the same (*Joseph und Aseneth*, 219).

115. Burchard, *Joseph und Aseneth*, 219. Palimpsest M clearly provides πορφυρα, likely refers to διαδημα (διαδη …), and at the very least, the large gap in the texts sug-

in her text, and she does not comment on the distinctions in the witnesses noted above.[116]

Burchard's reconstruction presents four materials (πορφύρα, ὑάκινθος, κόκκος, and βύσσος) that are also required in the production of Aaronid garments in LXX Exodus, and based on this correlation, Gideon Bohak argues that these bees represent Jewish priests and that the honeycomb signifies the Jewish temple in Heliopolis.[117] Only the Syriac translation of *Aseneth*, however, definitively provides all four of these elements, and the diversity of attestations that we find in the evidence may be best attributed to the kind of scribal redaction that Kraemer discusses. In the LXX/OG, these materials certainly are used in reference to the tabernacle/temple or to Aaronid priesthood (LXX Exodus, Leviticus, Numbers, and 2 Chronicles), but they are also used to describe wealth or royalty. A good example is LXX Isa 3:21–24, where the prophet Isaiah delivers a judgment oracle against the wealthy women of Jerusalem. "In that day," Isaiah warns, God will take away their expensive jewelry and luxurious clothing made of πορφύρα, ὑάκινθος, κόκκος, and βύσσος. Most importantly, the more commonly attested adjectives in our witnesses, πορφύρα and ὑάκινθος (and their respective cognates) often signify wealth and/or regal status in the LXX/OG.[118] Since all but L1 and *a* adorn the bees with diadems, the bees appear to be depicted in the likeness of royalty instead of priesthood, and the dominant readings of "purple" and "violet" only enhance a regal image. In the transmission of this scene, scribes may have tweaked it possibly to align it with other references, such as in the Syriac with (possibly) the Aaronid priesthood. A metaphorical reference to a Heliopolite, Jewish priesthood becomes less likely, though, when examining the individual

---

gests that M read something similar to the other witnesses (Fink, *Joseph und Aseneth*, 39).

116. Fink, *Joseph und Aseneth*, 185. The only distinction in Fink's text is that she is more confident that the word χρυσοϋφῇ should be in the text (providing, χρυσ<οϋφῇ> compared to Burchard's, <χρυσοϋφῇ>.

117. Bohak, *"Joseph and Aseneth,"* 10–12. In particular he cites the following passages: LXX Exod 25:3; 26:1, 31, 36; 27:16; 28:4–5, 8, 15; 35:6, 25 (11 n. 16).

118. ὑάκινθος (or cognate form): Sir 6:30; 40:4; Ezek 16:10; 23:6; 27:24. πορφύρα (or cognate form): Judg (A and Vat.) 8:26; 1 Esd 3:6; Esth 1:6; 8:15; Jdt 10:21; 1 Macc 8:14; 10:20, 62, 64; 11:58; 14:43, 44; 2 Macc 4:38, Song 3:10; 7:6; Ep Jer 11, 71; and Dan 5:7, 15, 29 (OG and Th); 6:4 (OG). ὑάκινθος and πορφύρα (and/or cognates) together: 1 Macc 4:23; Isa 3:21–24, Jer 10:9; and Ezek 27:7.

witnesses. The dependence upon a reconstructed text, then, can lead to untenable interpretations.

As I will discuss in the next chapter, most of the witnesses share a similar enough storyline, and, in places, similar enough phrases and descriptions, that we can discuss the narrative at its hypothesized earliest stage. Yet, to depend on Philonenko's, Burchard's, or Fink's reconstructions alone disregards the individual adaptations that are found in the manuscripts, and acknowledging this multiplicity may be the key to understanding the transmission of *Aseneth*. Relying on the analytical models of Standhartinger and Kraemer (which presume that the two reconstructions represent textual snapshots in the earlier stages of *Aseneth*'s transmission) conceals the variety of scribal activity preserved in the evidence. It is more precise to say that *some* witnesses exhibit scribal redactions of the narrative, and many of the alterations or expansions could have been made independently by several scribes. The assumed sequential order of the two reconstructions (whereby one represents the earliest text) also detracts from the idea that several different narrations of *Aseneth* could have existed at the same time, even during its earliest stages of existence. Burchard's and Fink's transmission histories of *Aseneth* also depend on a clear genealogical production of our witnesses, but many of the manuscripts could just as equally descend from contemporaneous scribal redaction and/or from more than two majuscules or minuscules. The transmission of *Aseneth* may have been more akin to that of the Apocryphal Acts whereby an overall plot was maintained but individual scenes were altered or expanded. Viewing the text of *Aseneth* in this way helps to maintain awareness about the diversity of the tradition while discussing the possible value of this story when it supposedly was composed.

3
The *Fabula* of *Aseneth*

The reconstructed texts of *Aseneth* mask the complexity of scribal transmission that is evident in the textual witnesses, and thus they have too often given the impression that scholars have a fixed, earliest text to examine. As I discussed in chapter 1, the distinct redactions found within each textual family make comparing the reconstructions of Burchard and Philonenko obsolete; the reconstructed texts do not adequately reflect two stages of scribal transmission, and so they fail to demonstrate how an earlier *Aseneth* narrative purposefully was expanded or altered. As I discussed in chapter 2, Burchard's and Fink's texts also conceal the diversity preserved in the witnesses, and their theory about the transmission of the *Aseneth* witnesses is not persuasive. Burchard tries to organize the transmission of *Aseneth* in a linear schema that the evidence cannot confirm, and even though Fink presents a more subtle stemma, she at times favors her theoretical stemma over and against the textual evidence. The two majuscule/minuscule hypothesis that Burchard and Fink promote is based primarily upon one verse (Bu/F 10:2), and as I discussed in chapter 2, there are other, equally viable ways how that verse may have evolved in the witnesses. Inevitably, for the application of Burchard's hypothesis and Fink's stemma to work, we need to admit that at different times, scribes of one text deleted a reading or scribes of another added it, and in the end, these scenarios yield little that is definitive. The idea behind one reconstructed text does not allow for multiple ways of recounting a scene, and if we accept Burchard's and Fink's linear schemata, we either must force the evidence to fit their precise arrangements or discard the reconstructed text all together. Although Fink corrects Burchard's text to fit his theory of transmission more accurately, her stemma restricts her textual choices even more than Burchard's does (whereby Fink presents a direct line of textual descent from $M2$ in the order of E, *f*, Mc, *a*, and *d*). Like Burchard, she also tinkers with the text or makes exceptions to her transmission theory in order to create her ideal text. Both Burchard's and Fink's texts betray a desire to create a comprehensive and cohesive narrative of the earliest, retrievable *Aseneth* text, but the textual witnesses reveal a muddled picture that could hint at a more complicated transmission process. The witnesses provide multiple tellings of a fairly fixed storyline, not multiple copies of a fairly fixed text.

Although in his publications Burchard does not seem to embrace the idea, even he agrees that there may have been multiple narrations of the story (when he suggested that the supposed predecessors of families *b*, *ad*, and *c* [β, αδ, and ζ] may have developed independently from one another).[1] Some of Fink's textual analysis (but not her overall argument) also supports the hypothesis that the evidence is too diverse to produce a reliable, initial Greek text. The four contaminations that she identifies complicate the more linear picture of Burchard's and Fink's transmission histories, and Fink's assessment of MS E is perhaps the most striking datum. Manuscript E possibly reflects earlier narrations of the story, but in its current form, it exhibits liberal scribal activity. It is characterized by substantial deletions and retellings such that Burchard had considered it of little textual value in producing his reconstruction. If Fink is correct about its importance, MS E is illustrative in showing how scribes understood the transmission of *Aseneth*; they considered it a pliable narrative that could be altered, bent, and stretched without harming the perceived integrity of the story.

There was likely an initial, written narrative of *Aseneth*, but the diversity of the textual witnesses makes it impossible to discover this original.[2]

---

1. Burchard, "Present State of Research," 34.
2. For an initial written narrative, see Burchard, "Joseph and Aseneth," 180. In response to Elder ("On Transcription and Oral Transmission," 119–42), I agree that orality was likely a part in how this narrative may have been produced and reproduced. His argument that the text demonstrates "strong residual orality," however, would have been more convincing if (1) he had developed it by examining the manuscript families and not simply by depending upon Burchard's reconstuction (he also seems unaware of Fink's adaptation of Burchard's text as well as Burchard's reclassification of the longer *b*-family); and (2) he had compared the relationship between the *Aseneth* manuscript evidence and Homeric scholarship in Alexandria during the Ptolemaic period. This comparison would have included the role of oral and written components in Greek education as well as related theories about the translation and production of Septuagint texts. As it stands, it is difficult to ascertain what would

Yet, the textual witnesses are extremely consistent in their presentation of the narrative, and as I will argue, the repeated storyline shared by the witnesses makes it possible to hypothesize about the significance of *Aseneth* when it was first composed. To identify this common storyline, I will present a model similar to that used by Thomas in her study on the Acts of Peter.[3] Like the textual evidence of *Aseneth*, the textual witnesses that preserve the narrative of the Acts of Peter do not reveal a discernible path back to a so-called original text. The manuscript evidence demonstrates that scribes considered the Acts of Peter to be somewhat fluid in nature, and so they often would alter or adapt it. Thomas contends that the reception of the Acts of Peter by ancient scribes and audiences was akin to how oral traditions are received; a general, fixed version of events was presumed, but at the same time, a variety of performances were transmitted (albeit in the case of the Acts of Peter, the performances were transmitted in written form.) I argue in this chapter that the manuscripts of *Aseneth* are best understood in this light; they are performances of a general storyline about Aseneth and particular events associated with her incorporation into Joseph's family.

In order to show how helpful Thomas's analysis is to examining *Aseneth*, I will first summarize the textual witnesses of the Acts of Peter and the way in which Thomas explains their relationship to one another. My purpose here is simply to illustrate how the problems posed by the *Aseneth* witnesses are not unique, that diversity in scribal transmission occurred with other narratives and that scribes often took liberty in how they transmitted stories. After this section, I will not return to the particular details of the Acts of Peter; I will only refer to the model that Thomas uses to interpret the textual evidence.

---

have been a standard intonation unit for intelligentsia in antiquity and why *Aseneth* preserves oral units instead of simply imitates septugintal style of narration. As I will argue in this chapter and the next, there is a purposeful connection made between *Aseneth* and Septuagint texts, and this connection is related to identity formulation. Furthermore, as I will present in this chapter, different tellings of a basic storyline existed in written forms in antiquity and not just through oral media.

3. Thomas, *Acts of Peter*.

Thomas's Study of the Acts of Peter

In one form or another, the Acts of Peter is preserved in Coptic, Greek, Latin, Syriac, Armenian, Ethiopic, Arabic, and Old Church Slavonic.[4] The Acts of Peter was likely composed in Greek, but the most significant witness to an early and extensive form of the story is preserved in Latin (see fig. 3.1). Referred to as Actus Vercellenses, this witness is found in a codex at Vercilli dated to the sixth-seventh centuries (cod. Ver 158), but based on historical and linguistic factors, it most likely was translated in the late fourth century.[5] The oldest witness of the Acts of Peter, the Greek P.Oxy. 6.849 (fourth century CE), and the other most reliable Greek witnesses (codices Patmos 48 [ninth century CE] and Vatopedi 79 [tenth-eleventh century CE]) seem to preserve excerpts of a longer version of the Acts of Peter, much like that of Actus Vercellenses.[6] The Coptic fragment of codex Papyrus Berolinensis 8502 (fourth–fifth centuries CE) preserves yet another scene of a longer narrative.[7] Latin contemporaries of Actus Vercellenses are (1) a martyrdom account of Peter that is attributed to bishop Linus of Rome (referred to by Thomas as the "Linus text"), and it closely resembles but adds to the account in Actus Vercellenses; and (2) a martyrdom account of Peter and Paul in a Latin rewriting of Josephus's *Jewish War* ("Pseudo-Hegesippos"), and it overlaps in content but alters some of the events in Actus Vercellenses and the Linus Text.[8] Two other Greek witnesses date to the fifth to sixth centuries CE, namely, the Passion of Peter and Paul (ascribed to Marcellus, so Thomas refers to it as "the Marcellus text") and the Acts of Nereus and Achilleus. The Marcellus

---

4. Thomas, *Acts of Peter*, 10, 40, 72.

5. Thomas, *Acts of Peter*, 10–11, 28; Jan Bremmer, "Aspects of the *Acts of Peter*: Women, Magic, Place, and Date," in *Acts of Peter: Magic, Miracles, and Gnosticism*, ed. Jan Bremmer, Studies on the Apocryphal Acts of the Apostles 3 (Leuven: Peeters, 1998), 1–20; and C. H. Turner, "The Latin Acts of Peter," *JTS* 32 (1931): 119–33.

6. The papyrus is a fragment of a longer text. P.Oxy. 6.849 coincides roughly with chs. 25–26 of Actus Vercellenses and the numbering on the fragment seems to indicate that it was a shortened version of the longer narrative (Thomas, *Acts of Peter*, 17). The codices present the martyrdom account at different places within the longer narrative's sequence of events (Thomas, *Acts of Peter*, 72).

7. This witness is also in fragmented form and recounts a story about Peter and his paralyzed daughter (which is a scene in the first part of the longer narrative, which takes place in Jerusalem) (Thomas, *Acts of Peter*, 10, 17–21).

8. Thomas, *Acts of Peter*, 42–44, 106–7.

text bears some resemblance to Actus Vercellenses in terms of its plot, provides scenes attested in Pseudo-Hegesippos but not in the Linus Text and Actus Vercellenses, and incorporates an account of Paul's martyrdom in its version of the Acts of Peter.[9] The Marcellus text is attested in several witnesses; the majority Greek text reflects the *Vorlagen* of the Armenian and Old Slavonic versions, and one (minority) Greek witness reflects the *Vorlage* of the Latin version.[10] The overall composition of the Acts of Nereus and Achilleus is unique to the storyline of the Acts of Peter, but it provides particular scenes evident in Actus Vercellenses, Pseudo-Hegesippos, and the Berlin Coptic papyrus.[11] A Latin translation was made from one Greek recension of Nereus and Achilleus in the seventh century CE.[12] Thomas considers all these witnesses (i.e., the oldest fragments and the later Greek and Latin witnesses) to be the most pertinent for her study of the earliest stages of the Acts of Peter tradition.[13]

Based upon a close textual critique of the witnesses, Thomas argues that Actus Vercellenses descends from (1) "an unredacted continuous

---

9. Both the Marcellus text and Pseudo-Hegesippus narrate the following events: (1) Simon dies immediately after his failed flight attempt, whereas Actus Vercellenses recounts that Simon is severely injured but dies later; (2) Peter's execution in Pseudo-Hegesippus and in the Marcellus text is a result of his involvement in the death of Simon, whereas in Actus Vercellenses and the Linus text, Peter's execution is a result of "Agrippa's anger over his changed relationship to his concubines;" and (3) Peter requests to be crucified upside down "because he considered himself unworthy to die in the same manner as Christ," whereas in *Actus Vercellenses* and the Linus text, Peter's reason is "to reveal the mystery of the cross and the first man" (Thomas, *Acts of Peter*, 44–5). For incorporating an acccount of the martyrdom of Paul, see Thomas, *Acts of Peter*, 44–45, 107.

10. Thomas, *Acts of Peter*, 44.

11. In particular, these common scenes are: an episode involving a talking dog, Simon, and Peter in Actus Vercellenses (see summary, Thomas, *Acts of Peter*, 29–31); a contest between Simon and Peter in resurrecting a corpse in Actus Vercellenses and Pseudo-Hegesippos; and a version of the episode with Peter and his paralyzed daughter in the Berlin Coptic papyrus (Thomas, *Acts of Peter*, 45).

12. Thomas, *Acts of Peter*, 40, 45, 107.

13. Thomas mentions that the Syriac witnesses portray a similar transmission history, in which individual witnesses reveal alterations, deletions, and additions to the general narrative tradition. She claims that the transmission history of the Syriac witnesses "developed independently" from the tradition of witnesses she investigates, but she does not explain exactly why these two traditions never overlapped (*Acts of Peter*, 136–37 n. 1)

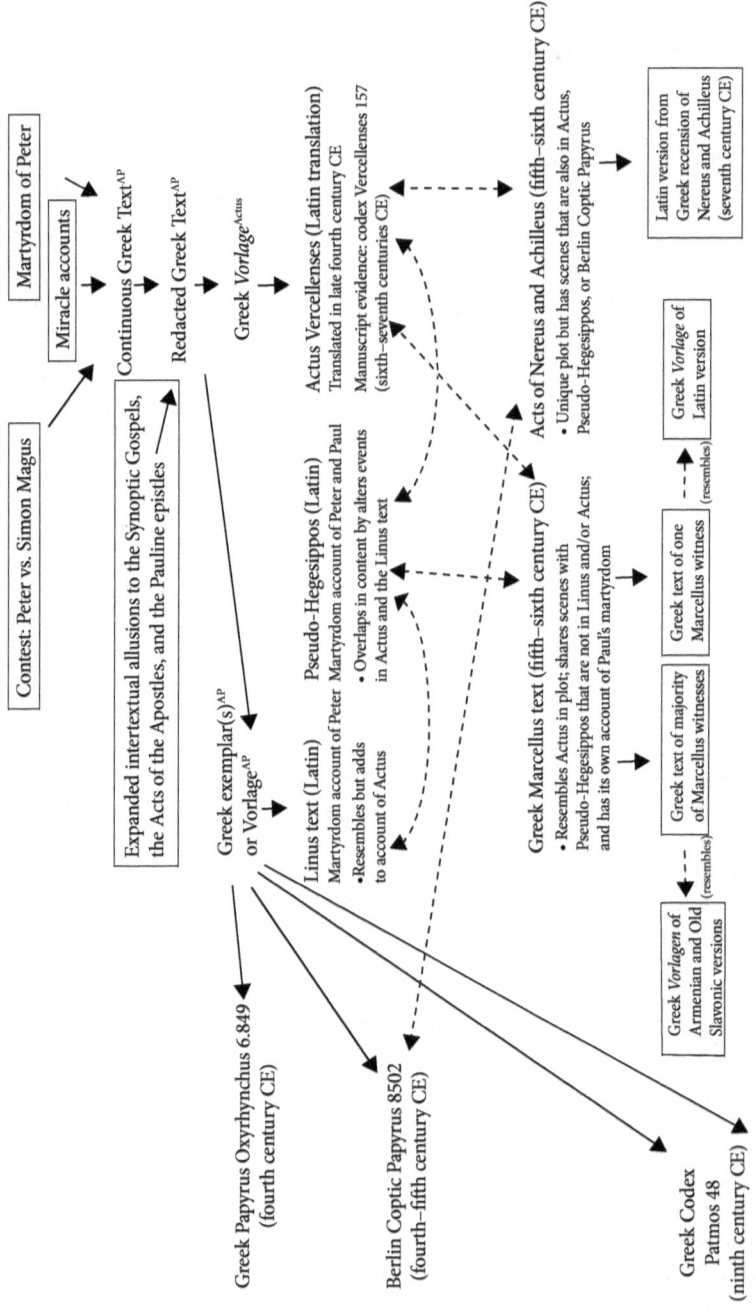

Fig. 3.1. Diagram of Thomas's proposal for the transmission of the Acts of Peter

Greek text" (hereafter referred to as "continuous Greek text"), from which (2) a redacted Greek text was made (see fig. 3.1).[14] The Greek *Vorlage* of Actus Vercellenses closely resembled the Greek exemplars or *Vorlagen* of several witnesses: P.Oxy. 6.849, Berlin Coptic Papyrus 8502, the Linus text, and codices Patmos 48, and Vatopedi 79.[15] Chapters 4–40 of Actus Vercellenses are a representation of the continuous Greek text, minus the interpolations that Thomas identifies in those chapters.[16] Thomas theorizes that the continuous Greek text was composed from three primary sources (miracle accounts, contest, and the martyrdom of Peter), which most likely contained references to particular passages in the Septuagint and to words attributed to Jesus. The creator of the continuous Greek text linked these sources together with reference to the Acts of the Apostles (Acts 2:46–47), and the redactor of the continuous Greek text then expanded the intertextual allusions to the Synoptic Gospels, the Acts of the Apostles, and the Pauline Epistles. The witnesses that come after the Greek redacted text, however, cannot be neatly aligned in a particular order of transmission. The witnesses presume a similar storyline and share many common scenes, yet the extent to which they differ exhibits a fluid style in their transmission. Quite early on in the life of the Acts of Peter tradition, scribes added to and altered the construction of the narrative and even tried to bring the narrative into conformity with other traditional writings and traditions.[17] Thomas concludes:

---

14. Thomas presents the details of this argument in ch. 2, "Time and Revision: Literary Processes at Work in the *Acts of Peter*" (*Acts of Peter*, 14–39). In particular, she argues that the Pauline interpolations in Actus Vercellenses (chs. 1–3 and 41, and portions of chs. 4, 6, 10, and perhaps 23) were additions/alterations that were composed in a redacted Greek text, and not by the author of Actus Vercellenses (as scholars had previously argued). Thomas contends that Actus Vercellenses in its entirety reads as a faithful translation of a Greek text, so it is less likely that these interpolations were the invention of the translator.

15. I have reconstructed the transmission history discussed in the paragraph from Thomas, chs. 1–3 (*Acts of Peter*, 3–71, with special attention given to pp. 27–39). As mentioned above, Pseudo-Hegesippos, the Marcellus text, and Nereus and Achilleus all depend on accounts similar to each other and/or to other witnesses, most notably, Actus Vercellenses.

16. Namely, portions of chs. 4, 6, 10, and perhaps 23 (see above). This representation is not exact, however. Thomas points out that Actus Vercellenses seems to abbreviate some portions of the text it translated (*Acts of Peter*, 42).

17. Thomas argues that the Pauline interpolations coincide well with the increased

Though all of the individuals who took part in this literary activity clearly treasured the story of Peter, none of them, apparently, felt constrained to retain the sources in precisely the form in which he or she received them. The transmission of the narrative is fluid. On the written level, the continuous reedition of the *Acts of Peter* in various written manifestations makes the recovery of the "original text" of any of the versions impossible from the standpoint of scholarly method. On the level of audience and reception, it is unclear what is to be considered the "real" *Acts of Peter*. Their multiformity, the nemesis of the scholar in search of *the* text, is a literary characteristic inseparable from the work itself.[18]

Although Thomas hypothesizes about a possible chronology for the transmission of this tradition, she hesitates to reconstruct an original text. More importantly, she suggests that the act of reconstructing an original text of the Acts of Peter would neglect an essential characteristic of how that story of Peter was perceived in antiquity. Even though one particular composition (the redacted Greek text) may have initiated the existence of the tradition, this does not necessarily mean that the earlier composition should be considered the authoritative form of the Acts of Peter narrative. In fact, Thomas attempts to elevate in importance the varieties of narration presented by the textual witnesses from late antiquity. All of these witnesses resemble each other, but none are exactly alike. The Coptic papyrus preserves a scene believed to have been in the redacted Greek text, but it is not preserved in Actus Vercellenses.[19] Although similar in their storyline, Actus Vercellenses and the Linus Text are linguistically different and do not share all events in common. Pseudo-Hegesippus is presented in an epitome-like form; Nereus and Achilleus recasts scenes similar to Pseudo-Hegesippos and Actus Vercellenses in a story about two Christians, Nereus and Achilleus; and the Marcellus text appears to derive from traditions preserved in Actus Vercellenses and Pseudo-Hegesippos but it also incorporates Paul into the story and organizes scenes in a unique way (such as presenting the *quo vadis* episode as a flashback by Peter at his death). Thomas posits that the storyline, and not a particular text, was most important in the transmission of the Peter narrative:

---

circulation of traditions about Paul's martyrdom in the late second century CE (see esp., *Acts of Peter*, 14–39).

18. Thomas, *Acts of Peter*, 39.
19. Thomas, *Acts of Peter*, 20.

> Though the Petrine texts are written texts, one finds present among them the hallmarks of oral transmission, such as the presence of multiforms, the telescoping of chronology, and the fluidity of the text. Just as important as the fluidity of the text are those elements that remain fixed, or rather, the relationship between fluid and fixed. The logic that determines which aspects of the narrative were fixed and which fluid is the most important indicator of the reason these texts altered so much from one version to the next. The multifarious versions of these works and their lack of verbal overlap suggest that it was the general line of the story, rather than the specific text at any given point, which was the significant aspect of these works. The fluidity of the narrative allowed it to be continually reshaped.[20]

Thomas suggests that ancient audiences received and applied the Acts of Peter tradition in a way similar to how they received and used oral narratives. She describes this phenomenon as the "performative aspect" of a tradition, in which each time a narrative was delivered, the narrator/author composed it in a particular and, often, unique way.[21] Precisely because we have a variety of related compositions that narrate Peter's martyrdom, it appears that ancient scribes viewed the Acts of Peter tradition as a source for independent expressions of this story.[22]

The flexibility of the Acts of Peter tradition, however, would be impossible to detect if not for its equally identifiable fixed components. Thomas claims that each text of the Acts of Peter tradition assumes a base narrative about the final stage of Peter's missionary work (which includes miracle stories about Peter), the contest between Peter and Simon Magus, and the eventual arrest and execution of Peter. The textual evidence also maintains the existence of certain secondary characters (e.g., Marcellus and Agrippa) and a shared set of "multiforms" that are applied in independent narrations of this tradition. Borrowing the term from Albert Lord's *The Singer of Tales*, Thomas defines a multiform as "one of the variant versions resulting from

---

20. Thomas, *Acts of Peter*, 41.
21. Thomas, *Acts of Peter*, 84–86.
22. Thomas also argues that the educational system of late antiquity included the instruction of expanding and epitomizing narratives, which would have been conducted in both oral and written forms (*Acts of Peter*, 85–86). Rabbinic schools also utilized similar didactic formats, as can be seen in midrashic texts. Examples are discussed in James L. Kugel, *In Potiphar's House: The Interpretive Life of Biblical Texts* (Cambridge: Harvard University Press, 1994); and David Stern, *Parables in Midrash: Narrative and Exegesis in Rabbinic Literature* (Cambridge: Harvard University Press, 1991).

multiple oral performances of a narrative."²³ In the Acts of Peter tradition, multiforms serve as mininarratives that aid the particular performance of the greater narrative. Some multiforms repeat in the narrative, as with Simon's flight over the city of Rome and with the resurrection of a young man, and other multiforms appear to have been more independent units that were also used in other writings.²⁴ For example, Peter's conversion of Roman officials' concubines/wives, and the consequences that ensue, share the same mininarrative (not characters) found in other apocryphal acts.²⁵ The Acts of Peter tradition, then, can be defined in terms of the basic plot *and* particular narrative elements that were considered to be essential to this tradition (e.g., the persistence of certain characters and scenes).

Thomas calls this fixed aspect of the tradition the "'story of the stories' within the *Acts of Peter* trajectory," and she explains this concept in terms of the Russian formalist term *fabula* as opposed to *sjuzhet*.²⁶ For Thomas,

> the fabula is the most generic form of a narrative trajectory: it denotes the events in their logical and chronological sequence and includes the basic elements of the narrative, such as situation, location, characters. In the case of the *Acts of Peter*, the fabula would be the sum of individual narratives about Peter, arranged in logical sequence according to the external dictates of his life. For example, events in Jerusalem precede those in Rome; the contest with Simon takes place before Peter's trial and execution, and the *quo vadis* story just before his arrest. A *sjuzhet*, or, as I will call it, *storyline*, is a particular rhetorical organization of a fabula that may readjust standard temporal or logical sequences. The materials of

---

23. Lord, *The Singer of Tales*, HSCL 24 (Cambridge: Harvard University Press, 1960); Thomas, *Acts of Peter*, 135 n. 139. Thomas also argues that the existence of multiforms in the *Acts of Peter* tradition suggest an original stage of oral transmission of the story, but she clarifies that regardless of this prewritten stage, the written tradition clearly maintains certain multiforms and sometimes treats individual versions of a multiform as separate historical accounts (*Acts of Peter*, 69).

24. Thomas, *Acts of Peter*, 65–69.

25. Thomas cites Virginia Burrus's work, *Chastity as Autonomy: Women in the Stories of the Apocryphal Acts*, SWR 23 (Lewiston, NY: Mellen, 1987), in which she discusses Agrippa's concubines and Albinus's wife, Xanthippe, in the Acts of Peter; Maximilla in the Acts of Andrew; Drusiana in the Acts of John; Thekla in the Acts of Paul and Thekla; Artemilla and Eubula in the Hamburg Papyrus of the Acts of Paul; the bride (first chapter), Mygdonia, and Tertia in the Acts of Thomas (Thomas, *Acts of Peter*, 66, and 143 n. 103).

26. Quotation from Thomas, *Acts of Peter*, 41.

the fabulas may be restructured, for example, by the technique of flashback; similarly, the motivations of the characters may not be presented in logical fashion. The Marcellus text preserves a unique storyline when it presents the *quo vadis* narrative as a flashback told by Peter as he is dying on the cross. To these two categories, narratologists have added a third, *text*, the storyline told on one occasion by a particular narrative agent, whether oral performance or manuscript.[27]

The story of the stories, then, is the *fabula* of a tradition, the individual manuscripts reveal different *sjuzhets* that organize the *fabula* differently, and each textual witness offers its own performance of a storyline (*text*). For Thomas, each textual witness of the Acts of Peter offers an individual performance of a basic narrative about Peter and his martyrdom (i.e., the *fabula*), and the evidence is best discussed in terms of how each witness expresses this *fabula* (and not in reconstructing the *Urtext*). In her work, Thomas discusses the earliest, attested forms of the Acts of Peter and posits the motivations of scribes behind their respective texts.

The textual evidence of the Acts of Peter clearly shows that the fixed quality of the story about Peter did not reside in one particular witness but rather in a *fabula* that was recast in several ways. The *fabula* of the Acts of Peter consisted of a basic narrative and other literary features that portrayed Peter's martyrdom and narrated the conflict between Christianity and Roman rule. The individual witnesses utilized this *fabula* in different ways, but they each presumed the same narrative chronology about Peter and shared similar characters and accounts. The key for understanding the transmission of *Aseneth* is similar; the best way to make sense of both the uniformity among and the distinctions between the witnesses is to produce a *fabula* that the evidence shares.

---

27. Thomas, *Acts of Peter*, 45–46 (emphasis original). Thomas credits Mieke Bal for adding the third category to the concepts of *fabula* and *sjuzhet* in *Narratology: Introduction to the Theory of Narrative*, trans. Christine van Boheemen (Toronto: University of Toronto Press, 1985) (*Acts of Peter*, 138 n. 22). See also Boris Èjxenbaum, "The Theory of the Formal Method," in *Readings in Russian Poetics: Formalist and Structuralist Views*, ed. Ladislov Matejka and Krystyna Pomorska (Cambridge: MIT Press, 1971), 3–37. Thomas also credits Richard Valantasis for being the first to apply these concepts to the Apocryphal Acts (Valantasis, "Narrative Strategies and Synoptic Quandaries: A Response to Dennis MacDonald's Reading of *Acts of Paul* and *Acts of Peter*," in *Society of Biblical Literature 1992 Seminar Papers*, SBLSPS 31 [Atlanta: Scholars Press, 1992], 234–39) (Thomas, *Acts of Peter*, 46).

Thomas's Model and the Textual Witnesses of *Aseneth*

Thomas's analysis of the Acts of Peter provides a helpful analogue for understanding the textual evidence of *Aseneth*. At first glance, *Aseneth*'s witnesses seem quite unlike those of the Acts of Peter tradition. Scribes were much more conservative at the textual (literal) level in the transmission of *Aseneth*, and even the plot arrangement appears to have been preserved intact among the witnesses.[28] Yet, as we have seen, there are enough variations attested in the evidence to make it impossible to detect the original text of *Aseneth*. For Thomas, the concept of a *fabula* enables her to discuss the individual witnesses on their own merit while maintaining the reasonable idea that these witnesses descend from a common story about Peter. For our purposes, the concept of a *fabula* enables us to discuss a possible earliest telling of the narrative even though we cannot reconstruct an original Greek text. As I will explain below, the concepts of *fabula* and *sjuzhet* are most conducive to discussing the witnesses of *Aseneth*. I do not incorporate Thomas's third category of *text*, which overlaps enough with my definition of *sjuzhet* to render it unproductive in my analysis.

Although in modern narratology, the term *fabula* is much debated, the term can still be helpful for understanding the transmission of ancient and medieval manuscripts.[29] I understand *fabula* much like Thomas does; *fabula* indicates a story that consists of irreducible components (such as characters, location, and situation) that are organized in particular, causal, and chronological ways.[30] The textual witnesses of *Aseneth* presume a core narrative (such as the same sequence of

---

28. Thomas also mentions that unlike the Acts of Peter tradition and the Alexander Romance, the *Aseneth* tradition was much less fluid in its transmission (*Acts of Peter*, 78).

29. See the helpful summary of the discussion up to 2001 by Richard Walsh, "Fabula and Fictionality in Narrative Theory," *Style* 35 (Winter 2001): 592–606; and the discussion of *fabulae* of "mimetic narratives," in Brian Richardson, "Unnatural Narrative Theory: A Paradoxical Paradigm," in *Emerging Vectors of Narratology*, ed. Per Krogh Hansen et al., Narratologia 57 (Berlin: de Gruyter, 2017), 193–206.

30. I have been most influenced by Boris Tomashevsky's article, "Thematics," in *Russian Formalist Criticism: Four Essays*, trans. Lee T. Lemon and Marion J. Reis (Lincoln: University of Nebraska, 1965), 61–95. See also Viktor Shklovsky, "On the Connection between Devices of *Syuzhet* Construction and General Stylistic Devices (1919)," in *Russian Formalism*, ed. Stephen Bann and John E. Bowlt, trans. Jane Knox (New York: Barnes & Noble, 1973), 48–72; and Èjxenbaum, "Theory of the Formal Method."

events, scenes, and characterizations) and share particular references in common (such as Aseneth's and Joseph's appearance) that are irreducibly part of the narrative. Each textual witness, however, is best understood as a particular performance of this core narrative. According to early Russian formalists, the *sjuzhet* is best associated with this idea of individual performance; the scribal creation of a particular *sjuzhet* of the *Aseneth* narrative pertains to how exactly the manuscript arranges the *fabula*, which includes how each manuscript extends or deletes certain features of the *fabula*. The abridgement of the ambush scene in the latter half of the narrative by many Armenian and L1 witnesses significantly changes the tone of the story, and therefore these witnesses produce distinct, artistic creations (*sjuzhet*) of *Aseneth*. Deletions in the witnesses, then, inevitably produced distinct performances of the *Aseneth* story. In family *f*, MS G omits 2:13b–10:1a and L1 omits Aseneth's preparation for Joseph's second arrival (Bu/F: 18:2–19:1); in family *d*, MSS B and D omit much of the marriage scene between Aseneth and Joseph (Ph: 21:2–7), and the Slavonic witness deletes much of the angelic figure's initial pronouncement to Aseneth (Ph: 15:6–14). As discussed in chapter 2, the remaining manuscript categories display their distinct creations as well. Although these witnesses share a common storyline, and at times most share the same or comparable wording, they nonetheless reveal their own individual expressions of the *Aseneth* story. Even Burchard admits, "Often the witnesses agree literally or to a degree that the general run of the text is unmistakable even if the wording is not."[31] In Russian formalism, *fabula* and *sjuzhet* are complimentary terms that are meant to identify the artistic achievement of individual compositions, and certainly there is much to glean in examining the witnesses of *Aseneth* in the way that Thomas studies the Acts of Peter (by comparing the *fabula* against the particular tellings of each witness). The consistency in the transmission of the *Aseneth* witnesses, however, makes it possible not only to formulate a well-defined *fabula* but also to posit the context of the narrative's initial composition. The remainder of this chapter will outline the *fabula* of *Aseneth*, and the next chapter will contextualize *Aseneth* in Hellenistic Egypt.

Unlike the Acts of Peter tradition, the witnesses of *Aseneth* uniformly present the chronological and causal events of the *fabula*; no witness

---

31. Burchard, "Joseph and Aseneth," 180.

employs the technique of in medias res or embeds smaller narrative units of *Aseneth* within a different story (as the Marcellus text and Nereus and Achilleus do with the Acts of Peter). At the linguistic level, the commonality among the witnesses is striking, but in comparison to a reconstructed text, a *fabula* can be more transparent about the limits of what the manuscript categories share. For the remainder of this chapter and the next, the term "manuscript categories" refers to the individual groupings of the witnesses that Burchard classified; so, the term is used for the following groups: Syr, Arm, L2, E, *f*, Mc, *a*, and *d*.

I will provide two examples how a *fabula* can reveal the multiplicity of the evidence while also demonstrating a basic storyline. The first example is with Bu/F 5:3, when Pentephres's household (except for Aseneth) greet Joseph. Burchard's text provides the following:

καὶ ἐξῆλθον εἰς συνάντησιν τοῦ Ἰωσὴφ Πεντεφρῆς καὶ ἡ γυνὴ αὐτοῦ καὶ πᾶσα ἡ συγγένεια αὐτοῦ
And Pentephres, his wife, and all of his kindred came out to greet Joseph.

The attestations of this line in the individual witnesses are as follows:[32]

Syr: *et omnes qui in domo eius*
Arm: "und alle Diener ihre"
L2: *et omnis famulatio eorum*
E: καὶ πᾶσα ἡ θεραπεία αὐτοῦ
F (*f*): καὶ πᾶσα ἡ συγγένεια αὐτῆς
W (*f*): καὶ πᾶσα ἡ συγγένεια αὐτῶν
L1 (*f*): *et omnis cognatio eius*
c (Mc): καὶ πᾶσα ἡ θεραπεία αὐτῶν
ACP (*a*): καὶ πᾶσα ἡ συγγένεια αὐτῶν καὶ ἡ θεραπεία
Q (*a*): καὶ πᾶσα ἡ συγγένεια αὐτοῦ
BSlav (*d*): καὶ πᾶσα ἡ συγγένεια αὐτοῦ
D (*d*): καὶ πᾶσα ἡ συγγένεια αὐτῶν

---

32. Burchard, *Joseph und Aseneth*, 100; Fink, *Joseph und Aseneth*, 268; Batiffol, *Le Livre de la Prière d'Aseneth*, 93; Philonenko, *Joseph et Aséneth*, 146. I am assuming that the Slavonic witnesses agree with MS B given what Burchard and Philonenko provide in their annotations.

Despite what Burchard provides, the witnesses disagree. The reading, "all kindred" (καὶ πᾶσα ἡ συγγένεια) is provided by *f* and *d*; a different reading of "all servants" is in Arm, L2, MSS E and *c* (πᾶσα ἡ θεραπεία or its equivalent); and the Syriac offers "all in the household" (*omnes qui in domo eius*). Burchard argues that the phrase, "and all of his kindred" (καὶ πᾶσα ἡ συγγένεια αὐτοῦ), is the best choice because servants are not mentioned later on in the story (as in 5:7; 7:2, 8; and 10:1).[33] In her reconstruction, Fink presents a combination of "kindred and servants" (καὶ πᾶσα ἡ συγγένεια αὐτοῦ καὶ ἡ θεραπεία αὐτοῦ), which she adapts from family *a*.[34] Here is a case where the two-majuscule theory does not help, though. For Fink's stemma to work, her reading must have existed at the majuscule stage, with the Syriac either demonstrating a free translation of its Greek *Vorlage* or reflecting a different Greek attestation, and then the remainder of the witnesses (all but for the majority of *a*) fell into two different groups. Some scribes deleted "kindred" (in *M1* or independently in Arm and L2; and then independently in MSS E and *c* [assuming that *M2* attested to it]); other scribes deleted "servants" (families *f* and *d*, independently from each other); and at least one scribe of *a* kept the two ("kindred and servants"). This kind of theorizing is unsatisfactory because it depends on too many unverifiable parts. Like the case with the suitors' actions in Bu/F 1:6 (when they either courted Aseneth or praised her through song), it is equally likely that two different ways of describing Bu/F 5:3 existed in the transmission of this story. For the *fabula*, we do not have to propose how the transmission occurred; we can simply summarize that Pentephres's household and/or relatives greeted Joseph.

The second example comes from Bu/F 4:7, when Pentephres begins to recount Joseph's exemplary qualities. Burchard and Fink provide the following in their texts:

καὶ αὐτός ἐστιν ἄρχων πάσης τῆς γῆς Αἰγύπτου καὶ ὁ βασιλεὺς Φαραὼ κατέστησεν αὐτὸν βασιλέα [Fink: ἄρχοντα] πάσης τῆς γῆς.
He is ruler of the entire land of Egypt and the king, Pharaoh, appointed him as king [Fink: ruler] of the entire land.

---

33. Burchard, *Joseph und Aseneth*, 100.
34. Fink, *Joseph und Aseneth*, 107–8. Fink also maintains that this reading in *a* is a contamination from Mc (*Joseph und Aseneth*, 50), which could explain how the *c* attestation of ἡ θεραπεία made it into *a*.

Here, we have two clauses that describe Joseph's authority in Egypt; the first clause describes Joseph as a ruler (ἄρχων), but the second claims he is either a king (βασιλεύς) or repeats the title of ruler (ἄρχων). The first clause appears to be represented well among the manuscript categories. Burchard does not provide all the attestations for this verse, but looking at the annotated texts and published witnesses, it appears that the following witnesses possibly copied or translated ἄρχων: Syr (*dominator*), Arm, L2 (*princeps*), E, *c*, *a*, and *d*.[35] Interestingly, family *f*—which typically matches Syr, Arm, and L2— does not mention ἄρχων in this clause. Manuscript F has ἔχων πάσης τῆς γῆς, MS W provides ἔχων ἐξουσίαν, and L1 indicates that Joseph was appointed "over" the land (*super universam terram*).[36] The weight of the evidence strongly suggests, though, that in the *fabula* of *Aseneth* Joseph was appointed as a ruler of sorts.

This consistency in the evidence cannot be said about the second clause. Burchard's choice of βασιλέα appears in *c* and as *regem* in MSS 436 (L2) and L1 (*f*); Fink's choice of ἄρχοντα appears in MSS FW (*f*), *d*, and seemingly group "a" of the Armenian (according to Burchard, [Arm^a] translates as "zum Herrn über," and Fink states that "Herrn" stands for ἄρχοντα); and family *a* and MS 671 (one of the modern Greek witnesses [Ngr] of family *f*) attest to both terms (ἄρχοντα καὶ βασιλέα, and ἄρχοντα καὶ βασιλεύς, respectively).[37] The remaining witnesses display more variations. The Syriac simply provides "over" the land (*super*); supposedly most Armenian witnesses have something similar to the Syriac ("zum über"); MSS 435& (L2) just mention that Pharaoh appointed Joseph (*a Pharaone constitutus* [Joseph]); and MS E instead provides, "(Pharaoh appointed Joseph) εἰς σωτηρίαν."[38] Fink proposes a compelling argument that the inclusion of the term "king" (βασιλέα) demonstrates redaction in the transmission of some of the witnesses (whereby an ancestor of *c* was used to alter an ancestor of *a*, and then a later copy of *a* influenced an alteration in the

---

35. Batiffol, *Le Livre de la Prière d'Asenerth*, 44; Brooks, *Historia ecclesiastica Zachariae Rhetori*, 17; Burchard, *Joseph und Aseneth*, 93; Fink, *Joseph und Aseneth*, 173 and 266; Philonenko, *Joseph et Aséneth*, 142; and Wright, "After Antiquity," 2:26 and 246. Because at this part of 4:7, Burchard only provides variant readings and both Arm and *c* attest to this verse in general, I am assuming that Arm and *c* had ἄρχων in their respective exemplars.

36. Burchard, *Joseph und Aseneth*, 93; Batiffol, *Le Livre de la Prière d'Aseneth*, 92. The attestation for L1 is taken from Batiffol since Burchard does not provide it.

37. Fink, *Joseph und Aseneth*, 66–67.

38. Burchard, *Joseph und Aseneth*, 93–94; Fink, *Joseph und Aseneth*, 66–67, 266.

Greek *Vorlage* of Ngr).³⁹ She maintains that ἄρχοντα (in the second clause) is authentic because Joseph refers to himself this way in Bu/F 20:9 (that Pharaoh had appointed him as ἄρχοντα), and the term aligns better with the LXX Genesis narrative than βασιλέα does since only Pharaoh is a "king" in the LXX story.⁴⁰ But Fink neither explains how MSS 436 (L2) and L1 (*f*) have *rex* instead of, for example, *princeps*, nor does she address how the Syriac, most of the Armenian, and MSS 435& of L2 mention no title in the second clause and instead refer to Joseph's authority as "appointed" and/or "over" the land. I will add that all the manuscript categories mention Pharaoh in this line and appear to use some form of καθίστημι or its equivalent in expressing Pharaoh's appointment of Joseph.⁴¹ Combining this evidence all together, then, the variations in this second clause only yield the general summary that Pharaoh granted Joseph authority over the land. So, the *fabula* of *Aseneth* for this line in Bu/F 4:7 is that Pentephres refers to Joseph as a ruler over Egypt (with the term ἄρχων being well-attested across most of the manuscript categories) and as granted authority by Pharaoh. Joseph's supposed administrative title as "king" does not make the *fabula*.

Some may argue that in cases like these, the story of *Aseneth* can seem to lose its luster. In focusing on the common denominator of the evidence, appealing descriptions and scenes are not included in the *fabula* and are transferred to the *sjuzhet* of individual witnesses. Delineating between the common plot and individual performances, though, provides a more transparent presentation of the evidence and inevitably forces us to rethink how narratives like *Aseneth* and the Acts of Peter were transmitted in antiquity.

The *Fabula* of *Aseneth*

In the remainder of this chapter, I propose the *fabula* for *Aseneth*. I first provide an outline of the plot and then I propose particular Greek liter-

---

39. Fink, *Joseph und Aseneth*, 66–67.
40. Fink, *Joseph und Aseneth*, 66–67.
41. The latter point is not verified by Burchard's annotations, but he does not mention variants of κατέστησεν (which implies shared attestations). I can also verify some form of the verb in the following manuscript categories: Syr, L2, MSS FW and L1 (*f*), MS E, *c*, *a*, *d* (so all the manuscript categories but Arm) (Batiffol, *Le Livre de la Prière d'Aseneth*, 92 [L1] 44 [MS A]; Brooks, *Historia ecclesiastica Zachariae Rhetori*, 17; and Burchard, *Joseph und Aseneth*, 94; Fink, *Joseph und Aseneth*, 266; Wright, "After Antiquity," 2:26 and 246).

ary features and vocabulary that can be reasonably associated with the *fabula*. As we will see, the *fabula* plotline is quite detailed, despite the challenges posed by the textual witnesses. For this reason, I include literary features and particular vocabulary that can arguably be included in my construction of the *fabula*. I propose that the *fabula* was highly influence by Greek prose in the Septuagint, and I echo other scholars in emphasizing the influence of particular septuagintal narratives in the story. That being said, my plot outline does not delve into every passage to provide a precise articulation of the common reading, and I do not present a comprehensive list of shared vocabulary. I spend most time on passages that I will then discuss in the next chapter.

In determining the *fabula*, I consulted the textual notes and discussions of Burchard, Fink, and Philonenko. Fink also provides Bu/F 16:13–29:9 of palimpsest M and a transcription of the subgroups of L2 (MSS 436 and 435&). Burchard's critical edition (2003) offers corrections to the texts produced by Brooks (on the Syriac), Batiffol (on MS A of family *a* and on L1), and Philonenko, but I refer to the latter three when Burchard and/or Fink lack reference to particular witnesses. I have also relied upon Wright's full transcriptions of MS E, MSS FW and G, and MS *c* when Burchard's annotations provide insufficient details about these witnesses.[42] Based upon the textual analyses by Burchard and Fink, I am convinced that the following manuscript categories are of tremendous value in producing this *fabula*: Syr, Arm, L2, family *f*, E, and Mc. In general, when a strong majority of these categories attest to a scene, I provide it in the *fabula*. A "strong majority" attestation is when, of the manuscript categories that can be considered (so excluding times when evidence is missing), (1) all of the categories attest to the scene or (2) all but one category attests to the scene, and the lack of the attestation in the outlier category can reasonably be understood as an abbreviation or alteration of the narrative. For example, there are several places where MS E appears to condense the narrative (skipping, e.g., much of the description of Aseneth's quarters in ch. 2), and at these times, I do not consider MS E when the remaining categories attest to the scene.

I do not include sole renderings of either family *a* or *d*. As I discussed in chapter 1 and as Fink has argued extensively, family *a* represents the longest performances of *Aseneth*, and its embellishments and alterations

---

42. Wright, "After Antiquity," vol. 2.

go beyond the core *fabula*. My exclusion of family *a* changes what many scholars have taken to be the original text because Burchard relied upon these readings in his reconstructed text, and as I discussed in chapter 2, even Fink keeps some of these readings, mostly to maintain her stemma. As for family *d*, Burchard and Fink have demonstrated that MSS B and D present an abridged story.[43] The B manuscript in particular does not seem to have a coherent narrative, and it was likely abbreviated for its inclusion in a hagiographical collection.[44] The Slavonic witnesses of family *d* also exhibit significant reduction, but they, along with MS B, indicate that scribes desired to flesh out their respective texts. Fink provides convincing evidence that the ancestor of MS G was consulted to produce the Greek *Vorlage* of the Slavonic witnesses, and MS A (of family *a*) was consulted in the production of the ancestor to MS B.[45] Nevertheless, contrary to either Burchard's or Fink's arguments, the manuscript evidence of family *d* is not necessarily secondary (beyond the contaminated portions of MS B) but rather presents particular performances of the *Aseneth fabula*. There is no evidence to suggest whether the ancestors of the *d* witnesses represented late or early tellings of *Aseneth* in the transmission process. Nevertheless, the *d* witnesses condense the *fabula*, so in my presentation, I include elements that are not attested in *d* but are well-attested in the other manuscript categories.

One final note about my textual considerations: because fewer witnesses from the manuscript categories attest to the second plot of the narrative (chs. 23–29), my discernment of the *fabula* in these chapters slightly differs from that of the former ones. In L2, only MS 436 extends beyond 21:9; from 25:4 to 27:11, only one Armenian manuscript (MS 332 or Arm^f) continues with this narrative (the remaining Armenian witnesses substitute this section with a pastiche of the passages from this portion of the story), and no Armenian witness extends beyond 29:7; since *c* ends at 16:17, we can only depend on the detectable portions of palimpsest M (16:13–17:3; 18:6–21:4; 24:15–28:3; and 29:3–9 [and the folio preserving this last passage is mostly indecipherable]); and since witnesses in family *f* show several gaps (particularly MSS FW and L1), MS G has greater impor-

---

43. Burchard, "Zum Text von 'Joseph und Aseneth,'" 13–28; Burchard, "Zum Stand der Arbeit," 5–24; Fink, *Joseph und Aseneth*, 87–96; and Fink, "Textkritische Situation," 40.
44. As Fink surmises, "Anhang: Erläuterung zum Stemma," 50.
45. Fink, *Joseph und Aseneth*, 53–63.

tance at those places in the story. Manuscript E remains helpful, but it consistently has gaps in its narrative. So, if *a* or *a* and *d* agree with the witnesses that provide the latter half of the narrative, I consider the attestation to be *fabula*-worthy.

Below is my proposed outline of the plot for the *Aseneth fabula*. In my summary of the scenes, I try to use vocabulary reflective of the common readings, but I will discuss particular Greek words and phrases later on in this chapter.[46] For sections I depend on in my next chapter, I provide further explanation of my *fabula* scenes in the notes. When necessary, I cite the versification of Fink's text (Bu/F) in order to help the reader locate the reference that I discuss.

The *Fabula* of *Aseneth*: The Core Storyline

1. The story begins during the first year of abundance in Egypt when Joseph begins his collection of grain. The characters Pentephres and Aseneth are introduced. Pentephres is a high-ranking official of Pharaoh and priest of Heliopolis. His daughter, Aseneth, is a *parthenos* and more beautiful than other *parthenoi* in the land. Aseneth's unsurpassable beauty is likened to Hebrew matriarchs (Sara, Rebecca, and Rachel), and she becomes renowned for her appearance. Sons of notables respond, and there is strife between them on account of her. (Bu/F 1:1–6)

2. Pharaoh's son asks Pharaoh if he could marry Aseneth, and Pharaoh rejects the idea. Aseneth is inferior to him, Pharaoh tells his son; he should instead marry the daughter of the Moabite king. (Bu/F 1:7–9)

3. Aseneth despises men and is boastful and arrogant. Unseen by any man, she lives in a tower in Pentephres's housing complex. Seven *parthenoi* also live with her and serve her. The narrator provides a description of Aseneth's exquisite quarters, her fine belongings, and her religious practices. She has an opulent bedroom with Egyptian representations, before which she performs sacrificial rituals daily. This bedroom overlooks a large, private courtyard with abundant fruit

---

46. Burchard presents an outline that is similar to mine, but he does not present it in terms of a *fabula* ("Der jüdische Asenethroman," 545–50).

trees and a water source, and it also overlooks the street. She has a second room containing her jewelry, fine clothes, and accessories, and a third room stores food. Each of the seven *parthenoi* have their own respective rooms. (Bu/F 2:1–12)

4. Joseph sends servants to announce his visit to Pentephres's home, and Pentephres enthusiastically prepares for Joseph's arrival. (Bu/F 3:1–4)

5. Aseneth hears that her parents are returning from their agricultural field, and she prepares to meet them. The narrator describes Aseneth dressing in fine attire with gold and costly accessories that included the names and images of Egyptian gods on them. She also places a diadem on her head and covers it with a cloth garment (veil).[47] (Bu/F 3:5–6)

---

47. All the manuscript categories seem to indicate that Aseneth's clothing had gold in it (interwoven or furnished with gold). All the manuscript categories refer to Aseneth's accessories having the names and images of gods on them. Burchard does not provide the attestations for τῶν θεῶν τῶν Αἰγυπτίων, but I take this to mean that no variants exist for this phrase. Because Burchard provides variants for the rest of Bu/F 3:6, I assume that all manuscript categories refer to representations of some sort. All manuscript categories except Syr and *a* have τὰ πρόσωπα τῶν εἰδώλων or its equivalent, but the Syriac seems to condense this scene, mentioning that the names and images were both inscribed and carved on her accessories [*et nomina atque imagines deorum multorum Aegyptiorum in eis undique inscripta et sculpta erant*]); and I can detect the reference to Egyptian gods in the following witnesses: Syr, L2, MSS FW and L1 (*f*), MS E, Mc, *a*, and *d* (Batiffol, *Le Livre de la Prière d'Aseneth*, 43 [MS A] and 92 [L1]; Brooks, *Historia ecclesiastica Zachariae Rhetori*, 17; Fink, *Joseph und Aseneth*, 264; Batiffol, *Le Livre de la Prière d'Aseneth*, 43 [MS A] and 92 [L1]; and Wright, "After Antiquity," 2:22 and 245) (Burchard, *Joseph und Aseneth*, 88–89). Burchard does not provide comprehensive notes on his phrase, "and she covered her head with a *theristron* [θέριστρον]," but he provides the variants for θέριστρον as well as witnesses that lack the term. Combining Burchard's notations with Philonenko's, as well as with the more accessible manuscripts, it appears that the term θέριστρον is well-attested among the manuscript categories. The word or its equivalent appears in Syr (*theristro*), MS 436 (L2, *amictu*), *f* (W [θέριστρον] and L1 [*theristro*]), E (θερίστρῳ), *a*, and *d* (both citing θερίστρῳ). Burchard notes that family Mc attests to θεθρίστρῳ, but Philonenko notes that MS H of *c* attests to θερίστρῳ and Wright lists *c* with θερίστρῳ. Since Burchard does not mention that the Armenian lacks a translation of θέριστρον, I am assuming that the Armenian attests to its equivalent (Batiffol, *Le Livre de la Prière d'Aseneth*, 43 [MS A] and 92 [L1]; Brooks, *Historica ecclesiastica Zachariae Rhetori*, 17; Burchard, *Joseph und Aseneth*, 89; Fink, *Joseph und Aseneth*, 265; Philonenko, *Joseph et Aséneth*, 140; and Wright, "After Antiquity," 2:246). On "diadem," see discussion further below.

6. The parents bring Aseneth produce from their field, and they and Aseneth greet one another. (Bu/F 4:1–2)

7. Pentephres declares to Aseneth Joseph's noble qualities and informs her that he will be handing her in marriage to Joseph. Pentephres states that Pharaoh appointed Joseph to collect and distribute the grain and that Joseph's god is with him. (Bu/F 4:3–8)

8. Aseneth vehemently refuses to marry Joseph and expounds upon his inferior qualities. She rehearses how Joseph is of another people (not hers) and that he was a slave who was caught sleeping with Potiphar's wife, imprisoned, and then released after interpreting Pharaoh's dreams.[48] Pentephres is ashamed at Aseneth's reaction. When it is announced that Joseph has arrived, Aseneth flees to her private quarters to watch Joseph's entrance into the courtyard; Pentephres and his household/relatives go out to meet Joseph. (Bu/F 4:9–5:3)

9. The narrator describes Joseph's royal appearance when he enters Pentephres's courtyard. He rides in Pharaoh's second chariot made of gold; wears elaborate, purple garb and has a gold crown on his head with the image of rays upon it; and he carries a royal staff in his hand.[49]

---

48. "Another people (not hers)": The manuscript categories mostly use ἀλλογενής for Aseneth's description of Joseph as a foreigner (Arm, L2, MSS FW [*f*], MS E, MS J [*c*], *a*, *d*), or provide both ἀλλόφυλος and ἀλλογενής (L1 [*f*], MSS HK [*c*], and MSS PQ [*a*]). Burchard chose ἀλλόφυλος for his text, and Fink has ἀλλογενής (Burchard, *Joseph und Aseneth*, 96; and Fink, *Joseph und Aseneth*, 173). The Syriac could have translated either Greek word (*non filio populi mei*, according to Burchard, or *nec populari meo*, according to Brooks; Burchard, *Joseph und Aseneth*, 96; Brooks, *Historia Ecclesiastica Zachariae Rhetori*, 17). See further in this chapter regarding references to Potiphar's wife, Joseph's imprisonment, and his dream interpretations.

49. Joseph's chariot: Burchard's annotations imply that the reference to Pharaoh's second chariot is strong among the manuscript categories; he only mentions that family *c* lacks τοῦ Φαραώ, which suggests that the rest of the categories that attest to this scene have "of Pharaoh" (which would include, then, Arm and MS E). The phrase, "Pharaoh's second chariot" or the like, is attested in Syr, L2 (435&; MS 436 just has *curru Pharaonis*), MS E, L1 (*f*), Mc, *a*, and *d* (Batiffol, *Le Livre de la Prière d'Aseneth*, 93 [L1] and 45 [MS A]; Brooks, *Historia ecclesiastica Zachariae Rhetori*, 18; Fink, *Joseph und Aseneth*, 268; Philonenko, *Joseph et Aséneth*, 146; and Wright, "After Antiquity," 2:33 and 248). All the manuscript categories provide that the chariot was made of gold. Joseph's dress and appearance: All the manuscript categories depict Joseph as impressive in dress and

The gates are closed, and Pentephres and his household/relatives greet Joseph. (Bu/F 5:4–7)

10. Looking out her window, Aseneth falls in love with Joseph at first sight and prays to the god of Joseph to ensure that she marries him. She confesses her ignorant words about Joseph, she identifies him as *helios* on a chariot from whom nothing can be hidden, and she asks Joseph's god for mercy.[50] (Bu/F 6:1–8)

11. Joseph prepares to dine with them, but he notices Aseneth and fears that she will annoy him like all the other women in Egypt (who were all taken by his beauty). Joseph repeatedly rejected their advances because he would not sin against his god, and Jacob told him to guard himself from associating with strange women. Joseph orders that Aseneth be removed from the premises. (Bu/F 7:1–6)

12. Pentephres tells Joseph that his daughter is not a strange woman and that she hates men. Joseph is convinced and invites her to meet him. (Bu/F 7:7–8)

---

appearance, but they are not always uniform. The description of Joseph wearing purple, however, seems well-attested. For the term "purple" in the phrase ἡ στολὴ τῆς περιβολῆς αὐτοῦ ἦν πορφυρᾶ ("the robe around him was purple"), Burchard only mentions Greek variants in Mc, *a*, and *d* (πορφυρά, πορφυρή, and πορφύρα), says that MS E paraphrases here, and two manuscripts show a gap here (MSS G from *f* and Q from *a*). Wright's text confirms that MS E provides "purple," however (καὶ περϊεζωσμένος πορφύραν καὶ βύσσον). The attestation for "purple" can also be confirmed in Syriac, L2, L1 (*f*), *a*, and *d* (Batiffol, *Le Livre de la Prière d'Aseneth*, 45 [MS A] and 93 [L1]; Brooks, *Historia ecclesiastica Zachariae Rhetori*, 18; Fink, *Joseph und Aseneth*, 268; Philonenko, *Joseph et Aséneth*, 146; and Wright, "After Antiquity," 2:248). "Crown" (στέφανος): The word appears in all manuscript categories. The particular word for "rays" (ἀκτίς or equivalent) will be discussed further below. "Royal staff": The manuscript categories differ in terms of a staff, rod, or scepter, but the modifier "royal/regal" remains constant. For the phrase ῥάβδος βασιλική in Burchard's text, Burchard only provides variants, all of which keep the royal aspect of what Joseph carries: FW (*f*) have ῥάβδος βασιλέως; *d* has σκῆπτρον βασιλικόν; and Syr has *sceptrum regni aureum*. I take this to mean that "royal staff/scepter" is well-attested among the manuscript categories, and it can also be confirmed in L2 (*virga regalis*), L1 (in family *f* providing *virga regia*), MS E, and Mc (Batiffol, *Le Livre de la Prière d'Aseneth*, 93; Fink, *Joseph und Aseneth*, 268; and Wright, "After Antiquity," 2:34 and 248) (Burchard, *Joseph und Aseneth*, 101).

50. The reference to *helios* on a chariot is discussed further below.

13. Aseneth approaches to greet Joseph, but when she reaches out to kiss him, he physically blocks her from coming closer. He then gives a lengthy reason as to why he cannot touch her: it is not fitting for those who revere God, praising God and partaking in life-giving bread, drink, and oil, to kiss those who praise dead idols and partake in idolatrous bread, drink and oil.[51] Because Aseneth engages in the latter, Joseph will not kiss her. (Bu/F 8:1–7)

14. Aseneth is upset, and Joseph responds by offering a prayer on her behalf. He prays to his god, the Most High, Mighty One, and creator of everything, to bless Aseneth, restore her to life, and to accept her as an adherent. (Bu/F 8:8–9)

---

51. "It is not fitting": This phrase always introduces a guideline that is affiliated with being allegiant to Joseph's god. In Bu/F 8:5–7, this phrase is well-represented among the manuscript categories. Burchard provides variants in *d* only, which implies that the manuscript categories are in agreement here (*Joseph und Aseneth*, 116). I can confirm that the phrase, "it is not fitting" (or its equivalent), appears in the following witnesses: Syr, L2, *f* (MSS FW and L1), MS E, Mc, *a*, and *d* (Batiffol, *Le Livre de la Prière d'Aseneth*, 96; Brooks, *Historia ecclesiastica Zachariae Rhetori*, 20; Fink, *Joseph und Aseneth*, 274; and Wright, "After Antiquity," 2:50 and 249). There are several dicta that begin with this phrase, as I will discuss below (Bu/F 8:5–7; 21:1; 23:9, 12; 28:10, 14; and 29:3). "Those who revere God" (θεοσεβής): Burchard does not provide information about variants in 8:5 (which implies that the manuscript categories agree), but he does show that in 8:6 (ἀλλ' ἀνηρ θεοσεβής φιλήσει), all the manuscript categories provide θεοσεβής or its equivalent (except for L2, but see below) (Burchard, *Joseph und Aseneth*, 116–17). I can verify that the term θεοσεβής or its equivalent is used in 8:5–7 in the following witnesses: Syr (participle of *timeo*), MSS FW and G (*f*); L1 (*f* providing the participle of *colo*), MS E, Mc, *a*, and *d* (Batiffol, *Le Livre de la Prière d'Aseneth*, 96 [L1] and 49 [MS A]; Brooks, *Historia ecclesiastica Zachariae Rhetori*, 21; Philonenko, *Joseph et Aséneth*, 154–56; Wright, "After Antiquity," 2:50 and 250). The witnesses from L2 consistently show *fidelis* here and elsewhere in the story where θεοσεβής and its equivalent can be confirmed (Fink, *Joseph und Aseneth*, 274), so I am assuming that its Greek *Vorlage* had θεοσεβής. I have chosen to translate the word as "one who reveres God" in hopes of capturing what θεοσεβής connotes. The concept, "to fear God," can be misleading in terms of what fear today often denotes, and "to worship God" attracts Christian overtones that also do not apply to this term. The term, θεοσεβής, corresponds better with the word "revere," which indicates both feelings and actions that are associated with giving honor to someone/something else ("to feel deep respect or admiration" for someone/something [New Oxford American Dictionary] or "to show devoted deferential honor to" someone/something [Merriam-Webster Dictionary]).

15. Aseneth rejoices at Joseph's gesture, and she returns to her quarters. She immediately begins a seven-day ritual of repentance, and she renounces her religious practices and allegiances. (Bu/F 9:1–2)

16. Meanwhile, Joseph dines with the rest of Aseneth's family, and afterward he and the family depart from the housing complex. (Bu/F 9:3–10:1)

17. Aseneth proceeds to go through her extensive process of mourning and repentance that will last seven days. She locks herself in her room, changes into mourning garb, sits in sackcloth and ashes, fasts, and cries. One of the *parthenoi* overhears Aseneth in distress and checks on her, but Aseneth sends her away. Through the street-facing window, Aseneth throws away her wealthy clothing and attire, all remnants of her gods, and all her sacrificial food and utensils. (Bu/F 10:1–16)

18. After her seven days of silence, Aseneth prays to the god of Joseph for forgiveness and protection. She describes her abandoned and vulnerable state as she had just destroyed her religious objects and renounced her allegiance to Egyptian gods. She appeals to God's mercy and confesses her sins. She recounts God's power, prays for protection, and asks to be with Joseph. (Bu/F 11:1–13:15)

19. When she finishes praying, the morning star rises, and seemingly from this star an angelic messenger appears in Aseneth's locked room. The narrator describes the appearance of the angel: he looks like Joseph but his face is like lightning, his eyes like the sun's rays/light, his hair like a flame of fire, and his extremities like glowing metal.[52] (Bu/F 14:1–10)

20. The angel and Aseneth have a few interchanges that appear in the following order:
    a. The angel's announcement to Aseneth and her initial response;
    b. His command to Aseneth that she change her clothing and wash her face and hands (which Aseneth proceeds to do);

---

52. See more below on the comparisons with the book of Daniel.

c. His confirmation that God heard her prayer, and the promise that her name will be written in a book of the living/life, she will be renewed and be able to partake in life-giving food, and she will marry Joseph;[53]
d. His announcement of Aseneth's name change, "City of Refuge"[54] because people will seek refuge in her;
e. The angel introduces the role of Metanoia, who has a close relationship with God;
f. The angel announces that he will also appear to Joseph and inform him of all that has happened, and the angel tells her to prepare for Joseph's arrival;
g. Aseneth requests that the angel remain for a meal. He agrees and asks for a honeycomb, which miraculously appears in Aseneth's storehouse. Aseneth brings the comb to the angel and identifies it with him. He then blesses Aseneth and declares that secret/inexplicable matters of God have been revealed to her.[55] Aseneth then eats a portion of this honeycomb, and the angel associates it with partaking in a life-giving meal and oil;
h. The angel causes bees to emerge from the comb. These bees appear dressed in wealthy garb with purple and they are adorned with

---

53. "Book of the living/life": Discussed further below when comparing *Aseneth* to the book of Daniel.

54. "City of Refuge": The attestations for καταφυγή (place of refuge) are discussed further below.

55. "Secret/inexplicable matters of God": Precisely what is revealed to Aseneth varies among the manuscript categories. Burchard's text reads, τὰ ἀπόρρητα μυστήρια τοῦ ὑψίστου ("the ineffable mysteries of the Most High"), but this phrase does not seem to appear in any single witness. The evidence is as follows: (1) Syriac = *secreta Altissimi*; (2) Arm = "die Geheimnisse [oder 'verborgenen (Dinge)'] Gottes des Höchsten"; (4) L2 = *inenarrabilia altissimi* (MS 436) or *mysteria altissima* (MSS 435&); (5) *f* = μυστήρια τοῦ ὑψίστου (MS F) or τὰ κρυπτὰ τοῦ ὑψίστου (MS G); (6) MS E = τὰ ἄρρητα τοῦ δεσπότου; (7) *c* = τὰ ἀπόρρητα τοῦ ὑψίστου; (9) *a* = τὰ ἀπόρρητα τοῦ θεοῦ μυστήρια; and (10) *d* = τὰ ἀπόρρητα τοῦ θεοῦ. Fink's text differs from that of Burchard, providing, τὰ ἄρρητα μυστήρια τοῦ ὑψίστου ("the unspeakable mysteries of the Most High"). Arguments could be made that the versions translated ἄρρητα (which Fink argues for the Syriac and MS 436 [L2]) or ἀπόρρητα (which Burchard seems to have concluded). For the *fabula*, I have chosen to emphasize concepts that these attestations share (secret and inexplicable) and that the source of this revelation is God (Burchard, *Joseph und Aseneth*, 210; Fink, *Joseph und Aseneth*, 121–22, 301).

diadems.⁵⁶ They encircle Aseneth from her head to her feet and make a comb like the former one upon her lips. The angel commands them to go to their place, which for some appears to be heaven. The other bees wish to harm Aseneth, but they die, and the angel summons them to rise and go to their place, and they reside in the trees in the courtyard.⁵⁷ After this, the angel confirms that Aseneth witnessed this event, and upon her confirmation, he sets the comb ablaze and its fragrance fills the room;

i. Aseneth asks him to bless the *parthenoi*, which he does; and
j. The angel commands Aseneth to put the meal table away, and when she turns to do so, he departs from her presence. Aseneth sees the angel riding something like a chariot with horses into the sky. In response to her encounter, Aseneth prays to God. (Bu/F 14:11–17:10)

21. Joseph's arrival is announced and Aseneth prepares to meet him. She changes into wealthy attire; she puts on jewelry (without inscriptions/engravings of Egyptian gods), a crown, and a cloth over her head (veil); and she takes a scepter in her hand.⁵⁸ The narrator also describes Aseneth's stunning appearance. (Bu/F 18:1–11)

---

56. See ch. 2 where I provide all attestations of this line from the witnesses. All the manuscript groups (including palimpsest M from Mc) provide some portion of this scene, except for MS E (which abbreviates 16:16 καὶ κέχρισαι–17:4 θάλαμον and does not mention the appearance of the bees; [Burchard, *Joseph und Aseneth*, 213]). All those that provide the scene provide "purple," and only family *a* definitively lacks "diadem."

57. "They encircle Aseneth ... to go to their place": Verses 19–22 in Bu/F 16 are well-represented across the manuscript categories but nonetheless exhibit scribal editing. Several witnesses abbreviate this scene or entirely skip it (MS 436 [L2], MS G [*f*], MS E, and *d*). Since family *c* ends at Bu/F 16:17, we can only rely on palimpsest M, which fortunately offers helpful attestations for these verses. The content from these verses that are included in the *fabula* derive from what is shared by Syr, Arm, 435& (L2), MS F (*f*), palimpsest M (Mc), and *a* (Burchard, *Joseph und Aseneth*, 220–21; Fink, *Joseph und Aseneth*, 39, 303–4; and Wright, "After Antiquity," 2:141–143).

58. "She changes into wealthy attire ... scepter in her hand": Manuscript E lacks Bu/F 18:5 (beginning at ὡς ἀστραπήν) to 18:9 (ἔκυψεν Ἀσενέθ), but all other manuscript categories refer to Aseneth's attire. None of these categories mention names or images of Egyptian gods on the accessories; all of them except for Mc (but the decipherable folio begins further down the line of Bu/F 18:6) mention a crown (στεφάνος or its equivalent); all (including palimpsest M) mention the head covering (θέριστρον);

22. When Joseph arrives at the housing complex, he and Aseneth intimately greet each other. She leads him into the house for a meal and washes his feet. (Bu/F 19:1–20:5)

23. Aseneth's parents and kindred arrive, and they are amazed at the sight of Joseph and Aseneth together, and they celebrate the forthcoming marriage. Pentephres and Joseph prepare for the wedding, and Joseph tells Pentephres that he (Joseph) will go to Pharaoh, who appointed him and is a father to him, and Joseph will tell him about Aseneth and ask Pharaoh to give her to him as a wife. (Bu/F 20:6–10)

24. Joseph stays with Pentephres that day and does not lie with Aseneth because Joseph said that it was not fitting for a God-revering man to lie with his wife before marriage. (Bu/F 21:1)[59]

25. Joseph goes to Pharaoh and tells Pharaoh to give Aseneth to him as a wife, and Pharaoh approves and declares that the union is fitting. When Aseneth is before Pharaoh, he is amazed at her beauty, and he administers the marriage of Joseph and Aseneth. He places gold crowns on their heads, blesses their union, and wishes the God Most High to bless them. Pharaoh gives a wedding feast for seven days and mandates that all celebrate it. (Bu/F 21:2–8)

---

and all but *a* and *d* mention the scepter (σκῆπτρον or equivalent) (Burchard, *Joseph und Aseneth*, 234–45; Fink, *Joseph und Aseneth*, 40).

59. "It was not fitting for a God-revering man to lie with his wife before marriage": Syr, L2, *f* (MSS FW, G, and L1), M (of Mc), *a*, and *d* (Burchard, *Joseph und Aseneth*, 256; and Fink, *Joseph und Aseneth*, 41). The Armenian shows some form of "it is not fitting" and "not to lie with one's wife before marriage," and I am presuming that it also has some form of "God-revering man" for the following reasons: For "God-revering man" (ἀνδρὶ θεοσεβεῖ), Burchard provides only the variants *viro fideli* in L2 and *homini deum colenti* in L1 (*f*) along with mentioning that MS E lacks this line (*Joseph und Aseneth*, 256). I infer from Burchard's annotations for this line that the phrase, "God-revering man," is well-attested across the manuscript families with the exception of MS E; as mentioned earlier, L2 consistently appears to translate θεοσεβής as *fidelis*, and *colenti* from L1 still fits my *fabula*. I can verify that the following witnesses provide some form of "God-revering man" in this line: Syr (which typically translates θεοσεβής as *deus timens*); MSS FW and G (*f*), M (Mc), *a*, and *d* (Batiffol, *Le Livre de la Prière d'Aseneth*, 71 [MS A]; Brooks, *Historia ecclesiastica Zachariae Rhetori*, 31; Fink, *Joseph und Aseneth*, 41; Wright, "After Antiquity," 2:168).

26. After this, Joseph and Aseneth lie together, and ultimately she gives birth to Manasseh and Ephraim. (Bu/F 21:9)

27. Aseneth confesses and offers praise to God. (Bu/F 21:10–21)

28. The seven years of abundance end, and in the second year of the famine, Joseph's father (Jacob/Israel) and family come and settle in Goshen. (Bu/F 22:1–2)

29. Aseneth tells Joseph that she wants to see his father, and they go to Goshen to meet Jacob/Israel. Joseph's brothers meet them and prostrate themselves before them. Aseneth is amazed at the sight of Jacob/Israel and prostrates herself before him.[60] Jacob calls her to him, blesses her and kisses her. Aseneth greets him with like affection. They share a meal, and then Aseneth and Joseph leave. (Bu/F 22:3–10)

30. The sons of Leah, Joseph's brothers, accompany them but not the sons of the slaves, Bilhah and Zilpah. Levi is at Aseneth's right and Joseph is at her left. Aseneth loves Levi, and he and she discuss secret matters of God the Most High. (Bu/F 22:11–13)

31. Pharaoh's son sees Joseph and Aseneth together, and he is greatly vexed because of her beauty. (Bu/F 23:1)

32. Pharaoh's son sends for Simeon and Levi. He recounts the destruction of Shechem that was conducted by the two, mentioning the many fighters whom they had cut down with their swords, and he promises them gold and silver and other assets if they help him. He has been insulted by Joseph's taking Aseneth as a wife, and he asks them to help him make war against Joseph and kill Joseph, and then Aseneth will become his wife. Do this, Pharaoh's son tells them, and they will be his brothers and friends. But if they hesitate to do this or reject it, Pharaoh's son will use his sword against them and he unsheathes his sword before them. (Bu/F 23:2–6)

---

60. "Joseph's brothers meet them and prostrate themselves": On the verb "prostrate" and its relation to the Joseph novella, see more below.

33. Levi and Simeon are stunned, and Simeon desires to strike Pharaoh's son because of what he had said. Levi figures out what Simeon has in mind and treads on Simeon's foot, signaling for him to stop his anger. He asks Simeon why he is angry and tells him that as God-revering people, it is not fitting for them to repay evil with evil.[61] (Bu/F 23:7–9)

34. Levi asks Pharaoh's son why he said such things and tells him that they are God-revering men and that their father and brother Joseph are close to God. How could they do this malicious matter? They will not do this act before God, their father, and their brother, Joseph. It is not fitting for God-revering men to do (unjustifiable) harm to another person.[62] If Pharaoh's son does this malicious matter, their swords will be against him. Levi and Simeon show their swords to Pharaoh's son, and Levi tells him that these are the swords they used against the

---

61. "It is not fitting for them to repay evil with evil": All manuscript categories except for Mc have some version of this guideline in Bu/F 23:9 (c ends at Bu/F 16:17, and we lack this portion of the narrative in palimpsest M). Of the witnesses that attest to this line, all but MS E provide some form of the phrase, "it is not fitting to repay evil for evil" (προσήκει ἀποδοῦναι κακὸν ἀντὶ κακοῦ), but MS E simply states μὴ ἀποδίδοντες κακὸν ἀντὶ κακοῦ. Given the dominant reading of "it is not fitting" in the other categories and given that MS E tends to paraphrase, I am including the phrase in the *fabula* (Burchard, *Joseph und Aseneth*, 285; and Fink, *Joseph und Aseneth*, 320). The phrase, "God-revering men" (ἄνδρες θεοσεβεῖς) or its equivalent appears in all the manuscript categories except for Mc and L2, but as I have indicated above, L2 consistently uses *fidelis* to translate θεοσεβής, as it does here in in this scene (*Aseneth* 23:10) (Fink, *Joseph und Aseneth*, 320; Burchard, *Joseph und Aseneth*, 285–86).

62. "It is not fitting for God-revering men to do (unjustifiable) harm to another person": I tentatively include this dictum in the *fabula* because it exists in some form in the following witnesses: Syr, Arm, MS 436 (L2), MSS FW (f), and a. Since MSS 435& (L2) ended at 21:9; MS E lacks 23:11 (from καὶ ἁμαρτήσομεν)–23:12; and the evidence for Mc is lost for this scene, we have fewer witnesses from the categories to incorporate. I am siding, however, with including the dictum in the *fabula* because the representation is strong across the manuscript families that attest to this scene (Brooks, *Historia ecclesiastica Zachariae Rhetori*, 34; Burchard, *Joseph und Aseneth*, 286–87; Fink, *Joseph und Aseneth*, 321; and Wright, "After Antiquity," 2:191). By "(unjustifiable) harm," I am implying that in the narrative, Levi's comment is understood to be that God-revering men do not act unjustly against another (ἀδικέω in the Greek), which is distinct from acting in self-defense (which Levi's and Simeon's unsheathed swords at the end of Levi's speech is meant to indicate).

Shechemites to avenge for the *hybris* committed against their sister, Dinah (which was defilement).[63] (Bu/F 23:10–14)

35. In response, Pharaoh's son is afraid and falls on the ground. Levi tells him to stand up and not fear but also not to consider this malicious matter against their brother. Simeon and Levi then leave. (Bu/F 23:15–17)

36. Pharaoh's son is afraid and in grief, and he is fixated on Aseneth's beauty. His servants tell him that the sons of Bilhah and Zilpah, the slaves of Leah and Rachel and wives of Jacob, are at enmity with Joseph and Aseneth, and they will do according to his will. (Bu/F 24:1–2)

37. Pharaoh's son summons the sons of Bilhah and Zilpah, and they come to him at night. Pharaoh's son tells them that they are powerful men, and Dan and Gad respond that they (all four of them) will listen and do his command. Pharaoh's son tells his slaves to stand back, because his word to the sons of Bilhah and Zilpah is secret, and the slaves stand back. Pharaoh's son tells them that they are powerful men who fight their enemies bravely. Then he tells them: he had heard Joseph say to his father (Pharaoh) that the sons of Bilhah and Zilpah are children of slaves, and after Joseph's father dies, Joseph would wipe them out because children of slaves should not inherit with him. According to Pharaoh's son, Joseph told Pharaoh that the sons of Bilhah and Zilpah sold him to the Ishmaelites, and Joseph would pay them back for the *hybris* they had committed.[64] According to Pharaoh's son, his father responded favorably to Joseph and promised to help him. (Bu/F 24:3–10)

38. The sons of Bilhah and Zilpah are upset, and they ask for Pharaoh's son to help them. The two parties make an agreement, and the sons of Bilhah and Zilpah say that they will do according to the will of Pharaoh's son. Pharaoh's son tells them that he will kill his father, who is like a father to Joseph; they (the sons of Bilhah and Zilpah) will kill

---

63. I discuss this passage more below, including the description of *hybris* in the story.

64. On the concepts of paying someone back and of *hybris*, see below.

Joseph, and he will take Aseneth as a wife. Pharaoh's son will then reward them as brothers and heirs. (Bu/F 24: 4–14)

39. Dan and Gad indicate that they and their brothers agree to the arrangement, and they tell Pharaoh's son that they heard Joseph tell Aseneth to go to their field of inheritance. Joseph had assigned six hundred battle-able men and fifty forerunners to go with Aseneth. Pharaoh's son gives each brother five hundred men and appoints each brother as leader over their assigned force. Dan and Gad tell Pharaoh's son that they (the four with their forces) will go and lie in wait at the wadi in the thicket of reeds. They tell him to take fifty archers and go in front at a distance. Aseneth will fall into their ambush, and they will kill the men with her. Aseneth will flee on the chariot (she is riding in), fall into the hands of Pharaoh's son, and he can do as he desires. Then the sons of Bilhah and Zilpah will kill Joseph and his children. Pharaoh's son rejoices, and he sends them off with their armed forces. They come to the wadi and set up there as planned. (Bu/F 24:15–20)

40. Pharaoh's son arises at night, and comes to his father to kill him. Guards keep him from entering (where the father is located) because they tell him that the father does not feel well and is resting. Pharaoh's son then goes out with the fifty riders/archers, just as he and the sons of Bilhah and Zilpah had planned. (Bu/F 25:1–4)

41. The younger brothers, Naphtali and Asher, ask Dan and Gad why they are acting wickedly again against their father and their brother, Joseph, whom the Lord/God protects. Did they not sell Joseph, and now he is king of the land, savior, and grain provider? If they try to do this wicked act, heavenly power will come to Joseph's aid and it will consume them. The older brothers become angry and respond saying, should they die like women? (Bu/F 25:5–8)

42. Aseneth arises at dawn and tells Joseph that she is going to the field of inheritance, as he had said, and her soul is afraid to be separated from him. Joseph tells her not to fear and go; the Lord/God will guard her. He is going on his way to distribute grain and supply food. The two then depart. (Bu/F 26:1–5)

43. Aseneth comes upon the place at the wadi with the six hundred men accompanying her, and the men waiting in ambush come out and fight the men protecting Aseneth. Those who had waited in ambush strike down those with Aseneth, and Aseneth flees ahead in the chariot. (Bu/F 26:5)

44. Levi reports to the (other) brothers about the danger Aseneth is in, and each takes his sword and goes at once to Aseneth. Meanwhile, Aseneth is fleeing ahead from the ambush site and Pharaoh's son and his men meet her. Aseneth looks and is afraid, and she calls upon the name of the Lord/God. (Bu/F 26: 6–8)

45. Benjamin is beside Aseneth in the chariot. He is a youth, and he is handsome and strong. He gets out of the chariot, takes a stone in his hand from the wadi, and hurls it at Pharaoh's son and strikes him in the head. Pharaoh's son is severely injured, and he falls to the ground. Benjamin tells the charioteer to give him stones from the wadi, which the charioteer does, and Benjamin kills all the men who were with Pharaoh's son.[65] (Bu/F 27:1–5)

46. The sons of Leah—Reuben, Simeon, Levi, Judah, Issachar, and Zebulun—are pursuing those who had lain in wait for Aseneth and they kill the men who had accompanied the sons of Bilhah and Zilpah. (Bu/F 27:6)

47. The sons of Bilhah and Zilpah flee, saying that their brothers have destroyed them, that Pharaoh's son was killed by Benjamin as well as the men with Pharaoh's son. They decide to kill Aseneth and Benjamin. They approach Aseneth with their swords in hand, and Aseneth sees them. She then addresses God as the one who brought her to life from death and who told her (that) her soul would live forever, and calls on God to deliver her from the sons of Bilhah and Zilpah. (Bu/F 27: 7–10)

48. The Lord hears Aseneth's voice, and the sons of Bilhah and Zilpah are disarmed (their swords fall out of their hands and disintegrate). The

---

65. This scene with Benjamin is discussed further below.

sons of Bilhah and Zilpah see this and they are afraid. They say that the Lord wages war against them on behalf of Aseneth, and they fall and prostrate themselves before her. They address her as their lady and queen, and they say that they had committed evil acts against her and that the Lord had repaid them for their deeds. They beg her to have mercy on them and deliver them from their brothers who are avenging the *hybris* that was committed against her and whose swords are against them.[66] (Bu/F 27:11–28:4)

49. Aseneth tells them not to fear because their brothers revere God.[67] She then tells them to go into the thicket of reeds; she will intervene and put an end to their brothers' anger, and God will judge them. The brothers then hide in the thicket. (Bu/F 28:7–8)[68]

50. The sons of Leah run onto the scene, and Aseneth meets them with tears. The sons prostrate themselves before her and weep loudly. Aseneth tells them not to do evil for evil, that God protected her and that their brothers' swords were rendered useless.[69] It is enough

---

66. The appeal by the sons of Bilhah and Zilpah are discussed further below, with special emphasis on the title, "queen" (βασίλισσα), the verb "to beg" (δεόμεθα), and the term *hybris* (ὕβρις).

67. "Because their brothers revere God": All manuscript categories that attest to this scene (except for Syr) provide the reason that "their brothers revere God" (providing θεοσεβής or its equivalent): Arm, MS 436 (L2), *f* (MSS FW and G), *a*, and *d*. These manuscripts attest some form of what Fink (and Burchard) provide: (that the brothers) εἰσιν ἄνδρες θεοσεβεῖς καὶ φοβούμενοι τὸν θεόν. Since the Syriac provides the latter phrase (*quoniam ipsi sunt timentes deum*) and not the former, it seems that its version abbreviates Aseneth's description of the brothers, and it nonetheless conveys a similar point about the brothers' reverence of their god. As discussed above, L2 provides *fidelis* for what appears to have been θεοσεβής in its *Vorlage*, and we lack a folio of this scene from palimpsest M (Burchard, *Joseph und Aseneth*, 323; Fink, *Joseph und Aseneth*, 195).

68. Burchard's text additionally provides 28:5–6: καὶ οἴδαμεν ὅτι οἱ ἀδελφοὶ ἡμῶν ἄνδρες εἰσὶ θεοσεβεῖς καὶ μὴ ἀποδιδόντες κακὸν ἀντὶ κακοῦ τινι ἀνθρώπῳ. λοιπὸν γενοῦ ἴλεως τοῖς δούλοις σου δέσποινα ἐνώπιον αὐτῶν (*Joseph und Aseneth*, 322). Fink correctly discards the lines from her reconstruction because they are only preserved in *a* and *d* (*Joseph und Aseneth*, 141, 195).

69. "Not to do evil for evil": All manuscript categories except for MS E and Mc provide some form of the phrase "not to do evil for evil" (most using some form of μὴ ποιέω κακὸν ἀντὶ κακοῦ, although *d* provides "do not do evil against them" [μὴ ποιήσητε αὐτοῖς κακόν]). Manuscript E abbreviates Bu/F: 28:1–17, and palimpsest M

that God fights them. Spare your brothers, Aseneth tells Leah's sons, because they are your father's sons. (Bu/F 28:8–11)

51. Simeon responds, asking Aseneth why she says this about their enemies. He and the rest of Leah's sons will destroy their brothers with their swords because they (the sons of Bilhah and Zilpah) had planned against their father, Joseph and Aseneth—who is queen.[70] Aseneth reaches out to Simeon and kisses him, and says not to do evil for evil and leave it for God to address their action of *hybris*.[71] Levi comes to her, touches her hand, and he knows that Aseneth is protecting the men. Levi knows that the men are hiding in the thicket, but he does not tell his brothers (the other of Leah's sons); he fears that they would kill the sons of Bilhah and Zilpah. (Bu/F 28:12–17)

52. Pharaoh's son remains alive, but he is injured. Benjamin runs over to Pharaoh's son and takes the sword of Pharaoh's son with the intent to kill him. Levi runs over to Benjamin and stops him by urging that he not do that act because as God-revering men, they do not repay evil for evil.[72] (Bu/F 29:1–4)

---

lacks a folio containing this line (Burchard, *Joseph und Aseneth*, 325; Fink, *Joseph und Aseneth*, 38–44).

70. The title, "queen," will be discussed further below.

71. "Not to do evil for evil" and "God to address their action of *hybris*": Although phrased slightly differently, in Bu/F 28:14 all manuscript categories except for MS E and Mc provide some form of the phrase "not to do evil for evil" (most using some form of μὴ ποιέω κακὸν ἀντὶ κακοῦ). All but MS E and Mc also provide the attestation that God will address the insult (ὕβρις or equivalent) that the sons of Bilahah and Zilpah had committed. Manuscript E abbreviates Bu/F: 28:1–17 (providing only 28:1–4 and 7); we lack 28:4–17 from palimpsest M; and *c* ends at 16:17 (Burchard, *Joseph und Aseneth*, 328; and Wright, "After Antiquity," 2:264–65).

72. All manuscript categories that decipherably attest to this scene (*fabula* 52) provide the plotline and equivalent wording as expressed in the *fabula* here; they provide some form of the dictum "it is not fitting to repay evil for evil" (οὐ προσήκει ἀποδοῦναι κακὸν ἀντὶ κακοῦ) and refer to such people as "God-revering men" (θεοσεβεῖς or its equivalent). (MS E only provides Bu/F 29:7–9 from this chapter, and palimpsest M is unreadable at this portion of the narrative.) A few clarifications, however, are in order: (1) "they revere God" (θεοσεβής or its equivalent) is the dominant attestation, but the only manuscript from L2 that attests to *Aseneth* after 21:9 (MS 436) provides *fideles*. As discussed above, L2 consistently uses *fidelis* where the other witnesses refer to "reverance of God" (8:5–6; 23:10; and 28:7), so I am assuming that θεοσεβής is behind this

53. Levi then asks Benjamin to help him heal Pharaoh's son; if the son lives, they will have good relations with Pharaoh and his son.[73] Levi tends to Pharaoh's son, brings him to his father, and reports to Pharaoh. Pharaoh arises from his throne and prostrates himself before Levi. (Bu/F 29:5–6)

54. Pharaoh's son dies, and his father mourns and then he becomes sick and dies.[74] Pharaoh leaves his diadem to Joseph, who reigns for forty-eight years. After this, Joseph gives the diadem to a male relative of Pharaoh.[75] (Bu/F 29:7–9)

---

translation. The Syriac uses the phrase "God-fearers" (*viri sumus qui Dominum timemus*), but as I explain above, "God-fearing" fits the concept of "God-revering" in the *fabula* (Brooks, *Historia ecclesiastica Zachariae Rhetori*, 39); and (2) that "God-revering men not repay evil for evil," is consistent among the manuscript categories, but MS 436 is illegible in parts of this phrase. According to Fink, what can be deciphered is, *quia nos viri fideles* then a gap of about twenty-eight characters followed by *tribuere malum pro malo* (then another gap); I am assuming that MS 436 originally provided something like what Fink proposes (*quia nos viri fideles <sumus et non convenit viro fideli> tribuere malum pro malo*) (*Joseph und Aseneth*, 324–25) (Burchard, *Joseph und Aseneth*, 330–31; Wright, "After Antiquity," 2:235).

73. "Levi asks Benjamin to help … good relations with Pharaoh and his son": All manuscript categories that attest to the end of this scene (so not MS E and palimpsest M) provide some form of this description (Burchard, *Joseph und Aseneth*, 331–32). Manuscript 436 (the only witness of L2 that extends beyond 21:9) is illegible in several parts of 29:3–5; what can be detected, however, indicates that this witness shares the basic content in the *fabula* here. Fink offers the following with her proposed readings in angled brackets: <*Et nunc converte*> *gladium in locum suum* <*et huc*> *adiuva* <*me et sanemus eum*> *a vulnere* <*eius et*> *si v*<*ivat, nobis*> *erit amicus post ea* <*et*> *Pharao erit tamquam pater* <*noster*> (*Joseph und Aseneth*, 325).

74. Among the Armenian manuscripts that preserve the second part of the narrative, all but MS 352 end their story at the death of Pharaoh's son (Bu/F 29:7, ending at "the son of Pharaoh died"), and MS 352 ends according to the ending of Bu/F 29:7 in Burchard's and Fink's texts where the cause of death is mentioned (Burchard provides the translation, "der war verwundet [durch den] Schlag vom Herrn"). The manuscript categories that preserve the remainder of the story are as follows: Syr, L2 (MS 436 only, but it is legible in these final verses), *f*, MS E, Mc (whereby it is clear that palimpsest M has 29:3–9, albeit not fully decipherable), *a*, and *d*. I consider these witnesses to provide strong enough support to include the remainder of the narrative in the *fabula* (Burchard, *Joseph und Aseneth*, 334).

75. All the remaining manuscript categories that are decipherable in this scene (so not Mc) attest to Joseph receiving a royal headpiece and then passing it on to Pharaoh's male relative, and all but L2 refer to the headpiece as διάδημα or its equiva-

Because the storyline of the *fabula* is so well-defined, the particular framework of the story can also be delineated. The entire narrative takes place in Egypt. The first part takes place in Heliopolis at Pentephres's housing complex where Aseneth resides, and in the second part, the story attends briefly to where Jacob and his family relocated in Egypt (Γεσέμ), then focuses on the location of Pharaoh's and his son's residence, the countryside road that leads to Aseneth's and Joseph's agricultural estate, and back to the pharaonic residence. As for the plot, the *fabula* presents the events that lead to the Egyptian woman, Aseneth, marrying Joseph (cf. Gen 41:45); the subsequent event that threatens the success of this union (the ambush attempt orchestrated by Pharaoh's son); and the conclusion with the reign of Joseph over Egypt for a fixed period of time. The cast of the *fabula* consists of Aseneth, Joseph, Pentephres and Aseneth's mother, the angelic figure, Pharaoh, Pharaoh's son, Levi, Simeon, the sons of Bilhah and Zilpah (Dan, Gad, Naphtali, and Asher), Benjamin and the remainder of Leah's sons (Reuben, Judah, Issachar, and Zebulun), God the Most High, a few unnamed servants, and hosts of Egyptian soldiers.

In the previous two chapters, I demonstrated the problems inherent in creating a reconstructed text of *Aseneth*. The witnesses are diverse enough to complicate a clear trajectory of transmission of this narrative, but they also share a common storyline that can be delineated in some detail. For this reason, the uniformity among the manuscript categories runs deep enough to identify particular Greek literary features and vocabulary as part of the *fabula*. Most dominant are the references to septuagintal writings, but I will also discuss other core terms in the narrative.[76]

---

lent (Syr, *f* [MSS FW and G], MS E, *a*, and *d*). Manuscript 436 (L2) provides *regnum* instead for both references in Bu/F 29:8–9, and L1 (*f*) refers to *regnum* for the first reference and *diadema* for the second. Since MS 436 and L1 provide *diadema* in Bu/F 3:6, I am taking the wording of *regnum* to be an interpretative move on the translator's part and not reflective of a different word for διάδημα in the Greek *Vorlage* of each respective manuscript group (Batiffol, *Le Livre de la Prière d'Aseneth*, 92 [MS A] and 115 [L1]; Burchard, *Joseph und Aseneth*, 335; and Fink, *Joseph und Aseneth*, 264).

76. In 1978, Delling presented a detailed analysis of how the Septuagint influenced the composition of *Aseneth* ("Einwirkungen der Sprache der Septuaginta," 29–56). Most of his observations do not apply to my discussion because he relied on Batiffol's Greek text (pp. 29–30 n. 2), but I will note when his ideas are helpful in producing the *fabula*.

The *Fabula* of *Aseneth*: Greek Literary Features and Vocabulary

The features of the *fabula* that are related to the Septuagint can be divided into two parts: (1) lexical similarities and (2) literary and/or linguistic connections to particular narratives. When looking at the lexical similarities between the Septuagint and *Aseneth*, the range of the Septuagint's influence on the compositional style of *Aseneth* is considerable. The narrative marker (καὶ) ἐγένετο (which translates the Hebrew temporal clause indicator, ויהי) is represented in all the manuscript categories at the start of the narrative (Bu/F 1:1), and the vast majority of the manuscript categories display similar narrative markers elsewhere in the story: καὶ ἐγένετο at Bu/F 3:1; καὶ ἐγένετο and/or μετὰ ταῦτα at Bu/F 22:1; and καὶ ἐγένετο at Bu/F 23:1.[77] Translating the particle הנה in the Septuagint, ἰδού is used several times (Bu/F 5:1; 12:9, 15; 14:1, 2, 9; 18:1; 19:1; and 26:7).[78] In Hebrew

---

77. Manuscript 436 (L2) does not begin its narrative until Bu/F 1:7 (beginning at "Pharaoh's son said to his father" [*Dixit filius Pharaonis ad patrem suum*]), and MSS FW (*f*) do not begin their narratives until verse 3 (beginning with, "There was a certain man" [ἦν τις]). Nevertheless, all the manuscript categories attest to the narrative marker, "it came to pass" (ἐγένετο or its translated equivalent) in Bu/F 1:1 (Syr, Arm, MSS 435& [L2], *f* [MS G and L1], MS E, Mc, *a*, and *d*). In Bu/F 3:1, all manuscript categories except for MS E provide ἐγένετο or its equivalent. In Bu/F 22:1, καὶ ἐγένετο μετὰ ταῦτα (and its equivalent) is attested in Syr, Arm, MS G (*f*), MS E, *a*, and *d*; μετὰ ταῦτα and its equivalent is attested in MS 436 (L2; MSS 435& stop at 21:9) and MSS FW (*f*). Palimpsest M is unreadable at chs. 22 and 23 and the reliable portion of *c* ends at ch. 16. All the remaining manuscript categories appear to attest to καὶ ἐγένετο or its equivalent in Bu/F 23:1 (Burchard, *Joseph und Aseneth*, 70, 85, 270, and 277). See also Delling, "Einwirkungen der Sprache der Septuaginta," 34.

78. In Bu/F 5:1, all the manuscript categories that provide the content of ch. 5 seem to use ἰδού somewhere in the verse (Burchard, *Joseph und Aseneth*, 98). The following witnesses attest to the particle in the servant's announcement of Joseph's sudden arrival: Syr, L2, *f* (MS F and L1), MS E, *c*, MS A (*a*), and *d* (Batiffol, *Le Livre de la Prière d'Aseneth*, 93 [L1] and 45 [MS A]; Brooks, *Historia ecclesiastica Zachariae Rhetori*, 18; Fink, *Joseph und Aseneth*, 267; Philonenko, *Joseph et Aséneth*, 146; Wright, "After Antiquity," 2:30). Burchard's annotations do not provide variations in Bu/F 12:9 for ἰδοὺ γάρ, which implies it is well-represented among the manuscript categories. I can confirm that the particle is attested in Syr, L2, *f* (MSS FW [MS F omites γάρ] and L1), *c*, *a*, and *d* (Batiffol, *Le Livre de la Prière d'Aseneth*, 101 [L1] and 55 [MS A]; Brooks, *Historia ecclesiastica Zachariae Rhetori*, 24; Fink, *Joseph und Aseneth*, 287; Philonenko, *Joseph et Aséneth*, 170; and Wright, "After Antiquity," 2:93). Manuscript E provides its own paraphrase of Aseneth's prayer, lacking 12:5 (starting at ἥμαρτον) to 13:13 Χαναάν in Burchard's text (*Joseph und Aseneth*, 157). In Bu/F 12:15, all the

prose, הנה marks someone's presence or a sudden action, or it emphasizes the current situation in the text; the particle ἰδού creates a similar function in septuagintal texts and the *fabula* applies this narrative device accordingly. The Septuagint also exhibits the use of a finite verb plus cognate noun, which oftentimes translates the Hebrew use of a finite verb with the infinitive absolute (but sometimes it reflects the Hebrew use of a verb plus the internal accusative).[79] Other Greek compositions that have been

---

manuscript categories except for MS E (but see above) provide ἰδού when Aseneth concludes her petition to God (Burchard, *Joseph und Aseneth*, 165). In ch. 14, the particle ἰδού emphasizes the appearance of the morning star in seemingly all manuscript categories except the Armenian (and the Syriac, which is missing folios that contain Bu/F 13:15 [starting at τῆς χάριτος] to Bu/F 16:7 [ending at βάδιζε]). Burchard provides only variants for this attestation, implying that the witnesses not mentioned attest to ἰδού (*Aseneth* 14:1; *Joseph und Aseneth*, 175). I can confirm attestation of the particle in Bu/F 14:1 in the following witnesses: L2, *f* (MSS FW, G, and L1), MS E, *c*, *a*, and *d* (Batiffol, *Le Livre de la Prière d'Asenath*, 101; Fink, *Joseph und Aseneth*, 291; and Wright, "After Antiquity," 2:104 and 253). Similarly, the attestation of the particle again in Bu/F 14:2 also applies; the Armenian seems to provide an equivalent of the particle, so all manuscript categories but the Syriac appear to use the particle in that line (Burchard, *Joseph und Aseneth*, 176; Batiffol, *Le Livre de la Prière d'Asenath*, 101; Wright, "After Antiquity," 2:105). Burchard does not provide variants for his attestation of ἰδού in 14:9, implying that it is common among the manuscript categories (except for Syriac) (*Joseph und Aseneth*, 179); other editions confirm that the particle is used in L2, *f* (MS G and L1), MS E, *c*, *a*, and *d* (Batiffol, *Le Livre de la Prière d'Asenath*, 102 [L1] and 59 [MS A]; Fink, *Joseph und Aseneth*, 292; Philonenko, *Joseph et Asénath*, 158; and Wright, "After Antiquity," 2:107 and 253). In Bu/F 18:1, all manuscript categories attest to ἰδού at least once. In Bu/F 19:1, all manuscript categories provide ἰδού; most provide it in the servant's announcement of Joseph's arrival, but MS E provides it in the narrator's voice (καὶ ταῦτα λέγοντος ἰδοὺ παιδάριον καὶ εἶπεν πρὸς ἀσενέθ; "and while saying these things, look, a servant [came] and said to Aseneth.") (Burchard, *Joseph und Aseneth*, 229; 241; and Wright, "After Antiquity," 2:257). In Bu/F 26:7, all manuscript categories but the Armenian provide ἰδού to mark the sudden presence of Pharaoh's son (when he and his cavalrymen attack Aseneth and her entourage). There is only one Armenian manuscript (MS 332 or Arm[f]), however, that attests to chs. 25–28 in ways similar to the other witnesses (the other Armenian witnesses instead provide a pastiche of the content in Bu/F 25:3–27:11) (Burchard, *Joseph und Aseneth*, 313). See also Delling, "Einwirkungen der Sprache der Septuaginta," 34; and Robert Helbing, who discusses the influence of Hebrew syntax in septuagintal texts, including the phrases, καὶ ἐγένετο and καὶ ἰδού (*Die Kasussyntax der Verba bei den Septuaginta: Ein Beitrag zur Hebraismenfrage und zur Syntax der Κοινή* [Göttingen: Vandenhoeck & Ruprecht, 1928]).

79. For a complete listing and discussion of the ways in which the infinitive abso-

influenced by the Septuagint also display this kind of clause, such as in the book of Judith, which could reflect a narrative style that was inspired by septuagintal texts.[80] A case in point is the translation in Isa 39:2, where the finite verb (וישמח) is rendered in the Greek with the cognate accusative plus the adjective "great" (καὶ ἐχάρη … χαρὰν μεγάλην).[81] Aseneth uses this verbal construction with a cognate noun at several points in the story: ἐχάρη(σαν) χαρὰν μεγάλην [Bu/F 3:3; 4:1; 7:8; 9:1; 15:11; 24:5]; ἐφοβεῖτο/ἐφοβήθη φόβον μέγαν [Bu/F 6:1; 10:1; 14:10]; ἔτρεμε τρόμον βαρύν [Bu/F 10:1]; and ἐτραυμάτισεν τραύματι βαρεῖ [Bu/F 27:2].[82] The effect of this

---

lute was translated in the Septuagint, see Emmanuel Tov, "Renderings of Combinations of the Infinitive Absolute and Finite Verbs in the LXX—Their Nature and Distribution," in *Studien zur Septuaginta—Robert Hanhart zu Ehren*, ed. Detlef Fraenkel, Udo Quast, and John William Wevers, MSU 20 (Göttingen: Vandenhoeck & Ruprecht, 1990), 64–73. Greek translations of this verbal phrase predominantly display a cognate noun in the dative, but the use of the cognate accusative also appears. Some examples of the Greek translation of the Hebrew internal accusative are: Num 11:4; Jonah 1:10 (1:16 with dative), and 4:6. See also Bruce K. Waltke and M. O'Connor, *An Introduction to Biblical Hebrew Syntax* (Winona Lake, IN: Eisenbrauns, 1990), 167.

80. See Deborah Levine Gera, *Judith*, CEJL (Berlin: de Gruyter, 2014), on this verbal expression (p. 84) but also on the original language of the book of Judith (pp. 79–97). I agree with Gera that for all practical purposes, the final form of Judith should be viewed as a Greek composition.

81. Mirjam Van der Vorm-Croughs (*The Old Greek of Isaiah: An Analysis of Its Pluses and Minuses* [Atlanta: SBL Press, 2014]) categorizes the additional phrase in Isaiah here as one of several times when the "the translator did not adopt elements from one *specific* biblical text, but merely adjusted his translation in line with locutions that figure in Scripture repeatedly" (450). Her discussion of this verse, however, does not quite confirm that χαίρω χαρὰν μεγάλην was repeated often in the MT or Septuagint. She wonders whether the Isaiah translator was influenced by the other places in the MT when it reads some form of שמח שמחה גדולה ("rejoice a great rejoicing"), but of the examples she gives, only one other text (Jon 4:6) translates the Hebrew to χαίρω χαρὰν μεγάλην. The other examples (3 Kgdms 1:40 [1 Kgs 1:40 MT]; 1 Chr 29:9; Neh 12:43) all translate the corresponding Hebrew phrase with some form of either εὐφραίνω εὐφροσύνην μεγάλην or εὐφραίνω μεγάλως (pp. 450–51). The additional phrase, χαίρω χαρὰν μεγάλην, may best be an indicator of a general septuagintal style of presenting a finite verb with cognate noun.

82. The phrase, "rejoice a great joy" (ἐχάρη[σαν] χαρὰν μεγάλην), appears to be in all manuscript categories in Bu/F 3:3; in all but MS E in 4:1 and 7:8; and in all but MS E and L2 in 24:5 (MS 436 only, since MSS 435& end at 21:9) (Burchard, *Joseph und Aseneth*, 87, 90, 113, 292). In Bu/F 9:1, all categories but MS E and Syriac attest to the phrase, but the Syriac may convey a translation of what the finite verb plus cognate accusative means (providing, *magnopere gavisa est*) (Brooks, *Historia ecclesiastica*

phrasing emphasizes the characters' emotions and was notable to scribes of *Aseneth* as well; family *a* adds that when Joseph asked Pharaoh that Aseneth be his wife, Pharaoh "rejoiced a great joy" (ἐχάρη χαρὰν μεγάλην in Bu/F 21:3 [Burchard's text only]), and MS G (family *f*) adds that when Aseneth saw Jacob she "rejoiced a great joy" (ἐχάρη χαρὰν μεγάλην; Bu/F 22:8).[83]

Zachariae Rhetori, 20; and Burchard, *Joseph und Aseneth*, 121). I am less certain about Bu/F 15:11, but with Wright's recent dissertation I can more confidently include it in the *fabula*. Both Burchard's and Fink's texts have ἐχάρη χαρὰν μεγάλην, and Burchard's annotations imply that all manuscript categories attest to the phrase, except for MS E and the Syriac (the latter because of lost folios) (*Joseph und Aseneth*, 196). I can now confirm that *f* (MSS FW and G), *c*, *a*, and *d* attest to this phrase (Wright, "After Antiquity," 2:123), but Fink's transcription of L2 provides an interesting alteration. Although L2 displays a more precise translation of ἐχάρη χαρὰν μεγάλην elsewhere (*gavisus/gavisa est gaudio magno* in Bu/F 3:3; 7:8; and 9:1; and *gavisi sunt gaudio magno* [435&] in 4:1), it does not in Bu/F 15:11 (providing *repleta est* [MS 436: *Asenec*] *gaudio magno* (Fink, *Joseph und Aseneth*, 263, 265, 272, 275). In Bu/F 6:1, the following witnesses attest to some form of ἐφοβεῖτο/ἐφοβήθη φόβον μέγαν: Syr, L2 (MS 436), *f* (MSS FW), *c*, *a*, and *d* (Brooks, *Historia ecclesiastica Zachariae Rhetori*, 18; Finks, *Joseph und Aseneth*, 269; and Wright, "After Antiquity," 2:36). In Bu/F 10:1, all manuscript categories but Syr, MS E, and *a* provide some form of the phrase, "fear a great fear," which is combined with ἔτρεμε τρόμον βαρύν ("tremble a deep trembling"). The Syriac could provide a summary rendering (*et erat in metu ac tremore*), and given the tendencies toward paraphrasing in MS E and toward editing in *a*, I tentatively place the reference of both "fear a big fear" and "tremble a deep trembling" from 10:1 in the *fabula* (Burchard, *Joseph und Aseneth*, 126). For Bu/F 14:10, all categories but Syr, MS E, *a*, and *d* provide ἐφοβήθη φόβον μέγαν or its equivalent. In this case, the folios for the Syriac are missing here, MS E just mentions μετὰ φόβου, and *d* provides a similar rendering to what the Syriac had in Bu/F 10:1 (ἐν φόβῳ μεγάλῳ καὶ τρόμῳ) (Burchard, *Joseph und Aseneth*, 181). Burchard's and Fink's texts also present the phrase, "to fear a great fear" (φοβέω φόβον μέγαν) in Bu/F 18:11, but the attestation does not carry enough across the manuscript categories (only definitively appearing in Syr, MS 436 of L2, and Arm) (Burchard, *Joseph und Aseneth*, 239; Fink, *Joseph und Aseneth*, 186). In Bu/F 27:2, all manuscript categories provide some form of "wound a severe wound" (ἐτραυμάτισεν τραύματι βαρεῖ), including the Armenian manuscript 332 (the only Armenian witness to attest to the full story of chs. 25–27) and palimpsest M (και ετραυ[ματισ]εν αυτον τραυματι βαθει) (Burchard, *Joseph und Aseneth*, 315; Fink, *Joseph und Aseneth*, 43). See also, Delling, "Einwirkungen der Sprache der Septuaginta," 31, but note that some of his references do not apply to my discussion.

83. Burchard, *Joseph und Aseneth*, 257, 273. Fink removes Pharaoh's reaction in Bu 21:3 from her text, since it only appears in family *a* (*Joseph und Aseneth*, 129).

Another subtle example of the Septuagint's influence is how *Aseneth* employs the Greek word εὐλογέω. In classical Greek, this verb typically means "to praise," but in the Septuagint, it is used to take on an extended meaning from the Hebrew verb, "to bless" (ברך).[84] At times the verb ברך is translated to εὐλογέω to indicate praise, as in Gen 24:48, "I praised [εὐλόγησα; ואברך] the Lord, God of my lord Abraham." In many cases, however, εὐλογέω implies what ברך typically means in the Hebrew: "to bless" or "to pronounce words held to confer special favor or well-being upon," as in Ruth 3:10, "and Boaz said, 'May you be blessed [εὐλογημένη; ברוכה] by the Lord God.'"[85] *Aseneth* also uses εὐλογέω in these two different ways; at times the verb indicates praise of a god (Bu/F 8:5 and 15:12), and at other times the verb describes the blessing of people (Bu/F 8:9; 17:4–5; 21:4, 6; and 22:9).[86]

---

84. For a summary of the scholarship on this point, see Sabine van den Eynde, "Blessed by God—Blessed Be God: Εὐλογέω and the Concept of Blessing in the LXX with Special Attention to the Book of Ruth," in *Interpreting Translation: Studies on the LXX and Ezekiel in Honour of Johan Lust*, ed. Florentino García Martínez and Marc Vervenne (Leuven: Peeters, 2005), 415–16.

85. Takamitsu Muraoka, *A Greek-English Lexicon of the Septuagint* (Leuven: Peeters, 2009), 301. For the use of εὐλογέω in the book of Ruth, see Van den Eynde, "Blessed by God," 415–36.

86. Burchard's annotations for Bu/F 8:5 do not provide variants for εὐλογεῖ, which I take to mean that the verb is well-attested among the manuscript categories (*Joseph und Aseneth*, 116–17). The verb appears in the following manuscripts: Syr, L2, MSS FW and L1 (*f*), MS E, *c* (Mc), *a*, and *d* (Batiffol, *Le Livre de la Prière d'Asenath*, 96 [L1] and 49 [MS A]; Brooks, *Historia ecclesiastica Zachariae Rhetori*, 20; Fink, *Joseph und Aseneth*, 274; Philonenko, *Joseph et Aséneth*, 154–56; and Wright, "After Antiquity," 2:50 and 249; see also, Delling, "Einwirkungen der Sprache der Septuaginta," 39–40).

In Bu/F 15:12, Burchard's and Fink's text provide, εὐλογημένος κύριος ὁ θεός σου (blessed is the Lord, your God), which is attested in *f* (MSS FW and 671 [Ngr]) and MS E. Other Greek manuscripts attest to εὐλογητός (MSS G [*f*], *c*, *a*, and MSS BD [*d*]). Both εὐλογημένος and εὐλογητός appear in the Septuagint for translating the *qal* passive participle of ברך (e.g., Gen 14:19–20), but in the Greek, the sense here is of praising and not that of a human giving special favor to a god. The Armenian attests to "gesegnet ist," and the Latin versions (L2 and L1 [*f*]) provide *benedictus*. The Syriac is missing folios from Bu/F 15:7 (at καταφυγῆς) to 15:12x (Burchard, *Joseph und Aseneth* (2003), 197).

In Bu/F 8:9, Burchard's annotations imply that Joseph's request that God bless (εὐλόγησον) Aseneth is well-attested; he only provides the variant readings for *a* and *d* (which add ζωοποίησον) and that MS G has gaps in this portion of the narrative (*Joseph und Aseneth*, 120). The equivalent of εὐλογέω is also attested in Syr, L2, and L1

3. The *Fabula* of *Aseneth* 165

Other word-pairings or phrases that are noteworthy: There is an expression of reverence in the Septuagint ("to fear God/gods" φοβέω θεόν/κύριον τὸν θεόν/θεοῦς) that reflects an equivalent Hebrew phrase and is not as commonly used in other Hellenistic writings.[87] In *Aseneth*, the phrase is used several times: Aseneth fears her gods (ἐφοβεῖτο) in Bu/F 2:3; Joseph is described as a man who fears God (φοβούμενος) in Bu/F 8:8; Benjamin is said to also fear the Lord/God (φοβούμενος) in Bu/F 26:1; and Aseneth describes the sons of Leah as men who fear God/the Lord (φοβούμενοι) in Bu/F 28:7.[88] Although used by several Hellenistic writers, the phrase "Do

---

(*f*) (Batiffol, *Le Livre de la Prière d'Aseneth*, 96; Brooks, *Historia ecclesiastica Zachariae Rhetori*, 20; Fink, *Joseph und Aseneth*, 275), and the verb appears in MSS FW (*f*) and *c* (Wright, "After Antiquity," 2:53).

In Bu/F 17:4, Aseneth's request that the angelic figure bless (εὐλόγησεις) her female attendants is attested in some form in Syr, L2 (435& only; MS 436 lacks Bu/F 16:16x–17:5), Arm, *f* (MSS FW, G, and L1), MS E, *a*, and *d*. In Bu/F 17:5, the angelic figure's prayer that God bless (εὐλογήσει) the women is attested in Syr, Arm, L2 (MSS 435& only), *f* (MSS FW, G, and L1), MS E, *a*, and *d*. Palimpsest M is missing the rest of ch. 17 after verse 3 (Burchard, *Joseph und Aseneth*, 225; and Fink, *Joseph und Aseneth*, 39–40).

In Bu/F 21:4, Pharaoh wishes that God bless Aseneth (εὐλογήσει), and the verb appears in Syr, Arm, L2, *f* (MSS FW, G, and L1), *a*, and Slavonic (*d*). Palimpsest M also provides the reading in Burchard's and Fink's text here (ευλογησει σε κυριος ο θεος) (Fink, *Joseph und Aseneth*, 41). Manuscript E condenses 21:4–5 (beginning at καὶ εἶδεν and ending at καὶ τὴν Ἀσενέθ in Burchard's text), but in its place, it has Pharaoh "blessing" (εὐλόγησεν) Joseph and Aseneth (Burchard, *Joseph und Aseneth*, 259).

In Bu/F 21:6, Pharaoh wishes that God bless (εὐλογήσει) Joseph and Aseneth, and the verb appears in Syr, Arm, L2, *f* (MSS FW, G, and L1), *a*, and Slav (*d*). Again, MS E is condensed, attesting to none of Bu/F 21:5 (from <εἰς> τὰς κεφαλάς) through the end of Bu/F 21:7; palimpsest M is missing after 21:4 (Burchard, *Joseph und Aseneth*, 258–61; and Fink, *Joseph und Aseneth*, 41–42). In Bu/F 22:9, Jacob blesses (εὐλόγησεν) Aseneth, and the verb appears in Syr, L2 (MS 436 only because MSS 435& end at 21:9), Arm, *f* (MSS FW and L1), *a*, and *d*. Palimpsest M lacks ch. 22 (Burchard, *Joseph und Aseneth*, 274; and Fink, *Joseph und Aseneth*, 41–42).

In Bu/F 22:9, Jacob blesses (εὐλόγησεν) Aseneth, and the verb appears in Syr, L2 (MS 436 only because MSS 435& end at 21:9), Arm, *f* (MSS FW and L1), *a* and *d*. Palimpsest M lacks chapter 22 (Burchard, *Joseph und Aseneth*, 274; and Fink, *Joseph und Aseneth*, 41–42).

87. According to TLG, there are forty-two times the phrase φοβέω θεόν/κύριον τὸν θεόν or φοβέω θεοῦς is mentioned in the LXX/OG but few times in non-Jewish, Greek texts (Lysias, *Orat. Pro milite* 17; and a fragment attributed to Theono [*Fragmenta*, letter to Rhodope]).

88. In Bu/F 2:3, all manuscript categories except for MS E provide some form of

not be afraid" (μὴ φοβέω [in the middle-passive or aorist passive forms]) appears more than one hundred times in the Septuagint, and some form of the phrase is used twice in *Aseneth* (when the angelic figure speaks to Aseneth in Bu/F 14:11 and 23:16).[89] The pairing of the words "fear and dread" (φόβος καὶ τρόμος) is a repeated phrase in the LXX/OG, and *Aseneth* uses the combination twice (Bu/F 9:1 and 10:1).[90] Another noticeable phrase in the Septuagint is "to pursue after someone" (καταδιώκω ὀπίσω τινός), which appears twice in *Aseneth* (Bu/F 26:6; 27:6) as well.[91]

φοβέομαι or its equivalent (Burchard, *Joseph und Aseneth*, 78). In Bu/F 8:8, all the manuscript categories appear to refer to Joseph as a "man who fears God" (φοβούμενος τὸν θεόν or its equivalent), but Burchard's annotations are incomplete (*Joseph und Aseneth*, 119). He gives no indication of variants, but the phrase is identifiable in Syr, L2, MSS FW and L1 (*f*), MS E, *c*, *a*, and *d* (Batiffol, *Le Livre de la Prière d'Aseneth*, 96 [L1] and 49 [MS A]; Brooks, *Historia ecclesiastica Zachariae Rhetori*, 20; Fink, *Joseph und Aseneth*, 275; Philonenko, *Joseph et Aséneth*, 156; and Wright, "After Antiquity," 2:52 and 249). In Bu/F 27:1, Benjamin "fears the Lord/God/the Lord God" in all the manuscript categories except for the Armenian (which only has one witness attesting to a full account of chs. 25–27 [MS 332]). The word φοβουμενος cannot be legibly detected in palimpsest M, but given that the witness provides (τ)ον κυριον σφοδρα with room for φοβουμενος, I agree with Fink that it likely attests to the verb (MSS FW, e.g., provide: καὶ [ἦν W] φοβούμενος τὸν κύριον σφόδρα) (Burchard, *Joseph und Aseneth*, 315; Fink, *Joseph und Aseneth*, 43). In Bu/F 28:7, all the manuscript categories attest to Aseneth's description of the sons of Leah as men who fear God/the Lord (Burchard, *Joseph und Aseneth*, 323). See also Delling, "Einwirkungen der Sprache der Septuaginta," 31–32.

89. TLG lists 102 times that some from of μὴ φοβέω appears in the LXX/OG. In Bu/F 14:11, μὴ φοβέω or its equivalent appears in all manuscript categories except for the Syriac, which is missing leaves for chs. 13–15. In 23:16, the phase (some form of μὴ φοβέω or its equivalent) is attested in all categories (Burchard, *Joseph und Aseneth*, 181, 289). See also Delling, "Einwirkungen der Sprache der Septuaginta," 31–32.

90. The word pairing appears in LXX Gen 9:2; Exod 15:16; Deut 2:25; 11:25; Jdt 2:28; 15:2; 1 Macc 7:18; Pss 2:11; 54:6; Isa 19:16; and also in 4 Macc 4:10. In Bu/F 9:1, all manuscript categories except for MS E, *a*, and *d* appear to have the pairing (φόβος καὶ τρόμος or its equivalent; families *a* and *d* lack "trembling") (Batiffol, *Le Livre de la Prière d'Aseneth*, 97; Brooks, *Historia ecclesiastica Zachariae Rhetori*, 21; Burchard, *Joseph und Aseneth*, 122; Fink, *Joseph und Aseneth*, 276; and Wright, "After Antiquity," 2:56). In Bu/F 10:1, all categories except MS E, *a*, and *d* convey the pairing of "fear and trembling," but of the witnesses that do, all but the Syriac expand the pairing in terms of the finite verb plus cognate accusative ("fear a fear and tremble a tremble") (Burchard, *Joseph und Aseneth*, 126). See also, Delling, "Einwirkungen der Sprache der Septuaginta," 32.

91. The phrase, καταδιώκω ὀπίσω τινός, appears thirty-four times in the Septuagint: LXX Gen 14:14; 31:36; 35:5; Exod 14:4, 8, 9; Deut 11:4; Josh 2:5, 7, 16; 8:16, 17

3. The *Fabula* of Aseneth 167

Along with the lexical associations that the manuscript categories demonstrate with the Septuagint, all the witness groups provide common literary and linguistic connections to the LXX Genesis story about Joseph (chs. 37, 39–50), and so these connections can be included in the *fabula*. Particular examples are the references to: (1) Joseph's gathering of grain during the time "of abundance" (τῆς εὐθηνίας or equivalent phrase) in Bu/F 1:1 and 3:1 (cf. LXX Gen 41:47, 53 ["the seven years τῆς εὐθηνίας"]);[92] (2) Joseph's enslavement mentioned in Bu/F 4:9, 24:9, and 25:5 (cf. LXX Gen 37:12–36 and 39:1–6);[93] (3) the accusation by Potiphar's wife, Joseph's

---

(2x); 10:19; 24:6; Judg 1:6; 7:23; 1 Kgdms 17:52; 23:25, 28; 24:15; 26:18; 30:8; 2 Kgdms 2:19, 24, 28; 17:1; 20:6; 1 Chr 10:1; 2 Chr 13:18; 1 Macc 10:78; 12:30; Sir 27:17; and Jer 52:8. The phrase, κατεδίωξαν ὀπίσω τῆς Ἀσενέθ or its equivalent in Bu/F 26:6, is attested in L2 (only MS 436, since MSS 435& end at 21:9), *f*, MS E, *a*, and *d*, and although the Syriac uniquely provides an extended description of the scene, its *Vorlage* may have had κατεδιώκω at least (the Syriac provides, *et statim persecuti sunt et cito ad Āsyath pervenerunt*). Only MS 332 in the Armenian provides an extensive narration of chs. 25–27, and in this verse it presents much of the same as Burchard's text, but it uses the verb "to go" instead of "to pursue" (Burchard translates the Armenian as "gingen"). According to Fink, Palimpsest M legibly provides, κατεδ[ιω]ξαν οπισω] της ασενεχ δρομω [...] (whereby indecipherable letters are in brackets). The evidence weighs heavily in favor of the phrase, κατεδίωξαν ὀπίσω τῆς Ἀσενέθ, being associated with the *fabula* (with the Armenian as the sole outlier) (Burchard, *Joseph und Aseneth*, 313; and Fink, *Joseph und Aseneth*, 43). In Bu/F 27:6, all manuscript categories except for L2 provide the phrase καταδιώκω ὀπίσω ("those lying in ambush") or its equivalent, and I include here Fink's decipherment of palimpsest M (κατεδιωξαν [ο]πι[σω των] ανδρ[ων τω]ν εν εδρευ[...]). Manuscript 436 (the only witness of L2 that preserves beyond ch. 21) seems to have skipped the verb of its *Vorlage*, stating that the "sons of Jacob" (not Leah, as in all other manuscript categories) *post insidiatores illos* (Burchard, *Joseph und Aseneth*, 217; Fink, *Joseph und Aseneth*, 43 and 323). See also, Delling, "Einwirkungen der Sprache der Septuaginta," 31.

92. In Bu/F 1:1, all the manuscript categories appear to reference Joseph's gathering of grain during the years of abundance in some form. Burchard does not provide variants, and I can detect the reference in the following: Syr, MSS 435& (L2; MS 436 does not begin until Bu/F 1:7), *f* (L1 and perhaps MS G, which reads εὐτηνείας), MS E *c* (Mc), *a*, and *d* (Batiffol, *Le Livre de la Prière d'Aseneth*, 39 [MS A] and 89 [L1]; Brooks, *Historia ecclesiastica Zachariae Rhetori*, 15; Fink, *Joseph und Aseneth*, 259; Wright, "After Antiquity," 2:2 and 244). In Bu/F 3:1, all the manuscript categories refer to Joseph gathering the grain, and all but MS E make a reference to the years of plenty (Burchard, *Joseph und Aseneth*, 70–71, 85).

93. It appears that all manuscript categories refer to Joseph's enslavement in Bu/F 4:9, dominantly using the verb πέρνημι or its equivalent. Burchard only provides variants in his critical edition, which implies that the verb is well-attested across the

imprisonment and subsequent release after he had interpreted Pharaoh's dreams in Bu/F 4:10 (cf. LXX Gen 39:6–41:36);[94] (4) Joseph's oversight of the collection and distribution of grain, referred to in Bu/F 4:7 and 25:5 (cf. LXX Gen 41:46-49, 53–57); and I also include here the references that Pharaoh appointed (κατέσησεν) Joseph (cf. LXX Gen 41:41 [καθίστημί σε]; and 42:43 [κατέστησεν αὐτόν]); Joseph rode Pharaoh's second chariot; and Joseph was "saving" Egypt (cf. especially the reference of σωτήρ in Bu/F 25:5 with LXX Gen 47:25 [σέσωκας ἡμᾶς]);[95] (5) Pharaoh oversee-

---

manuscript categories. I can confirm that the following categories provide it: Syr, L2, ƒ (MSS FW and L1), MS E, c (Mc), a, and d (Batiffol, *Le Livre de la Prière d'Aseneth*, 44–45 [MS A] and 93 [L1]; Brooks, *Historia ecclesiastica Zachariae Rhetori*, 17; Burchard, *Joseph und Aseneth*, 96; Fink, *Joseph und Aseneth*, 267; Philonenko, *Joseph et Aséneth*, 144; and Wright, "After Antiquity," 2:28 and 246). In Bu/F 24:9, all the manuscript categories except for Mc relay that Joseph was sold (πεπράσκασι or its equivalent). The palimpsest M, however, is unreadable in this portion of ch. 24 and family c ends at ch. 16 (Burchard, *Joseph und Aseneth*, 294). In Bu/F 25:5 of Burchard's and Fink's texts, Naphtali and Asher make reference to when Joseph's brothers sold him into slavery. All the manuscript categories appear to attest to this reference. Burchard's annotations provide no variants for πεπράκατε, but the verb or its equivalent is attested in Syr, L2 (MS 436 only, since MSS 435& end at 21:9), ƒ (MSS FW and G), MS E, a, and d (Batiffol, *Le Livre de la Prière d'Aseneth*, 79; Brooks, *Historia ecclesiastica Zachariae Rhetori*, 36; Burchard, *Joseph und Aseneth*, 307; Fink, *Joseph und Aseneth*, 322; Philonenko, *Joseph et Aséneth*, 210; Wright, "After Antiquity," 2:211 and 262). Fink's transcription of palimpsest M suggests that the witness had πεπράκατε, but all that is decipherable is the letter ρ and the final ε. It does, however, clearly provide ἅπαξ before the word and ιωσηφ after, aligning well with other attestations. Cf., e.g., ιδου απαξ [πεπ]ρ[ακατ]ε ιωσηφ και (M) with ἰδοὺ ἅπαξ πεπράκατε αὐτὸν καί in MSS FW and G (Fink, *Joseph und Aseneth*, 42; and Wright, "After Antiquity," 2:211).

94. All manuscript categories refer to the accusation that Joseph slept with Potiphar's wife (and in MS E, Aseneth describes the accusation as Joseph raping Potiphar's wife [βιάζων τὴν κυρίαν αὐτοῦ]); and all the categories appear to mention Joseph's imprisonment and cause for his release (Burchard's critical edition only provides minor variants that do not conflict with this summary). I can verify that the latter description appears in Syr, L2, ƒ (MSS FW and L1), MS E, c (Mc), a, and d (Batiffol, *Le Livre de la Prière d'Aseneth*, 44–45 [MS A] and 93 [L1]; Brooks, *Historia ecclesiastica Zachariae Rhetori*, 17–18; Burchard *Joseph und Aseneth*, 96–97; Fink, *Joseph und Aseneth*, 267; Philonenko, *Joseph et Aséneth*, 144; and Wright, "After Antiquity," 2:29 and 246).

95. Although the content is phrased differently, all manuscript categories appear to refer to the appointment of Joseph by Pharaoh (κατέστησεν or its equivalent) and Joseph's oversight of the grain in preparation for the coming famine (with all but the Syriac using a form or equivalent of σιτοδοτέω). In Bu/F 25:5, however, all categories

ing the marriage between Joseph and Aseneth in Bu/F 21:2–8 as well as the fact that Aseneth is identified as the daughter of a Heliopolite priest in Bu/F 1:3–4 (cf. LXX Gen 41:45);[96] (6) Aseneth giving birth to Ephraim and Manasseh during the years of abundance in Bu/F 21:9 (cf. LXX Gen 41:50–52);[97] (7) the shift from the years of abundance to the years of the famine and Jacob's relocation to Egypt and settlement in Goshen (Γεσέμ) in Bu/F 22:1–2 (cf. LXX Gen 41:53–42:2; 46–47);[98] and (8) God's favor of Joseph, mentioned by Pentephres in Bu/F 4:7 and by Naphtali and Asher in Bu/F 25:5–6 (cf. LXX Gen 39:2–5, 21–23; 41:38–39; 45:4–8; 50:19–21).[99]

There are other features in the *fabula* that interweave memorable scenes from the Joseph novella into the story about Aseneth. In chapter 5, Pentephres and all his kindred (except Aseneth) prostrate before Joseph with their faces on the ground (προσεκύνησαν τῷ Ἰωσὴφ ἐπὶ πρόσωπον

---

attest to calling Joseph some form of σιτοδότης, even palimpsest M. Pharaoh's second chariot in Bu/F 5:4 is a clear reference to LXX Gen 41:43, in which Joseph receives τὸ ἅρμα τὸ δεύτερον belonging to Pharaoh (see note to *fabula* 9, above). In Bu/F 4:7, all categories provide the description of Joseph "saving" or being a "savior" (and all but the Syriac and Armenian use a form of the verb σώζω or its equivalent). In Bu/F 25:5, all (including palimpsest M) but the Syriac refer to Joseph as σωτήρ or its equivalent, but the Syriac refers to Joseph "saving" (*servat*) (Batiffol, *Le Livre de la Prière d'Asenath*, 44 [MS A] and 92 [L1]; Brooks, *Historia ecclesiastica Zachariae Rhetori*, 17; Burchard, *Joseph und Aseneth*, 94, 307; Fink, *Joseph und Aseneth*, 42, 266; and Philonenko, *Joseph et Aséneth*, 142).

96. All manuscript categories refer to Pharaoh's authority over the marriage of Joseph and Aseneth and his blessing of the union, although some witnesses provide lengthier scenes than others (Burchard, *Joseph und Aseneth*, 258–61; and Fink, *Joseph und Aseneth*, 41). All manuscript categories refer to Pentephres as a priest of Heliopolis (I take *solis civitatis* in MSS 435& [L2] to be a translation of Ἡλιουπόλεως), and all categories identify Aseneth as his daughter (Burchard, *Joseph und Aseneth*, 71).

97. All manuscript categories, except for Mc (but only because c ends at ch. 16 and palimpsest M is unreadable at this portion of the narrative), make reference to Aseneth bearing Manasseh and Ephraim (Burchard, *Joseph und Aseneth*, 263).

98. Although not uniform in their presentation of this scene, all the manuscript categories mention the years of famine (λιμός or its equivalent) and Jacob's residence in Goshen (Γεσέμ) (Burchard, *Joseph und Aseneth*, 270–71).

99. All manuscript categories attest to Pentephres's stating how God's spirit and/or God's favor is in/with Joseph (Burchard, *Joseph und Aseneth*, 95). In ch. 25, Naphtali and Asher argue that "God guards" Joseph (διαφυλάσσω or its equivalent) and that if they (the sons of Bilhah and Zilpah) execute the ambush attack, God will destroy them. These accounts are well-attested across the manuscript categories (Burchard, *Joseph und Aseneth*, 307; Fink, *Joseph und Aseneth*, 42).

ἐπὶ τὴν γῆν, 5:7), which echoes the actions of Joseph's brothers in LXX Gen 42:6 and 43:26 (προσεκύνησαν αὐτῷ ἐπὶ πρόσωπον ἐπὶ τὴν γῆν) and is reflected in the brothers' behavior in *Aseneth* (they prostrate before Joseph and Aseneth [Bu/F 22:5, προσεκύνησαν αὐτοῖς ἐπὶ πρόσωπον ἐπὶ τὴν γῆν]; the sons of Bilhah and Zilpah prostrate before Aseneth when they beg her for protection [Bu/F 28:2, προσεκύνησαν or the equivalent]; and the sons of Leah fall and prostrate before Aseneth as well [Bu/F 28:9, προσεκύνησεν ἐπὶ τὴν γῆν or the equivalent]).[100] Aseneth also prostrates before Jacob (Bu/F 22:8, προσεκύνησεν) as does Pharaoh before Levi (Bu/F 29:6, προσεκύνησε).[101] The deception of Pharaoh's son in *Asen.* 24 (*fabula* 37) is believable because he creates a scenario that resonates with what Joseph's brothers fear in the book of Genesis. In LXX Gen 50:15, the broth-

---

100. In Bu/F 5:7, the phrase, προσεκύνησαν τῷ Ἰωσὴφ ἐπὶ πρόσωπον ἐπὶ τὴν γῆν or its equivalent is evident in L2, *f* (MSS FW and L1), MS E, *a*, and *d* (Batiffol, *Le Livre de la Prière d'Aseneth*, 46 [MS A] and 94 [L1]; Burchard, *Joseph und Aseneth*, 103; Fink, *Joseph und Aseneth*, 269; and Philonenko, *Joseph et Aséneth*, 146; Wright, "After Antiquity," 2:35 and 247). The Syriac and family *c* provide a shorter rendition of this line but include προσκυνέω or its equivalent and the object of Joseph; the Syriac lacks reference to "their faces" (*et Ioseph in terra adoraverunt*), and family *c* just has προσεκύνησαν τῷ Ἰωσήφ (Brooks, *Historia ecclesiastica Zachariae Rhetori*, 18; Wright, "After Antiquity," 2:35). Burchard does not provide variants for this phrase, and given the attestations I can detect from the other manuscript categories, I assume that it also appears in Arm (Burchard, *Joseph und Aseneth*, 103). In Bu/F 22:5, all the manuscript categories but MS E and *d* attest to προσεκύνησαν αὐτοῖς ἐπὶ πρόσωπον ἐπὶ τὴν γῆν or its equivalent, but family *d* attests to προσεκύνησαν ἐπὶ τὴν γῆν (Burchard, *Joseph und Aseneth*, 271). In Bu/F 28:2, all the manuscript categories but Arm narrate that the sons of Bilhah and Zilpah fell to the ground and prostrated (Syr, MS 436 [L2], *f* [MSS FW], MS E, M [Mc], *a*, and *d*). The Armenian seems to abbreviate the description by only providing, "und fielen vor Asanēt" (Burchard, *Joseph und Aseneth*, 321; and Fink, *Joseph und Aseneth*, 43). In Bu/F 28:9, all manuscript categories except MS E and Mc provide προσεκύνησαν ... ἐπὶ τὴν γῆν or its equivalent. Palimpsest M is unreadable in this portion of the story; *c* ends at ch. 16; and MS E significantly abbreviates Bu/F 28 (providing only 28:1-4 and 7) (Burchard, *Joseph und Aseneth*, 325). The phrase, προσκυνέω πρόσωπον (τινι) ἐπὶ τὴν γῆν, also appears in LXX Gen 19:1 (with τῷ προσώπῳ); 48:12 (with ἐπὶ τῆς γῆς); 1 Kgdms 25:41; 2 Kgdms 14:33; 18:28; 24:20; 3 Kgdms 1:23; 1 Chr 21:21; 2 Esd 18:6. The phrase, προσκυνέω τῷ προσώπῳ (τινος), is in Num 22:31 and Jdt 14:7.

101. All manuscript categories but MS E and *d* provide that Aseneth prostrates (προσκυνέω or its equivalent) before Jacob in Bu/F 22:8. All manuscript categories that decipherably attest to the scene in ch. 29 (so not Mc or MS E, the latter of which only attests to Bu/F 29:7-9) provide the verb or its equivalent in Bu/F 29:6 (Burchard, *Joseph und Aseneth*, 273, 321, 333; and Fink, *Joseph und Aseneth*, 43).

ers worry that Joseph bears a grudge and, now after Jacob's death, Joseph will "pay them back" (ἀνταποδῷ) for all the evil things they had done. In *Aseneth*, Pharaoh's son reports that he heard Joseph say to Pharaoh that, after Jacob's passing, "I will pay them back" (ἀνταποδώσω or its equivalent) for the *hybris* of the sons of Bilhah and Zilpah selling him into slavery (Bu/F 24:9).[102] (Further, when in defeat before Aseneth, the sons of Bilhah and Zilpah interpret their fate as the Lord repaying them [ἀνταπέδωκεν or its equivalent] for their deeds [28:3].)[103] In particular, Pharaoh's son mentions the selling of Joseph into slavery as the cause of Joseph's ire (Bu/F 24:9), which is similarly implied in the brothers' conversation in LXX Gen 50.[104] The difference, though, is that all the brothers are culpable in Genesis, but Pharaoh's son spins a tale in which Joseph only blames the sons of Bilhah and Zilpah.

This lie plays off of another narrative in Genesis, one that does not factor into the Joseph story but does in *Aseneth*. Dan and Naphtali are sons of Rachel's slave, Bilhah, and Gad and Asher are sons of Leah's slave, Zilpah (Gen 30:1–13), but all four sons are legitimate heirs of Jacob in the book of Genesis. They are not treated as peculiarly subordinate to Jacob's other sons; reflective of ancient Near Eastern customs, Bilhah and Zilpah satisfied a legitimate way that wealthy patriarchs maintained their heritage.[105] But in *Aseneth*, the narrative creates the perception that these sons were

---

102. All manuscript categories except for MS E and Mc refer to ἀνταποδίδωμι or an equivalent (*retribuam* in MS 436 [L2], and *ulciscar* in the Syriac). Manuscript E provides a paraphrase of the speech of Pharaoh's son, and we lack the folio from palimpsest M with this scene. Although not uniformly expressed, all manuscript categories except for Mc refer to the timing that Joseph (supposedly) planned to take revenge on the sons of Bilhah and Zilpah after his father's death. Burchard's annotations imply that the Syriac does not attest to this idea, but Brooks translation does mention it (*simul ac luctus patris mei accesserit, eos ulciscar*) (*Historia ecclesiastica Zachariae Rhetori*, 35; Burchard, *Joseph und Aseneth*, 294–95). I deal with the term *hybris* further below.

103. All manuscript categories refer to ἀνταπέδωκεν or its equivalent in Bu/F 28:3 (Burchard, *Joseph und Aseneth*, 322; Fink, *Joseph und Aseneth*, 43).

104. In particular, all the manuscript categories except for Mc attest to Pharaoh's son adding that Joseph said his brothers με πεπράκασι or an equivalent (Burchard, *Joseph und Aseneth*, 294). Although LXX Gen 50:15 does not use πέρνημι and instead refers to the evil things that the brothers had done (τὰ κακά), it is clear in the story that the brothers primarily are referring to their selling Joseph into slavery.

105. Marten Stol, *Women in the Ancient Near East*, trans. Helen Richardson and Mervyn Richardson (Boston: de Gruyter, 2016), 168–70.

secondary to the sons of Leah (especially compared to Levi and Simeon). Dan, Gad, Naphtali, and Asher are consistently mentioned as sons of *slaves* (παιδίσκαι or its equivalent in Bu/F 22:11; 24:2, 8; as Bilhah and Zilpah are identified in LXX Gen 30:3–13; and 35:25–26) and Joseph's other brothers (except for Benjamin) are referred to as "the sons of Leah" (Bu/F 22:11; 27:6; 28:8).[106] The dichotomy between "sons of slaves" and "sons of Leah" implies a distinction of status that Pharaoh's son includes in his lie. Joseph, so Pharaoh's son reports, does not want the sons of Bilhah and Zilpah to have a share of the inheritance since they are children of slaves (24:8).[107] That the sons believe the lie confirms that they, too, suspect that they are considered inferior to the other brothers; in other words, the narrative establishes the perceived secondary status of Bilhah's and Zilpah's sons. In association with their status, these sons are known for their disloyalty in *Aseneth*. They do not accompany Joseph and Aseneth after their visit with Jacob (as Leah's sons do; Bu/F 22:11); Pharaoh's son is advised that they are at enmity with Joseph and Aseneth and therefore would be likely to do his

---

106. In Bu/F 22:11, all manuscript categories except for MS E, M*c*, and *d* identify Dan, Gad, Naphtali, and Asher as the sons of Bilhah and Zilpah "slaves of Leah and Rachel" (παιδισκῶν or its equivalent). Palimpsest M is missing folios for this portion of the story and *c* ends at ch. 16, so only MS E and family *d* definitely lack the reference. For the same verse, all categories except for M*c* and *d* mention that the "sons of Leah" accompany Joseph and Aseneth (Burchard, *Joseph und Aseneth*, 275). In Bu/F 24:2, all manuscript categories except for M*c* identify the men as sons of slaves (παιδισκῶν or its equivalent). In Bu/F 24:8, the Syriac has Pharaoh's son report Joseph calling the sons "my slaves" (*servi mei*), and the remainder of the categories (except for M*c*) mention the sons as "children of slaves" (τέκνα παιδισκῶν or its equivalent). We lack evidence for both Bu/F 24:2 and 24:8 in palimpsest M (folio 80r begins its side with Bu/F 24:15) (Burchard, *Joseph und Aseneth*, 294; and Fink, *Joseph und Aseneth*, 42). In Bu/F 27:6, all manuscript categories except for L2 attest to "sons of Leah" (Syr, Arm [MS 332], *f* [FW and G], MS E, M[M*c*], *a*, and *d*). Manuscript 436, the only L2 witness to attest to the story beyond 21:9, provides "sons of Jacob" (Burchard, *Joseph und Aseneth*, 317; and Fink, *Joseph und Aseneth*, 43). In Bu/F 28:8, all manuscript categories except for MS E and M*c* refer to the "sons of Leah" (who rush in on the scene to rescue Aseneth). Palimpsest M is unreadable at this portion of the story; *c* ends at ch. 16, and MS E only provides vv. 1–4 and 7 of Bu/F 28 (Burchard, *Joseph und Aseneth*, 325; Fink, *Joseph und Aseneth*, 38).

107. Although not phrased identically, all the manuscript categories but MS E and M*c* attest to Joseph (supposedly) saying that Dan, Gad, Naphtali, and Asher should not receive inheritance since they are children of slaves. Palimpsest M is unreadable at this portion of the story and *c* ends at ch. 16, so only MS E definitively lacks this reference (Burchard, *Joseph und Aseneth*, 294).

3. The *Fabula* of Aseneth 173

will (Bu/F 24:2); and they engage in the ambush attempt with Pharaoh's son and ultimately try to kill Aseneth (Bu/F 25–28).[108]

The *fabula* also depends on knowledge of Gen 34, which is used to develop the characterization of Levi and Simeon and to feed the suspense of the latter half of the narrative. In Gen 34, Levi and Simeon (who are "sons of Leah," 34:14), kill all the males in Shechem after its prince, Shechem, had raped their sister, Dinah. Similarly, in *Aseneth*, Levi describes his and Simeon's actions against Shechem as God avenging the defilement (μιαίνω) of Dinah (Bu/F 23:14), which echoes the brothers' sentiments in LXX Gen 34:13 (when they lie to Shechem and Hamor because, the narrator tells us, their sister had been "defiled" [ἐμίαναν]).[109] It is also striking that *Aseneth* describes the rape of Dinah as an act of *hybris* (ὕβρις/ὑβρίζω or its equivalent), which I will discuss further below and in the next chapter. In the Genesis story, Jacob worries that his household's reputation in Canaan had been jeopardized by his sons' actions (Gen 34:30), but in *Aseneth*, the sons' reputation attracts the attention of Pharaoh's son. He

---

108. Although not sharing identical phrasing, the following manuscript categories mention that sons of Leah escorted Joseph and Aseneth but not the sons of Bilhah and Zilpah in Bu/F 22:11: Syr, Arm, MS 436 (L2; MSS 435& end at 21:9), *f* (MSS FW and G), and *a*. It is undetermined whether palimpsest M originally had this scene (the folios provide nothing from Bu/F 22 or 23), and *c* ends at ch. 16; MS E and family *d* narrate slightly different scenes without mention of the sons of Bilhah and Zilpah. I tentatively include the mention of the sons and Bilhah and Zilpah as part of the *fabula* since E and *d* typically shorten the narrative and the remaining witnesses that have this scene strongly attest to it (Burchard, *Joseph und Aseneth*, 275; and Wright, "After Antiquity," 2:182). In Bu/F 24:2, all manuscript categories except for M*c* attest to the slaves of Pharaoh's son telling him that the sons of Bilhah and Zilpah are at enmity with Joseph and Aseneth and so they will do his will. Palimpsest M is missing a part of ch. 24 (folio 80r begins at Bu/F 24:15), and family *c* ends at ch. 16 (Burchard, *Joseph und Aseneth*, 290–91). The narration of the ambush attempt and ultimate attack against Aseneth is depicted in all manuscript categories (even M*c* [palimpsest M]), albeit differently (Burchard, *Joseph und Aseneth*, 303–21; Fink, *Joseph und Aseneth*, 38–43).

109. All manuscript categories but M*c* provide some form of Levi's summary about the attack of Shechem in Bu/F 23:14, in particular that the brother's actions were to avenge what happened to Dinah (ἐκδικέω or equivalent), and all but the Syriac and M*c* mention that God was the primary avenger. All but M*c* and Syriac specifically mention that Dinah was "defiled" (ἐμίανε or equivalent), but the Syriac does refer to the dishonoring of Dinah (*ignominiam Dinae sororis nostrae*). Palimpsest M is missing folios in this portion and *c* ends at ch. 16 (Burchard, *Joseph und Aseneth*, 288).

had heard about their single-handed defeat of the Shechemites, and he promises them great reward for helping him to kidnap Aseneth and kill Joseph (Bu/F 23:2–4).[110] To Pharaoh's son surprise, Simeon and Levi react strongly against his plan (Bu/F 23:6–13), to the extent that Simeon considers striking down the man immediately (Bu/F 23:7).[111] This scene sets up the first time we hear some form of the dictum that as God-revering men, "it is not fitting to repay evil for evil," which Levi states to Simeon to calm his rage (23:8–9). The dictum is paraphrased in Bu/F 23:12 (by Levi to Pharaoh's son) and in Bu/F 28:10 and 28:14 (by Aseneth to Leah's sons), and repeated in Bu/F 29:3 (by Levi to Benjamin).[112] In the next chapter, I will discuss this dictum further as well as the interplay between Levi's and Simeon's actions in Gen 34 as compared to their actions in *Aseneth*. For now, I simply indicate how the *fabula* design of *Aseneth* depends on knowledge of Gen 34.

The *fabula* contains references to other septuagintal texts as well, displaying a knowledge of particular stories and phrases. One example is the characterization of Benjamin in *Aseneth*.[113] In the book of Genesis, Joseph's brother, Benjamin, is a static character, but *Aseneth* portrays him in the image of David. Alluding to when David fought Goliath, Benjamin is introduced as a "youth" (παιδάριον or its equivalent) and handsome (κάλλος or its equivalent) in Bu/F 27:1, which compares with the description of David in 1 Kgdms 17 (LXX) //1 Sam 17 (MT) (esp. 17:42, where Goliath sees that David is a "boy [παιδάριον] … with beauty of eyes [μετὰ κάλλους ὀφθαλμῶν]").[114] Like when David fought Goliath, Benjamin takes stones from the wadi (λίθοι ἐκ τοῦ χειμάρρου or its equivalent [Bu/F 27:2,

---

110. All manuscript categories except for MS E and Mc have Pharaoh's son specifically refer to the Shechemite incident, and all categories but Mc attest to Pharaoh's proposal to Levi and Simeon. Since palimpsest M is missing folios at this portion of the story, and c ends at ch. 16, only MS E definitively lacks mention of Gen 34 (Burchard, *Joseph und Asenath*, 279–81; and Fink, *Joseph und Asenath*, 34–36).

111. Although phrased differently, all manuscript categories but Mc refer to the brothers' shock at the request of Pharaoh's son and to Simeon's desire to strike down Pharaoh's son (Burchard, *Joseph und Asenath*, 283). We lack any evidence for ch. 23 in palimpsest M (Fink, *Joseph und Asenath*, 41–42).

112. See notes to *fabula* 33–34, 50–52.

113. Several scholars have discussed this allusion to 1 Kgdms 17, including Angela Standhartinger, "Humour in *Joseph and Aseneth*," *JSP* 24 (2015): 254–56; and Hicks-Keeton, *Arguing with Aseneth*, 80–87.

114. "Youth" (παιδάριον or equivalent) and "handsome" (κάλλος or equivalent)

4]; cf. 1 Kgdms 17:40, 49 where David retrieves λίθοι and uses one against Goliath), strikes Pharaoh's son in the head (πατάσσω or equivalent; cf. 1 Kgdms 17:49 where David strikes [πατάσσω] Goliath between the eyes), and Pharaoh's son falls to the ground (ἔπεσεν ἐπὶ τὴν γῆν; cf. 1 Kgdms 17:49 when Goliath falls on his face on the ground [ἔπεσεν ... ἐπὶ τὴν γῆν]).[115] After the sons of Leah find Aseneth, Benjamin runs over to Pharaoh's son and takes the sword of Pharaoh's son (ἔδραμεν ἐπ'αὐτὸν βενιαμὶν καὶ ἔλαβε τὴν ῥομφαίαν αὐτοῦ; Bu/F 29:2).[116] This action imitates that of

---

are attested in all manuscript categories, even Mc (palimpsest M attests to both Greek words) (Burchard, *Joseph und Aseneth*, 315; and Fink, *Joseph und Aseneth*, 43).

115. All manuscript categories seem to present these basic points and terms (or their equivalents). For the phrase, λίθος ἐκ τοῦ χειμάρρου or its equivalent, the manuscript categories are in more agreement with Bu/F 27:4 than with 27:2, but the different attestations in the latter could arguably be paraphrasing. In Bu/F 27:2, the majority of the manuscript categories provide λίθον στρογγύλον or equivalent (Arm [MS 332], L2 [MS 436], *f* [MSS FW and G], Mc [palimpsest M clearly shows στρογγυλον and indicates λιθον (ελαβε λιθον εκ του χειμαρρου στρογγυλον)], *a*, and *d* [in 1 Kgdms 17:40, David picks up λίθους λείους]). The Syriac only has *calculos*, MS E provides στρογγυλοῦν, and MS G (*f*) only has λίθον or its equivalent (as does also Slav in *d*). Burchard does not provide attestations for ἐκ τοῦ χειμάρρου in Bu/F 27:2 (which implies uniformity among the manuscript categories), but I can verify that the phrase appears in the following: Syr, MS 436 (L2), *f* (MSS FW and G), MS E (ἀπὸ τοῦ χειμάρρου), *a*, and *d*. In Bu/F 27:4, Benjamin commands to give him λίθους ἐκ τοῦ χειμάρρου (or its equivalent) in all the manuscript categories (including Mc). Burchard provides no variants for πατάσσω (to strike) in Bu/F 27:2, which implies it is used across the manuscript categories. It is attested in Syr, MS 436 (L2), *f* (MSS FW and G), MS E, Mc (palimpsest M), *a*, and *d*. Finally, the phrase, ἔπεσεν ἐπὶ τὴν γῆν, appears in all manuscript categories except for *d* (which only mentions that Pharaoh's son falls [ἔπεσεν] from his horse) (Batiffol, *Le Livre de la Prière d'Aseneth*, 81 [MS A]; Brooks, *Historia ecclesiastica Zachariae Rhetori*, 37; Burchard, *Joseph und Aseneth*, 315–16; Fink, *Joseph und Aseneth*, 43 [M] and 323 [L2]; Philonenko, *Joseph et Aséneth*, 214; and Wright, "After Antiquity," 2:219, 263). See also Delling, "Einwirkungen der Sprache der Septuaginta," 51.

116. All the manuscript categories except for MS E provide ἔδραμεν ἐπ'αὐτὸν βενιαμίν or equivalent, and all the categories but Syriac and MS E provide καὶ ἔλαβε τὴν ῥομφαίαν αὐτοῦ or equivalent. Concerning the latter phrase, the Syriac conveys a similar action (*Et Beniamin ad eum accurrit, et gladium filii Pharaonis strinxit eumque in pectore ferire volebat* [Brooks, *Historia ecclesiastica Zachariae Rhetori*, 38–39]), and MS E abbreviates much of ch. 29, only providing vv. 7–9. Also, it appears that the Armenian may give the sense that Benjamin unsheathes *his* sword, not that of Pharaoh's son. The rest of the manuscript categories that attest to this scene clarify that Benjamin had no sword himself (providing some equivalent to what Burchard and

David, for when he strikes down Goliath with the stone, he runs over to him and takes Goliath's sword (ἔδραμεν Δαυιδ καὶ ἐπέστη ἐπ'αὐτὸν καὶ ἔλαβεν τὴν ῥομφαίαν αὐτοῦ [1 Kgdms 17:51]). Unlike David's reaction to Goliath, however, Benjamin does not slay Pharaoh's son, which is a point I will discuss in the next chapter.

Another septuagintal connection is demonstrated by Aseneth's engagement with the angel, which reveals literary echoes of divine encounters in the Septuagint. In chapter 14, the messenger's address ("Aseneth, Aseneth") and her response ("Here I am") are reminiscent of scenes in Gen 22 and 1 Kgdms 3 (cf. καὶ ἐκάλεσαν αὐτὴν ... καὶ Ἀσενὲθ Ἀσενέθ. καὶ εἶπεν· ἰδοὺ ἐγώ κύριε [Bu/F 14:6–7] and καὶ ἐκάλεσεν αὐτὸν ἄγγελος κυρίου ... καὶ εἶπεν αὐτῷ Αβρααμ, Αβρααμ. ὁ δὲ εἶπεν ἰδοὺ ἐγώ [LXX Gen 22:11] and καὶ ἐκάλεσαν κύριος Σαμουηλ Σαμουηλ· καὶ εἶπεν ἰδοὺ ἐγώ [1 Kgdms 3:4].)[117] Just like Abraham and Samuel, Aseneth is also called more than once by the divine figure.[118]

More prominently, Aseneth's encounter with the angelic figure imitates Daniel's encounter with Gabriel in the book of Daniel. When Aseneth first sets eyes on the angel, he looks like Joseph except his face is like lightning (dominantly provided in the manuscript categories as τὸ πρόσωπον

Fink have: διότι Βενιαμὶν ῥομφαίαν οὐκ εἶχεν). The Armenian may imply, then, that "he took his sword" means that Benjamin took Benjamin's sword. Given that Syr, L2 (MS 436), *f*, *a*, and *d* strongly attest to Benjamin taking the sword of Pharaoh's son, this narrative point is included in the *fabula* (Burchard, *Joseph und Aseneth*, 330–31; and Wright, "After Antiquity," 2:265).

117. The manuscript categories are not uniform in what Burchard and Fink provide for Bu/F 14:4 and 14:6–7; e.g., not all use the verb καλέω or its equivalent both times and not all have the angel repeat Aseneth's name both times he calls her. All but the Syriac, however, provide in some way what I have quoted from 14:6–7 (Burchard, *Joseph und Aseneth*, 177–78). Since the Syriac is missing folios that would have covered Bu/F 13:15 τῆς χάριτός—16:7 βάδιζε, it is unclear what it originally preserved. In Gen 22:1, God also says, "Abraham, Abraham," but the use of εἶπεν instead of ἐκάλεσαν weakens the literal association (although the general association would have likely been identified by listeners/readers familiar with Gen 22). See also Kraemer, *When Aseneth Met Joseph*, 34; 47 n. 56; 59.

118. Most of the manuscript categories refer to the angel calling a "second" time (ἐκ δευτέρου in Arm, *f* [MSS FW and L1], *c*, and *d*; πάλιν ἐκ δευτέρου in MS G [*f*] and *a*; and *iterum* in L2) (cf. LXX Gen 22:15 with δεύτερον), but MS E refers to a third time (ἐκ τρίτου), perhaps echoing 1 Kgdms 2/1 Sam 2 (MT) (cf. 1 Kgdms 2:8, which has ἐν τρίτῳ). The Syriac folios for this section are missing (see above note) (Burchard, *Joseph und Aseneth*, 174, 178).

αὐτοῦ ἦν ὡς ἀστραπή, or its equivalent), his eyes are like the sun's rays/ light, his hair like a flame of fire, and his extremities like glowing metal (*Asen.* 14:9).[119] This description of the angel shares close affinities with the

---

119. The phrase, "his face was the appearance of lightning" (τὸ πρόσωπον αὐτοῦ ἦν ὡς ἀστραπή or its equivalent) is attested across all manuscript categories that provide ch. 14 (so not Syriac, see above note); the phrase appears in Arm, L2, *f* (MS G and L1), MS E, *c*, *a*, and *d*. Manuscripts F and W from *f* do not attest to Bu/F 14:8 τὰ ῥήματά μου–11. The phrase, "his eyes were like the light/ray of the sun," is attested in all manuscript categories except for MS E and the Syriac (but see above). Both Burchard and Fink provide the phrase, ὡς φέγγος ἡλίου, which is attested in *c*, *a*, and *d*; L2 refers to *lumen solis*, and Arm and L1 (*f*) refer to the sun's rays ("wie Strahlen der Sonne" and *radius solis*, respectively). The *fabula* settles on the general reference only and not on particular terms. I am presuming that the phrase, "hairs of his head was like a flame of fire," appears to be attested in all manuscript categories except for MS E and the Syriac. Burchard provides no indication of variations here, but the notations indicate that MS E lacks any mention in 14:9 from καὶ οἱ ὀφθαλμοὶ to τῶν ποδῶν αὐτοῦ (in Burchard's text). I can confirm that the phrase is attested in L2 (MSS 435&); *f* (MS G and L1); *c* (Mc), *a*, and *d* (Batiffol, *Le Livre de la Prière d'Aseneth*, 59 [MS A] and 102 [L1]; Fink, *Joseph und Aseneth*, 239; Philonenko, *Joseph et Aséneth*, 178; and Wright, "After Antiquity," 2:108). Both Burchard and Fink provide an additional modifier to the "hairs of his head." The angel's hair was either like a flame of fire "that is kindled in a window" (or some sort of opening) (ὑπολαμπάδος καιομένης, attested only in MS A from family *a* and provided by Burchard), or like a flame of fire "that is kindled by a torch" (ὑπὸ λαμπάδος, attested in *c* and MS P [family *a*] and provided by Fink). Manuscript 436 of L2 mentions a "torch" (*facula*), but the image describes the angel's hands and feet, not his hair (*et sicut a facula scintille emicabant a manibus et pedibus eius*). Regardless of placement, the modifying image is lacking in several manuscript categories (Arm, *f*, MS E, and *d*), and so I do not include it in the *fabula*. Burchard promotes the change that Fink makes to her text, and he rightfully advises that the possible meaning of "torch" for ὑπολαμπάς be removed from Denis's concordance as well as Bauer's and Lampe's Greek-English lexicons (*Joseph und Aseneth*, 180). All manuscript categories but Syriac (missing folios) and MS E (which abbreviates the description) mention the hot glow of the angel's hands and feet. Of the categories that mention this description, all but *f* describe the image of glowing iron (but there is only one manuscript [MS G] in family *f* that attests to this image; MSS F and W lack 14:8–11 and L1 stops at the flaming hair [Batiffol, *Le Livre de la Prière d'Aseneth*, 102]). Burchard and Fink provide, "like iron that is shining from a fire" (ὥσπερ σίδηρος ἐκ πυρὸς ἀπολάμπων), which comes from *c* and *a*. The Armenian refers to "glowing" iron ("wie Eisen glühendgemachtes"); L2 and Slavonic (*d*) refer to ignited iron (*tamquam ferrum* [+ *candens*, MS 436] *cum ab igne flagrat*, and "wie Eisen entzündent (durch) Feuer," respectively), and the only witness attesting to this phrase from family *f* (MS G) just mentions that his hands and feet were like fire (ὁμοίως ὡς τὸ πῦρ). So, the reference to "fire" is most common, and "iron" is also dominant (Burchard, *Joseph und Aseneth*, 179–80; and Fink, *Joseph und Aseneth*, 181, 293).

description of Gabriel in chapter 10 of LXX/OG Daniel.[120] Gabriel's face was "like the appearance of lightning" (καὶ τὸ πρόσωπον αὐτοῦ ὡσεὶ ὅρασις ἀστραπῆς [OG/Th]); his eyes were "like flaming torches" (καὶ οἱ ὀφθαλμοὶ αὐτοῦ ὡσεὶ λαμπάδες πυρός [OG/Th]); and his arms and feet (legs [Th]) were "like the appearance of gleaming bronze" (καὶ οἱ βραχίονες αὐτοῦ καὶ οἱ πόδες ὡσεὶ χαλκὸς ἐξαστράπτων [Th: οἱ βραχίονες αὐτοῦ καὶ τὰ σκέλη ὡς ὅρασις χαλκοῦ στίλβοντος) (OG/Th Dan 10:6). As Gerhard Delling notes, both texts describe the angel's appearance in the same order (face, eyes, and extremities/limbs), and the descriptions share very close affinities (the appearance of lightning [ἀστραπή], fire-like effects, and glowing metal).[121]

What is more, the entire encounter of Aseneth with the angel echoes similar scenes between Daniel and Gabriel (and even between Daniel and God). When Aseneth sees the bright manifestation in the sky, she falls on her face (ἔπεσεν ἐπὶ πρόσωπον, or its equivalent), and after the angel speaks to her, she looks and sees a man (εἶδε καὶ ἰδοὺ ἀνήρ, or equivalent) before her, looking in every way like Joseph except for the gleaming and lightning flashes explained above (Bu/F 14:3 and 14:9).[122] In response to the angel's appearance, Aseneth looks and falls upon her face once more (Bu/F

---

120. Delling, "Einwirkungen der Sprache der Septuaginta," 48. The angelic figure in Dan 10 is likely Gabriel (John J. Collins, *Daniel: A Commentary on the Book of Daniel*, Hermeneia [Minneapolis: Fortress, 1993], 373; Louis Francis Hartman and Alexander A. Di Lella, *The Book of Daniel*, AB 23 [Garden City, NY: Doubleday, 1978], 279).

121. Delling, "Einwirkungen der Sprache der Septuaginta," 48.

122. All manuscript categories except for the Syriac (missing folios) provide that Aseneth fell (ἔπεσεν, or its equivalent) toward the ground. All categories except for Syriac and family *c* mention that she fell upon her face. In family *c*, however, after the angel speaks to Aseneth (14:6–8), Aseneth "raises her face" (ἐπάρασα δὲ τὸ πρόσωπον), which implies that she had her face down when she fell down in 14:3. For "she looked, and see, a man" (εἶδε καὶ ἰδοὺ ἀνήρ), all manuscript categories except the Syriac (missing folios) provide εἶδε or equivalent. Burchard provides no annotations for ἰδού, but given the detailed information he provides for this verse and that the more accessible witnesses attest to it, I am assuming ἰδού is well-attested (except for Syriac). The Greek word or its equivalent appears in L2, *f* (MS G and L1), MS E, M*c* (*c*), *a*, and *d*. For the word, "man" (ἀνήρ), Burchard only provides variant readings and witnesses that lack the reference; L2 (MS 436, *vir*), *f* (MS G and L1), MS E, *c* (M*c*), *a*, and *d* all attest to the word, so I am assuming that it is well-attested among the manuscript categories (minus the Syriac) (Batiffol, *Le Livre de la Prière d'Aseneth*, 59 [MS A] and 102 [L1]; Fink, *Joseph und Aseneth*, 292; Philonenko, *Joseph et Aséneth*, 178; and Wright, "After Antiquity," 2:107 and 253) (Burchard, *Joseph und Aseneth*, 176, 179).

14:10).¹²³ Similarly, in LXX/OG Dan 10:5, Daniel looks and sees a man (εἶδον καὶ ἰδοὺ ἄνθρωπος [ἀνήρ Th]) before him, dressed in linen and also depicted as bright as lightning and gleaming like hot metal (see above). In response to the angel's appearance, Daniel falls upon his face (ἐγὼ ἤμην πεπτωκὼς ἐπὶ πρόσωπόν μου [OG 10:8]) or at least, has his face to the ground (πρόσωπόν μου ἐπί τὴν γῆν [OG/Th 10:8]). In chapter 10, Daniel's response to Gabriel repeats how he reacted when Gabriel comes to him in chapter 8; there, Daniel also falls on his face when Gabriel approaches him (ἔπεσα [Th: πίπτω] ἐπὶ πρόσωπόν μου [OG/Th 8:17]). In fact, the reaction of "falling on one's face" is a common phrase in the Septuagint, appearing almost fifty times and vastly more than in any other Greek literary source before the second century CE.¹²⁴ Notably, several times the phrase is used when a character responds to encountering an angel or the Israelite God (Abraham in LXX Gen 17:3, 17; Manoah and his wife in LXX Judg 13:20 [Alexandrinus and Vaticanus]; Ezekiel in LXX Ezek 1:28; and of course, the Daniel examples above).

After Aseneth is bent down on the ground, the angel tells her "not to fear" (some form of φοβέω or its equivalent), to get up, and "I will tell my words" to her (λαλήσω τὰ ῥήματά μου or its equivalent) (*Aseneth* 14:8 and/or 14:11).¹²⁵ Likewise, in LXX/OG Dan 10, Gabriel consoles Daniel

---

123. All the manuscript categories except for Syriac (missing folios) provide some form of Aseneth "looking" (with some form of ὁράω or its equivalent being most dominant; family *c* appears to be unusual with its attestation of καθορῶσα). All but MS E and Syriac narrate that Aseneth fell "upon her face" (MS E has Aseneth "fall at his feet," ἔπεσεν πρὸς τοὺς πόδας αὐτοῦ) but there is no agreement as to the phrase that follows. Burchard and Fink provide, "at his feet on the ground" (ἐπὶ τοὺς πόδας αὐτοῦ ἐπὶ τὴν γῆν), which is only attested in MSS 435& of L2 (*ad pedes eius in pavimentum*). The Armenian only mentions the ground ("auf die Erde"); L1 (the only witness from *f* attesting to some form of this phrase); the Greek witnesses MS E and *d* just mention the angel's feet (*ad pedes eius* and τοὺς πόδας αὐτοῦ, respectively); and *c* and *a* narrate how Aseneth was unable to stand on *her* feet (μηδ᾽ [μὴ *c*] ὅλως [> *c*] δυνηθεῖσα στῆναι ἐπὶ [ὑπὸ *c*] τοὺς πόδας αὐτῆς). Although Burchard does not provide annotations for "fell" (ἔπεσεν in his text), it appears to be attested across all manuscript categories except for Syriac. The verb or its equivalent is attested in L2 (MSS 435&), *f* (MS G and L1), MS E, M*c* (c), *a*, and *d* (Batiffol, *Le Livre de la Prière d'Asenath*, 59 [MS A] and 102 [L1]; Fink, *Joseph und Aseneth*, 293; Philonenko, *Joseph et Aséneth*, 178; and Wright, "After Antiquity," 2:108 and 253) (Burchard, *Joseph und Aseneth*, 180–81).

124. According to TLG, out of roughly seventy attestations of πίπτω ἐπὶ πρόσωπον dated prior to the second century CE, the Septuagint provides forty-eight of them.

125. The phrase "not to fear" (using φοβέω or its equivalent) is attested in all man-

by helping him up and telling him to understand the words he is telling Daniel (λαλήσω) and "not to fear" (μὴ φοβοῦ) (OG/Th: 10:11–12). Gabriel then proceeds to reveal God's plan to Daniel. He explains in detail the imperial rise of the Ptolemaic and Seleucid dynasties, the time of persecution under Antiochus IV Epiphanes, and the ultimate salvation for the righteous (Dan 10:14–12:4). At that time, Michael will appear, and "everyone who is found written in the book" will be delivered (OG: ὃς ἂν εὑρεθῇ ἐγγεγραμμένος ἐν τῷ βιβλίῳ; Th: πᾶς ὁ εὑρεθεὶς γεγραμμένος ἐν τῇ βίβλῳ; LXX/OG Dan 12:1). In *Aseneth*, after the angel consoles her, he tells her to change her attire and after she returns, he promises that her name is written in the book of the living/life (γράφω ἐν [τῇ] βίβλῳ τῶν ζώντων [ζωῆς], or its equivalent; Bu/F 15:4), and he outlines the benefits of her future.[126] She will partake in the practices associated with Joseph's god, she will be called "City of Refuge" (πόλις καταφυγῆς), and she will marry Joseph (Bu/F 14:12–15:10).[127] Although the particulars promised to Daniel differ from what Aseneth receives, both protagonists receive special information from an angel about their respective futures.

The *fabula* of *Aseneth*, then, exhibits an extensive use of the lexical and literary design of septuagintal literature. It demonstrates the prose tech-

---

uscript categories except for Syriac (missing folios). In Bu/F 14:8 and 14:11, Burchard and Fink provide, "arise and stand" (ἀνάστηθι καὶ στῆθι), but the manuscript categories are not uniform in presenting this couplet (once or even twice). All the manuscript categories except for the Syriac have the angel tell Aseneth to "arise" (ἀνάστηθι or its equivalent) at least once, so the *fabula* simply includes this verb. At least once (in Bu/F 14:8 and many categories repeat in Bu/F 14:11), all manuscript categories except the Syriac and *d* attest to "my words" (τὰ ῥήματά μου). Burchard provides no variants or gaps for "I will speak" (λαλήσω), but I assume that the verb is well-attested among the manuscript categories (except for Syriac). The verb or its equivalent appears in L2, *f* (MSS FW, G, and L1), MS E, Mc (*c*), *a*, and *d* (Batiffol, *Le Livre de la Prière d'Aseneth*, 59 [MS A] and 102 [L1]; Fink, *Joseph und Aseneth*, 292-93; Philonenko, *Joseph et Aséneth*, 178-80; and Wright, "After Antiquity," 2:107 and 253) (Burchard, *Joseph und Aseneth*, 179-181).

126. All manuscript categories except for Syriac (missing folios) attest to some form of γράφω or its equivalent and to the phrase "in the book of the living/life" (ἐν [τῇ] βίβλῳ τῶν ζώντων [ζωῆς] or its equivalent) (Burchard, *Joseph und Aseneth*, 188-89).

127. The phrase, "city of refuge" in 15:7 (πόλις καταφυγῆς or its equivalent) is attested in all manuscript categories except for Syriac (missing folios) (Burchard, *Untersuchungen zu Joseph und Asenath*, 56; and Burchard, *Joseph und Aseneth*, 190-92). See below and the next chapter for further discussion.

3. The *Fabula* of Aseneth   181

niques found in septuagintal narratives (καὶ ἐγένετο, ἰδού), and it shares vocabulary and phrases of septuagintal literature (such as εὐλογέω, expressions with φοβέω, and the verbal construction with cognate noun). It alludes to stories in the Septuagint, not only by referring to specific scenes but also by repeating particular vocabulary that links *Aseneth* to those stories (such as προσκυνέω and ἀνταποδίδωμι in LXX Gen 37–50; μιαίνω in LXX Gen 34; παιδάριον, λίθος ἐκ τοῦ χειμάρρου, πατάσσω, and τρέχω in 1 Kgdms 17; πρόσωπον [like] ἀστραπή, ἔπεσεν ἐπὶ πρόσωπον, λαλῆσω, and μὴ φοβοῦ in LXX/OG Dan 10; and γράφω ἐν τῷ βιβλίῳ in LXX/OG Dan 12). It even constructs its plot off of assumed knowledge of particular characters or events in septuagintal texts (such as the sons of the slaves, Bilhah and Zilpah, and the avenging actions by Levi and Simeon). There are a few more images and terms that are strongly attested among the manuscript categories, and so I also include them as part of the *fabula*. I will close this chapter by briefly discussing each of the following: ἀκτίς (Bu/F 5:5); ἥλιος (Bu/F 6:2); καταφεύγω/καταφυγή (15:7); ὕβρις (Bu/F 23:14; 24:9; 28:4, 14); βασίλισσα (Bu/F 28:2); δέομαι (Bu/F 28:4); διάδημα (Bu/F 3:6 for Aseneth, Bu/F 29:9 for Joseph) and βασιλεύω (Bu/F 29:9). This is not an exhaustive vocabulary list; I include them in the *fabula* because of the reasonable probability that they were part of the initial telling of the story, and in the next chapter, I will explain in more detail their importance for contextualizing *Aseneth*. For now, I will outline the particulars of each word in the manuscript evidence.

In chapter 5, we see Joseph in this story for the first time. He enters Pentephres's complex riding the second chariot of Pharaoh (cf. LXX Gen 41:43), which is made of gold (Bu/F 5:5). Joseph is cloaked in purple material, he wears a crown with rays (ἀκτίς) extending from it, and he holds a royal staff in his hand.[128] In the next chapter, I will discuss in more detail the regal references to Joseph, but the particular use of the word "rays" (ἀκτίς)

---

128. The particular word for "rays" (ἀκτίς or equivalent) appears in the following categories: Syr, L2, *f* (MSS FW), *c* (Mc), *a*, and *d*. The Armenian provides a slightly different phrase, which nonetheless implies radiant beams ("goldene strahlende Figuren"), similar to the Syriac, which is most explicit in associating the rays with the sun (*ut radii solis fulgentes*). Manuscript E lacks the full radiant-like description of Joseph's crown in Burchard's/Fink's texts, but given the strong attestation of "rays" in the rest of the categories, I include the term in the *fabula* (Burchard, *Joseph und Aseneth*, 101). See notes to *fabula* 9 above for textual details regarding the other regal references in Bu/F 5.

upon the crown of a man who commands a chariot immediately reminds of Helios, the sun god.[129] The association is not lost on Aseneth either, who upon watching Joseph's entrance, refers to him as ἥλιος (helios/Helios) in a chariot (Bu/F 6:2).[130] The angel who looks much like Joseph (Bu/F 14:9) also appears to ride a heavenly chariot (Bu/F 17:8), which echoes Joseph's appearance as described by Aseneth. In verse 7 of chapter 15, the angel gives Aseneth a new name, "City of Refuge" (πόλις καταφυγῆς) and tells her that people will seek refuge in her (καταφεύξονται). The angel does not elucidate further what this title means for Aseneth, but it is well-attested among the manuscript categories.[131] In the latter half of the narrative, several times characters refer to the effects of violent actions on a victim as *hybris* (ὕβρις in Bu/F 23:14; 24:9; 28:4, 14).[132] By the Hellenistic period,

---

129. Several have made the correlation between Helios and Joseph's crown: Burchard, "Joseph and Aseneth," 208 n. k; Philonenko, *Joseph et Aséneth*, 79–80; and Kraemer, *When Aseneth Met Joseph*, 156–67.

130. In Burchard's and Fink's text, Aseneth says the following, καὶ νῦν ἰδοὺ ὁ ἥλιος ἐκ τοῦ οὐρανοῦ ἥκει πρὸς ἡμᾶς ἐν τῷ ἅρματι αὐτοῦ ("and now, the sun/Sun from heaven has come to us in his chariot"). Although the manuscript categories tweak this phrase a bit (Syr, MSS 435& [L2], and MSS FW [*f*] do not have "from heaven"), all the categories refer to Joseph as ἥλιος, and all but MS E appear to mention him as ἥλιος on a chariot. For the reference to a chariot, Burchard only mentions variant readings (Arm lacks "his" in reference to the chariot, and the Syriac says "from" instead of "in"). I take this to mean that "chariot" is well-attested, and it can also be confirmed in Syr, L2, *f* (MSS FW and L1), Mc (*c*), *a*, and *d* (Batiffol, *Le Livre de la Prière d'Asenath*, 46 [MS A] and 94 [L1]; Brooks, *Historia ecclesiastica Zachariae Rhetori*, 18; Fink, *Joseph und Aseneth*, 269; Philonenko, *Joseph et Aséneth*, 150; and Wright, "After Antiquity," 2:37) (Burchard, *Joseph und Aseneth*, 105).

131. All manuscript categories except the Syriac (missing folios) attest to "City of Refuge" (πόλις καταφυγῆς or its equivalent). The verb καταφεύγω or its equivalent appears in all manuscript categories except for Syriac as well; it is attested in Arm, L2, *f* (MSS FW, G, and L1), MS E, *a*, and *d* (Burchard *Untersuchungen zu Joseph und Aseneth*, 56; Wright, "After Antiquity," 2:118 and 254). (In his critical edition, Burchard does not provide variants for the καταφεύξονται, because it seems that the manuscript categories agree here [*Joseph und Aseneth*, 191].)

132. Disregarding Mc (given its constraints in missing folios for ch. 23), all manuscript categories except for Syr refer to the rape of Dinah as ὕβρις and/or as an action of ὑβρίζω or its linguisitic equivalent (Bu/F 23:14): Arm, MS 436 (L2, *iniurias*), *f* (MSS FW and G), MS E, *a*, and *d* (Burchard, *Joseph und Aseneth*, 288; Fink, *Joseph und Aseneth*, 321; and Wright, "After Antiquity," 2:192 and 260). The Syriac abbreviates Levi's summary of their attack that emphasizes the brothers' avenging actions: *His duobus gladiis ignominiam Dinae sororis nostrae a Sichimitis ulti sumus* (Brooks, *Historia ecclesiastica*

3. The *Fabula* of *Aseneth*   183

this was a recognizable legal term, and I will explain in the next chapter its significance to the context of Hellenistic Egypt. At the end of the narrative, the sons of Bilhah and Zilpah appeal to Aseneth for protection from their brothers (Bu/F 28:1–4), and in particular, they call her "queen" (βασίλισσα) and beg (δεόμεθα) her to help them in their plight.[133] Next chapter, I will explain in more detail the importance of these terms as well. The final two Greek words that I highlight here also relate to the royal implications of Aseneth and Joseph. In chapter 3, when Aseneth prepares to meet her parents, she wears a diadem on her head (διάδημα or its equivalent), and at the end of the chapter, Joseph receives Pharaoh's diadem (διάδημα or its equivalent) and then passes it on to Pharaoh's male kin after forty-eight years (Bu/F 3:6 and 29:9, respectively).[134] Finally, all the manuscript cat-

---

Zachariae Rhetori, 34). In Bu/F 24:9, Pharaoh's son tells the sons of Bilhah and Zilpah that Joseph referred to his being sold into slavery as *hybris*. The term ὕβρις or its equivalent appears in Arm, L2 (MS 436), *f* (MSS FW and G), and *a*. Manuscript E provides a paraphrase (simply referring to the sons of Bilhah and Zilpah doing evil/harm, κακία), and the folio for this scene is missing from M (*c* ends at ch. 16). Both here and in Bu/F 23:14, the Syriac provides *ulciscar* when the speaker refers to avenging an action that the remainder of the manuscript categories define as *hybris*. The Syriac appears to be more in line with the other categories in Bu/F 28 (see below), but given the broad attestation of ὕβρις in chs. 23 and 24, I lean toward including the term in the *fabula* here as well (Burchard, *Joseph und Aseneth*, 295; and Wright, "After Antiquity," 2:261). In Bu/F 28:4, the sons of Bilhah and Zilpah refer to their actions against Aseneth as *hybris* that their brothers will avenge. The term ὕβρις or its equivalent appears in Syr, Arm, L2 (MS 436), *f* (MSS FW and G), MS E, *a*, and *d*; the folio with palimpsest M ends at ανταπεδωκεν ημιν from Bu/F 28:3, so it is unverified if Mc attests to the word (Burchard, *Joseph und Aseneth*, 322–23). In Bu/F 28:14, Aseneth refers to the actions of the sons of Bilhah and Zilpah as *hybris*. Since Burchard provides no information in his critical edition about the attestations for the term ὕβρις or its equivalent, I am assuming that it is well-represented among the manuscript categories. I can confirm it appears in Syr, L2 (MS 436), *f* (MSS FW and G), *a*, and *d*. Manuscript E abbreviates this chapter, providing only 28:1–4 and 7, and we lack folio from palimpsest M that preserves anything from Bu/F 28:3 (after ανταπεδωκεν ημιν) to 29:3 (supposedly beginning at κακον αντι κακου) (Brooks, *Historia ecclesiastica Zachariae Rhetori*, 38; Burchard, *Joseph und Aseneth*, 328; Fink, *Joseph und Aseneth*, 44, 324; and Wright, "After Antiquity," 2:264–65).

133. All the manuscript categories except for *d* attest to βασίλισσα and its equivalent; given the tendency of *d* to abbreviate the text, I am inclined to consider βασίλισσα as part of the fabula. All the manuscript categories attest to δέω or its equivalent (Burchard, *Joseph und Aseneth*, 322).

134. The following manuscript categories attest to διάδημα or its equivalent in Bu/F 3:6: Arm, L2, *f*, E, *c*, *a*, and *d*. The Syriac attests to *klyl'*, which Burchard suggests

egories that conclude this narrative in a decipherable way (so neither the Armenian nor Mc) provide that Joseph reigned (ἐβασίλευσεν or its equivalent) in Egypt (Bu/F 29:9).[135]

The Implications of a *Fabula* of *Aseneth*

Despite the difficulties of creating one reconstructed text of *Aseneth*, it remains possible to identify a detailed storyline, literary style, and particular vocabulary of this story that the manuscript categories share in common. I have referred to this selection of a common narrative and its traits the *fabula* of *Aseneth*, building off of Russian formalists' understanding of the term and Thomas's application of it in her study of the Acts of Peter. My proposed *fabula* derives from careful attention to the individual manuscripts as best as I can discern from publications of annotated, reconstructed texts and/or reproductions of individual witnesses. In this chapter, I outlined an extensive *fabula* that not only includes a detailed storyline but also connects with narrative styles and content in the Septuagint. It is noteworthy that storytelling and scenes from the Septuagint

---

could refer to either *coronam* or *diadema*, but it is possible that the Syriac translated some form of "crown" (perhaps τιάραν). Nevertheless, given the strong attestation of διάδημα in all other manuscript categories, I am inclined to include διάδημα in the *fabula*. Burchard and Fink also provide a second headpiece in their reconstructions because several manuscripts provide it, but this second headpiece is not as well-attested or even identical in the manuscripts. The following manuscript categories provide two headpieces: for the Armenian, Burchard gives "Kopfputz" (which he surmises translated τιάραν) and διάδημα; in L2, MS 436 provides *tyaram* and *diademate*, and MSS 435& give *mitram* and *dyademate*; and families c and a provide τίαραν and διάδημα. The rest of the manuscript categories only attest to one headpiece, and all the Greek manuscripts here provide διάδημα: f, MS E, d, and possibly Syr (see comment above). For the *fabula*, I am focusing on the most common headpiece among the witnesses (Burchard, *Joseph und Aseneth*, 89; and Fink, *Joseph und Aseneth*, 172, 264–65). For the evidence for διάδημα in ch. 29, see footnote to the *fabula* plot 54 above.

135. As discussed in ch. 2, one of the most reliable Armenian witnesses (MS 332 which constitutes Burchard's classification of Arm[f]) ends at Bu/F 28:13; the remaining witness groups substitute Bu/F 25:3–27:11 with a pastiche of passages from these chapters, with groups Arm[c] and Arm[g] ending at Bu/F 27:11 and the rest ending at Bu/F 29:7. The verb βασιλεύω or its equivalent, however, is attested in the rest of the manuscript categories save Mc (Burchard, *Joseph und Aseneth*, 335). Palimpsest M indicates that it concluded the narrative at 29:9, but the particulars are indecipherable (Fink, *Joseph und Aseneth*, 38–44).

are interwoven tightly into the *fabula*, and this core feature points to an origin where septuagintal texts and reinterpretations of those texts were studied and discussed. Given the extent of what the manuscript categories share, I also identified particular vocabulary that offers clues to the context of *Aseneth*'s beginnings. My proposed *fabula* is not meant to be exhaustive, but it serves as the basis for hypothesizing the earliest location for the composition of this story. As I will argue in the next chapter, this narrative makes most sense as a Judean composition written within the landscape and social environment of Ptolemaic and early Roman Egypt. From this time period, we have evidence of Judean intellectuals studying septuagintal texts, reworking them, and composing new material from them, and the fragmentary works of Artapanus provide a helpful comparison with the *fabula* of *Aseneth* in this regard. There are also particular references in the *fabula* that are best understood in Hellenistic Egypt, which leads to the conclusion that *Aseneth* began as a Judean composition there.

4
Aseneth and the Landscape of Ptolemaic and Early Roman Egypt

What has led many scholars to propose that *Aseneth* was composed in Hellenistic Egypt still holds with the *fabula* of *Aseneth*. The story not only takes place in Egypt but also depicts varying relationships between Egyptians and Hebrews, reflecting a cultural landscape in the pharaonic past that could imply similar negotiations of *ethnos* identity in Hellenistic Egypt. The narrative also addresses the challenge of maintaining devotion to the Israelite God outside of the Judean, ancestral homeland, which although was not a challenge that was exclusive to Judeans in Egypt, it was nonetheless a reality that they faced. Yet, there is more that can be said as to why this story so aptly fits a Judean origin in Hellenistic Egypt. During the Ptolemaic period, several non-Egyptians recast their ancestral identities through the lens of Egyptian traditions, and *Aseneth* reflects such an effort from a Judean perspective. This impulse to connect to the pharaonic or primeval Egyptian past was attractive to many, among them the Ptolemaic court, Alexandrian intellectuals, and Judean writers in Egypt. Oftentimes their efforts produced new discourses that could have only developed through the collision and confluence of diverse cultural traditions; examples include the dynastic cult of Arsinoe II in Egyptian temples, the evolution of the Serapis cult in Memphis, Hecataeus's presentation of Sesostris, and Artapanus's characterization of Moses. But for these new discourses to effectively communicate to people who lived in the diverse setting of Egypt, they needed to be rooted in everyday experience. The highly ritualized and public activity of Egyptian temples throughout the *chora* and its reflected importance even in Alexandria provided ways for all inhabitants of Egypt (not just Egyptians) to learn about key Egyptian narratives and traditions. This activity also promoted multiple discourses about Ptolemaic royalty, which then were repeated through images on coins and buildings as well as in common administrative texts. *Aseneth* builds upon such daily experiences in Egypt and carves out a new ancestral tradition for Judeans in Egypt. I will argue in this chapter that the *fabula* of *Aseneth* creates a new discourse about Judean heritage in Egypt by utilizing Greek literary techniques and Ptolemaic strategies of legitimation and power, by borrowing Ptolemaic legal language and Egyptian images, and by rooting its narrative in septuagintal compositions to communicate the greatness of the Judean past in Egypt and to construct ways for Judeans to negotiate their everyday life there.

This chapter is divided into two parts. First, I argue that *Aseneth* is best understood within the intellectual, narrative tradition that Greek-speaking inhabitants, including Judeans, utilized in Egypt. The legacy of pharaonic Egypt was renowned, and Greek writers sought to insert their ancestral traditions into the broader landscape of Egyptian history, which inevitably combined these writers' ancestral stories with their interpretations of contemporary Egyptian (and Ptolemaic-Egyptian) traditions. Through this activity, they produced new, self-ascribed identities that distinguished them in Egypt from those in their homelands. In this section, I focus on the writings of Hecataeus of Abdera and Artapanus and discuss the implications of comparing the two works with *Aseneth*. In the second part of the chapter, I focus on key touch points in the *Aseneth fabula* that are best understood in the landscape of Hellenistic Egypt to illustrate how *Aseneth* makes most sense as a Judean narrative from Egypt.

Rewriting Ancestral Identity into the Pharaonic Past

Even before the rise of Alexander, Egypt held sway in the minds of many. Certainly Near Eastern and Mediterranean powers coveted its economic and political assets, but Herodotus perhaps encapsulates best the awe outsiders felt when witnessing the grandeur of Egyptian buildings, the full-scale production of its rituals, and the intellectual traditions of its priests and scribes. In book 2 of the *Historiae*, Herodotus discusses in detail Egyptian religious practices, describes some of Egypt's immense structures, records the extensive chronicles of the Egyptian educated elite on the history of Egypt, and clearly identifies Egypt as impressive. For one thing, Egypt's religious traditions were "more than any other people," and, from among all those whom Herodotus interviewed, the Egyptian elite were the most skilled in preserving memory of the past (*Hist.* 2.37, 77). This is not to say that Greek writers always referred positively to Egyptians

4. *Aseneth* and the Landscape of Ptolemaic and Early Roman Egypt 189

and their traditions (as evident in Aeschylus's *Suppliants* and Euripides's *Helen*), and as Phiroze Vasunia has demonstrated, Herodotus's configuration of Egyptian space makes room for a dominant, Greek voice.[1] But Herodotus the traveler, the one who made contact with Egyptian intellectuals, is notably different than his Greek peers. In coming into contact with Egyptian space, time, and tradition, Herodotus's view changed. As Ian Moyer has argued, Herodotus's historical consciousness as a Greek in the fifth century BCE was sparked by his interactions with Egyptian priests, whose own consciousness of *their* antiquity led Herodotus to plot Greek traditions after Egyptian ones.[2] The name of Heracles, for example, hailed from Egypt as did many of the names of Greek gods, and several Greek customs apparently derived from Egypt (*Hist.* 2, esp. §§2–3, 43–64, and 99–182). Herodotus's writings, then, demonstrate a tension between a respect for Egyptian customs and traditions, on the one hand, and a desire to connect one's foreign identity to Egypt, on the other. By the Ptolemaic period, this tension becomes magnified in the voices of Greek-speaking intellectuals in Egypt, including Judeans.

I will illustrate this tension by primarily focusing on the writings of the Judean author, Artapanus, but I will first provide significant comparative material. Beginning with Herodotus, Greek-educated writers became acquainted with the prowess of an Egyptian king they called Sesostris, and in particular, Artapanus redacted a particular version of the Sesostris tale that Hecataeus of Abdera also knew. I will first trace the development of this tale from Herodotus to Hecataeus to Artapanus, and then I will comment upon the grander designs of Hecataeus's *Aegyptiaca* and Artapanus's Ἰουδαϊκά. The narrative trajectories each writer presents are in alignment with their respective backgrounds, and I argue that *Aseneth* shares a similar methodological approach to that of Artapanus. I close this section articulating my theoretical base for understanding how Greek-educated writers, including Judeans, rescripted their place in Ptolemaic Egypt.

According to Herodotus, Egyptian priests told him about Sesostris's military expeditions, how he had ordered the construction of the temple of Ptah (Hephaestus) and the formation of irrigation canals, and how he had parceled out land ownership and established the Egyptian tax system (*Hist.*

---

1. Vasunia, *The Gift of the Nile: Hellenizing Egypt from Aeschylus to Alexander*, Classics and Contemporary Thought 8 (Berkeley: University of California Press, 2001).
2. Moyer, *Egypt and the Limits of Hellenism*, 42–83. See also Susan Stephens, *Seeing Double*, 44–49.

2.102–109). Herodotus's account derives from Egyptian retellings of a pharaoh named Senwosret, who was portrayed as an ideal king of the Egyptian past and who lay in sharp contrast with the contemporary, Persian rulers.³ Perhaps this tale originated from the histories of Senwosret I or Senwosret III (pharaohs of the Twelfth Dynasty), but by the time of Herodotus's visit, it grew to encompass more. Herodotus conversed with Egyptian priests at a time when they were producing an archaized view of their heritage, which in the face of Persian rule created a form of resistance.⁴ According to the priests, Herodotus tells us, the priest of Ptah had blocked Darius from placing his statue in front of statues of Sesostris and his family in the temple of Ptah, because Darius "had achieved nothing equal to the deeds of Sesostris the Egyptian" and so his statue did not deserve to be placed before that legendary king (§110). Darius, apparently, complied with the priests' demands, which narrates a moment (however fictional) of Persian admission of Egyptian superiority. In Egyptian circles, then, this Sesostris tradition produced an opposing view to foreign rule, and it seemed to have carried meaning for Egyptian elite into the Roman period, as we have hints that Sesostris narratives continued in Demotic script.⁵

Herodotus, though, introduced Sesostris to Greek (and later Roman) intelligentsia who for centuries after were intrigued by the person and the narrative.⁶ One author in particular studied Herodotus's description

---

3. Alan B. Lloyd, *Herodotus, Book II: Commentary 99–182*, EPRO 43, 2nd ed. (Leiden: Brill, 1993), 16–18; Moyer, *Egypt and the Limits of Hellenism*, 42–83; Stephens, *Seeing Double*, 34–36.

4. Moyer, *Egypt and the Limits of Hellenism*, 68–74.

5. Most notably in the fragments of P.Carlsberg 411 and P.Carlsberg 412 (first–second centuries CE) and ostracon Leipzig UB 2217 (suggested date between first century BCE and first century CE) (Kim Ryholt, "A Sesostris Story in Demotic Egyptian and Demotic Literary Exercises [O. Leipzig UB 2217]," in *Honi Soit Qui Mal Y Pense: Studien zum pharaonischen, griechish-römischen und spätantiken Ägypten zu Ehren von Heinz-Josef Thissen*, ed. Hermann Knuf, Christian Leitz, and Daniel von Recklinghausen, OLA 194 [Leuven: Peeters, 2010], 429–38; and Ghislaine Widmir, "Pharaoh Maâ-Rê, Pharaoh Amenemhat and Sesostris: Three Figures from Egypt's Past as Seen in Sources of the Graeco-Roman Period," in *Acts of the Seventh International Conference of Demotic Studies*, ed. Kim Ryholt, CNI 27 [Copenhagen: Museum Tusculanum Press, 2002], 377–93). Hecataeus also mentions that both Greek writers and Egyptian priests and poets provide "conflicting stories" about Sesostris (Diodorus Siculus, *Bib. hist.* 1.53.1).

6. Michel Malaise discusses the bulk of the evidence in, "Sésostris, Pharaon de légende et d'histoire," *CE* 41.82 (1966): 244–72.

4. *Aseneth* and the Landscape of Ptolemaic and Early Roman Egypt   191

of Egypt and extensively expanded the story about Sesostris.⁷ Hecataeus of Abdera lived at the turn of the third century BCE, and he became known as a philosopher and writer.⁸ We know of three of his works, *On*

---

7. On a summary of the evidence, see Gregory E. Sterling, *Historiography and Self-Definition: Josephos, Luke-Acts and Apologetic Historiography*, NovTSup 64 (Leiden: Brill, 1992), 65–69.

8. For an extensive review of the evidence, see Sterling, *Historiography and Self-Definition*, 59–61. At some point in his education, he was associated with Pyrron (Diogenes Laertius, 9.6), but see the more cautious reading by Bazalel Bar-Kochva (*Pseudo-Hecataeus "On the Jews": Legitimizing the Jewish Diaspora*, HCS 21 [Berkeley: University of California Press, 1997], 8 n. 5). Most scholars agree that Hecataeus's *Aegyptiaca* is preserved in book 1 of the *Bibliotheca* by Diodorus Siculus. The fundamental arguments were laid out by Eduard Schwartz, Felix Jacoby, and then expanded upon by Oswyn Murray (Schwartz, "Hekataeos von Teos," *Rheinisches Museum für Philologie* 40 [1885]: 223–62; Jacoby, *FGrHist* 264; Murray, "Hecataeus of Abdera and Pharaonic Kingship," *JEA* 56 [1970]: 145–50). Further defense is provided by Bar-Kochva, *Pseudo-Hecataeus*, 14–15, 289–90; Stanley M. Burstein, "Hecataeus of Abdera's History of Egypt," in *Life in a Multi-Cultural Society: Egypt from Cambyses to Constantine and Beyond*, ed. Janet H. Johnson, SAOC 51 (Chicago: Oriental Institute of the University of Chicago, 1992), 45 n. 1; Oswyn Murray, review of *Book I: A Commentary by Diodorus Siculus* by Anne Burton, *JHS* 95 (1975): 214–15; and Sterling *Historiography and Self-Definition*, 61–64. There has been a growing debate, however, about how much of Hecataeus's work can be detected in that of Diodorus. Anne Burton argues against the broad assumption that Diodorus mostly copies Hecataeus in book 1, but she admits that at least chs. 69–95 are in large part borrowed from Hecataeus (*Diodorus Siculus Book I: A Commentary*, EPRO 29 [Leiden: Brill, 1972]). More recently Kenneth S. Sacks claims that the question about Diodorus's sources has dominated scholarship too much, and he focuses on Diodorus the author (and not the compiler) (*Diodorus Siculus and the First Century* [Princeton: Princeton University Press, 1990]). Sacks, though, does not examine carefully Diodorus's sources for book 1. Most recently, Charles E. Muntz has tried to tackle the issue of whether or not Hecataeus's work can be detected in book 1, but his argument focuses more on the weaknesses of scholarly arguments (especially Murray's) than it promotes a way for understanding the literary design of book 1 ("The Sources of Diodorus Siculus, Book 1," *ClQ* 61.2 [2011]: 574–94). I am sympathetic to the idea of treating Diodorus's work from his perspective, regardless of the sources that he used, but the counteropinions to Hecataeus as a source are not beyond dispute. These scholars do not address the issue of how Artapanus could so clearly be using a source that Diodorus had used; given the fair certainty of Alexander Polyhistor's dating, it seems that Artapanus wrote before Diodorus. I agree with Holgar M. Zellentin that if indeed Diodorus was not using Hecataeus, he inevitably used a source that other intellectuals (like Artapanus) knew ("The End of Jewish Egypt—Artapanus's Second Exodus," in *Antiquity in Antiquity: Jewish and Christian Pasts in the Greco-Roman Period*, ed. Gregg Gardner and Kevin

the *Poetry of Homer and Hesiod*, *On the Hyperboreans*, and *Aegyptiaca* (*On the Egyptians*), the last of which he likely wrote between 320 and 305 BCE, possibly under the patronage of Ptolemy, son of Lagus (who would become Ptolemy I Soter).[9] Hecataeus apparently traveled throughout Egypt and consulted with Egyptian priests, and even though he depended on Herodotus's account, he distanced himself from it in his own work on the Egyptians (Diodorus Siculus, *Bib. hist.* 1.69.7).[10] Hecataeus also improved Herodotus's account; he aligned Herodotus's Egyptian king list more closely to Egyptian chronology; corrected Herodotus's spelling to better reflect Egyptian pronunciation (as Seoösis [Σεσόωσις] more accurately reflects the pronunciation of Senwosre, for example); and expanded some of Herodotus's descriptions.[11]

Looking more closely at Hecataeus's narrative about Sesostris, there are obvious expansions and additions.[12] Hecataeus describes Sesostris's training as a youth and his chosen status as a ruler (Diodorus Siculus, *Bib. hist.* 1.53). Sesostris meticulously chose his troops and treated them well,

---

Lee Osterloh, TSAJ 123 [Tübingen: Mohr Siebeck, 2008], 48–49). For now, then, I am siding with the argument that Hecataeus was a primary source for Diodorus, book 1.10–98, except for the insertions listed in Murray, "Hecataeus of Abdera," 146. See also Alan B. Lloyd who takes issue with Burton's argument on Hecataeus (review of *Diodorus Siculus Book 1: A Commentary*, by Anne Burton," *JEA* 60 [1974]: 287–90); some of Lloyd's critique could be applied to Muntz's recent discussion as well.

9. Murray, "Hecataeus of Abdera," 142–44; Bar-Kochva, *Pseudo-Hecataeus*, 9. Josephus refers to the patronage of Hecataeus under Ptolemy I (*Ag. Ap.* 1.183); Hecataeus was "at once a philosopher and a highly competent man of affairs, who rose to fame under King Alexander, and was afterwards associated with Ptolemy, son of Lagus."

10. "Not only the priests of Egypt give these facts from their records, but many also of the Greeks who visited Thebes in the time of Ptolemy son of Lagus and composed histories of Egypt, one of whom was Hecataeus agree with what we have said" (Diodorus Siculus, *Bib. hist.* 1.46.8 [Oldfather]). Jacoby also ascertained that Hecataeus had consulted priests at Heliopolis, Memphis, and Thebes (Murray, "Hecataeus of Abdera," 151 n. 3).

11. Burstein, "Hecataeus of Abdera's History of Egypt," 46–48.

12. Hecataeus maintains some of Herodotus's observations, but the differences are more striking. Places where Hecataeus agrees with Herodotus: (1) Sesostris's campaigns reached far into Asia and Europe, several monuments document these campaigns, and the Colchians descend from Egyptians (*Hist.* 2.102–106; Diodorus Siculus, *Bib. hist.* 1.55); (2) captured peoples performed heavy labor on behalf of Sesostris (*Hist.* 2.108; Diodorus Siculus, *Bib. hist.* 1.56.2–4; and (3) his brother's failed assassination attempt (*Hist.* 2.107; Diodorus Siculus, *Bib. hist.* 1.57.6–7).

distributing the best of the *chora* to them, and he showed goodwill to all Egyptians, forgiving past grievances and providing benefits (Diodorus Siculus, *Bib. hist.* 1.54.1–2, 4–6). Herodotus's Sesostris divided the land into parcels that were taxed annually (*Hist.* 2.109), but Hecataeus tell us that Sesostris divided the land into thirty-six nomes (νομός) and appointed a nomarch to supervise each through the collection of taxes and administration of daily affairs (Diodorus Siculus, *Bib. hist.* 1.54.3). The first military campaign of Hecataeus's Sesostris (as king) was waged against Ethiopia and then, "as the first Egyptian to build warships," he overtook the Red Sea and conquered as far as India (Diodorus Siculus, *Bib. hist.* 1.55.1–4); Herodotus's Sesostris first campaigned with a navy fleet against Arabian peoples (*Hist.* 2.102), and then he eventually ruled over Ethiopia (*Hist.* 2.110.1).[13] Hecataeus's Sesostris also has more foresight and purpose; his innovations were meant for the security of Egyptians and their land (Diodorus Siculus, *Bib. hist.* 1.56.1, 57.2–4). Like the Sesostris of Herodotus, the one of Hecataeus promulgated the construction of irrigation canals to improve Egyptians' lives (cf. *Hist.* 2.108 and Diodorus Siculus, *Bib. hist.* 1.57.2), but the accomplishments of the latter Sesostris stand out more. Under his watch, every city had a temple built to its local god (Diodorus Siculus, *Bib. hist.* 1.56.2); Sesostris built a large fortification on the east side of Egypt to protect against Syria and Arabia (Diodorus Siculus, *Bib. hist.* 1.57.4); and he was a great patron and devotee of Egyptian temples, providing lavish votive offerings to all temples but especially to those in Thebes and in Memphis (Diodorus Siculus, *Bib. hist.* 1.55.11; 57.5, 8). Hecataeus's Sesostris was more renowned than the one whom Herodotus describes. He maintained a powerful hold over the conquered peoples of his campaigns; they regularly paid him homage and he consistently demonstrated his dominance over them (Diodorus Siculus, *Bib. hist.* 1.58.1–3).

Several writers appeared to have studied Hecataeus works, such as Diodorus Siculus, but we also have evidence of a Judean writer in Egypt who seemed to have known Hecataeus's *Aegyptiaca*.[14] During the second

---

13. Hecataeus mentions that prior to his ascension to the throne, Sesostris was sent with an army by his father to conquer Arabia (Diodorus Siculus, *Bib. hist.* 1.53.5–6).

14. Murray proposes the possible influence of Hecataeus on Theophrastus, Alexinus, Crantor, and in Egypt, on Apollonius (*Argonautica*) and Theocritus (*Idyll 17, Encomium to Ptolemy*) ("Hecataeus of Abdera," 168). See also Stephens, *Seeing Double*, esp. 32–44, 122–70. Zellentin is persuaded by Burton and Sacks in not assigning Hecataeus as the dominant source for book 1 of Diodorus Siculus's *Bibliotheca historica*, but

century BCE, Artapanus wrote a Greek work with either the title, Ἰουδαϊκά or Περὶ Ἰουδαίων, and the compiler, Alexander Polyhistor copied it in the mid-first century BCE.[15] Centuries later, Clement of Alexandria (late second century CE) and then Eusebius (early fourth century CE) preserved selections of Artapanus's work, and they seem to have copied from a common Polyhistor text (in that they provide the same information in the same order); Eusebius in particular reliably transmitted Polyhistor's works.[16] We only have fragments of what was supposedly a larger work, but these fragments appear to be authentic to Artapanus. The largest portions of Artapanus's work are preserved in Eusebius's *Praeparatio Evangelica*,

---

he admits that there is a common source shared by Diodorus and Artapanus (what I and most scholars refer to as Hecateaus's work) ("End of Jewish Egypt," 48–51). On the debate whether or not Artapanus is a Jewish author, see Howard Jacobson, "Artapanus Judaeus," *JJS* 57 (2006): 210–21; and my rebuttal, Ahearne-Kroll, "Constructing Jewish Identity in Ptolemaic Egypt: The Case of Artapanus," in Harlow, *"Other" in Second Temple Judaism*, 434–56. The vast majority of scholars continue to agree that Artapanus was a Jewish intellectual in Egypt; see, e.g., John J. Collins, "Artapanus Revisited," in *From Judaism to Christianity: Tradition and Transition; a Festschrift for Thomas H. Tobin on the Occasion of His Sixty-Fifth Birthday*, ed. Patricia Walters, NovTSup 136 (Boston: Brill, 2010), 59–68; Erich S. Gruen, *Diaspora: Jews amidst Greeks and Romans* (Cambridge: Harvard University Press, 2002); Rob Kugler, "Hearing the Story of Moses in Ptolemaic Egypt: Artapanus Accommodates the Tradition," in *The Wisdom of Egypt: Jewish, Early Christian, and Gnostic Essays in Honour of Gerard P. Luttikhuizen*, ed. A. Hilhorst and Geurt Hendrik van Kooten, AGJU 59 (Leiden: Brill, 2005), 67–80; and Zellentin, "End of Jewish Egypt."

15. On Alexander Polyhistor, see J. Freudenthal, *Alexander Polyhistor und die von ihm erhaltenen Reste jüdischer und samaritanischer Geschichtswerke*, Hellenistische Studien 1–2 (Breslau: Grass, 1874–1875); Sterling, *Historiography and Self-Definition*, 144–52; and John Strugnell, "General Introduction, with a Note on Alexander Polyhistor," *OTP* 2:777–79, and related bibliographies. On the cultural context of Polyhistor and his work, see William Adler, "Alexander Polyhistor's *Perio Ioudaiōn* and Literary Culture in Republican Rome," in *Reconsidering Eusebius: Collected Papers on Literary, Historical, and Theological Issues*, ed. Sabrina Inowlocki and Claudio Zmagni (Leiden: Brill, 2011), 225–40.

16. On the reliability of Polyhistor's works, see Strugnell, "General Introduction," 778. According to Sterling, Clement provides excerpts from Eupolemos, Artapanus, and Ezekiel the Tragedian in the precise order that Eusebius does (see Clement, *Strom.* 1.23.153–55; Eusebius, *Praep. ev.* 9.26–28), and Eusebius cites Polyhistor as the source for these passages (*Historiography and Self-Definition*, 147). On the reliability of Eusebius's quotations, see Freudenthal, *Alexander Polyhistor*, 3–16, and Sabrina Inowlocki, *Eusebius and the Jewish Authors: His Citation Technique in an Apologetic Context*, AGJU 64 (Leiden: Brill, 2006), 276.

4. *Aseneth* and the Landscape of Ptolemaic and Early Roman Egypt 195

in which we find selections from Artapanus's narratives about Abraham, Joseph, and Moses in Egypt that significantly alter septuagintal stories.

In a brief telling about Abraham, Artapanus provides the etymology of the Greek word Ἰουδαῖοι, and he describes Abraham's activity when he and his household came to Egypt (cf. LXX Gen 12:10–20). In contrast to the Genesis account, Artapanus narrates how Abraham taught the Egyptian king astrology, lived in Egypt for twenty years, and how, when he returned to Syria, some members of his household remained in Egypt (*Praep. ev.* 9.18.1). In a longer rendition about Joseph, Artapanus tells how Joseph came to Egypt and rose to leadership, and again, his version alters the Genesis story. Here, Joseph anticipated his brothers' plot against him and he himself sought transportation to Egypt from traveling Arabs, and once in Egypt, he became the financial administrator (διοικητής) for all of Egypt (cf. LXX Gen 37, 39–41 and *Praep. ev.* 9.23.1–2). Artapanus bypasses all remnants of jealousy, treachery, enslavement, and revenge that Genesis portrays in Joseph's rise to greatness. Even though the book of Genesis credits Joseph for redistributing the land and establishing its agricultural tax (LXX Gen 47:13–26), Artapanus's Joseph divides the land in more equitable ways (implied by the fact that prior to his divisions, the strong treated the weak "unfairly") and utilizes more of the land (making it tillable) (*Praep. ev.* 9.23.2). In LXX Genesis, Joseph left alone the priests' land (47:22), but in Artapanus, he assigns some of the land (ἄρουραι) to the priests (*Praep. ev.* 9.23.2). Joseph was loved by the Egyptians, he married Aseneth, the daughter of a priest of Heliopolis, and his family joined him in Egypt and settled in Heliopolis and Sais (*Praep. ev.* 9.23.3 and cf. LXX Gen. 41:45, 45–46).

In Artapanus's longest excerpt, he talks about Moses's life. Like in the book of Exodus, pharaoh's daughter takes Moses as her own and gives him the name of "Moses" (cf. LXX Exod 2:5–10), but Artapanus names the daughter (Merris), has her betrothed to a man named Chenephres (who becomes Moses's archenemy), and says that she took in "one of the children of the Ἰουδαῖοι [Judeans]" because she was barren (*Praep. ev.* 9.27.3). Although Merris's father (Palmanothes) "dealt meanly with Ἰουδαῖοι [Judeans]" (*Praep. ev.* 9.27.2), Artapanus does not mention pharaoh's command to kill male Hebrew infants nor Moses's mother placing him in a papyrus basket in the river (cf. LXX Exod 1:15–2:4). For the next thirteen lines, Artapanus breaks away from the Exodus narrative and provides a unique picture of Moses. The name "Moses" (Μωϋσος) was also known to the Greeks, who instead referred to him as "Mousaios" (Μουσαῖος), and

Moses was the teacher of Orpheus (*Praep. ev.* 9.27.3–4). In several Greek traditions, Orpheus and Mousaios are closely associated, and the insertion of the Hebrew Moses here foreshadows other ways Artapanus alters the past.[17] Moses also founded much of pharaonic Egypt's infrastructure—from its ritual centers and academic life to its military technology and successful campaigns.

In fact, Artapanus's Moses looks a lot like Hecataeus's Sesostris.[18] He invents ships, divides the land into thirty-six nomes, fights against the Ethiopians, commands an army with success, and gains approval from the Egyptian masses (cf. Diodorus Siculus, *Bib. hist.* 1.54.1–3, 55.1–2 and *Praep. ev.* 9.27.4, 6–8). Several factors of Egypt's industry are attributed to Moses, much like Hecataeus's Sesostris. Moses created instruments for watering (cf. Sesostris establishing irrigation canals, Diodorus Siculus, *Bib. hist.* 1.57.2) and invented Egyptian weapons, military training, and machines for moving stones (cf. Sesostris creating a formidable army [Diodorus Siculus, *Bib. hist.* 1.54.4–5] and constructing great works [Diodorus Siculus, *Bib. hist.* 1.56.1, 57.4–5]) (*Praep. ev.* 9.27.4). Moses also assigned a god in each nome to be revered, and in particular Moses and his army consecrated the ibis in the city of Hermopolis (*Praep. ev.* 9.27.4, 9; cf. Sesostris building a temple in each city for its local god [Diodorus Siculus, *Bib. hist.* 1.56.2]). But unlike Hecataeus's account (or even that of Herodotus), the practice of male circumcision descends from Moses and not from Egyptians in Sesostris's military campaigns; Ethiopians learned the practice from Moses himself (*Praep. ev.* 9.27.10; cf. Diodorus Siculus, *Bib. hist.* 1.55.4–5; *Hist.* 2.104).

Artapanus's Moses compares beyond Hecataeus's account of Sesostris; he is also like Hecataeus's Hermes.[19] The Egyptians, Hecataeus tells us, believed that the god Hermes invented their language and established the honors and offerings accorded to the gods, and the Greeks called

---

17. Orpheus and Mousaios are associated in the canonical lists of Hesiod and Homer; Plato calls them the "offspring of the Moon and the Muses" (*Resp.* 364e); and Diodorus Siculus states that Orpheus is the father of Mousaios (4.25.1) (Fritz Graf, "Musaeus (1)," *Oxford Classical Dictionary*, ed. Simon Hornblower and Antony Spawforth, 4th ed. (Oxford: Oxford University Press); doi: 10.1093/acref/9780199545568.001.0001.

18. The most thorough treatment of the influence of the Sesostris tradition in Artapanus is by David Lenz Tiede, *The Charismatic Figure as Miracle Worker*, SBLDS 1 (Missoula, MT: Society of Biblical Literature, 1972), 153–68.

19. Tiede, *Charismatic Figure*, 155–56.

4. *Aseneth* and the Landscape of Ptolemaic and Early Roman Egypt 197

him "Hermes" because he taught them "how to expound their thoughts [διδάξαι τὰ περὶ τὴν ἑρμηνείαν]" (Diodorus Siculus, *Bib. hist.* 1.16.1–2). As mentioned above, Artapanus's Moses assigned the god to be worshiped in each nome, but he also assigned the "sacred writings" to the priests and he was called "Hermes" because of "his ability to interpret the sacred writings [διὰ τὴν τῶν ἱερῶν γραμμάτων ἑρμηνείαν]" (*Praep. ev.* 9.27.4, 6). Moses and his army also established a city in the nome of Hermopolis, calling it by the same name, "City of Hermes" (Ἑρμοῦ πόλις) (*Praep. ev.* 9.27.9). The priests tell Hecataeus that Hermes discovered education and the arts (παιδεῖαι and τέχναι; Diodorus Siculus, *Bib. hist.* 1.43.6), and Artapanus tells us that Moses invented philosophy (τὴν φιλοσοφίαν ἐξευρεῖν; *Praep. ev.* 9.27.4). Hecataeus tell us that according to the Egyptians, Hermes was first a mortal in Egypt who attained immortality through his sagacity and the benefits that he bestowed on humans (Diodorus Siculus, *Bib. hist.* 1.13.1–2), and for Artapanus, Moses was given honors like a god (ἰσοθέου τιμῆς) by the Egyptian priests, which is partially why he was called, "Hermes" (*Praep. ev.* 9.27.6).

Artapanus also tells us that Moses assigned cats, dogs, and ibises as Egyptian gods, and he assigned land exclusively to the priests (*Praep. ev.* 9.27.4). These actions are reminiscent to Hecataeus's account about Isis. According to the priests, Isis instituted the payment of honors to Osiris throughout Egypt, and she also ordered the priests to consecrate native animals in their districts, to pay honors to them in life like they had of Osiris, and then to provide mortuary rituals for them in death like they had for Osiris (Diodorus Siculus, *Bib. hist.* 1.21.6). Isis allotted to the priests one third of the land to fund this ritual activity, and "to this day" it had continued (μέχρι τοῦ νῦν) (Diodorus Siculus, *Bib. hist.* 1.21.7, 9). According to Hecataeus, this practice was ordered by Isis to the priests in private (Diodorus Siculus, *Bib. hist.* 1.21.6), but the particular honors paid to the sacred bulls, Apis and Mnevis, were introduced to all Egyptians because of the general benefits the bulls had given to Egypt's agricultural life (Diodorus Siculus, *Bib. hist.* 1.21.10–11). Artapanus also mentions the sacred bull, Apis, which was honored in the city of Memphis, but the source of worshiping Apis was not Moses. Chenephres (Merris's husband and then pharaoh) asked Moses if "there was anything else useful for humans," and Moses recommended a "breed of oxen" because it was used to till the land. Chenephres, however, named a bull "Apis," commanded the people to dedicate a temple to it, and ordered that all the animals that Moses had consecrated be buried at Memphis, "wishing to conceal the ideas of Moses" (κατακρύπτειν θέλοντα τὰ τοῦ Μωῦσου ἐπινοήματα; *Praep. ev.* 9.27.12). So Moses had instituted much of the ritual activity in Egypt (like Isis had in Hecataeus's account) save that which focused on Apis and other Memphite, necropolite cults.

Moses's association with Egyptian animal cults has been an obstacle for many scholars when considering Artapanus as a Jewish (or in my terms, Judean) writer.[20] As I have argued elsewhere, the fact that Artapanus disassociates Moses from the Apis cult is a targeted critique that supplements his elevation of his Judean ancestors and god.[21] As Hecataeus mentions, the veneration of Apis and Mnevis was public, and in Memphis, the cultic activity around Apis was dominant.[22] The Memphite economy, especially during the Ptolemaic period, was fueled by the activities of the temple of Ptah in the city proper and at the necropolis, just west of the city. During the Ptolemaic period, an Apis bull would die about every twenty years, and after each death, the cultic functionaries of the temple of Ptah would conduct an elaborate set of mortuary rituals lasting seventy days.[23] At its conclusion, a public ceremony would reenact the rejuvenation of Apis, and the bull would be taken in a public procession to the necropolis to be buried. This spectacle was grand and the involvement was high. As the location of Osiris-Apis, the mortuary complex of the deceased Apis bull in the necropolis became a popular site not only for Egyptians but for Greek immigrants as well. As early as the Persian period, Greek inhabitants in Memphis (Hellenomemphites) revered the god, and after the rise of the Ptolemies, several associations were made between Osiris-Apis

---

20. Jacobson, "Artapanus Judaeus"; and summarized by Erkki Koskenniemi, "Greeks, Egyptians and Jews in the Fragments of Artapanus," *JSP* 13 (2002): 26–31.

21. Ahearne-Kroll, "Constructing Jewish Identity in Ptolemaic Egypt."

22. A helpful summary of the Apis cult during the Ptolemaic period can be found in Thompson, *Memphis under the Ptolemies*, 177–96; Stefan Pfeiffer, "The God Serapis, His Cult and the Beginnings of the Ruler Cult in Ptolemaic Egypt," in *Ptolemy II Philadelphus and His World*, ed. Paul Mckechnie and Philippe Guillaume, Mnemosyne Supplementum 300 (Leiden: Brill, 2008), 387–408.

23. There were thirteen Apis bulls during the Ptolemaic period, and Thompson's list of evidence suggests that the bulls lived for about twenty years on average (Thompson, *Memphis under the Ptolemies*, 263–83). A description of the Apis mortuary ritual is provided by P.Vindob. 3837, which appears to be an official manual with commentary (See R. L. Vos, *The Apis Embalming Ritual: P.Vindob. 3837*, OLA 50 [Leuven: Peeters, 1993]). See Thompson's discussion as well (*Memphis under the Ptolemies*, 184–88).

and Dionysos.²⁴ The Ptolemies were significant patrons of the Memphite practices at the temple of Ptah and the necropolis; any inhabitant near Memphis (which includes those living in the Fayum) would have known about the cities' main cultic practices.²⁵ Veneration of the god Serapis had its origin at the Memphite necropolis (where the mortuary complex of Osiris-Apis was called the "Serapeum" in papyri), and the early Ptolemies forged close connections between their rule and the protective powers of Serapis.²⁶ In Alexandria, at least by the time of Ptolemy III (but perhaps earlier), the royal court promoted cultic activity around Serapis; Ptolemy III funded the temple complex of Serapis that included a temple to the god, a colonnade court, and several other building structures. One of those structures enclosed an entrance to underground passages that share architectural similarities with those attached to the Serapeum in the Memphite necropolis.²⁷ It is clear, then, that the Ptolemies favored the Apis cult, and Greek-speaking and Egyptian inhabitants revered the cult in its varied forms.

---

24. Thompson summarizes the tendency as follows: "The Hellenomemphites of the city had long taken part in this essentially Egyptian festival [the burial of the Apis bull], and with the great influx of Greeks following the conquest of Alexander, attempts were made to interpret these Memphite rituals in terms of Dionysiac mysteries, with Memphis now located within the traditional Greek topography of Hades. The Lake of Pharaoh, which the Apis crossed, was that of Acherousia. The staffs and scepters of the priests become Dionysiac *thyrsoi*, while the dress that the men of Anoubis wore were *nebrides*, the fawn skins, of the Bacchic revelers. The great gates of the Serapeum were those of Lethe and of Kokytos, bound in bronze and found within the temple of Hekate. The Greek Dionysiac statuary of the avenue to the Serapeum stood as a forerunner to the syncretic accounts of later writers" (*Memphis under the Ptolemies*, 188). A case could be made that Artapanus was also aware of this association, and he purposely switched the order of influence between Mousaios and Orpheus so to suggest that Moses was the founder of Dionysiac mysteries as well (undercutting Greek originality of what were considered to be sacred, ritual traditions).

25. For a summary of the evidence of Ptolemaic patronage in Memphis, see Thompson, *Memphis under the Ptolemies*, 106–17.

26. Pfeiffer, "God Serapis," esp. 390; Philippe Borgeaud and Youri Volokhine, "La formation de la légende de Sarapis: une approche transculturelle" *ARelG* 2 (2000): 37–76.

27. Judith S. McKenzie, Sheila Gibson, and A. T. Reyes, "Reconstructing the Serapeum in Alexandria from the Archaeological Evidence" *JRS* 94 (2004), 73–121, esp. 111. Pfeiffer argues that Ptolemy I had established a sanctuary to Serapis at the site ("God Serapis," 400–403).

In my opinion, Artapanus critiques the Ptolemaic-Egyptian priesthood establishment in Memphis by narrating that, for spite, the archenemy of Moses (Chenephres) created what in Artapanus's time were dominant cultic practices. Chenephres is clearly the antihero in the story, and so the Memphite traditions associated with him are equally unfavorable. From the beginning, Chenephres was envious of Moses and sought to kill him, despite the fact that Moses had produced all of his inventions "for the sake of keeping the monarchy stable for Chenephres" (*Praep. ev.* 9.27.5,7). Chenephres sent Moses to lead an untrained group of men against the Ethiopians, and after he had failed to dispose of Moses in this way, he "plotted against [Moses]" again (*Praep. ev.* 9.27.7–11). Chenephres's actions, though, achieved nothing. Right after the Memphis episode, Chenephres was banished by Egyptians, his officials did not obey his order to kill Moses, and only after being censured by the king did Chanethothes attempt to execute Chenephres's command (*Praep. ev.* 9.27.13–18). After Moses fled Egypt, Chenephres chastised Judeans in Egypt, and he ended up dying from elephantiasis because of this (implying that his death was a divine punishment) (*Praep. ev.* 9.27.20). As Artapanus tells it, Moses established security and prosperity in Egypt under Chenephres's reign, which in Egyptian kingship ideology translates as Moses providing Maat and not Chenephres.[28] At the same time, Artapanus also rehearses the exodus narrative: he provides the Israelite god's call to Moses, Moses's performance of miracles before (a different) pharaoh, and the Judeans' ultimate escape from Egypt (*Praep. ev.* 9.21–37; cf. Exod 3–15). In the end, much of Egypt's magnificence is destroyed; during the battle of the plagues (cf. Exod 7–11), "all the houses and most of the temples collapsed" (*Praep. ev.* 9.27.33). The Moses narrative ends, then, with the victory of the Israelite god and deliverance of the Hebrew people from Egypt, coinciding precisely with Judean ancestral tradition.

But as Artapanus would have it, the great heritage of Egypt (minus the Memphite cultic traditions) was established by Moses, not Sesostris, Hermes, or Isis. In fact, when we include all the preserved fragments from Artapanus's work, much of Egypt's legacy descended from Hebrew patriarchs. Hecataeus tells us that, according to Egyptian priests, Belus appointed Babylonian priests, called "Chaldeans," who observed the stars

---

28. For a succinct description of the relationship between Egyptian kingship and Maat, see James P. Allen, *Middle Egyptian: An Introduction to the Language and Culture of Hieroglyphs*, 3rd ed. (Cambridge: Cambridge University Press, 2014), 147–49.

4. *Aseneth* and the Landscape of Ptolemaic and Early Roman Egypt 201

"following the example of the Egyptian priests, physicists, and astrologers" (Diodorus Siculus, *Bib. hist.* 1.28.1). According to the book of Genesis, though, Abraham comes from Ur of the Chaldeans (LXX Gen 11:27–32), and for Artapanus, it is Abraham who taught the Egyptian king astrology (*Praep. ev.* 9.18.1). So too, Artapanus's Joseph brings bureaucratic stability to the land in ways reminiscent to Sesostris (Diodorus Siculus, *Bib. hist.* 1.54.3); he became the chief administrator who redistributed the land and maximized its use (*Praep. ev.* 9.23.2; cf. LXX Gen 47: 13–26). If we add what Artapanus spins about Moses, we are left to think that pharaonic infrastructures descend from the Hebrews.

We can see, then, how Artanapus borrows associations with Egypt that echo Hecataeus's account, but each writer conveys a different story that is directly related to the social capital each writer enjoyed. If we return to Hecataeus's *Aegyptiaca*, he not only demonstrates how Egyptians had rich mythic traditions (e.g., Diodorus Siculus, *Bib. hist.* 1.11–14, 16), proof of their imperial past (e.g., Diodorus Siculus, *Bib. hist.* 1.47–49), and an established legacy of conquest, expansion, and success (e.g., Diodorus Siculus, *Bib. hist.* 1.45–68), but he also inserts Greek predecessors into that history.[29] Famous Greeks, like Musaeas, Homer, and Plato, had visited Egypt long ago in order to partake in Egyptian customs and learning (νόμιμος καὶ παιδεία) (Diodorus Siculus, *Bib. hist.* 1.96).[30] Hecataeus implies that the distinguished wisdom and learning of the Greeks descended from the Egyptians, but now, in *his* time, Ptolemy controlled that place. As innocent as Hecataeus's account seems (simply describing the records of a foreign *ethnos*), the fact that he produces this history at the start of Ptolemaic rule conveys that more was at stake. In essence, he narrates the extent to which Ptolemy was bestowed with Egypt's power and importance.[31] Whether or not Hecataeus was a court writer, his presentation of the cultural and

---

29. I do not include Diodorus's insertions in book 1 that Murray proposes ("Hecataeus of Abdera," 146). The following are insertions that I leave out of my discussion: 1.11.3–4; 13.4; 44.1, 2–5; 46.7; 50.6–7; 52.3; 56.5–6; 58.5; 61.4; 63.5; and 68.6. Where Hecataeus refers to his Egyptian sources, see Diodorus Siculus, *Bib. hist.* 1.13.3; 21.1–2; 26.1; 43.6; 45.1; 46.7–8; 53.1; 62.2–3; and 69.7.

30. Hecataeus lists Orpheus, Musaeus, Melampus, Daedalus, Homer, Lycurgus of Sparta, Solon, Plato, and Pythagoras, Eudoxus, Democritus of Abdera, and Oenopides of Chios, and claims that the Egyptian priests have proof in their sacred books and on statues and inscriptions that recorded these visits.

31. Sterling provides a succinct summary of the likely political benefits Hecataeus's work had on the early Ptolemaic regime (*Historiography and Self-Definition*,

historical greatness of Egypt ultimately bolstered Ptolemaic claims to that land. Further, it is insufficient to describe Hecataeus's work (or that or Herodotus) as providing an *interpretatio Graeca* of Egypt.[32] His contact with Egypt brought about new configurations of Greek relations with Egypt, which his near contemporaries in Alexandria also produced (most notably Callimachus and Theocritus).[33] But when these writers perpetuated stories about the Egyptian origin of Greek myths, genealogies, and cultic practices, they did so from a dominant social location; if not involved with Greek imperial powers, they partook in and cast their identities in terms of dominant, Hellenistic traditions.

This was not the case with Artapanus, who was a Greek-educated, Judean writer familiar with the *chora* of Lower Egypt. In particular, the content and vocabulary of Artapanus's text considerably helps us to posit his background. First, Artapanus's identification of Joseph as a διοικητής is apt for a Ptolemaic-era writer to use. The διοικητής was a privileged position under Ptolemaic rule; he was the chief financial officer and administrator of all the nomes in the *chora*.[34] In the book of Genesis, Joseph is "second in command" over all of Egypt because he becomes the main administrator of grain in the land, and he saves Egyptians and dependent economies in the Levant during seven years of famine (chs. 41–47). The fact that Artapanus uses the term διοικητής tells us that he likely knew its Ptolemaic usage. Second, a similar case can be made with Artapanus's reference

---

73–75). See also Murray, "Hecataeus of Abdera"; and Bar-Kochva, *Pseudo-Hecataeus*, 15–18.

32. John Dillery, "Hecataeus of Abdera: Hyperboreans, Egypt, and the 'Interpretatio Graeca,'" *Historia* 47 (1998): esp. 255–60.

33. See Stephens, *Seeing Double*, 74–170.

34. Although Zellentin mentions that the title, διοικητής, stands for "the manager of a private estate" ("'Artapanus,' Edition, Translation, and Commentary," *BNJ* 726), the term actually had a higher administrative function in Ptolemaic Egypt. He was the chief financial officer of the empire, but his office also oversaw legal disputes and the appointment and supervision of regional officers. In P.Rev.Laws (259 BCE), the stipulations for taxation of oil production are outlined and the document is marked as "being corrected" in the office of Apollonius, the διοικητής (cols. 38–56). Apollonius the διοικητής is the owner of the land estate managed by Zenon in Philadelphia, Egypt (P.Cairo Zen. 59012, 59021, 59034, and 59816), and he is mentioned in other documentation as well (P.Lond. 1954; PSI 488; P.Corn. 1; P.Col. 54; P.Hib. 110). Other evidence for the Ptolemaic, administrative position of the διοικητής can be found in P.Tebt. 1.5 (C.Ord.Ptol. 53; 118 BCE), P.Yale 36, W.Chrest. 411, and P.Tebt. 11 (which mentions the appointment of Menches as village scribe of Kerkeosiris by the διοικητής).

that Joseph assigned ἄρουραι (land) to Egyptian priests (*Praep. ev.* 9.23.2). The term *aroura* (ἄρουρα) is the standard land measurement in Ptolemaic papyri, often used to describe the size of land ownership.[35] Both διοικητής and ἄρουρα were not derived from the biblical story about Joseph; in the Septuagint, διοικητής shows up only four times and never in the book of Genesis, and ἄρουρα appears only three times in the Septuagint and never in the Joseph story.[36] Third, given all the Greek associations present in Artapanus's work, he appears to have received some form of Greek education (which included reading Hecataeus's work or at least a work that Diodorus Siculus also used) along with gaining extensive knowledge of the books of Genesis and Exodus. Finally, Artapanus also was active in the *chora* sufficiently enough to know about the role of a διοικητής, the land measurement of ἄρουρα, and Memphite cultic practices.

It is safe to say that Artapanus's work was not written from a dominant cultural or political perspective. Artapanus's motives have been described as defensive, that he was addressing his contemporary, hostile environment, but the Artapanus fragments do not decisively prove this.[37] Only the story of Moses describes hostility against Judeans, but the moments of strife in the story coincide with times of Egyptian oppression as described in the book of Exodus; Artapanus may have been following the Exodus

---

35. The papyrological evidence is overwhelming in confirming that the ἄρουρα was the basic land measurement (one ἄρουρα was equivalent to about 0.66 acre). For a more recent discussion of the land economy of Ptolemaic Egypt, see Andrew Monson, *From the Ptolemies to the Romans: Political and Economic Change in Egypt* (Cambridge: Cambridge University Press, 2012).

36. According to TLG, διοικητής only appears in 2 Esd 8:36, Tob 1:22 (codices Vaticanus, Alexandrinus, and Sinaiticus), and OG Dan 3:2. The term ἄρουρα appears in Gen 21:33; 1 Sam 22:6; 31:13.

37. Koskenniemi contends that Artapanus negotiates between the Greek and Egyptian cultures, and that he characterizes Egyptians as "common and simple people led by a wicked and treacherous king," ("Greeks, Egyptians and Jews," 26); and John J. Collins posits that Artapanus responds to Manetho-like accusations or at least to an environment that included anti-Jewish sentiments (*Between Athens and Jerusalem: Jewish Identity in the Hellenistic Diaspora*, 2nd ed., BRS [Grand Rapids: Eerdmans, 2000], 37–46). On the other hand, Barclay places "Artapanus" under his category of "cultural convergence" in Ptolemaic Egypt, and both he and Carl Holladay propose that Artapanus reflected Jewish populations who did not find polytheistic traditions threatening (Barclay, *Jews in the Mediterranean*, 127–32; Holladay, *Historians*, vol. 1 of *Fragments from Hellenistic Jewish Authors*, SBLTT 20 [Chico, CA: Scholars Press, 1983], 193).

plot and not necessarily reflecting contemporary social relations.[38] Otherwise, the Hebrew ancestors fare well in Egypt. Many who came with Abraham remained in the land because they were "attracted by the prosperity of the *chora*" (*Praep. ev.* 9.18.1); Joseph was loved by the Egyptians and his descendants prospered in the land (*Praep. ev.* 9.23.3); and Moses was loved by Egyptians (*Praep. ev.* 9.27.6). Artapanus's motives are more along the lines of what Collins has called "competitive historiography," in which Artapanus utilized contemporary methods of legitimizing ancestral heritage.[39] Artapanus, though, was writing from a less powerful position. His connection with Egypt was not to legitimize contemporary, Judean control over the land, or to narrate from the dominant perspective of Greek education and cultic practices in the Mediterranean. Rather, he choose to articulate the important contributions Judean ancestors had made to Egypt despite the Judean story of Egypt's ultimate defeat.

I suspect that a catalyst for Artapanus to produce his narrative was the fact that he was likely living well in Egypt but that his Judean tradition depended on the story of Egypt's downfall. Perhaps Artapanus was responding to critics like Manetho, but he also could have simply created a way for Judeans to have a positive view of their heritage in Egypt.[40] The story about Egyptian oppression and God's supremacy over Egypt and its pharaoh reverberates throughout septuagintal (biblical) texts. Genesis hints at it; Exodus provides its renditions; Leviticus, Numbers, and Deuteronomy remind the reader about it as do the historical books; the prophets recall the story, promise a victory and renewed relationship that echo the story, or even warn about new Egyptian oppression; and the psalms and other texts also recall the narrative.[41] Much of Israelite

---

38. Cf. *Praep. ev.* 9.27.2 and LXX Exod 1:8–12; *Praep. ev.* 9.27.18–20 and LXX Exod 2:11–25; and *Praep. ev.* 9.27.22–37 and LXX Exod 7–14. Although the two stories do not agree on the content of the king's hostility against the Judeans (in Artapanus) or the Israelites (in Exodus), both appear to be aligned in terms of when the hostility occurs (before Moses's adoption, after Moses kills the Egyptian, during the drama of the plagues, and in the final chase at the sea).

39. Quotation from Collins, *Between Athens and Jerusalem*, 46.

40. Bar-Kochva makes a similar argument for the purpose of Pseudo-Hecataeus's work (*Pseudo-Hecataeus*, 232–48).

41. Gen 15; Exod 1–40; Lev 11:45; 18:2; 19:36; 22:33; 26:45; Num 1:1; 9:1–5; 14:11–25; 15:41; 24:8; Deut 4:34; 5:6; 6:12, 20–25; 7:18–20; 8:11–18; 9:25–29; 15:15; 16:1–12; 20:1; 24:17–18, 21–22; 26:5–10; 28:68; 29:1–2; Josh 24:5–7; Judg 2:12; 6:7–10, 13; 1 Sam 12:6; 1 Kgs 9:9; 12:28; 2 Kgs 17:7; 23:21–23. Examples of references in the

identity is expressed against the backdrop of a malevolent Egypt, but in Artapanus's time, a sizeable number of Judeans prospered there. By the first century BCE, thousands of Judeans lived in Alexandria and the *chora*, and especially in the Fayum and around Memphis, there were scores of Judeans living in villages and cities, as soldiers, farmers, shepherds, police personnel, and potters.[42] They had designated prayer houses (προσευχαί), and in Herakleopolis (a city at the entrance to the Fayum), a Judean community had its own *politeuma*.[43] The foundational stories of Judean ancestry and cultic life expound about the evils of Egypt, and yet, Judeans

---

prophetic books: (1) recalling the story: Amos 2:10; Hag 2:2-9; Jer 2:4-19; 7:21-26; 11:1-8; 31:32; Ezek 20; (2) telling of repeated promise: Hos 2:14-20; Jer 23:7-8; Isa 43:16-21; 52:3-10 (3) warning of repeated oppression: Hos 8:13; 9:3; and Jeremiah particularly prophesies against emigration to Egypt, to the extent that God will punish exiles who go there (chs. 42-44). References in other biblical texts: Pss 78; 80; 81; 105; 106; 114; 136; Ezra 6:19-22; Neh 9:9-25; and Dan 9:15.

42. Joseph Mélèze Modrzejewski estimates that at the time of Rome's arrival in Egypt, there were 6.5 million Egyptians and 1.5 million Greek-speaking inhabitants of which about 300,000 were Jewish, and that Alexandria had a population of at least 500,000 of which 100,000-130,000 were Jewish (*The Jews of Egypt: From Rameses II to Emperor Hadrian*, trans. Robert Cornman [Princeton: Princeton University Press, 1995], 73-74). Brian McGing, however, has demonstrated the problems of deducing accurate demographic readings of Jewish populations in the ancient world ("Population and Proselytism: How Many Jews Were There in the Ancient World?," in *Jews in the Hellenistic and Roman Cities*, ed. John R. Bartlett [London: Routledge, 2002], 100-118), so the best we can postulate is from the documentary and epigraphical evidence. As I discuss below (see 234 and n. 113), Christelle Fischer-Bovet posits a more conservative demographic count, in which the entire population of Egypt by the start of the first century BCE was 4 million, of which roughly 200,000 were Greek-speaking. Based on epigraphical and papyrological evidence, the Judean population was at least in the thousands and arguably constituted a sizeable minority in Egypt (see more below). See also Andrew Monson, who summarizes the more recent discussions about demographic estimates for the Ptolemaic period (*From the Ptolemies to the Romans*, 33-72).

43. For papyrological evidence about Judaean life in Egypt, see *CPJ*; Cowey and Maresch, *Urkunden des Politeuma der Juden von Herakleopolis*; and the additional references in Willy Clarysse, "Jews in Trikomia," in *Proceedings of the Twentieth International Congress of Papyrologists (Copenhagen, 23-29 August 1992)*, ed. Adam Bülow-Jacobsen (University of Copenhagen: Museum Tusculanum Press, 1994), 193-203. For epigraphical evidence of Judean προσευχαί, see Horbury and Noy, *Jewish Inscriptions*, nos. 13, **22**, **24**, **25**, **27**, **28**, **117**, 125, and 126. The inscriptions in bold indicate examples where a προσευχή is explicitly designated for 'Ιουδαῖοι (Judeans); the remainder are assumed to refer to Judaean prayer houses because there is no evidence for any other self-ascribed group in Egypt referring to their own προσευχή (Horbury

were living for generations in that supposed despotic place. Artapanus, though, recasts a better picture of their ancestral past in that land.

Artapanus constructs his story by utilizing techniques at his disposal, imitating the ways in which his contemporaries persuasively communicated their stories. Like Hecateaus, Artapanus accepts the legacy of Egyptian history, but he implants his *ethnos*-associations in it. Beginning with the ancient tradition of his ancestry (septuagintal stories), Artapanus recalibrates the narratives about Abraham, Joseph, and Moses to connect his heritage with that of Egypt's. Even though his results differ from his Greek counterparts (in that Egyptians were not the sources of influence), the technique of tracking trajectories of influence from the epic past is the same. Artapanus also hints at the legitimation of at least Moses as a successful ruler of Egypt's past, whereby Moses (in the model of Sesostris) performs the duty of a pharaoh better than the Egyptian pharaoh (Chenephres) does. Again, his motive may not have been antagonistic. Hecateaus, and Diodorus Siculus after him, wrote from a dominant vantage point; Hecateaus shared language, narratives, and cultic traditions with the Ptolemies whether or not he was a court historian. As foreign conquerors, the challenge for the Ptolemies was to plug themselves into the legacy of Egyptian culture, and narratives linking Greek heritage to Egypt created a discourse of "coming home"; they produced the fiction that the Ptolemies were meant to rule over Egypt. But Artapanus wrote from a secondary vantage point; although he was Greek-educated, his ancestral traditions differed from those of Ptolemaic-supported Greek institutions.[44] Whether or not Artapanus exercised political or economic influence, his ancestral narratives lay outside of those shared by the Ptolemaic court and Macedonian/Greek administrators. To express the greatness of his heritage, Artapanus spun how Hebrew patriarchs surpassed (not descended from) historic Egyptian leaders. Perhaps the greatest indicator of Judean supremacy lies tucked away in Artapanus's rendition of the plagues against Egypt. When Moses strikes the Nile with his staff, the river does not change color (as it does in the book of Exodus) but rather it floods the land; "It was from that time that the flooding of the Nile began" (*Praep. ev.* 9.27.28; cf.

---

and Noy, *Jewish Inscriptions*, 215). Note the interesting case of the Fayum village, Trikomia, where the majority were Judaean (Clarysse, "Jews of Trikomia").

44. As best demonstrated by tax-exemptions given to teachers of Greek or to those participating in the performing arts or athletic contests. For more, see Clarysse and Thompson, *Counting the People*, 2:123–205.

LXX Exod 7:14–25). The inundation of the Nile was not only essential to the agricultural life of Egypt but—going back to the Old Kingdom—its regularity was used to mark the seasons, guide ritual activity, and signify mythic beginnings.[45] For one of the core features of Egyptian identity, space, and time, Egyptians apparently had Moses to thank.

As I have suggested with the works of Hecataeus and Artapanus, the cultural landscape of pharaonic Egypt became a source for the Ptolemies and Greek-speaking writers to formulate their identities and to construct their placement in society (especially in terms of associating with power, both real and perceived). This leads to my final point in this section. As other scholars have noted in detail, Hecataeus and Artapanus are two of several examples that we have of Greek-educated writers reconstructing their respective, cultural identities in Hellenistic Egypt.[46] At their disposal were various discourses, which I define as any form of communication, whether it is literary or visual and whether mediated through a combination of sensate experiences (as with ritual activity).[47] The discourses that the Ptolemies and Greek-speaking writers utilized were visual and visceral (seen on images on coins and buildings, statues and other artifacts; and experienced in witnessing processions and rituals), practical and formal (in terms of everyday economic transactions, contract resolutions, and procedures for appeals), and literary (in public documents and decrees as well as narratives and poetry). To borrow the concept of Pierre Bourdieu, the social space of Ptolemaic Egypt entailed the reproduction and consumption of these discourses, many of which were identified by agents as containing significant social power. Most of these discourses were initiated

---

45. Anthony J. Spalinger, "Calendars," *OEAE* 1:224–27. The central role of the Nile in Egyptian temple life is well documented; see, e.g., Byron E. Shafer, ed., *Temples of Ancient Egypt* (Ithaca, NY: Cornell University Press, 1997).

46. Examples include Scott Noegel, who argues for the influence of Egyptian solar mythology in Apollonius's *Argonautica* ("Apollonius' *Argonautika* and Egyptian Solar Mythology," *CW* 97 [2004], 123–36); Stephens who examines the works of Callimachus, Theocritus, and Apollonius of Rhodes in their Ptolemaic, Alexandrian context (*Seeing Double*); and Dan Seldon, who discusses in detail the Egyptian influences on Callimachus's *Lock of Berenice* and *Hymn to Apollo* ("Alibis," *ClAnt.* 17 [1998]: 289–412).

47. My use of the term *discourse* is influenced by the work of Bruce Lincoln, esp. *Discourse and the Construction of Society: Comparative Studies of Myth, Ritual, and Classification* (New York: Oxford University Press, 1989); and Lincoln, *Theorizing Myth: Narrative, Ideology, and Scholarship* (Chicago: University of Chicago Press, 1999).

and perpetuated by rulers and patrons, but inhabitants of Egypt (so not just those of Greek-speaking ancestry) acknowledged these discourses as having real capital in this social space. Most notably in this regard was the discourse of pharaonic greatness; those who associated with the legendary past of Egypt and its pharaohs, which included its rituals and mythic traditions, communicated *their own* (the agents') elevated worth. In the case of the Ptolemies, the association also communicated their actual, demonstrated power.[48]

The dynamics of this social space were such that different agents could access these discourses, and in so doing, their regenerations formulated meanings not necessarily meant by their host creators.[49] Mary Louise Pratt calls this phenomenon the "slipperiness of signifiers" that inevitably occurs when cultures interact through contact on varying levels of interac-

---

48. I depend here upon the following works by Bourdieu: *Outline of a Theory of Practice* (Cambridge: Cambridge University Press, 1977); Bourdieu, "The Social Space and the Genesis of Groups," *Theory and Society* 14 (1985): 723–44; and Bourdieu, "Social Space and Symbolic Power," *Sociological Theory* 7 (1989): 14–25.

49. By producing their own pharaonic images, the Ptolemies regenerated pharaonic discourse, which appeared as visual images on temple walls, and as titles on official decrees, which included descriptions of Ptolemaic rule in pharaonic terms (protecting the land, ensuring the seasons, and administering justice). For examples, see Paul Edmund Stanwick, *Portraits of the Ptolemies: Greek Kings as Egyptian Pharaohs* (Austin: University of Texas Press, 2002). How all of these signifiers were received by Egyptians versus Greek-speaking inhabitants likely differed (Ludwig Koenen, "The Ptolemaic King as a Religious Figure," in *Images and Ideologies: Self-definition in the Hellenistic World*, ed. Anthony W. Bulloch et al., HCS 12 [Berkeley: University of California Press, 1993], 25–115). Likewise, although Callimachus, Theocritus, and possibly Apollonius utilized mythic Egyptian traditions in rewriting a Greek, epic past, their end products likely did not echo Egyptian sentiments. But some regenerations appear to have found favor with several different groups, as has been well-demonstrated by the Arsinoe cult. The dynastic traditions established in honor of Arsinoe II in the early Ptolemaic period lasted for centuries and seemed to have appealed to Egyptian inhabitants of Greek-speaking ancestry (Jan Quaegebeur, "Documents Concerning a Cult of Arsinoe Philadelphos at Memphis," *JNES* 30 (1971): 239–70; Quaegebeur, "Ptolémée II en adoration devant Arsinoè II divinisée," *BIFAO* 69 (1971): 191–217; Quaegebeur, "Reines ptolémaïques et traditions égyptiennes," in *Das ptolemäische Ägypten: Akten des Internationalen Symposions 27.–29. September 1976 in Berlin*, ed. Herwig Maehler and Volker Michael Strocka [Mainz: von Zabern, 1978], 245–62; and Quaegebeur, "Cleopatra VII and the Cults of the Ptolemaic Queens," in *Cleopatra's Egypt: Age of the Ptolemies*, ed. Robert Bianchi and Robert Fazzini [Brooklyn: Brooklyn Museum, 1988], 41–54).

tion.[50] In Ptolemaic Egypt, the economy of discourses (to adapt Bourdieu's discussion about the economy of social goods) functioned within relationships of varying power; soldiers with significant land ownership, financial officers, policeman, priests, and scribes, all of different self-ascribed *ethnoi* ("Macedonian," "Egyptian," "Judean," etc.), male and female, utilized different discourses for the purpose of having real effects in their social spaces. The same discourse could have implied different meanings for different agents, depending upon their intent and/or influence in their social spaces. This phenomenon includes what Ludwig Koenen calls the double meanings in Ptolemaic discourse and what Stephens describes as the "copresence" of Egyptian and Greek traditions in Alexandrian writings.[51] I prefer Pratt's use of the term "contact," however, to articulate the range of activity and meaning-making in the social space of Hellenistic Egypt. In linguistics studies, contact refers to the reality when agents from different linguistic systems must communicate with each other; the effects can vary—collision, reformulation, or agreement—but the respective linguistic systems are inevitably altered by virtue of this interaction.[52] Neither side is unaffected by the encounter. In her work, Pratt expanded the linguistic term to describe what occurs when discourses are produced by different agents in a colonized social space, which she calls the "contact zone."[53] For our purposes, the social space of Ptolemaic Egypt included dominant agents that had power over other agents in varying degrees,

---

50. Pratt, "Linguistic Utopias," in *The Linguistics of Writing: Argument between Writing and Literature*, ed. Nigel Fabb et al. (New York: Methuen, 1987), 48–66. Similarly, Bourdieu mentions how once symbolic capital is used in a social space, it has an "elasticity" whereby the understanding of it is not inherently stable ("Social Space and Symbolic Power," 20).

51. Koenen, "Ptolemaic King as a Religious Figure," esp. 25–29; Stephens, *Seeing Double*, 194–208. Stephens borrows the term "copresence" from Pratt's discussion of what she calls the "contact zone" of imperial Spain in Latin America (Mary Louise Pratt, *Imperial Eyes: Travel Writing and Transculturation* [New York: Routledge, 1992]).

52. See Raymond Hickey, "Language Contact: Reconsideration and Reassessment," 1–28, and other essays in *The Handbook of Language Contact*, ed. Raymond Hickey, BHL (Chichester: Wiley-Blackwell, 2010).

53. First expressed in Pratt, "Linguistic Utopias," and elaborated upon in Pratt, *Imperial Eyes*. I am not implying that the societal and political conditions of Ptolemaic Egypt equate with the histories of European imperialism across the globe. Postcolonial critiques, however, offer helpful theoretical models that best incorporate the range of influences that occur when a foreign power conquers and rules over an indigenous population and their land.

which in essence created a contact zone that fits Pratt's use of the term. A foreign power had rule over Egypt; the vast majority of its population were native to that controlled land; and elite indigenous inhabitants as well as those who could claim nonindigenous ancestry (i.e., Greek-speaking subjects) had varying statuses of local power.[54]

It is within this social context of Ptolemaic Egypt that I place the creation of *Aseneth*, and *Aseneth* is methodologically similar to Artapanus's work. As I demonstrated in the last chapter, *Aseneth* displays a learned understanding of septuagintal (and thus Judean, ancestral) traditions, and as I will argue in the next section, *Aseneth* particularly rewrites Hebrew ancestors in Egypt as heroes in the pharaonic past. *Aseneth* shares the same vantage point as that of Artapanus (Judean and thus nonrepresentative of dominant, imperial traditions), and it arguably paints the rosiest picture of Hebrew life in Egypt. The ruling establishment is not an enemy of the ancestors, and noble leadership is mostly reserved for Aseneth, Joseph, and some of Jacob's other sons. *Aseneth* achieves this positive portrayal by interweaving into its story dominant discourses that existed in Hellenistic Egypt. The characterizations of Aseneth and Joseph borrow Ptolemaic discourses of royalty and power to create the memory of Joseph and Aseneth as a pharaonic couple, and the depiction of the bees, who are associated with the mysterious honeycomb, further enhances Aseneth's royal connections. At the same time, *Aseneth* focuses on Judean history. Its extensive use of septuagintal literary styles and texts produces an imitation of Judean, ancestral traditions, but its delineation of Judean identity in an Egyptian environment establishes boundaries that would have been effective in Hellenistic Egypt. In the end, *Aseneth*, like Artapanus, promotes the greatness of the Judean ancestors as connected to the legacy of Egypt much like Hecataeus did for the Ptolemies and Greek immigrants in Egypt.

The Narrative Landscape of *Aseneth* and the Environment of Ptolemaic Egypt

As demonstrated in chapter 3, *Aseneth* is written in a septuagintal style, utilizing particular narrative features that one finds in septuagintal texts, and it not only refashions the Joseph narrative in the book of Genesis but

---

54. Stephens also uses Pratt's model in her work, *Seeing Double*, but she applies it differently than I do.

it also alludes to other septuagintal narratives (most notably Gen 34; 1 Sam 17; and Dan 10). Like Artapanus's stories, *Aseneth* is rooted in Judean traditions. There are images and phrases, however, that resonate less with septuagintal texts and more with Ptolemaic images and legal language. That a Judean writer would be familiar with these factors is not unlikely. Just as septuagintal vocabulary reflects Koine Greek that is evident in contemporary papyri and inscriptions, Judean writers in Egypt also drew upon contemporary usages of Greek in Egypt.[55] Artapanus demonstrates this point with his use of the terms διοικητής and ἄρουρα, but he also indicates awareness about local cultic practices of his time, and as I have argued, he likely understood the extent of Memphis's influence. In like manner, *Aseneth* borrows discourses from Hellenistic Egypt to craft its story about an ancestral couple and to echo the lives of Judeans in Egypt.

In this section, I will discuss four relationships between *Aseneth* and its Hellenistic Egyptian context. First, Aseneth's title as a "City of Refuge" is often read as a symbol of her as a model convert who protects proselytes, but I argue that the phrase associates her with the protection that Ptolemies granted to plaintiffs and reflects what Aseneth actually provides in the story. Second, the portraits of Aseneth and Joseph foreshadow their royal status at the close of the narrative, and these portraits share resemblances with Ptolemaic royal imagery and affiliations; most notable are the headpieces that Aseneth and Joseph wear. Third, the extraordinary bees that Aseneth encounters present a particularly rich example of the contact between Egyptian and Judean traditions, but the end result simply bolsters the unique picture of Aseneth as an epic Judean ancestor. Finally, the story of *Aseneth* echoes interests that many Judeans in Hellenistic Egypt shared. The fact that Jacob's sons are so skilled in combat would have resonated with Judean communities there, since a considerable percentage of Judean males were associated with the military. Unlike Artapanus's history, *Aseneth* also produces directives about how an adherent of the God Most High should interact in a multi-*ethnos* environment. These directives make sense in the context of Hellenistic Egypt, where we have evidence of Judeans who dealt with people of other *ethnoi* and who were involved in legislative matters of dispute or offense. Put all together, these four sets of inferences demonstrate how *Aseneth* used dominant images of power in

---

55. James K. Aitken provides a helpful summary of the scholarship on inscriptions in *No Stone Unturned: Greek Inscriptions and Septuagint Vocabulary*, CrStHB 5 (Winona Lake, IN: Eisenbrauns 2014), 1–33.

Egypt to construct a story of Judean influence and success in the pharaonic past. In the discussion below, when I refer to the storyline of *Aseneth*, I cite the portions as represented in my *fabula* along with the respective passages in Fink's reconstructed text (Bu/F).

Aseneth as a City of Refuge

After Aseneth's week of prayer and fasting, an angel visits her (*fabula* 19–20; Bu/F 14–17). He gives her a new name, "City of Refuge" (πόλις καταφυγῆς) and explains that people will seek refuge (καταφεύξονται) in her (*fabula* 20.d; Bu/F 15:7). Scholars have focused mostly on the possible allusions this title and role make to septuagintal texts, which concern the import of personified Jerusalem or the protection guaranteed in "cities of refuge." In LXX Zech 2:15, the city of Jerusalem (θύγατερ Σιών) is promised that "all nations will seek refuge in the Lord [καταφεύξονται ἐπὶ τὸν κύριον]" and they will dwell in the midst of the city. Although Zion is not personified in LXX Jer 27:5 (MT Jer 50:5), the passage nonetheless echoes the concept of the city being the location of refuge in God; the prophet declares that Israelites and Judahites will ask for the way to Zion, and they will come and "seek refuge in the Lord God [καταφεύξονται πρὸς κύριον τὸν θεόν]." In LXX Isa 54:15, in a rendering that differs from that of the Masoretic Text, the barren city is promised that προσήλυτοι "will approach you through me [the Lord] and they will seek refuge in you [ἐπί σε καταφεύξονται]." The term προσήλυτος has typically been translated as "proselyte" or "convert," but evidence suggests that in septuagintal usage (at least in the Old Greek) the term simply meant "stranger" or "immigrant" (I will discuss this more below.) In any case, the connection of LXX Zech 2, Jer 27, and Isa 54 to Aseneth's new name leads Bohak to conclude that Aseneth becomes an "eschatological Jerusalem" where Jews and proselytes will live.[56] Burchard interprets Aseneth's status as being "Zion of the proselytes," and Aseneth's title, "City of Refuge," and her new identity has dominantly been viewed in scholarship as Aseneth becoming a model convert.[57] Certainly Aseneth, as

---

56. Bohak, "*Joseph and Aseneth*," 76–80. Bohak's reading of "City of Refuge" depends upon more than what my *fabula* allows, and it is motivated by his overarching argument that the story particularly addresses the community of Onias in Egypt and the Leontopolis temple therein.

57. Quotation from Burchard, *Untersuchungen zu Joseph und Aseneth*, 119. George W. E. Nickelsburg refers to Aseneth as a "prototype of future proselytes" (*Jewish*

a convert herself, could have signified for converts their legitimate status within the community.[58] "Way back when," a prominent convert was welcomed by Joseph's family and became significant in their lives. In this way, the characterization of Aseneth underscores what Joseph meant by his imperative about intermarriage (*fabula* 13; Bu/F 8:5–7). For *Aseneth*, one's familial descent does not matter when constructing Judean identity, but what is required is one's allegiance and devotion to God the Most High. Aseneth is Egyptian, but after she converts, Joseph marries her.

Another conceptual connection with Aseneth's name is the notion about the cities of refuge in the Septuagint.[59] In LXX Num 35:9–15, the Lord designates six cities as places of refuge for those who commit involuntary manslaughter (ἔσονται αἱ πόλεις αὗται εἰς φυγαδευτήριον, LXX Num 35:15). Everyone can seek refuge there (φυγεῖν ἐκεῖ παντί), whether it be the sons of Israel, the resident alien (πάροικος), or the προσήλυτος (LXX Num 35:15). The book of Deuteronomy also mentions cities of refuge for the same purpose as in Numbers; the Israelites are to establish three to six cities (πόλεις) to be set aside as places of refuge (καταφυγή) to which such agents flee (καταφεύξεται) (LXX Deut 19:1–10). The book of Joshua narrates the establishment of six such cities of refuge, and discusses their purpose with language similar to that of Numbers. The cities of refuge are called πόλεις τῶν φυγαδευτηρίων, and the sons of Israel or the προσήλυτος residing among them can seek refuge there (καταφυγεῖν ἐκεῖ παντί) (LXX

Literature between the Bible and the Mishnah: A Historical and Literary Introduction, 2nd ed. [Minneapolis: Fortress, 2005], 334), Collins suggests that the title of "City of Refuge" and her story of conversion present Aseneth as "the representative proselyte" (*Between Athens and Jerusalem*, 236–37); and Barclay offers similar sentiments in which Aseneth is a "paradigmatic convert" (*Jews in the Mediterranean Diaspora*, 214). Although Chesnutt argues that the ritual scene in *Aseneth* 16 does not reflect actual Jewish initiation rituals, he interprets *Aseneth* primarily as a narrative that addressed converts and the Jewish communities who had received them; for Chesnutt, Aseneth is a "city of refuge" for "future converts" (*From Death to Life*, 169). Anathea E. Portier-Young focuses on Aseneth's act of mercy at the end of the narrative and proposes that as a "City of Refuge," Aseneth is a refuge for sinners and converts alike ("Sweet Mercy Metropolis: Interpreting Aseneth's Honeycomb," *JSP* 14 [2005]: 137). My argument comes very close to Portier-Young's, but I argue that Aseneth's title does not imply anything in particular about converts at all.

58. Chesnutt, *From Death to Life*, esp. 118–50.

59. Burchard, *Untersuchungen zu Joseph und Aseneth*, 92–95; Kraemer, *When Aseneth Met Joseph*, 36; Philonenko, *Joseph et Aséneth*, 183; Portier-Young, "Sweet Mercy Metropolis," 135–38.

Josh 20:9). The idea that Aseneth is a model convert is likely influenced, in part, by understanding the word προσήλυτος in LXX Num 35, Josh 20, and perhaps also Isa 54:15 to mean "proselyte." As a convert to Judaism, she then becomes a city for other converts, understood through the reference to προσήλυτοι.

There is no convincing evidence, however, that προσήλυτος meant a proselyte in Septuagint texts during the Hellenistic period. In LXX Num 35 and Josh 20, the word προσήλυτος translates the standard word for "sojourner" in Hebrew (גר), but for the last century, much of biblical scholarship has rendered the Greek word to mean "proselyte."[60] Even though גר refers to "proselyte" in rabbinic literature, it does not denote a conversion to Israelite religious practices in biblical texts (even within ritual regulations like the Holiness Codes).[61] It also does not convincingly imply conversion to Judaism in the Dead Sea Scrolls; the term גר signified an outsider who was incorporated at the lowest ranks of the community, but it is not clear whether a גר became a full member of the sect.[62] Furthermore, looking at the Greek translation of גר as προσήλυτος, the lexical evidence strongly suggests that Septuagint translators presumed προσήλυτος to mean "newcomer" or "sojourner."[63] The association of Aseneth with cities of refuge, then, may have nothing to do with προσήλυτοι, however defined.

---

60. David M. Moffitt, C. Jacob Butera, and Matthew Thiessen provide convincing evidence how in the late nineteenth and early twentieth centuries, scholars typically understood the Septuagint use of προσήλυτος to mean "sojourner," but W. C. Allen's 1894 essay advocated for the meaning "proselyte," and his argument became the dominant position in Western scholarship for over a century (Allen, "On the Meaning of ΠΡΟΣΗΛΥΤΟΣ in the Septuagint," *Expositor* 4 (1894): 264–75; Moffitt and Butera, "P.Duk. Inv. 727r: New Evidence for the Meaning and Provenance of the Word Προσήλυτος," *JBL* 132 [2013]: 160–70; and Thiessen, "Revisiting the προσήλυτος in 'the LXX,'" *JBL* 132 [2013]: 333–50).

61. On rabbinical use of גר see, Marcus Jastrow, *A Dictionary of the Targumim, the Talmud Bavli and Yerushalmi, and the Midrashic Literature* [London: Luzac; New York: Putnam's Sons, 1903], s.v. "גר." On the rending of the term in biblical scholarship, see Jutta Jokiranta, "Conceptualizing GER in the Dead Sea Scrolls," in *In the Footsteps of Sherlock Holmes: Studies in the Biblical Text in Honour of Anneli Aejmelaeus*, ed. Kristin De Troyer, T. M. Law, and Marketta Liljeström, CBET 72 (Leuven: Peeters, 2014), 659–62.

62. Jokiranta, "Conceptualizing GER," 665–77.

63. Moffit and Butera, "New Evidence," 170–78; Thiessen, "Revisiting the προσήλυτος," 333–50; and Aitken, *No Stone Unturned*, 46.

4. Aseneth and the Landscape of Ptolemaic and Early Roman Egypt 215

For one thing, no textual witness of *Aseneth* uses the word προσήλυτος or any equivalent to "sojourner" or even "proselyte." So even if Aseneth's name, "City of Refuge," was inspired by biblical concepts, the concepts of "sojourner" or "convert" do not seem to have been the compelling connections. Aseneth also does not protect according to the rubrics for the cities of refuge as described in Numbers, Deuteronomy, and Joshua. She protects the sons of Bilhah and Zilpah who intended to kill her (not who attempt to commit involuntary manslaughter). These sons of Jacob also are neither converts nor sojourners. Aseneth's role as "city" and how she protects those who seek refuge actually has nothing to do with proselytes. She behaves in a manner assumed by administrators in Egypt, and her association with the concept καταφυγή is most telling in this regard.

From Ptolemaic Egypt, we have hundreds of petitions in Greek that were sent from inhabitants of Egypt to administrators in hopes of getting their perceived injustices resolved. People from all sectors of society produced these petitions: those employed by Ptolemaic institutions (farmers, soldiers, or officials), priests, self-employed professionals, prisoners, orphans, widows, and other women and men who reported their misfortunes.[64] These appeals were sent to administrators (such as the στρατηγός or ἐπιστάτης) to generate responses to the respective complaints, and many appeals were addressed to the Ptolemaic king or couple.[65] With the evidence spanning from the mid-third century BCE into the mid-first century BCE, this kind of legal petition clearly developed into a well-known

---

64. John Bauschatz, *Law and Enforcement in Ptolemaic Egypt* (Cambridge: Cambridge University Press, 2013), 189–97.

65. Ana di Bitonto Kasser provides the most recent treatment of classifying and discussing the genre of these petitions (ἐντεύχεις [when the appeal was formally made to the king or Ptolemaic couple] or ὑπομνήματα [when the appeal was made to a Ptolemaic administrator]), and she identifies 173 petitions that were addressed to the Ptolemaic king (ἐντεύχεις) and about 200 that were addressed to other Ptolemaic officials (ὑπομνήματα). My summary of the basic genre of these petitions is based on her analysis ("Le petizioni al re: Studio sul formulario," *Aegyptus* 47 [1967]: 5–57; and di Bitonto Kasser, "Le petizioni ai funzionari nel periodo tolemaico: Studio sul formulario," *Aegyptus* 48 [1968]: 53–107). A helpful summary of the genre in English can also be found in Bauschatz, *Law and Enforcement*, 160–217. Petitions sent to the Ptolemies appear to have been handled by the office of the *strategos* or other Ptolemaic officials (Naphtali Lewis, *Greeks in Ptolemaic Egypt: Case Studies in the Social History of the Hellenistic World* [Oakville, CT: American Society of Papyrologists, 2001], 58; Bauschatz, *Law and Enforcement*, 193 n. 77).

genre that scribes utilized and officials understood how to interpret. Although it appears to have been more a part of Ptolemaic bureaucracy, the petition continued to be used into the Roman period.[66] The basic format of these appeals included the following: a formal address (to the Ptolemies [βασιλεῖ or βασιλεῖ καὶ βασιλίσσῃ] or to another official [like a στρατηγός]), a description of the plaintiff's plight, a request (typically introduced by δέομαι or ἀξιῶ) that orders be sent to particular local officials so that the situation would be addressed (and oftentimes, the plaintiff specifies how he/she wants the situation resolved), and then a final appeal and closing salutation. When addressing the Ptolemies or an official, the plaintiff typically expressed his/her situation with *pathos* in an attempt to persuade the official to respond; in these cases, the plaintiff emphasized his or her hardship (i.e., insufficient protection [as with an orphan or widow], obstruction of one's livelihood, or being treated with contempt by an adversary) or physical suffering (i.e., starvation or the effects of old age).[67] Based on the comments recorded in many of the petitions, orders were issued to those with power to resolve the problem, and it appears that plaintiffs' complaints tended to be swiftly addressed.[68] At the very least, the submission of a formal petition was a standard way that inhabitants of Ptolemaic Egypt sought restitution and justice.

There are four points of contact between these petitions and the *Aseneth fabula*. Near the end of the *Aseneth* story, the sons of Bilhah and Zilpah find themselves at a treacherous impasse (*fabula* 45–51; Bu/F 27–28). Their ambush attempt has failed; their armed forces had been decimated by the sons of Leah, Pharaoh's son was incapacitated, and his accompanying force had been killed by Benjamin. In a panic, Dan, Gad,

---

66. In SB 18.13087 (4 BCE) the plaintiff petitions a police official (ἐπιστάτῃ φυλακιτῶν); SB 1 5232 (15–16 CE) is sent to an official in Soknopaiou Nesos; and P.Oxy. 19.2234 (31 CE) to the centurion, Quintos Gaius Passer.

67. Di Bitonto Kasser, "Le petizioni al re," 49–50; and di Bitonto Kasser, "Le petizioni ai funzionari," 99–100.

68. Di Bitonto Kasser, "Le petizioni ai funzionari," 105–106; Bauschatz, *Law and Enforcement*, 212–14. Bauschatz provides compelling examples to demonstrate how the swift responses were part of Ptolemaic bureaucracy: a same day response by the office of a *strategos* in Magdola (P.Enteux. 8; 221 BCE); a one-day response of a *strategos* office in Memphis (UPZ 1.7; 163 BCE), and a one-day response of a *strategos* office in Herakleopolite (BGU 8.1832; 51 BCE) (*Law and Enforcement*, 214 n. 127). These examples, of course, do not confirm whether or to what extent the orders were carried out.

Naphtali, and Asher decide that they should kill Aseneth and Benjamin, but when they approach Aseneth with their swords drawn, she prays to God and their weapons fall from their hands and disintegrate before their eyes. At this point, they prostrate themselves before Aseneth and beg her to help them. They appeal to her as their queen (calling her βασίλισσα), they admit their wrongdoings—that they had acted wickedly against her and that God had paid them back—and they plead for Aseneth to take pity on them and protect them from their brothers (*fabula* 48; Bu/F 28:2–4). They issue their request with the introductory verb δέομαι (δεόμεθά σου) that appear in many legal petitions (δέομαι οὖν σου), meaning "I beg you, therefore, to (respond to the problem as requested by the plaintiff)."[69] In fact, this introductory formula is predominant in petitions that are addressed to the Ptolemies (instead to other officials), which helps make sense of the sons' address to Aseneth as "queen" (βασίλισσα).[70] Although by the end of the narrative Aseneth becomes a queen (by implication of Joseph's kingship), the men's use of the term here is a surprise. In official petitions, however, the address to both a king and queen had been used for centuries, and so the inclusion of calling Aseneth "queen" may have been understood as a common enough trope in actual appeals to make the men's words believable in the fictional appeal to Aseneth. The only women who are addressed in Ptolemaic petitions are queens, and since the title also foreshadows Aseneth's position at the end of the narrative, the title is a fitting one for the sons of Bilhah and Zilpah to use.

Along with calling Aseneth "queen" and using the formulaic plea (δεόμεθα), the sons of Bilhah and Zilpah describe their situation with some element of *pathos*. They fully admit their grave error, but they also describe their vulnerable state in which their brothers seek vengeance with their swords (*fabula* 48; Bu/F 28:3–4). In describing the level of violence that they face, the men explain that the sons of Leah want to avenge the *hybris* (ὕβρις) that the sons of Bilhah and Zilpah had committed (*fabula* 48; Bu/F 28:4). In legal petitions from Ptolemaic Egypt, complaints of *hybris* were common; this term indicated severe actions

---

69. Di Bitonto Kasser, "Le petizioni al re," 15–16. Although most petitions are written on behalf of one individual (using the phrase, δέομαι σου), some represent more than one plaintiff, using the phrase, δεόμεθα: e.g., Menches and Poleman appeal to "King Ptolemy, Queen Cleopatra the sister, and Queen Cleopatra the wife," and beg them for protection (δεόμεθα) (P.Tebt. 1.43 [117 BCE]).

70. Di Bitonto Kasser, "Le petizioni al re," 15–16.

of insult or violence against the plaintiff, which oftentimes resulted in injuries and other offenses. Petitions with complaints about *hybris* do not necessarily refer to the Greek noun (in these cases the plaintiff provides extensive descriptions of what they had endured), but the nominal and verbal forms (ὕβρις/ὑβρίζω) are used enough in the petitions to signify that it was a legal category.[71] *Hybris*, so defined, accurately describes the violent actions that the sons of Bilhah and Zilpah intended to commit, and the sons' depiction of their brothers seeking to avenge *hybris* with swords communicates how dire the situation had become for these plaintiffs. Only an equally violent response would avenge their crime of *hybris*. It is important to add here the other times in the *Aseneth fabula* that ὕβρις is used: to describe the assault against Dinah (*fabula* 34; Bu/F 23:14), the supposed description by Joseph on being sold into slavery by his brothers (as told by pharaoh's son, *fabula* 37; Bu/F 24:9), and Aseneth's description of the actions committed by the sons of Bilhah and Zilpah (*fabula* 51; Bu/F 28:14). All the actions signified by ὕβρις in *Aseneth* fit what the term implied in legal petitions.[72]

As the *Aseneth* story unfolds, Aseneth assures the sons of Bilhah and Zilpah of her protection, and she ultimately convinces the sons of Leah to desist from their violent intent (*fabula* 49–51; Bu/F 28:8–17). Although the narrative at this point does not use the word, καταφυγή, Aseneth provides the sons of Bilhah and Zilpah refuge. Clearly, these sons of Jacob did not convert, but they beg for protection and she grants it; she secures their safe harbor. In many of the legal petitions, plaintiffs appeal to the benevolence of those addressed by saying that they (the plaintiffs) "have taken refuge" in the addressee; these petitions typically use either a participial phrase (καταφυγῶν/καταφυγοῦσα or καταπεφευγώς/καταπεφευγυῖα ἐπὶ σέ) or a

---

71. Di Bitonto Kasser, "Le petizioni ai re," 22–24, and di Bitonto Kasser, "Le petizioni ai funzionari," 75–77; Naphtali Lewis, "*Notationes Legentis*," *BASP* 34 (1997): 31–33; and LSJ, s.v. "ὕβρις," II.3. Beyond what di Bitonto Kasser provides, other petitions that use (1) the nominal form (ὕβρις) are: BGU 10.1903 (mid-third century BCE); P.Sorb. 3.112 (219 BCE); P.Fay. 12 (104–103 BCE); SB 18.13087 (4 BCE); and (2) the verbal form (ὑβρίζω); BGU 10.1903 (mid-third century BCE); UPZ 1.6 (163 BCE); UPZ 1.8 (161 BCE); UPZ 1.12 and 1.13 (158 BCE); UPZ 1.15 and 1.16 (156 BCE).

72. Standhartinger discusses the implications of ὕβρις in her adaptations of Philonenko's text (*der Kurtztext*) and Burchard's text (*der Langtext*), but she does not incorporate contemporary legal examples into her discussion (*Das Frauenbild im Judentum*, 167–79).

4. *Aseneth* and the Landscape of Ptolemaic and Early Roman Egypt 219

phrase with the nominal form καταφυγή (ποιέω ἐπὶ σὲ καταφυγήν).[73] I do not think it is a coincidence that Aseneth is renamed a "City of καταφυγή" and then later in the narrative she provides the kind of protection that the Ptolemaic bureaucracy was perceived to ensure; that is, she resolves the plaintiffs' complaint of *hybris*. She enacts what is expressed in legal petitions, that she—as a queen—ensures justice. Now, we cannot verify whether or not plaintiffs in Ptolemaic petitions were as innocent as they claimed to have been, but certainly, the sons of Bilhah and Zilpah are at fault. Even though they were deceived by Pharaoh's son, they ultimately decided to act as they did (*fabula* 38–39, 41, 43, 46–47; Bu/F 24–27). Likewise, official responses to actual petitions do not promise protection of violent perpetrators, as does Aseneth. My point here is that the *fabula* utilizes familiar discourses of Ptolemaic Egypt to construct a narrative about Aseneth and Joseph, not that it imitates those discourses precisely as they were used in real life.

Aseneth as a city of refuge has been a puzzling reference for scholars, and I propose that the phrase is built only in part from biblical associations. Situating this narrative within Hellenistic Egypt, the term echoes the legal concept of a plaintiff receiving justice. *Aseneth* borrows inferences of protection and restitution that "refuge" implies in septuagintal texts and in Ptolemaic appeals, but it also generates its own idea. Aseneth protects men who attempted murder, and her words and actions convince Levi to save pharaoh's son—the perpetrator of the violence against them (*fabula* 51–53; Bu/F 28:15–29:5). As I mentioned in the previous chapter, Levi persuades Benjamin to stand down, and Benjamin's imitation of David slaying Goliath is halted (cf. *fabula* 52 [Bu/F 29:1–4] and LXX 1 Kgdms 17:51). The

---

73. Di Bitonto Kasser, "Le petizioni ai re," 51–52; di Bitonto Kasser, "Le petizioni ai funzionari," 70–71. Although not exhaustive, I have identified twenty-three petitions using the verbal phrase with καταφεύγω dating from mid-third to mid-second centuries BCE, and thirty-two petitions using the nominal form καταφυγή dating from the mid-second century BCE into the first century CE (with the bulk coming from the latter half of the second century BCE). (1) Petitions with καταφεύγω: P.Col. 4.83; P.Enteux. 12, 13, 14, 15, 26, 46, 51, 60, 62, 69, 70, 71, 78, 82, 85, 89, 112; P.Heid. 6.376; P.Hib. 2.238; P.Petr. 3.27; P.Sorb. 3.104; and P.Yale 1.46. (2) Petitions with καταφυγή: BGU 8.1823; 8.1836; 8.1858; 20.2845; P.Dion. 9; P.Dryton 1.33; P.Enteux 24; P.Erasm. 1.2, 1.3; P.Fay. 11; P.Giss.Univ. 1.1; P.Oxy. 19.2234; P.Münch. 3.51; P.Rein. 1.18; 1.19; P.Tebt. 1.43; 3.1.785; 3.1.789; P.Tor.Choach. 8; SB 16.12305; 20.14708; 22.15546; UPZ 1.8; 1.12; 1.14; 1.17; 1.19; 1.106; 1.107 (copy of 1.106); 1.208; 2.191; 2.192 (copy of 2.191).

disruption of Benjamin replaying David's first military victory highlights what *Aseneth* promotes; it is at this point in the story that Levi repeats the dictum that God-revering men "do not repay evil for evil" (*fabula* 52; Bu/F 29:3). Earlier in the narrative, when Pharaoh's son had solicited Levi's and Simeon's assistance, Levi had declared it unfitting for God-revering men to do (unjustifiable) harm to another person, which for Levi did *not* include retribution against pharaoh's son (*fabula* 34; Bu/F 23:10–14). Now, at the end of story, Aseneth has changed Levi's mind. Just as Aseneth does not provide refuge in the Pentateuchal sense, she (and then Levi) enact justice differently than what Ptolemaic appeals reflect (which never support the accused) and what septuagintal cities of refuge required (which do not protect offenders of murder). According to *Aseneth*, restraint best characterizes the person devoted to God the Most High, even when it concerns severe family grievances. Aseneth best models this behavior, and the narrative conveys her authority in terms of a Ptolemaic queen—how plaintiffs seek refuge in her and how she brings about justice.

Royal Portraits of Aseneth and Joseph

I will now turn to the royal depictions of Aseneth and Joseph. The *fabula* hints at Aseneth's royal essence beyond her association with regal, judicial power. It extensively describes her wealth (*fabula* 3 and 5; Bu/F 2 and 3:5–6), and there are notable items that Aseneth wears when she prepares to greet her parents. She is decked out in regal attire—a garment of violet interwoven with gold, costly jewelry with Egyptian gods represented on them, and a diadem (διάδημα) around her head covered by a cloth garment (*fabula* 5; Bu/F 3:6). Later in the story, when Aseneth changes her attire to greet Joseph a second time, she again dresses in wealthy clothes and accessories sans images of Egyptian gods, but she instead wears a crown with a head covering and she carries a scepter (*fabula* 21; Bu/F 18:6). Both depictions in the story echo portraits of Ptolemaic queens, most notably on coins.

Ptolemy I Soter is credited with establishing a closed-currency economy in Egypt, minting gold, silver, and eventually, bronze coins.[74] Early Ptolemies displayed images of both kings and queens on gold coins, and

---

74. Sitta von Reden, *Money in Ptolemaic Egypt: From the Macedonian Conquest to the End of the Third Century BC* (Cambridge: Cambridge University Press, 2007), 31–57.

subsequently these images were minted on silver coins as well. On these coins, the king consistently bears a diadem on his head (more on this below). The diadem was a flat band worn around the head and knotted in the back, and by the Hellenistic period it became the signature image for imperial rule.[75] Coin portraits of Ptolemaic queens also displayed them with diadems along with other items. Beginning with Berenike I, but most popularized with the portrait of Arsinoe II that continued into the late Ptolemaic period, queens were portrayed wearing a diadem or crown (στεφάνη) or both, with most wearing a veil and many depicted with a scepter.[76] We have evidence of these coins issued into the late Ptolemaic period, although the bulk of the coins date to the third to second centuries BCE. Even though bronze coinage became the primary currency in the *chora* in the third century BCE (when cash was used), gold coins were issued to the military, and both silver and gold coins entered the regular economy in the *chora* (such as with large payments).[77] As we will see, a high percentage of Judean men were associated with the military and some may have been recipients of such large payments. Bronze coinage typically depicted Alexander the Great or Ammon (with the legend, "of the King Ptolemy"), but we have evidence of Ptolemaic portraits on bronze coins, specifically of Ptolemy I bearing a diadem, Arsinoe with a crown (στεφάνη) and veil, and Cleopatra VII bearing a diadem with the legend,

---

75. R. R. R. Smith, *Hellenistic Royal Portraits*, Oxford Monographs on Classical Archaeology (Oxford: Clarendon, 1988), 34–38. Stanwick, *Portraits of the Ptolemies*, 35.

76. I. N. Svoronos, Τα νομίσματα του κράτους των Πτολεμαίων [The coins of the Ptolemaic state], 4 vols. (Athens, 1904–1908). With only a diadem: Arsinoe II and Berenike I (nos. 603–6, 608–9, 613–14, 616a, 618, 621, 934, 1247–48); Berenike II (nos. 962–63); and Cleopatra VII (as ruler of Egypt) (nos. 1871–73). Wearing a diadem and a veil: Berenike II (nos. 972–73, 978–82, 986–91, 1113–16). Wearing crown (στεφάνη) and veil: Arsinoe II (no. 935); Berenike II (nos. 983–85). Wearing a crown (στεφάνη) and veil, with scepter: Arsinoe II (nos. 408–10, 419–21, 428–29, 432–32a, 434–35, 443–45, 454–56, 459–61, 471, 475–77, 486–90, 492, 495–96, 502, 502a, 503, 508, 512–13, 517–18, 520, 936–61); Cleopatra I (nos. 1241–42, 1374). Wearing a combination of a diadem and crown (στεφάνη) and veil, with scepter: Arsinoe II (nos. 1120, 1442, 1444, 1447, 1449, 1452, 1464, 1468, 1470), Ptolemaic queens depicted as Arsinoe II (Cleopatra II: no. 1498; Cleopatra III: nos. 1499–1500; and two undetermined Ptolemaic queens, nos. 1726 and 1841).

77. Von Reden, *Money in Ptolemaic Egypt*, 31–57. On the monetization of the Ptolemaic economy, see J. G. Manning, "Coinage as 'Code' in Ptolemaic Egypt," in *The Monetary Systems of the Greeks and Romans*, ed. Willaim Harris (Oxford: Oxford University Press, 2008), 84–111.

"of the Queen" (ΒΑΣΙΛΙΣΣΗΣ).[78] It is possible, then, that Judeans came across these images and understood some if not all of what these coins signified. In addition, we have examples of Ptolemaic seal impressions of queens wearing diadems and at least of one wearing a crown, and given that seals were used in contracts, receipts, wills, and other types of administrative documents, it is possible that Judeans in Egypt came across such royal images in this way.[79]

It is fair to say that Aseneth's attire in both scenes (*fabula* 5 [Bu/F 3:6] and *fabula* 21 [Bu/F 18:6]) implies her regal and noble status in the story, and I propose that her headpieces were construed from actual imagery of Ptolemaic queens but their distinctions in the story are meant to convey Aseneth's transference of allegiance to the God Most High. At first she bears a diadem and veil (*fabula* 5), but after her encounter with the angel, she bears a crown and veil and carries a scepter (*fabula* 21). The most common coin portraits of Arsinoe II depict her with a diademed crown (στεφάνη), veil, and scepter, and given Arsinoe II's popularity throughout Egypt as a deified queen, the resemblance of the new Aseneth with Arsinoe II is striking.[80] It is Aseneth, and not Arsinoe, who is associated

---

78. Svonoros, Τα νομίσματα του κράτους. Bronze coins depicting a diademed Ptolemy I: nos. 192, 212, 214, 216–17, and 549; bronze coins depicting Arsinoe II with crown and veil: nos. 346, 351–52, 383, 386–87; and of a diademed Cleopatra: nos. 1871–73.

79. Seal impressions of Ptolemaic queens with diadems exist in a hoard purchased by the Royal Ontario Museum in Toronto (J. G. Milne, "Ptolemaic Seal Impressions," *JHS* 36 [1916]: 87–101; see esp. nos. 192–99, and 204). The hoard was supposedly discovered in Edfu in 1905/1906, and 330 sealings were sold to Toronto and 317 of the same hoard were given to the Allard Pierson Museum in Amsterdam. The finding dates to the late Ptolemaic period (Ptolemy V and Cleopatra I to Cleopatra VII), and although it includes hieroglyphic seals, the vast majority is in Greek or with Greek/Greek-Egyptian imagery. The bulk of the Amsterdam hoard has not been published, but Dimitris Plantzos has discussed female portraits in that hoard that include seals of a young woman (possibly Cleopatra I) and Cleopatra VII wearing a diadem and Cleopatra II with a crown (στεφάνη) ("Female Portrait Types from the Edfu Hoard of Clay Seal Impressions," in *Archives et Sceaux du monde hellénistique*, ed. Marie-Françoise Boussac and Antonio Invernizzi, BCHSup 29 [Athens: Ecole Française d'Athènes, 1996], 307–13 and pls. 48–53). For a general introduction to the function, representation, and evidence of seals in Ptolemaic and early Roman Egypt, see K. Vandorpe, "Seals in and on the Papyri of Greco-Roman and Byzantine Egypt," in Boussac and Invernizzi, *Archives et Sceaux*, 231–91 and pls. 45–47.

80. On the coin portraits, see above. On the iconography of queens on Ptolemaic coinage, see Agnieszka Fulińska, "Iconography of the Ptolemaic Queens on Coins:

with divine power, as Aseneth's encounter with the divine bees also proves (which I will discuss further below).

If Aseneth is fit to be a queen, then most certainly should Joseph be a king, which ultimately happens at the end of the story. Just as the *fabula* foreshadows Aseneth's royal nature, so does the story hint at Joseph's. The first time Aseneth lays eyes on him, the *fabula* considerably enhances the depiction of Joseph as described in Genesis. In LXX Genesis, Joseph is given Pharaoh's ring, fine linen (στολὴν βυσσίνην) and gold collar (κλοιὸν χρυσοῦν), and he is bestowed with Pharaoh's second chariot to ride (47:42–43). In *Aseneth* (*fabula* 9; Bu/F 5:4–6), Joseph enters Pentephres's complex in this supposed second chariot, but here, it is made entirely of gold. So too, his appearance is far more exquisite than in LXX Genesis; he wears elaborate, purple garb and a gold crown with rays emanating from it, and he carries a royal staff in his hand. As explained in chapter 3, the manuscript categories predominantly emphasize the color purple as well as designate that Joseph carries some sort of regal staff. In antiquity, a purple cloak or tunic oftentimes signified a position of high rank (including but not exclusively of kings), as it is often used in Septuagint texts (LXX Judg [Alexandrinus and Vaticanus] 8:26; Esth 8:16; 1 Macc 8:14; 10:20, 62, 64; 11:58; 14:43, 44; Dan [OG and Th] 5:7, 15, 29).[81] But when combined with a royal staff of some sort and an elaborate crown that is more than a celebratory wreath, there is little doubt that Joseph's purple cloak hints at royalty.[82]

The crown that Joseph wears is quite distinct; as I mentioned in the last chapter, the particular description of rays (ἀκτίς) emanating from his crown alludes to Helios, the sun god. Upon seeing Joseph, Aseneth describes him as ἥλιος in a chariot (*fabula* 10; Bu/F 6:2), which clearly associates the image of Joseph with a legendary image of Helios in Greek traditions (both in art and literature). As early as the sixth century BCE,

---

Greek Style, Egyptian Ideas?," *Studies in Ancient Art and Civilization* 14 (2010): 73–92. On Arsinoe II and her cult that was instituted by Ptolemy II, see Quaegebeur, "Documents Concerning a Cult of Arsinoe"; and Quaegebeur, "Ptolémée II en adoration."

81. For a discussion about purple clothing and its signification in antiquity, see Meyer Reinhold, *History of Purple as a Status Symbol in Antiquity* (Brussels: Latomus, 1970).

82. Smith contends that the scepter, purple, and diadem were the primary symbols of royalty in the Hellenistic period (*Hellenistic Royal Portraits*, 34–38). Even though Joseph does not wear a diadem in this scene, I will explain how his crown hints at a regal one.

we have images of Helios riding a chariot with a solar disk above his head, and by the fifth century BCE, Helios was being depicted with rays emanating from his head.[83] These images of Helios continued into the Hellenistic period, as best indicated by Rhodian silver drachms from the early third century BCE and the metope of Helios on the temple of Athena at Troy.[84] The reference to Helios on his chariot is repeated in literary traditions, most notably in The Homeric Hymn to Helios, where the god rides a "golden-yoked chariot" from which he gazes at everything of the cosmos (both of mortals and gods); he wears a finely worked garment and golden helmet (κόρυς); and rays (ἀκτῖνες) shine off from him. The Hymn to Demeter repeats this picture of Helios; here, too, he rides a chariot, and Demeter attains the truth about her daughter from him since he is the watchman of both gods and humans (lines 62–89).[85] The tales about Helios's son, Phaethon, also repeat the notion of Helios's chariot and his surveying the earth by day.[86] Most telling for our purposes are Apollonius's references to Helios in the *Argonautica*, a Greek hexameter epic composed in the third century BCE in Ptolemaic Egypt. In Apollonius's retelling of Jason, Medea, and the Argonauts, he mentions Helios and his chariot several times. Helios had taken Hephaestus in his chariot after the Gigantomachy (3.233–34); Helios's son, Aeetes, the king of Colchis, mentions riding it (3.309–311); Helios gave Aeetes his chariot horses (4.220); and the myth of Phaethon on Helios's chariot is recounted (4.595–626). The *Argonautica* also alludes to Helios's radiating image; Aeetes puts on a gold helmet (κόρυς, cf. Hymn to Helios) that "[shines] like the round light of the sun [ἥλιος] when it first rises from Ocean" (3.1227–1230), and the children of Helios all have a "radiance from their eyes" that casts a "gleam like that of gold" (4.727–729).

---

83. Herbert Hoffmann, "Helios," *JARCE* 2 (1963): 117–24, especially pl. 23. In particular Hoffmann mentions Helios with a solar disk riding a chariot on a skyphos (in Taranto) and a black-figured lekythos (in Boston), and Helios with rays on Rhodian coinage.

84. Hoffman, "Helios," pl. 26.

85. Helios rides a chariot in the Homeric Hymn to Hermes as well (line 68).

86. In the myth of Phaethon, the son of Helios and Clymene loses control of the sun chariot and is killed by Zeus to prevent the world setting on fire (literally). For a summary of the evidence, see Euripides, *Fragments: Oedipus-Chrysippus, Other Fragments*, ed. and trans. Christopher Collard and Martin Cropp, LCL (Cambridge: Harvard University Press, 2008), 323–29.

In Ptolemaic Egypt, Helios was also a Greek reference to the Egyptian sun god, Re, and the image of Helios riding across the sky echoed Egyptian solar traditions recounting the cyclical journey of Re.[87] Hecataeus of Abdera claims that Helios reigned first in Egypt (Diodorus Siculus, *Bib. hist.* 1.13.2; 1.26.1), which matches Egyptian mythology that places Re as the first king and all subsequent kings as a "son of Re" (as indicated on royal titulature).[88] The Canopus decree (238 BCE) translates Re as Helios in the Greek, and the Memphis decree (196 BCE) associates Re/Helios with Ptolemy V.[89] Re/Helios is the primordial king and Ptolemy V is declared "king like Re/Helios;" the sun god's might is with Ptolemy V (Greek and Demotic read, "to whom Helios/Re gave/has given victory"); and following traditional Egyptian titulature, Ptolemy V is identified as a son of Re/Helios.[90] Panagiotis Iossif and Catharine Lorber argue that the images on *mnaieia* (gold coins worth one hundred silver drachms each) of Ptolemy III, Euergetes I, and Ptolemy V Epiphanes were meant to associate these kings with Egyptian mythic solar traditions of kingship.[91] Each coin depicts the king with rays radiating from his diadem, and in the second century BCE, Ptolemy VIII was depicted similarly on at least silver coinage minted in Cyprus.[92] The solar images connect these Ptol-

---

87. Stephens and Noegel both present compelling arguments about the Egyptian solar mythology in Apollonius's *Argonautica* (especially in book 4) (Stephens, *Seeing Double*, 171–237; Noegel, "Apollonius' *Argonautika*"). Even though Apollonius does not correlate Helios with Re, he nonetheless demonstrates significant knowledge of Egyptian mythology and incorporates it in an Alexandrian telling of Jason and the Golden Fleece. The *Argonautica* exemplifies the kind of cultural product I have been discussing; it combines ancestral traditions with Egyptian/Ptolemaic discourses to produce a new story.

88. Maya Müller, "Re and Re-Horakhty," *OEAE*, 3:123–26. A concise introduction to Egyptian royal titulature can be found in Allen, *Middle Egyptian*, 81–83.

89. For the Canopus decree, see Stefan Pfeiffer, *Das Dekret von Kanopos (238 v. Chr.): Kommentar und historische Auswertung eines Dreisprachigen Synodaldekretes der Ägyptischen Priester zu Ehren Ptolemaios' III. und seiner Familie*, APFB 18 (Munich: Suar, 2004), 163–66. Both the Demotic and hieroglyphic texts provide "Re."

90. Greek text: *OGIS* 90; demotic text: R. S. Simpson, *Demotic Grammar in the Ptolemaic Sacerdotal Decrees* (Oxford: Griffith Institute, 1996), 258–59. The beginning of the hieroglyphic text is missing on the Rosetta Stone, which provides the most complete, triliteral copy of the Memphis decree.

91. Iossif and Lorber, "The Rays of the Ptolemies," *RN* 6 (2012): 197–224.

92. Iossif and Lorber, "Rays of the Ptolemies," 198–99 nn. 1–3. Iossif and Lorber cite the following examples: (1) portraits of Ptolemy III: Svoronos, nos. 1117–19,

emies with Horus's kingship and Re's regeneration of the land and cosmos. Iossif and Lorber also identified five seals with radiating images of late Ptolemaic kings (one seal from Paphos and four from Edfu) and two gems with radiating images of Ptolemy VIII.[93] This phenomenon of blending recognizable iconography of a sun god (Helios rays) with the significance of a sun god's role in the cosmos (Re) created a new discourse that tapped into influential native Egyptian traditions but at the same time signified the rule of these Ptolemaic kings. Furthermore, the contact of Greek and Egyptian discourses that created the new image does not fit precisely into the source culture of either; in the social space of Hellenistic Egypt, a new discourse developed.

The Ptolemaic investment in perpetuating their pharaonic significance in Egypt did not go unnoticed, especially in the *chora*. As already mentioned, the Egyptian priesthood worked in tandem with the Ptolemies to expand ritual practices and temple industries in Egypt, all of which incorporated Ptolemaic rule into Egyptian narratives and art. As I discussed earlier in the chapter, this activity was noticed by non-Egyptians as well (in the case of Artapanus), and another interesting example also comes from Memphis. In the mid-second century BCE, Ptolemaios had become a recluse (ἐν κατοχῇ) in the Serapeum at Memphis; he was a self-ascribed Macedonian and son of Glaukias, a cleruch who had settled in Psichis (Herakleopolite nome).[94] Ptolemaios had some form of Greek education; he could read and write in Greek, and he sent several petitions on behalf of himself, family, and friends. In two petitions to King Ptolemy VI Philometor and Queen Cleopatra II, he addressed the king as Ἥλιε βασιλεῦ (O

1132–34, 1184; (2) Ptolemy V: Svoronos, nos. 1254, 1257; and a *mnaieion* outside of Svonoros's collection (Christie's sale, 9 October 1984, lot 304); and (3) Ptolemy VIII: Svoronos, no. 1507 (didrachm), and a tetradrachm of Ptolemy VIII not known to Svoronos (Leu 36, May 1985, lot 220). See also, R. A. Hazzard, *Ptolemaic Coins: An Introduction for Collectors* (Toronto: Kirk & Bentley, 1995), 7, 11. Beginning with Antiochus IV Epiphanes, Seleucid rulers sometimes portrayed themselves with the Helios crown on coins (Smith, *Hellenistic Royal Portraits*, 42). Iossif and Lorber argue that the coinage of Ptolemy III and Ptolemy V are distinct, and although it may have influenced the Seleucid coinage, Antiochus's discourse was unrelated to what the Ptolemies signified.

93. Iossif and Lorber, "Rays of the Ptolemies," 198–99 n. 3.

94. On Ptolemaios, his brother Apollonius, and life in the Memphite Serapeum, see Lewis, *Greeks in Ptolemaic Egypt*, 69–87; and Thompson, *Memphis under the Ptolemies*, 197–246.

Helios, King), and he closed the petitions echoing Egyptian ideology, mentioning how Helios (Re) watches over the land (πάσης χώρας ἧς ὁ Ἥλιος ἐφορᾶι) and praying that Isis and Serapis (and in *UPZ* 16, the twelve gods of Herakleopolis as well) grant the Ptolemaic couple and their children rulership over Egypt forever (*UPZ* 1 15 and 16). Ptolemaios appears to adapt a phrase from Homer (*Il.* 3:277 ['Ἥλιός θ', ὃς πάντ' ἐφορᾷς]; and similarly in *Od.* 11:109; 12:323), but he clearly associates Helios with Re (who protects *the land* [χώρα]) and conflates the mythic traditions about Re with Ptolemy VI's reign.[95] Interestingly, Aseneth identifies Joseph as ἥλιος on a chariot who *sees* everything; she frets about how she could hide her arrogance since nothing can be hidden from him (*fabula* 10, *Asen.* 6:6).[96] Joseph appears, then, to be and look like Helios/Re, and thus in the context of Ptolemaic discourse, to be like a king.

What I propose here is that the author of *Aseneth* utilized mythic images of kingship as proliferated by the Ptolemies and created a believable foreshadow of Joseph as king. Joseph's image imitates Helios, and Helios's arrayed crown and chariot are common associations that make their way to Egypt (the *Argonautica* being a prime example). The Ptolemaic conflation of Helios as king (Re) was known to Greek writers (Hecataeus) and scribes (as demonstrated in Ptolemaic decrees and by Ptolemaios). Joseph's *helios* crown, purple garment, and royal staff solidify the *fabula*'s claim about his regal qualities, which by the end of the narrative he fulfills. It turns out that Pharaoh's son dies, and soon after, so does Pharaoh, who leaves his diadem (διάδημα) for Joseph. Subsequently, Joseph reigns (ἐβασίλευσαν) for forty-eight years (*fabula* 54, *Asen.* 29:8–9). There is no surprise at the end of the story, then, about Joseph's rule, since he ultimately wears *the* signature feature of Hellenistic kingship (διάδημα). As I mentioned above, early on Ptolemaic kings portrayed themselves with a diadem on silver and gold coins, and our evidence stretches from the

---

95. I wonder whether scribes of families *a* and *d* changed Aseneth's speech to better fit this Homeric correlation of the sun seeing everything. These manuscript families alter Bu/F 6:2–7 in the order of vv. 5–7, 2–4 (which constitutes Ph 6:2–7). Aseneth describes Joseph as ἥλιος in Bu/F 6:2 and Joseph's all-seeing eye in Bu/F 6:5–6; families *a* and *d* echo classical Helios imagery by bringing these verses closer together (Ph: 6:2–3, 5).

96. In all manuscript categories except MS E, Aseneth recounts that nothing is hidden from Joseph's sight, and although not uniform in its placement, all categories have Aseneth refer to what Joseph "sees" (ὁράω or its equivalent appears in Syr, Arm, L2 [MS 436], *f* [FW, L1], *c*, *a*, and *d*) (Burchard, *Joseph und Aseneth*, 106).

reigns of Ptolemy I (304–283 BCE) to Ptolemy XIII (51–47 BCE).[97] As mentioned earlier, although bronze coinage was the more common currency and usually depicted a god or Alexander the Great on the obverse, some bronze coins portray Ptolemy I with a diadem.[98]

The association of the diadem as a significant royal headpiece also appears to have been known to Judean translators and writers. In the LXX, διάδημα was used to translate Hebrew words for a royal turban (כתר מלכות in Esth 1:11 and 2:17, or צניף in Isa 62:3), or διάδημα was used to signify sovereignty (such as in Sir 11:5 and 47:6 [the latter in reference to David's reign]. The royal διάδημα is also mentioned in the Wisdom of Solomon (5:16), and 1 Maccabees consistently uses the term to signify Hellenistic rule (1:9; 6:15; 8:14; 11:3 [3x], 54; 12:39; and 13:32). It is interesting to note that in LXX Esther, where Mordecai's role is more enhanced than in the Masoretic Text, Mordecai goes about Shushan wearing both a gold crown and a diadem (καὶ στέφανον ἔχων χρυσοῦν καὶ διάδημα), but he only wears a gold crown in the Hebrew text (עטרת זהב) (8:15). To accentuate Mordecai's regal character, the Greek Esther adds the clearly royal signature of a diadem.

To summarize, *Aseneth* portrays both Aseneth and Joseph as royalty far before they actually become rulers over Egypt. Each wears particular headpieces that resemble portraits of Ptolemaic queens (with a διάδημα and/or crown, and oftentimes with a veil) or of kings (with a διάδημα, and for a few,

---

97. Svoronos (Τα νομίσματα του κράτους) lists portraits of Ptolemaic kings with diadems issued between the reigns of Ptolemy I and Ptolemy XIII, with most portraying Ptolemy I. I provide here Svonoros's classifications for gold and silver coins minted in Egypt, but Svonoros also provides coinage minted in other Ptolemaic territories, which would add to this list: nos. 181–83, 185, 187, 190–91, 194–95, 196A–201, 203–5, 207–11, 218, 222–25a, 227–29, 231–34, 236, 240–68, 322–31, 333–37; 341a–44, 348–50, 353–55, 357–59, 361–62, 364–76, 378, 380, 388–407, 411, 430, 433, 436, 524–48, 551–52, 555, 558–59, 566–67, 569–70, 573–75, 578–79, 583–85, 588, 590–92, 595–97, 599, 607, 995–96, 1001, 1121–22, 1135, 1137, 1205–28, 1230–31, 1249, 1250, 1394, 1431–41, 1443, 1445–46, 1448, 1450–51, 1453–63, 1465–67, 1469, 1471–85, 1489–90, 1727–31, 1815–37, and 1839–40. Diademed Ptolemaic kings portrayed alongside the Ptolemaic queen: nos. 603–6 (this group alone covers over one hundred coins), 608–9, 613–14, 616a, 618, 621, 934, 1229, and 1247–48. The bulk of this evidence was issued under the reign of Ptolemy II, but later Ptolemies issued versions of Ptolemy II and Arsinoe II on the obverse and Ptolemy I and Berenike I on the reverse (issued under the reigns of Ptolemies III, IV, and V; this covered the time frame from the third century into the beginning of the second century BCE).

98. Svonoros, nos. 192, 212, 214, 216–17, and 549.

with a Helios, radiating crown). Having Aseneth and Joseph wear similar headpieces bolsters the characterizations that they were of royal stock and meant to rule, like the Ptolemies who came long after this Judean pair.

Aseneth and the Royal Bees

There is one more reference in *Aseneth* that is pertinent to dominant Ptolemaic discourse in Egypt. When Aseneth encounters the angelic figure, she asks him to stay for a meal, and in her interchange with him, a honeycomb miraculously appears in her storehouse. Aseneth brings the comb to the angel and identifies it with him, and he then blesses Aseneth. He declares that secret/inexplicable matters of God have been revealed to her, and he feeds her a portion of this honeycomb, which he associates with partaking in a life-giving meal and oil. He then summons bees from the comb, and their wings seem like expensive clothing in purple and their heads are adorned with diadems. (*fabula* 20.g–h; Bu/F 15:13–16:18) As mentioned above, diadems typically signify royalty, and when paired with purple clothing, they unmistakably refer to rulership.

The visual image of a bee also reinforces the idea of kingship in Egypt. As early as the Fifth Dynasty, the bee was used to signify royalty in the hieroglyphic writing of the throne name (or prenomen) that always began with hieroglyph unit, *nswt-bjt*, literally translated as "he to whom the sedge and bee belong," and meaning, "the king of Upper and Lower Egypt."[99] The official title of every pharaoh consisted of five titles: the Horus name, the Two Ladies name, the Gold Falcon name, the throne name, and the Son of Re name. For much of the pharaonic period, the throne name became the most significant title; it typically would display the hieroglyphic unit, *nswt-bjt*, followed by a cartouche that enclosed the royal name of the king (the name given upon coronation and signifying the continuation of the divine office).[100] In Henri Gauthier's list of royal

---

99. Allen, "The King's Names," in *Middle Egyptian*, 82–83. As the titulature suggests, the sedge plant is associated with Upper Egypt, and the bee signifies Lower Egypt and can also stand for the Red Crown of Lower Egypt (Jean LeClant, "Biene," *Lexikon der Ägyptologie*, edited by Wolfgang Helck, Otto Eberhard, and Wolfhart Westendorf [Wiesbaden: Harrassowitz, 1975], 1:787).

100. For an explanation of the perception of the divine office of the king in ancient Egypt, see Lanny Bell, "The New Kingdom 'Divine' Temple: The Example of Luxor," in Shafer, *Temples of Ancient Egypt*, 127–84.

titulatures, he lists over one hundred examples on temple reliefs as well as on statues and stelae of Ptolemaic Egyptian titulatures containing *nswt-bjt*.[101] The bulk of these examples are spread fairly evenly in mentioning Ptolemy II through Ptolemy VIII, during a time when the Ptolemies were significant patrons of Egyptian temples and cultic life (285–116 BCE).[102] Although most examples have been best preserved from Upper Egypt, sufficient examples exist from Lower Egypt as well; most notably in copies of the Canopus decree that were discovered at Tanis, Kom el-Hisn, and Tell Basta (Bubastis), and the Memphis decree that was discovered at el-Rashid (Rosetta) and Naucratis.[103] Although hieroglyphic examples are few, there are Ptolemaic seals that provide *nswt-bjt* and the throne name of a Ptolemaic king.[104] The demotic texts of the Canopus and Memphis

---

101. Henri Gauthier, *Le livre des rois d'Égypte: Recueil de titres et protocoles royaux, noms propres de rois, reines, princes, princesses et parents de rois, suivi d'un index alphabétique, vol. 4: De la XXV e dynastie à la fin des Ptolémées*, MIFAO 20 (Cairo: Imprimerie de l'Institut français d'archéologie orientale, 1915–1916), 199–203 and 214–406. The examples begin with Alexander the Great, the titulature of whom has been greatly expanded upon by Francisco Bosch-Puche ("The Egyptian Royal Titulary of Alexander the Great, I: Horus, Two Ladies, Golden Horus, and Throne Names," *JEA* 99 [2013]: 131–54; and Bosch-Puche, "The Egyptian Royal Titulary of Alexander the Great, II: Personal Name, Empty Cartouches, Final Remarks, and Appendix," *JEA* 100 [2014]: 89–109).

102. Dieter Arnold, *Temples of the Last Pharaohs* (New York: Oxford University Press, 1999), 143–224; Günther Höbl, *A History of the Ptolemaic Empire* (London: Routledge, 2001), esp. 77–124, 160–77, and 257–303; and for Memphite traditions in particular, see Thompson, *Memphis under the Ptolemies*, 99–143.

103. Examples listed in Gauthier, *Le livre des rois d'Égypte*: (1) Ptolemy I: stela found in Lower Egypt; (2) Ptolemy II: stela discovered at Tell el-Maskhuta (Heroonpolis); fragments found at Thmuis-Mendes; on a statue of the king found in Heliopolis; fragments found at Sebennytos; stela of Ptolemy II and Arsinoe II at Tanis; on three statues found in Alexandria; (3) Ptolemy III: copies of the Canopus decree (as mentioned above); and on a relief from a temple near Sebennytos; (4) Ptolemy IV: in the Raphia decree (Memphis stela); and on a dedicatory plate found in Alexandria; (5) Ptolemy V: in the Memphis decree (Rosetta Stone and Damanhur Stela [found at Naucratis]); stela of Apis; and on a stela at the Memphite Serapeum; (6) Ptolemy VI: on a stela at the Memphite Serapeum; and on a stela found in Memphis (Mit-Rahineh); and (7) Ptolemy VIII: on a stela at the Memphite Serapeum and three funerary stelae dedicated to different Apis bulls.

104. One of Ptolemy V: Ellen Doetsch-Amberger, "Ein Siegel Ptolemaios' V," *GM* 142 (1994): 67–68. The provenance of this seal is unknown and was privately owned (in 1994 at least), but Doetsch-Amberger provides the results of material analysis of

decrees translate the hieroglyphic phrase *nswt-bjt* as *pr-ʿꜣ* ("pharaoh," the standard word for "king" in Demotic papyri), and the Greek texts translate *nswt-bjt* as βασιλεύς.[105] It appears that by the Ptolemaic period, *nswt-bjt* was understood as a linguistic unit that referred to the king, and so the visual image in *Aseneth* of bees dressed in royal garb with diadems would noticeably imply this connection.

It is conceivable that Ptolemaic inhabitants who were not fluent in Egyptian hieroglyphic could have understood the bee-royalty association in *Aseneth*. For one thing, the sacerdotal decrees mentioned above were placed in the outer courtyards of Egyptian temples for people of all ranks to see, and given that the *nswt-bjt* hieroglyphs on those decrees

---

the seal that confirmed that the atomic make-up of the seal matched more verifiably dated, ancient Egyptian seals. Two of Ptolemy VI (but both of unknown provenance): one kept in the Egyptian Museum in Cairo (first discussed in Auguste Mariette, *Monuments divers recueillis en Égypte et en Nubie* [Paris: Franck, 1872], pl. 48e) and another in the Pier Collection (first discussed in Garrett Chatfield Pier, *Egyptian Antiquities in the Pier Collection* [Chicago: University of Chicago Press, 1906], 27, no. 233). Both examples are provided and discussed in Martina Minas, *Die Hieroglyphischen Ahnenreihen der Ptolemäischen Könige: Ein Vergleich mit den Titeln der eponymen Preister in den demotischen und griechischen Papyri* (Mainz: von Zabern, 2000), 40–41, and Dok. 97 and 98. The Los Angeles County Museum of Art (LACMA) has a clay seal presenting the throne and "Son of Re" names of Ptolemy I Soter (with *nswt-bjt* hieroglyphs), but I have not found any scholarly analysis about its validity; the item appears to have been in private hands until it was acquired by the museum (M.80.202.291).

105. Canopus decree (I refer here to the copy found at Tanis): (1) line 1 in Greek (with participle, βασιλεύοντος), demotic, and hieroglyphic; (2) line 7 in Greek, line 8 in the demotic, and line 4 in hieroglyphic; (3) lines 21 in Greek and demotic, and line 11 in hieroglyphic; (4) line 25 in Greek, line 26 in demotic; line 13 in hieroglyphic; (5) line 35 in Greek, line 34 in demotic, and line 17 in hieroglyphic; (6) line 46 in Greek, line 45 in demotic, line 23 in hieroglyphic (Pfeiffer, *Das Dekret von Kanopos*). Memphis decree (I refer here to the Rosetta Stone, which has a significant portion of the hieroglyphic missing): (1) line 9 in Greek and line 5 in demotic [hieroglyphic is missing]; (2) line 38 in Greek, line 22 in demotic, line 6 in hieroglyphic; and (2) line 41 in Greek, line 24 in demotic, line 7 in hieroglyphic (André Bernand, *Le prose sur pierre dans l'Égypte hellénistique et romaine*, vol. 1 [Paris: Centre National de la Recherche scientifique, 1992]; and Stephen Quirke and Carol Andrews, *The Rosetta Stone: Facsimile Drawing* [London: British Museum, 1988]). For the meaning of *pr-ʿꜣ* in demotic, see Janet J. Johnson, ed., *The Demotic Dictionary of the Oriental Institute of the University of Chicago* (Chicago: Oriental Institute of the University of Chicago, 2001), https://oi.uchicago.edu/research/publications/demotic-dictionary-oriental-institute-university-chicago.

were typically adjacent to the quite identifiable royal cartouche, even an untrained eye could have associated the bee with the king.[106] Given the economic industry of temples in the *chora* and the general public spectacle of Egyptian festivals, it would not be surprising if Judeans caught glimpses of hieroglyph designs on outer temple walls or within the public courtyards therein.[107] The Memphite necropolis alone provided opportunities for inhabitants (including Judeans) to witness a varying array of visuals and ritual activity simply because of their occupations (as traders, scribes, policemen, and soldiers) and not just because of devotional interest or desperate need (such as asylum).[108] Furthermore, as Herodotus and Hecataeus conversed with Egyptian priests, other Greek intellectuals likely did as well. In the first century CE, the Egyptian-Greek priest and philosopher, Chaeremon of Alexandria, wrote the Greek work *Hieroglyphica*, obviously for the Greek-educated to consult, and in it he identified the bee hieroglyph as signifying "king."[109] Alexandria, too, was not devoid of Egyptian influences; Egyptian sculptures were incorporated in the Alexandrian Serapeum, two colossal statues of a Ptolemaic couple portrayed as Egyptian royalty flanked the entrance to the harbor, and the oldest trilingual, priestly decree from the Ptolemaic period was composed in Alexandria (in 243 BCE).[110] Especially for the educated composer of *Aseneth*, it is reasonable to conclude that the writer understood the bee's significance in Egypt.

---

106. For the placement of the sacerdotal decrees, see Höbl, *History of the Ptolemaic Empire*, 106.

107. For a general overview of temple life during the Ptolemaic period, see Ragnhild Bjerre Finnestad, "Temples of the Ptolemaic and Roman Periods: Ancient Traditions in New Contexts," in Shafer, *Temples of Ancient Egypt*, 185–237. For a detailed example of the relationship between temple activity and the local economy in Ptolemaic Egypt, see Thompson, *Memphis under the Ptolemies*.

108. For a thick description of the Memphite necropolis, see Thompson, *Memphis under the Ptolemies*.

109. Renata Landgráfová, "Ars Memoriae Aegyptiaca? Some Preliminary Remarks on the Egyptian Hieroglyphs and the Classical Art of Memory," in *Visualizing Knowledge and Creating Meaning in Ancient Writing Systems*, ed. Shai Gordin, BBVO 23 (Gladbeck: PeWe-Verlag, 2014), 133–53.

110. On the colossal finds, see Jean-Yves Empereur, "Alexandrie (Égypte)," *BCH* 120 (1996): 967; and Stanwick, *Portraits of the Ptolemies*, 115–16. On the Alexandrian Serapeum, see McKenzie, Gibson, and Reyes, "Reconstructing the Serapeum," 73–121. On the Alexandria decree, see Yahia El-Masri, Hartwig Altenmüller, and Heinz-Josef Thissen, *Das Synodaldekret von Alexandria aus dem Jahre 243 v. Chr.* (Hamburg: Buske, 2012).

4. *Aseneth* and the Landscape of Ptolemaic and Early Roman Egypt   233

The fact that the bees in *Aseneth* are connected with the divine realm also reflects the author's awareness of the close correspondence between Egyptian royal titles (such as with the *nswt-bjt* throne name) and the inclusion of the Ptolemaic couples in the pharaonic line (as portrayed and repeated in Egyptian ritual). As depicted on temple reliefs and described in the sacerdotal decrees of the early Ptolemaic Empire, the dynastic cult in Egyptian temples conveyed how the Ptolemies tapped into the divine power granted to the pharaohs of the past and were included in the divine realm as the pharaonic ancestors were already perceived to be.[111] Likewise, the repetition and public spectacle of Egyptian festivals cannot be overstated here. No one in Egypt could have avoided these celebrations, and in witnessing them, the connections between the Ptolemies and divine world could have been ascertained. The bees in *Aseneth* are affiliated with the divine realm as well in their supernatural state and from their production of the life-giving comb (*fabula* 20g–h; Bu/F 15:13–17:4).

I am not suggesting here, however, that the creator of *Aseneth* completely understood Egyptian rituals and the incorporation of the dynastic cult in Egyptian temples. Pratt's reference to the "slipperiness of signifiers" can be helpful in this case. My point is that the creator of *Aseneth* and even those who received the narrative in Egypt could have recognized in the bee scene a royal connection to the divine realm as it seemed believable to them in their cultural background of dominant, Ptolemaic-funded ritual practices. From a Judean perspective, the choice of the honeybee in particular is ingenious. The correspondence between honey and wisdom, or between honey and divine knowledge has deep roots in Judean literary traditions, which makes the royal *honey*bees in *Aseneth* connect to both the visuals of the dominant, Ptolemaic environment and rich, Judean references. In particular, LXX Pss 18:8–11; 118:97–104; LXX Prov 24:13–14; and Sir 24:13–22 equate honey with God's teaching (νόμος) and/or wisdom, and LXX Ezek 3 associates honey with divinely bestowed knowledge (in that Ezekiel consumes God's prophecies).[112] The royal bees

---

111. Descriptions of Ptolemaic investment and presence in Egyptian temples can be found in Finnestad, "Temples of the Ptolemaic and Roman Periods," 185–237; and Höbl, *History of the Ptolemaic Empire*, 77–123, 160–77, and 257–303.

112. The connections between the honeycomb in *Aseneth* and Judean references have been discussed by many scholars, most thoroughly by Portier-Young, "Sweet Mercy Metropolis," 133–57. See also, Ahearne-Kroll, "*Joseph and Aseneth* and Jewish Identity," 250–62. On the possible associations between Ezek 3 and the comb

are connected to divine knowledge and power (as Ptolemies/pharaohs were presented to be) yet that power in *Aseneth* is attributed to the jurisdiction of the God Most High. The bee scene in *Aseneth*, then, conveys the uniqueness of Aseneth; how she repudiated her Egyptian religious practices, repented to God, and then was chosen by God to receive divine knowledge and to be incorporated in a special way in heaven (since her name will be inscribed in the book of the living/life, *fabula* 20.c; Bu/F 15:4). In Ptolemaic-Egyptian terms, she rightfully becomes a queen (as did the Ptolemaic queens, who were incorporated into the divine realm), but she becomes a queen on Judean terms (i.e., Aseneth does not become a goddess but eats of the special, life-giving comb that comes from the God Most High).

Aseneth and Judean Life in Egypt: Soldier Families and Directives of Negotiation

There is a striking feature in *Aseneth* that echoes the life experience of many Judean families in Hellenistic Egypt: that of a soldier. According to Christelle Fischer-Bovet, Greek-speaking inhabitants accounted for only about 5 percent of the population during the first two centuries of Ptolemaic rule (roughly 184,000 Greeks among 4 million total), but over half of the adult males from this small percentage were associated with the military in some capacity (a maximum of 40,000).[113] Clearly, a majority of the male immigrants came to Egypt to enroll in the Ptolemaic army, and among those whose ethnic identity is ascribed in documentation, Ἰουδαῖοι are listed as third among the top-ten provenance identifications of immigrants in Ptolemaic Egypt.[114] Although the number of ethnic designations is small (1600), it remains noticeable that the number of Ἰουδαῖοι mentioned in this sample is high (102 times with Ἰουδαῖοι compared to 199 references

---

in *Aseneth*, see Delling, "Einwirkungen der Sprache der Septuaginta," 54; and Standhartinger, *Das Frauenbild im Judentum*, 119–21 and n. 275.

113. Christelle Fischer-Bovet, "Counting the Greeks in Egypt: Immigration in the First Century of Ptolemaic Rule," in *Demography and the Greco-Roman World: New Insights and Approaches*, ed. Claire Holleran and April Pudsey (Cambridge: Cambridge University Press, 2011), 135–54.

114. Katja Mueller, *Settlements of the Ptolemies: City Foundations and New Settlement in the Hellenistic World*, Studia Hellenistica 43 (Leuven: Peeters, 2006), 166–74 esp. 170 n. 85.

to Thrace, and 201 to Cyrenaica).¹¹⁵ Significantly, and especially in the Fayum, which consisted of a high percentage of immigrants, papyrological documentation proves the existence of self-ascribed Judeans who were soldiers, members of military families or designated as possible recruits (as the designator "of the descent" [τῆς ἐπιγονῆς] implied).¹¹⁶ Judean military service in Egypt is also mentioned by Judean writers. Albeit a fictionalized account, the Letter of Aristeas mentions Judean military employed by the Ptolemies and by previous rules of Egypt (§§12–13), some details of which can be confirmed by papyrological records.¹¹⁷ Even Artapanus echoes the legend of Judeans as skilled in warfare; Moses himself led the Egyptian forces with an ability akin to that of Sesostris (*Praep. ev.* 9.27.4–10).

Given this backdrop of Judeans in Egypt, it is not a coincidence that *Aseneth* emphasizes the military prowess of Jacob's sons and provides a story about military pursuit and defeat (*fabula* 31–54; Bu/F 23–29). Levi and Simeon are renowned for their defeat of the Shechemites (*fabula* 32; Bu/F 23:2–6); Benjamin single-handedly disables pharaoh's son and terminates his accompanying troops (*fabula* 45; Bu/F 27:1–5); and in general, Jacob's sons prove to be better fighters than Egyptian forces. Under the leadership of Dan, Gad, Asher, and Naphtali, *their* Egyptian forces

---

115. Mueller lists in full, based primarily on the evidence compiled by Csaba A. Láda (*Foreign Ethnics in Hellenistic Egypt*, Studia Hellenistica 38 [Leuven: Peeters, 2002]): Cyrenaica (201), Thrace (199), *ioudaioi* (102), Crete (80), Attica (63), Thessaly (58), Caria (53), Arabia (49), Pamphylia (40), and Ionia (37) (Mueller, *Settlements of the Ptolemies*, 166–174 esp. p.170 n. 85). Mueller's analysis does not include the identifiers "Hellenes," "Macedonians," or "Persians," which all signified a social status other than ethnicity (Csaba A. Láda, *Ethnic Designations in Hellenistic Egypt*, 2 vols. [PhD diss., Cambridge, 1997]).

116. *CPJ* 1.147–78. Aryeh Kasher, *The Jews in Hellenistic and Roman Egypt: The Struggle for Equal Rights*, TSAJ 7 (Tübingen: Mohr, 1985), 38–55; Fischer-Bovet, *Army and Society in Ptolemaic Egypt*, 169–95. On the designator τῆς ἐπιγονῆς and related terms, see Csaba A. Láda, "Who Were Those 'of the Epigone'?," in *Akten des 21. Internationalen Papyrologenkongresses, Berlin, 13.–19.8 1995*, ed. Bärbel Kramer et al., APFB 3 (Stuttgart: Teubner, 1997), 1:563–69.

117. For a discussion about the letter's claim of Ptolemaic enslavement and later conscription into the army, see Benjamin G. Wright III, *The Letter of Aristeas: "Aristeas to Philocrates" or "On the Translation of the Law of the Jews,"* CEJL (Berlin: de Gruyter, 2015), 125–36. Most notably, the Elephantine papyri, dated to the Persian period, preserve documentation of Judean mercenary households (Bezalel Porten, *The Elephantine Papyri in English: Three Millennia of Cross-Cultural Continuity and Change*, 2nd ed., DMOA 22 [Atlanta: Society of Biblical Literature, 2011]).

dominate Aseneth's armed guard (*fabula* 39 and 43; Bu/F 24:15-20 and 26:5), but soon the sons of Leah decimate those soldiers who had been accompanying the sons of Bilhah and Zilpah (*fabula* 46; Bu/F 27:6). Within the narrative, the particular skills of Levi and Simeon are most acute since they are not only actualized against Egyptian forces (*fabula* 46), but their threats are believable to the narrator and other characters. Unbeknownst to pharaoh's son, Simeon almost kills him (*fabula* 33; Bu/F 23:7-9); pharaoh's son is intimidated by Levi's and Simeon's sword-drawn warning (*fabula* 34-35; Bu/F 23:10-17); and Simeon's expressed intention of revenge against the sons of Bilhah and Zilpah sets up, if only for a moment, the perception that Aseneth will fail in persuading the sons of Leah to desist (*fabula* 51; Bu/F 28:12-17). This latter part of *Aseneth* provides an entertaining tale of jealousy, ego, honor, and combat that showcases Judean skill in warfare.

But *Aseneth* does not conclude with a typical military victory. By its dictum to "not repay evil for evil," it instructs how to resolve disputes especially in response to violence, aggression, and *hybris*. As already discussed in this chapter, the corpus of legal petitions recorded from Ptolemaic Egypt demonstrate that regional administrative bodies facilitated solutions for such disputes, and *Aseneth* associates restraint with proper allegiance to the God Most High. The abrupt shift of Benjamin shadowing David's character in the Goliath story is a stark case in point how *Aseneth* alters the picture of the legendary Judean ancestors.[118] Here, the Goliath character is not killed in battle; instead, there is an effort to save his life (*fabula* 52-53; Bu/F 29:1-6). It is also important to emphasize that *Aseneth* portrays intra- *and* interfamilial hostility; Pharaoh's son instigated the attack, but the sons of Bilhah and Zilpah willingly agreed, and they would have been killed by Leah's sons if Aseneth had not interceded. For this reason, the teaching "not to repay evil for evil" does not necessarily allude to actual hostility towards Judeans (or converts to Judaism) in particular. Certainly within the story, Levi and Aseneth apply the dictum in response to hostility toward themselves or toward their family (*fabula* 33, 50-52; Bu/F 23:8-9; 28:10, 14; 29:3), but they are never threatened because of their *ethnos* identity, including their religious practices. Pharaoh's son is motivated by his desire to have Aseneth as his wife, and the sons of Bilhah and Zilpah are

---

118. See also Gordon Zerbe, *Non-Retaliation in Early Jewish and New Testament Texts: Ethical Themes in Social Contexts*, JSPSup 13 (Sheffield: Sheffield Academic, 1993), 78-80.

motivated first by the lie that Joseph will soon eliminate them and then by their own desire to escape a failed ambush (*fabula* 31, 36–38, and 47; Bu/F 23:1; 24:1–14; and 27:7–10). Levi and Simeon apparently acted as they did at Shechem because of the *hybris* committed against their sister (*fabula* 34; Bu/F 23:10–14), but they do not identify their *ethnos* as a cause. Given the legal implications of the term, *hybris* here likely refers to the violence committed against Dinah, and so when Aseneth persuades Simeon, Levi, and the rest of the sons of Leah to desist, she extends what "not repaying evil for evil" means (*fabula* 50–51; Bu/F 28:9–17). The sons of Bilhah and Zilpah definitively committed *hybris* against Aseneth, Joseph, and the sons of Leah (*fabula* 48; Bu/F 28:1–4), but Aseneth convinces the sons of Leah not do what Levi and Simeon did at Shechem. Levi is persuaded, and he in turn prevents Benjamin from killing Pharaoh's son (*fabula* 51–53; Bu/F 28:12–29:6). The dictum, "not to repay evil for evil," then, appears to address the idea of how an adherent of the Hebrew god should respond to any injustice, no matter the cause and no matter the perpetrator.

Ptolemaic legal appeals demonstrate many cases of perceived aggression and exploitation, and as is the case with the aggression in *Aseneth*, most grievances were reportedly done by people the plaintiffs knew.[119] Greek-speaking inhabitants and Egyptians all lodged complaints and were the subjects of complaints, and Judeans in Egypt knew about the administrative procedure of filing appeals.[120] Most telling is the fact that some Judeans in the Herakleopolite region made appeals in the petition form of a ὑπόμνημα to archons of a Judean *politeuma*.[121] This type of appeal was

---

119. Bauschatz, *Law and Enforcement*, 160–280.

120. A good example comes from a second-century BCE appeal from Philadelphia in the Fayum (P.Ryl. 578 and *CPJ* 1.43; in the form of a ὑπόμνημα). Judas, son of Dositheos, Ἰουδαίου, appeals to Zopyrus, the ἐπιμελητής (financial officer) to attend to the unfair raising of his annual rent for leasing farmland by Marres, the κωμογραμματεύς (the village scribe). See also: P.Tebt. 800 (*CPJ* 1.133; ὑπόμνημα); and perhaps P.Enteux. 59 (*CPJ* 1.37; if Theodotos, Gaddaios, and Phanias were Judean, as Tcherikover suggests [*CPJ*, 184 n.1]; in the petition form of an ἔντευξις). In P.Enteux. 2 (*CPJ* 1.38; ἔντευξις), a Judean is listed as the accused (Harmiysis, a wool-merchant in Krokodilopolis complains about a Judean shepherd named Seos in a wool transaction).

121. P.Heid. Inv. G 4927 (P.Polit.Iud. 1; Alexandros, a member of the *politeuma*, issues a complaint about Nikarchos, a person "from the harbor" [a nonmember of the *politeuma*] who verbally abused him in public); P.Heid. Inv. G 4877 (P.Polit.Iud. 2; Petaus, a Ἰουδαῖος, petitions the *politeuma* to advocate for his release from prison); P.Köln Inv. 20986 (P.Polit.Iud. 3; Protomachos appeals to the archons to resolve a

typically used to address a petition to a Ptolemaic administrator, which the archons of the Herakleopolite *politeuma* were not.[122] A custom developed, then, in how inhabitants of Egypt addressed disputes and experiences of wrongdoing. Likewise, as mentioned above, actions of *hybris* occurred enough for it to be a legal category; many people of all walks of life dealt with conflict and offensive behavior. Within this social context, *Aseneth* promotes the action of restraint in the face of hostility as a strategy for living in Egypt, and *Aseneth* associates this behavior with what it means to observe the Hebrew god. In the end, *Aseneth* tells us, restraint also pays off.

---

marriage contract negotiated by him and the bride's father, Euphranor); P.Heid. Inv. G 4931 (P.Polit.Iud. 4; A member of the *politeuma*, Philotas, appeals to the archons to resolve a dispute with Lysimachos over a reneged marriage contract; since Philotas requests that the archons have the "Judeans in the village" send Lysimachos to resolve the dispute, it appears that Lysimachos may also be Judean); P.Köln Inv. 21046 (P.Polit.Iud. 6; Theodotos, Ἰουδαῖος, appeals to the archons on behalf of his mother to request that they follow through demanding the judicial decision of an investigation performed by Judean judges of the town of Onnês); P.Köln Inv. 21038 (P.Polit.Iud. 7; Dorotheos, a member of the *politeuma*, makes an appeal against Jonas, the wife of his brother-in-law, and the archons' decision is written on the verso); P.Köln Inv. 21041 (P.Polit.Iud. 8; Theodotos, Ἰουδαῖος, petitions the *politeuma* to resolve a payment dispute with Plusia and Dorotheos, who are Ἰουδαῖοι from the village of Teis in the Oxyrhynchite region); P.Köln Inv. 21031 (P.Polit.Iud. 9; a Judean woman, Berenike, from the Aphrodite polis appeals to the archons against a Judean man, Demetrios, who failed to fulfill promised payment of sold labor [a slave, his children, and other hired labor]); P.Heid. Inv. G 4928 (P.Polit.Iud. 10; Ptolemaia appeals to the archons to compel Tetous, a female spinner "from the harbor," to complete an order she had arranged); P.Heid. Inv. G 4934 (P.Polit.Iud. 11; a Judean man named Ptolemaios appeals to the archons to resolve a dispute with a woman "from the harbor" who reneged in a transaction); and P.Vindob. G 57704 (P.Polit.Iud. 12; a Judean named Nikanor appeals to the archons to resolve a dispute with another Judean, Andromachos, who had failed to make payment on leased land). Several formulae in these appeals echo the language in other known ὑπομνήματα. Comparing these to di Bitonto Kasser's analysis ("Le petizioni ai funzionari"), particular similarities are: (1) all the above appeals use the introductory verb ἀξιῶ as is common in Ptolemaic appeals; (2) several use the common, reverential phrase ἐὰν φαίνηται (nos. 3, 4 [φάνηται], 6, 7, 8, 9) (cf. ἐάν σοι φαίνηται in other ὑπομνήματα); and (3) almost all the above use common verbs used to request administrative action; the examples are: συντάξαι (nos. 6, 9), συντάξαι γράψαι (nos. 4, 8), ἀνακαλέσασθαι (nos. 6, 7, 10), and/or προσκαλέσασθαι (nos. 11 and perhaps 12).

122. Di Bitonto Kasser, "Le petizioni ai funzionari," 53–107.

Levi's attempt to save Pharaoh's son gains Pharaoh's blessings, and shortly thereafter, Joseph reigns as king (*fabula* 53–54; Bu/F 29:6–9).

A word must be said about the fact that the story sanctions the marriage of the Hebrew Joseph and the Egyptian Aseneth. Joseph's dicta that a man who reveres God can only be intimate with a woman who reveres God and vice-versa summarize precisely how Aseneth's status changes. She remains an ancestral Egyptian but her sole allegiance shifts to Joseph's god. *Aseneth* does not require that Hebrews must marry among those of the same ancestral background; the narrative never erases the fact that Aseneth is the daughter of an Egyptian priest. In this way, *Aseneth* appears far more open to the intermarriage between Judeans and non-Judeans than when we compare the guidelines of texts such as Jubilees (cf. *Aseneth* with Jub. 30). This distinction has been a focal point for several scholars, where such intermarriage signifies outreach to converts or gentiles, or simply echoes believable scenarios in the Second Temple period.[123] The Elephantine texts of the Persian period demonstrate that some Judeans intermarried, and at the very least, documentation evidence in the Ptolemaic period hints at the possibility of intermarriage between Judeans and non-Judeans.[124] I agree that how *Aseneth* negotiates legitimate marriage

---

123. In his comprehensive study of Aseneth's conversion scene (Bu/F 10–17), Chesnutt argues that *Aseneth* fundamentally promotes the inclusion of converts into the Jewish community with a secondary purpose of instructing Jews about negotiating life in a gentile environment (*From Death to Life*, esp. 254–65). At the time of his monograph, Chesnutt was refuting a popular stance in Second Temple scholarship that *Aseneth* was missionary propaganda, aimed primarily at converting gentiles to Judaism (see references in *From Death to Life*, 257 n.1). Chesnutt proposed a more nuanced understanding of Joseph's dictum about marriage and of Aseneth's shift of allegiance, and my argument is very close to the core of Chesnutt's position in that *Aseneth* negotiates Judean identity in a multi-*ethnos* environment. Hicks-Keeton expands on Chesnutt's argument but in a direction different than my own. She argues that *Aseneth* produces a new paradigm in which the Ἰουδαῖος/Ἰουδαία affiliation becomes obsolete; *Aseneth*'s paradigm promotes gentile inclusion by redefining what affiliation with the Hebrew god means (it is to associate with the "living God" and not with the god of a particular *ethnos*) (*Arguing with Aseneth*). Another tack has been proposed by Matthew Thiessen, who argues that Aseneth undergoes an ontological transformation in chs. 10–17 to promote gentile conversion ("Aseneth's Eight-Day Transformation as Scriptural Justification for Conversion," *JSJ* 45 [2014]: 229–49). Collins argues that *Aseneth*'s focus on intermarriage aligns well with Second Temple Jewish concerns ("*Joseph and Aseneth*," 97–112).

124. On Elephantine, see the helpful, updated discussion by Annalisa Azzoni, "Women of Elephantine and Women in the Land of Israel," in *In the Shadow of Bezalel:*

within the parameters of proper devotion to the Judean god resonates with the social environment in Hellenistic Egypt, but there is little solid evidence to prove whether intermarriage was common among Judeans in Egypt. What is clear is that *Aseneth* teaches that intermarriage is acceptable if the outsider changes allegiance.

Conclusion

Returning to the topic at the start of this chapter, *Aseneth* is a narrative meant for more than just welcoming converts. It recasts the history of Jacob's family in Egypt in a more positive and significant light, and its tale inevitably competes with other ancestral stories that promoted legitimate connections of Greek-speaking peoples to the Egyptian pharaonic past. Much like Artapanus's work, *Aseneth* emphasizes Hebrews' contributions to the contemporary infrastructure of Hellenistic Egypt. Aseneth, the Egyptian wife of Joseph and future queen of Egypt, mediated peaceful solutions to violent altercations; the sons of Jacob were skilled soldiers; and Joseph became a pharaoh. This narrative portrays the ancestors according to ideal models of status, power, and influence in Hellenistic Egypt; the regal attire and appearance of both Aseneth and Joseph confirm the legitimacy of their rule at the end of the narrative, and the bee scene of chapter 16 in particular portrays Aseneth as a worthy queen who can mediate with the divine realm. *Aseneth* also provides explicit instructions about Judean marriage and responses to severe grievances, which could have addressed real issues that Judeans in Hellenistic Egypt faced, and the story narrates how epic figures of the Judean past followed them. Yet, much like Hecataeus's retelling of Greek origins in Egypt, *Aseneth* also inserts Judean ancestral traditions into the pharaonic past, and in so doing it creates the idea that Judeans share in the historic legacy of Egypt and could honorably feel at home living there. Keeping in mind my discussion about Ἰουδαία/Ἰουδαῖος at the start of this monograph, we can put it another way: *Aseneth* transforms the Judean "myth of common descent"

Aramaic, Biblical, and Ancient Near Eastern Studies in Honor of Bezalel Porten, ed. Alejandro F. Botta, CHANE 60 (Leiden: Brill, 2013), 3–12. Azzoni discusses the evidence for Mibtahiah and her marriage to the Egyptian, Eshor, and the marriage of the Egyptian slave, Tamut, to Anani. On possible examples of intermarriage from the Herakleopolite papyri, see Stewart Moore's summary and references in, *Jewish Ethnic Identity and Relations in Hellenistic Egypt: With Walls of Iron?*, JSJSup 171 (Leiden: Brill, 2015), 86–88.

to include a significantly greater stay in Egypt than the book of Genesis allows, and it delineates boundaries of Judean identity in Egypt that made it possible to settle and thrive there.

5
Conclusion

"But I don't want to go among mad people," Alice remarked.
"Oh, you can't help that," said the Cat: "we're all mad here. I'm mad. You're mad."
"How do you know I'm mad?" said Alice.
"You must be," said the Cat, "or you wouldn't have come here."
—Lewis Carroll, *Alice's Adventures in Wonderland*

Those of us who have surveyed the textual witnesses of *Aseneth* can very well relate with both Alice and the Cheshire Cat. The absurd and unexpected scenarios that Alice encounters in Wonderland match the experience I have had in managing the challenges of the *Aseneth* witnesses. I know that others can relate; Christopher Brenna recently described to me that making sense of the *Aseneth* witnesses is like walking ten cats. The evidence is unpredictable and oftentimes does not confirm interpretations of the story, and too many scholars continue to depend upon reconstructed texts (especially that of Burchard). We who have gone to *Aseneth*'s Wonderland surely echo the Cheshire Cat's comments, too. We are mad to have gone so far into the obscurity of the textual witnesses, but there is no other path to take if one wants to examine the narrative with accuracy.

My monograph attempts to answer how *Aseneth* began. After demonstrating how it is impossible to reconstruct the earliest *Aseneth* text, I proposed a way to talk about the story in an earlier setting. The philosopher's critique most certainly will be that I replaced one reconstruction with another. My response is that I do not propose a reconstructed text; I propose the core of what the witnesses share (the *fabula* of *Aseneth*) and, unlike the reconstructions of *Aseneth*, I inform the reader how I chose each core element, especially with regard to linguistic units. In this way, I have been transparent in how I have used the textual witnesses, and I have pointed readers to them if they wish to see for themselves. In other words, I force the reader to see the madness of variations among the witnesses, and I propose a way to make sense of it. The consistent storyline that the witnesses present makes this possible, and I argue that this storyline accords closely with Judean life in Hellenistic Egypt.

The *fabula* of *Aseneth* reflects how Greek-educated populations rewrote their identities in Hellenistic Egypt, and Artapanus also echoes this impulse. Both *Aseneth* and Artapanus rely on the literary traditions of septuagintal texts, implying the ancestral importance of those texts, but they also contextualize the Judean past as one that benefited Egypt. This narrative spin breaks away from the dominant story about Egypt in septuagintal texts but resonates with the more varied, and for centuries more positive, lived experience of Judeans in Hellenistic Egypt. Both Artapanus and *Aseneth* plant Judean heritage into the pharaonic past, and *Aseneth* utilizes several linguistic and visual connections to Ptolemaic power to construct the memory of the ancestors, Aseneth and Joseph, as a royal couple (the role of Aseneth as a legal protector of καταφυγή; Aseneth's attire akin to Ptolemaic queen portraits, and Joseph's association with Ptolemaic connections to Helios/Re as well as his ultimate pharaonic rule). The mediation of conflict in *Aseneth* aligns well with the documented evidence in Ptolemaic Egypt that included Judeans (esp. legal petitions that sought justice from actions of *hybris*), and *Aseneth*'s interest in the combat skills of Jacob's sons is believable in the context of Hellenistic Egypt where a high majority of Judean males were associated with the military. The *fabula* also defines Judean, *ethnos*-identity to include people from other *ethnoi*, but this inclusion is best understood as a transference of *ethnos*-identity whereby incomers abandoned ancestral associations with previous gods and embraced solely the god of Joseph. Given the polyethnic environment of Hellenistic Egypt, such inclusion likely occurred although our evidence for it is scarce. At the very least, if we combine *Aseneth*'s rescription for intermarriage with the rest of the features mentioned above, the context of Judeans in Hellenistic Egypt is a convincing setting for the creation of *Aseneth*.

I am unconvinced by Kraemer's and Nir's arguments for a late antique Christian setting, mostly because their readings do not take into account the entire narrative or they too loosely connect *Aseneth* to their proposed settings.[1] Kraemer's identification of the Septuagint's influence on *Aseneth*

---

1. As mentioned in my introduction, several scholars have raised these critiques about Kraemer's monograph, *When Aseneth Met Joseph*, but I cover these points in detail in my dissertation, "*Joseph and Aseneth* and Jewish Identity," 149–69. In chs. 2

is not necessarily a late antique phenomenon, and the same can be said about the association of Joseph's headpiece in *Asen.* 5 with Helios. Her proposals that *Aseneth* reflects adjuration practices or mystical traditions, or that Neoplatonic cosmological thought underlies the bee scene in *Asen.* 16 are not clearly evident at the literal level of the story, and Nir's proposal demonstrates similar shortcomings. Nir sees *Aseneth* as an allegory in which Aseneth symbolizes the Christian church, Joseph symbolizes Jesus, and ideals set forth in the latter part of the narrative echo Christian ideals. Even though Nir deals with the entire narrative, and not just *Asen.* 10–17, her reading requires interpreting the story beyond its literal level. The narrative of *Aseneth* is quite understandable and relatable on its own without searching for hidden meanings in its story, and I have argued that the story in its entirety would have been quite appealing to Judeans in Hellenistic Egypt.

I need to also address a particular challenge Kraemer raised about *Aseneth*, which is: since the manuscript evidence does not date earlier than the sixth century CE, and since we have no attestations referencing Aseneth prior to the third century CE, then we should start at the assumption that *Aseneth* was composed in late antiquity.[2] In the case of *Aseneth*, I believe her argument obscures the distinction between the origination and preservation of literature in antiquity. Although the works of Philo were primarily preserved and transmitted by later Christian writers, the study of Philo's writings in their hypothetical, original context has contributed a great deal to the study of Second Temple Judaism. The earliest witnesses we have of Philo's works date to the third century CE, and although the data are significant (forty-four folios in one codex and fifteen folios belonging to another), they are incomplete.[3] Medieval manuscripts (in the

---

and 3, Kraemer addresses the septuagintal connections to the shorter and longer texts; in chs. 4–6, she proposes her hypothesis about *Aseneth*'s connections to adjuration practices, mystical traditions, Helios, and Neoplatonic thought (*When Aseneth Met Joseph*). A helpful synthesis of the limitations of Nir's proposal can be found in Hicks-Keeton, *Arguing with Aseneth*, 24–26.

2. Kraemer, *When Aseneth Met Joseph*, 225–44. In his *Commentary on Genesis*, Origen refers to a story about Aseneth (cited in Kraemer, *When Aseneth Met Joseph*, 230, 235); see also V. Aptowitzer, "Asenath, Wife of Joseph: A Haggadic Literary-Historical Study," *HUCA* 1 (1924): 257; and Philonenko, *Joseph et Aséneth*, 38–39.

3. LDAB 3540 (P.Oxy. 9.1173, P.Oxy. 11.1356, PSI 11.1207, P.Oxy. 18.2158, P.Haun. 8, and P.Oxy. 82.5291) and LDAB 3541 (Parisinus supp. gr. 1120). LDAB 3540 contains *De sacrificiis Abelis et Caini, Legum allegoriae 1* and *2, De Pietate, De ebrietate*

West) are believed to descend from a fourth-century exemplar, more than a quarter of the manuscript evidence is in Armenian, and some of Philo's works are preserved only in Armenian (*Quaestiones et solutiones in Genesin 1–4*, *Quaestiones et solutiones in Exodum 1–2*, *De providentia 1–2*, *De animalibus*).[4] Certainly many early Christian writers refer to Philo, and his historical writings substantiate claims for the dating of his works.[5] The actual texts that scholars study, however, date centuries after Philo's time. The origin of Philo's best textual witnesses confirms that the preservation of a literary piece in later times indicates little (if anything) about when the piece was first composed.[6]

When considering periods about which we lack sufficient evidence, the historical dating of a composition relies on more factors than just what the textual evidence suggests. My point here is not to beg the reader to take a leap of faith to verify the hypothesis that *Aseneth* was composed earlier than the third century CE. Rather, my point is that when we are working with time periods from which we only have pockets of concentrated information, we are left with highly fragmented pictures of the literary life of that culture and time period. When we factor in our partial knowledge about literary production in antiquity, it becomes an even more difficult enterprise to produce a hypothesis about when (and why) a literary text was first composed. This is not to say, though, that such carefully constructed hypotheses are unproductive; much of classical scholarship relies

---

1 and 2, *De posteritate Caini*, and *Quod deterius potiori insidari soleat*). LDAB 3541 contains *Quis rerum divinarum heres sit* and *De sacrificiis Abelis et Caini*. The other papyrus is from Oxyrhynchus and contains fragments of Philo's writings (James R. Royse, "The Oxyrhynchus Papyrus of Philo," BASP 17 [1980]: 155–65).

4. Royse, "Oxyrhynchus Papyrus of Philo," 155; Anna Sirinian, "'Armenian Philo': A Survey of the Literature," in *Studies on the Ancient Armenian Version of Philo's Works*, ed. Sara Mancini Lombardi and Paola Pontani, SPhA 6 (Leiden: Brill, 2011), 7; and David T. Runia, *Philo in Early Christian Literature: A Survey*, CRINT 3 (Assen: Van Gorcum, 1993), 27.

5. Runia provides a survey of Philo's influence in both Eastern and Western writers up until the fifth century CE (*Philo in Early Christian Literature*).

6. Collins raises a similar point about the inherent problems of determining the designation and provenance of ancient writings based upon the dating of the textual witnesses alone. As examples, he refers to the textual witnesses of Enoch and Jubilees, which, before the discoveries of the Dead Sea Scrolls, were only known to be preserved by Christian scribes. In addition, the most extensive witnesses of these books are from Ethiopia, which is not the place of origin most scholars propose for these books ("*Joseph and Aseneth*," 98–99, 109).

heavily on Byzantine or medieval manuscripts that are believed to preserve the initial compositions of far more ancient texts than *Aseneth*.[7]

Although my monograph focuses on *Aseneth*'s beginnings, I also argue that *Aseneth* scholarship is at a point where it has to pay more attention to the individual witnesses. The evidence for *Aseneth* provides too complicated a web of connections for us to construct a comprehensive Greek text of *Aseneth*, which also means we cannot present a convincing order of *Aseneth*'s textual transmission. We must abandon detailed linear schemata of *Aseneth*'s textual history. We can only be certain of the chronological order of the manuscripts themselves (if verifiably dated), but we do not have enough evidence to posit the order in which exemplars were produced; and with the actual dating of the manuscripts, we can only assess the possible use of those texts in their respective historical times and places. An illustrative example is Ruth Nisse's analysis of *Aseneth* in the Latin MS 288 of Cambridge, Corpus Christi College (Burchard's designated MS 431 of the L1 group of family *f*).[8] In this thirteenth-century manuscript, *Aseneth* is compiled alongside of *Vindicta Salvatoris* (*Vengeance of the Savior*, which narrates the fall of Jerusalem); a pseudo-Augustine sermon on the Jews; the Life of Adam and Eve, Infancy Gospels of Matthew and Thomas; and apocalyptic narratives including Matthew Paris's rendering of the Mongol invasion of 1241 from his *Chronica Majora*. Nisse argues that *Aseneth* was part of a collection of "alternative narratives" that helped

---

7. A case in point is the manuscript evidence for Thucydides's *Historiae*. Although late antique papyrological evidence indicates that the medieval copies are likely fairly faithful to earlier copies, it is nonetheless the case that the primary Greek text that students and scholars examine is built off of witnesses dated to the eleventh through the thirteenth centuries. The version from the Loeb Classical Library depends on Karl Hude's edition (*Thucydides Historiae*, ed. maior 2 vols. [Leipzig: Teubner, 1898–1901]), which relies upon seven medieval manuscripts (Thucydides, *History of the Peloponnesian War*, trans. C. F. Smith, 4 vols., LCL [Cambridge: Harvard University Press, 1919–1923]). In the more recent edition by Giovanni B. Alberti, he too seems to rely on medieval manuscripts even though he incorporates papyrological evidence (*Thucydides Historiae*, 3 vols. [Rome: Typis Officinae Polygraphicae, 1972, 1992, and 2000]). There are thirty-one papyri that preserve portions of Thucydides' *Historiae*, and the evidence ranges between the first and sixth centuries CE. The earliest portions we have, then, date a little over four hundred years after Thucydides wrote. For the full list, see, Peter Stork, *Index of Verb Forms in Thucydides* (Leiden: Brill, 2008), xiii–xiv.

8. Ruth Nisse, *Jacob's Shipwreck: Diaspora, Translation, and Jewish-Christian Relations in Medieval England* (Ithaca, NY: Cornell University Press, 2017), 102–26; Burchard, *Joseph und Aseneth*, 6.

the Benedictine monks of Christ's Church Canterbury reinterpret their age (which included the contemporary escalation of hostility against Jews in England). Although too late for me to fully consider in this monograph, Wright's recent dissertation also examines the distinct versions and manuscripts of *Aseneth*.[9] The future of *Aseneth* studies is best suited to go in this direction.[10] Looking at how *Aseneth* is construed in each manuscript that also provides the so-called Life of Joseph could be most fruitful.

I want to close by expressing how indebted I am to the wealth of scholarship produced by Burchard and to the meticulous analyses of Standhartinger, Kraemer, and especially Fink. I clearly disagree with these scholars on several fronts, but I hope my respect for their work has been visible in this monograph. Standhartinger and Kraemer set forth a more serious critique than most *Aseneth* scholars have appreciated, and to repeat a point I have already made: no reputable argument can be made about *Aseneth* without a careful treatment of Fink's monograph, *Joseph und Aseneth* (2008). Burchard's critical edition (2003) is still essential for its copious apparatus, but Burchard's reconstruction is now obsolete. It is my hope that all reconstructions of *Aseneth* will soon be abandoned, but for now Fink's adaptation of Burchard's text should be used.[11]

Aseneth has certainly attracted attention, in the Christian East and West as well as into our era. I have proposed from whence this story came, but we are just starting to appreciate the distinct variations that this story has played out over time.

---

9. Wright, "After Antiquity."

10. As also pointed out by Standhartinger, "Recent Scholarship," 386–88.

11. As Eckart Reinmuth's edited volume promotes as well (*Joseph und Aseneth*, SAPERE 15 [Tübingen: Mohr Siebeck, 2009]).

Bibliography

Adler, William. "Alexander Polyhistor's *Perio Ioudaiōn* and Literary Culture in Republican Rome." Pages 225–40 in *Reconsidering Eusebius: Collected Papers on Literary, Historical, and Theological Issues*. Edited by Sabrina Inowlocki and Claudio Zmagni. Leiden: Brill, 2011.

Ahearne-Kroll, Patricia. "Constructing Jewish Identity in Ptolemaic Egypt: The Case of Artapanus." Pages 434–56 in *The "Other" in Second Temple Judaism: Essays in Honor of John J. Collins*. Edited by Daniel C. Harlow, Karina Martin Hogan, Matthew Goff, and Joel S. Kaminsky. Grand Rapids: Eerdmans, 2011.

———. "Joseph and Aseneth." Pages 2525–89 in vol. 3 of *Outside the Bible: Ancient Jewish Writings Related to Scripture*. Edited by Louis H. Feldman, James L. Kugel, and Lawrence H. Schiffman. 3 vols. Lincoln: University of Nebraska Press, 2013.

———. "*Joseph and Aseneth* and Jewish Identity in Greco-Roman Egypt." PhD diss., University of Chicago Divinity School, 2005.

———. "Multiple Witnesses, the 'Original Text,' and the Historian's Challenge: How to Make Sense Out of 'Joseph and Aseneth.'" Paper presented at the Annual Meeting of the Society of Biblical Literature. Chicago, IL, 20 November 2012.

———. "The Portrayal of Aseneth in Joseph and Aseneth: Women's Religious Experience in Antiquity and the Limitations of Ancient Narratives." Pages 39–58 in *Women and Gender in Ancient Religions: Interdisciplinary Approaches*. Edited by Stephen P. Ahearne-Kroll, Paul A. Holloway, and James A. Kelhoffer. WUNT 263. Tübingen: Mohr Siebeck, 2010.

———. "The Use of the Septuagint in *Joseph and Aseneth*." Paper presented at the Annual Meeting of the New England Region of the Society of Biblical Literature. Andover-Newton Theological School, Boston, May 2003.

Aitken, James K. *No Stone Unturned: Greek Inscriptions and Septuagint Vocabulary*. CrStHB 5. Winona Lake, IN: Eisenbrauns 2014.
Alberti, Giovanni B. *Thucydides Historiae*. 3 vols. Rome: Typis Officinae Polygraphicae, 1972, 1992, 2000.
Allen, James P. *Middle Egyptian: An Introduction to the Language and Culture of Hieroglyphs*. 3rd ed. Cambridge: Cambridge University Press, 2014.
Allen, W. C. "On the Meaning of ΠΡΟΣΗΛΥΤΟΣ in the Septuagint." *Expositor* 4 (1894): 264–75.
Aptowitzer, V. "Asenath, the Wife of Joseph: A Haggadic Literary-Historical Study." *HUCA* 1 (1924): 239–306.
Arnold, Dieter. *Temples of the Last Pharaohs*. New York: Oxford University Press, 1999.
Assemanus, Josephus S. *Sancti patris nostri Epharem Syri Opera Omnia quae extant Graece, Syriace, Latine*. 6 vols. Rome, 1732–1746.
Azzoni, Annalisa. "Women of Elephantine and Women in the Land of Israel." Pages 3–12 in *In the Shadow of Bezalel: Aramaic, Biblical, and Ancient Near Eastern Studies in Honor of Bezalel Porten*. Edited by Alejandro F. Botta. CHANE 60. Leiden: Brill, 2013.
Bal, Mieke. *Narratology: Introduction to the Theory of Narrative*. Translated by Christine van Boheemen. Toronto: University of Toronto Press, 1985.
Bar-Kochva, Bezalel. *Pseudo-Hecataeus "On the Jews": Legitimizing the Jewish Diaspora*. HCS 21. Berkeley: University of California Press, 1997.
Barclay, John M. G. "Ἰουδαῖος: Ethnicity and Translation." Pages 46–58 in *Ethnicity, Race, Religion: Identities and Ideologies in Early Jewish and Christian Texts, and in Modern Biblical Interpretation*. Edited by Katherine M. Hockey and David G. Horrell. London: T&T Clark, 2018.
———. *Jews in the Mediterranean Diaspora: From Alexander to Trajan (323 BCE–117 CE)*. HCS 33. Berkeley: University of California Press, 1996.
Batiffol, Pierre. *Le Livre de la Prière d'Aseneth*. Studia Patristica 1–2. Paris: Leroux, 1889–1890.
Bauschatz, John. *Law and Enforcement in Ptolemaic Egypt*. Cambridge: Cambridge University Press, 2013.
Bell, Lanny. "The New Kingdom 'Divine' Temple: The Example of Luxor." Pages 127–84 in *Temples of Ancient Egypt*. Edited by Byron E. Shafer. Ithaca, NY: Cornell University Press, 1997.

Bernand, André. *Le prose sur pierre dans l'Égypte hellénistique et romaine.* Vol. 1. Paris: Centre National de la Recherche scientifique, 1992.

Bitonto Kasser, Anna di. "Le petizioni ai funzionari del periodo tolemaico: Studio sul formulario." *Aegyptus* 48 (1968): 53–107.

———. "Le petizioni al re: Studio sul formulario." *Aegyptus* 47 (1967): 5–57.

Bloch, René. "Take Your Time: Conversion, Confidence and Tranquility in *Joseph and Aseneth*." Pages 77–96 in *Anthropologie und Ethik im Frühjudentum und im Neuen Testament.* Edited by Matthais Kondradt and Esther Schläpfer. WUNT 322. Tübingen: Mohr Siebeck, 2014.

Bohak, Gideon. *"Joseph and Aseneth" and the Jewish Temple in Heliopolis.* EJL 10. Atlanta: Scholars Press, 1996.

Borgeaud, Philippe, and Youri Volukhine, "La formation de la légende de Sarapis: Une approche transculturelle." *ARelG* 2 (2000): 37–76.

Bosch-Puche, Francisco. "The Egyptian Royal Titulary of Alexander the Great, I: Horus, Two Ladies, Golden Horus, and Throne Names." *JEA* 99 (2013): 131–54.

———. "The Egyptian Royal Titulary of Alexander the Great, II: Personal Name, Empty Cartouches, Final Remarks, and Appendix." *JEA* 100 (2014): 89–109.

Bourdieu, Pierre. *Outline of a Theory of Practice.* Cambridge: Cambridge University Press, 1977.

———. "Social Space and Symbolic Power." *Sociological Theory* 7 (1989): 14–25.

———. "The Social Space and the Genesis of Groups." *Theory and Society* 14 (1985): 723–44.

Braginskaya, Nina. "*Joseph and Aseneth* in Greek Literary History: The Case of the 'First Novel.'" Pages 79–106 in *The Ancient Novel and Early Christian and Jewish Narrative: Fictional Intersections.* Edited by Marília P. Futre Pinheiro, Judith Perkins, and Richard Pervo. Groningen: Barkhuis Publishing & Groningen University Library, 2012.

Bremmer, Jan. "Aspects of the *Acts of Peter*: Women, Magic, Place, and Date." Pages 1–20 in *Acts of Peter: Magic, Miracles, and Gnosticism.* Edited by Jan Bremmer. Studies on the Apocryphal Acts of the Apostles 3. Leuven: Peeters, 1998.

Brock, Sebastian P. Review of *Joseph et Aséneth: Introduction, texte critique, traduction et notes*, by Marc Philonenko. *JTS* 20 (1969): 588–91.

Brooke, George J. "Men and Women as Angels in Joseph and Aseneth." *JSP* 14 (2005): 159–77.

Brooks, E. W. *Joseph and Aseneth.* TED 2. London: SPCK, 1918.

———. *Historia ecclesiastica Zachariae Rhetori vulgo adscripta*. CSCO 87. Scriptores Syri 41. Leuven: Peeters, 2003.

Burchard, Christoph. "Character and Origin of the Armenian Version of Aseneth." Pages 73–90 in *Apocryphes arméniens: Transmission—traduction—création—iconographie; actes du colloque international sur la littérature apocryphe en langue arménienne, Genève, 18–20 septembre, 1997*. Edited by Valentina Calzolari Bourvier, Jean-Daniel Kaestli, and Bernard Outtier. Lausanne: Zèbre, 1999.

———. "Ein neuer Versuch zur Textgeschichte von Joseph und Aseneth." Pages 237–46 in *Der Freund des Menschen: Festschrift für Georg Christian Macholz zur Vollenung des 70. Lebensjahres*. Edited by Arndt Meinhold and Angelika Berlejung. Neukirchen-Vluyn: Neukirchener Verlag, 2003.

———. "Ein vorläufiger griechischer Text von Joseph und Aseneth." *DBAT* 14 (1979): 2–53.

———. "Joseph and Aseneth." *OTP* 2:177–247.

———. *Joseph und Aseneth*. Assisted by Carsten Burfeind and Uta Barbara Fink. PVTG 5. Leiden: Brill, 2003.

———. "Joseph und Aseneth neugriechisch." *NTS* 24 (1977): 68–84.

———. "Der jüdische Asenethroman und seine Nachwirkung: Von Egeria zu Anna Katharina Emmerick oder von Moses aus Aggel zu Karl Kerényi." *ANRW* 20.1:543–667.

———. *A Minor Edition of the Armenian Version of "Joseph and Aseneth."* Leuven: Peeters, 2010.

———. "Neues von Joseph und Aseneth auf Armenisch." Pages 139–59 in *Gesammelte Studien zu Joseph und Aseneth*. SVTP 13. Leiden: Brill, 1996.

———. "The Present State of Research on Joseph and Aseneth." Pages 31–52 in vol. 2 of *Religion, Literature, and Society in Ancient Israel, Formative Christianity and Judaism*. Edited by Jacob Neusner. NPAJ 1–2. Lanham, MD: University Press of America, 1987.

———. "Überlieferung, Gestalt und textkritischer Wert der zweiten lateinischen Übersetzung von Joseph und Aseneth." Pages 1–18 in *Religionsgeschichte des Neuen Testaments: Festschrift für Klaus Berger zum 60. Geburtstag*. Edited by Axel von Dobbeler, Jurt Erlemann, and Roman Heiligenthal. Tübingen: Francke, 2000.

———. *Untersuchungen zu Joseph und Aseneth: Überlieferung-Ortsbestimmung*. WUNT 8. Tübingen: Mohr, 1965.

———. *Unterweisung in erzählender Form: Joseph und Aseneth.* JSHRZ 2.4. Gütersloh: Mohn, 1983.

———. "Zum Stand der Arbeit am Text von Joseph und Aseneth." Pages 1–28 in *Das Ende der Tage und die Gegenwart des Heils: Begegnungen mit dem Neuen Testament und seiner Umwelt.* Edited by Michael Becker and Wolfgang Fenske. AGJU 44. Boston: Brill, 1999.

———. "Zum Text von 'Joseph und Aseneth.'" *JSJ* 1 (1970): 3–34.

———. "Zur armenischen Übersetzung von Joseph und Aseneth." *Revue des Études Arméniennes* 17 (1983): 207–40.

Burfiend, Carsten. "Der Text von *Joseph und Aseneth* im Palimpsest Rehdiger 26 der Universitätsbibliothek Wroclaw (Breslau)." *JSJ* 32 (2001): 42–53.

Burrus, Virginia. *Chastity as Autonomy: Women in the Stories of the Apocryphal Acts.* SWR 23. Lewiston, NY: Mellen, 1987.

Burstein, Stanley M. "Hecataeus of Abdera's History of Egypt." Pages 45–49 in *Life in a Multi-Cultural Society: Egypt from Cambyses to Constantine and Beyond.* Edited by Janet H. Johnson. SAOC 51. Chicago: Oriental Institute of the University of Chicago, 1992.

Burton, Anne. *Diodorus Siculus Book I: A Commentary.* EPRO 29. Leiden: Brill, 1972.

Capponi, Livia. *Il tempio di Leontopoli in Egitto: Identità politica e religiosa dei Giudei di Onia (c. 150 a.C.–73 d.C.).* Pubblicazioni della Facoltà di Lettere e Filosofia dell'Università di Pavia 118. Pisa: ETS, 2007.

Chesnutt, Randall D. *From Death to Life: Conversion in "Joseph and Aseneth."* JSPSup 16. Sheffield: Sheffield Academic, 1995.

———. Review of *When Aseneth Met Joseph: A Late Antique Tale of the Biblical Patriarch and His Egyptian Wife, Reconsidered,* by Ross Shepard Kraemer. *RBL* 119 (2002): 760–62.

Clarysse, Willy. "Jews in Trikomia." Pages 193–203 in *Proceedings of the Twentieth International Congress of Papyrologists (Copenhagen, 23–29 August 1992).* Edited by Adam Bülow-Jacobsen. University of Copenhagen: Museum Tusculanum Press, 1994.

Clarysse, Willy, and Dorothy J. Thompson. *Counting the People in Hellenistic Egypt.* 2 vols. Cambridge: Cambridge University Press, 2006.

Collins, John J. "Artapanus Revisited." Pages 59–68 in *From Judaism to Christianity: Tradition and Transition; a Festschrift for Thomas H. Tobin on the Occasion of His Sixty-Fifth Birthday.* Edited by Patricia Walters. NovTSup 136. Boston: Brill, 2010.

———. *Between Athens and Jerusalem: Jewish Identity in the Hellenistic Diaspora*. 2nd ed. BRS. Grand Rapids: Eerdmans, 2000.

———. *Daniel: A Commentary on the Book of Daniel*. Hermeneia. Minneapolis: Fortress, 1993.

———. "*Joseph and Aseneth*: Jewish or Christian?" *JSP* 14 (2005): 97–112.

Cowe, S. Peter. "The Bible in Armenia." Pages 143–60 in *The Bible from 600–1450*. Vol. 2 of *The New Cambridge History of the Bible*. Edited by Richard Marsden and E. Ann Matter. Cambridge: Cambridge University Press, 2012.

———. "A Typology of Armenian Biblical Manuscripts." *Revue des Études Arméniennes* 18 (1984): 49–67.

Cowey, James M. S., and Klaus Maresch, eds. *Urkunden des Politeuma der Juden von Herakleopolis (144/3–133/2 v.Chr.) (P.Polit.Iud.)*. Abhandlungen der Nordrhein-Westfälischen Akademie der Wissenschaften, Sonderreihe Papyrologica Coloniensia 29. Wiesbaden: Westdeutscher, 2001.

Dain, Alphonse. *Les manuscrits*. Collection d'Etudes Anciennes. Paris: Les Belles Lettres, 1964.

Delling, Gerhard. "Einwirkungen der Sprache der Septuaginta in 'Joseph und Aseneth.'" *JSJ* 9 (1978): 29–56.

Detienne, Marcel. "Orphée au miel." *QUCC* 12 (1971): 7–23.

Dillery, John. "Hecataeus of Abdera: Hyperboreans, Egypt, and the 'Interpretatio Graeca.'" *Historia* 47 (1998): 255–75.

Diodorus Siculus. *Library of History, Volume 1: Books 1–2.34*. Translated by C. H. Oldfather. LCL. Cambridge: Harvard University Press, 1933.

Docherty, Susan. "*Joseph and Aseneth*: Rewritten Bible or Narrative Expansion?" *JSJ* 35 (2004): 27–48.

Doetsch-Amberger, Ellen. "Ein Siegel Ptolemaios' V." *GM* 142 (1994): 67–68.

Èjxenbaum, Boris. "The Theory of the Formal Method." Pages 3–37 in *Readings in Russian Poetics: Formalist and Structuralist Views*. Edited by Ladislov Matejka and Krystyna Pomorska. Cambridge: MIT Press, 1971.

Elder, Nicholas A. "On Transcription and Oral Transmission in *Aseneth*: A Study of the Narrative's Conception." *JSJ* 47 (2016): 119–42.

El-Masri, Yahia, Hartwig Altenmüller, and Heinz-Josef Thissen. *Das Synodaldekret von Alexandria aus dem Jahre 243 v. Chr.* Hamburg: Buske, 2012.

Empereur, Jean-Yves. "Alexandrie (Égypte)." *BCH* 120 (1996): 959–70.

Eynde, Sabine van den. "Blessed by God—Blessed Be God: Εὐλογέω and the Concept of Blessing in the LXX with Special Attention to the Book of Ruth." Pages 415–36 in *Interpreting Translation: Studies on the LXX and Ezekiel in Honour of Johan Lust*. Edited by Florentino García Martínez and Marc Vervenne. Leuven: Peeters, 2005.

Euripides. *Fragments: Oedipus-Chrysippus, Other Fragments*. Edited and translated by Christopher Collard and Martin Cropp. LCL. Cambridge: Harvard University Press, 2008.

Fink, Uta Barbara. "Anhang: Erläuterung zum Stemma." Pages 45–54 in *Joseph und Aseneth*. Edited by Eckart Reinmuth. SAPERE 15. Tübingen: Mohr Siebeck, 2009.

———. *Joseph und Aseneth: Revision des griechischen Textes und Edition der zweiten lateinischen Übersetzung*. FSBP 5. Berlin: de Gruyter, 2008.

———. "Textkritische Situation." Pages 33–44 in *Joseph und Aseneth*. Edited by Eckart Reinmuth. SAPERE 15. Tübingen: Mohr Siebeck, 2009.

Finkelberg, Margalit. "Regional Texts and the Circulation of Books: The Case of Homer." *GRBS* 46 (2006): 231–48.

Finnestad, Ragnhild Bjerre. "Temples of the Ptolemaic and Roman Periods: Ancient Traditions in New Contexts." Pages 185–237 in *Temples of Ancient Egypt*. Edited by Byron E. Shafer. Ithaca, NY: Cornell University Press, 1997.

Fischer-Bovet, Christelle. *Army and Society in Ptolemaic Egypt*. Cambridge: Cambridge University Press, 2014.

———. "Counting the Greeks in Egypt: Immigration in the First Century of Ptolemaic Rule." Pages 135–54 in *Demography and the Greco-Roman World: New Insights and Approaches*. Edited by Claire Holleran and April Pudsey. Cambridge: Cambridge University Press, 2011.

Freudenthal, J. *Alexander Polyhistor und die von ihm erhaltenen Reste jüdischer und samaritanischer Geschichtswerke*. Hellenistische Studien 1–2. Breslau: Grass, 1874–1875.

Fulińska, Agnieszka. "Iconography of the Ptolemaic Queens on Coins: Greek Style, Egyptian Ideas?" *Studies in Ancient Art and Civilization* 14 (2010): 73–92.

Gauthier, Henri. *Le livre des rois d'Égypte: Recueil de titres et protocoles royaux, noms propres de rois, reines, princes, princesses et parents de rois, suivi d'un index alphabétique, Vol. 4: De la XXV e dynastie à la fin des Ptolémées*. MIFAO 20. Cairo: Imprimerie de l'Institut français d'archéologie orientale, 1915–1916.

Gera, Deborah Levine. *Judith: Introduction, Translation, and Commentary.* CEJL. Berlin: de Gruyter, 2014.

Graf, Fritz. "Musaeus (1)." *Oxford Classical Dictionary.* Edited by Simon Hornblower and Antony Spawforth. 4th ed. Oxford: Oxford University Press, 2012. doi: 10.1093/acref/9780199545568.001.0001.

———. "Sacred Times and Spaces: Introduction." Pages 243–44 in *Religions of the Ancient World: A Guide.* Edited by Sarah Iles Johnston. Cambridge: Harvard University Press, 2004.

Gruen, Erich S. *Diaspora: Jews amidst Greeks and Romans.* Cambridge: Harvard University Press, 2002.

Hacham, Noel. "*Joseph and Aseneth:* Loyalty, Traitors, Antiquity and Diasporan Identity." *JSP* 22 (2012): 53–67.

Hall, Jonathan M. *Hellenicity: Between Ethnicity and Culture.* Chicago: University of Chicago Press, 2002.

Hartman, Louis Francis, and Alexander A. Di Lella. *The Book of Daniel: A New Translation with Introduction and Commentary.* AB 23. Garden City, NY: Doubleday, 1978.

Haslam, Michael. "Homeric Papyri and the Transmission of the Text." Pages 55–100 in *A New Companion to Homer.* Edited by Ian Morris and Barry Powell. Mnemosyne Supplementum 163. Leiden: Brill, 1997.

Hazzard, R. A. *Ptolemaic Coins: An Introduction for Collectors.* Toronto: Kirk & Bentley, 1995.

Helbing, Robert. *Die Kasussyntax der Verba bei den Septuaginta: Ein Beitrag zur Hebraismenfrage und zur Syntax der Κοινή.* Göttingen: Vandenhoeck & Ruprecht, 1928.

Hezser, Catherine. "'Joseph and Aseneth' in the Context of Ancient Greek Novels." *FJB* 24 (1997): 1–40.

Hickey, Raymond, ed. *The Handbook of Language Contact.* BHL. Chichester: Wiley-Blackwell, 2010.

Hicks-Keeton, Jill. *Arguing with Aseneth: Gentile Access to Israel's Living God in Jewish Antiquity.* New York: Oxford University Press, 2018.

———. "Aseneth between Judaism and Christianity: Reframing the Debate." *JSJ* 49 (2018): 189–222.

Hirschberger, Martina. "Aseneths erstes Brautkleid, Symbolik von Kleidung und Zeit in der Bekehrung Aseneths (JosAs 1–21)." *Apocrypha* 21 (2011): 179–202.

Höbl, Günther. *A History of the Ptolemaic Empire.* London: Routledge, 2001.

Hoffmann, Herbert. "Helios." *JARCE* 2 (1963): 117–24.
Holladay, Carl R. *Historians*. Vol. 1 of *Fragments from Hellenistic Jewish Authors*. SBLTT 20. Chico, CA: Scholars Press, 1983.
Holtz, Traugott. Review of *Joseph et Aséneth*, by Marc Philonenko. *OLZ* 67 (1972): 49–55.
Horbury, William, and David Noy, eds. *Jewish Inscriptions of Graeco-Roman Egypt*. Cambridge: Cambridge University Press, 1992.
Hude, Karl. *Thucydides Historiae*. Ed. maior. 2 vols. Leipzig: Teubner, 1898–1901.
Inowlocki, Sabrina. *Des idoles mortes et muettes au dieu vivant: Joseph, Aséneth et le fils de Pharaon dans un roman du judaïsme hellénisé*. Turnhout: Brepols, 2002.
―――. *Eusebius and the Jewish Authors: His Citation Technique in an Apologetic Context*. AGJU 64. Leiden: Brill, 2006.
Iossif, Panagiotis, and Catharine Lorber. "The Rays of the Ptolemies." *RN* 6 (2012): 197–224.
Istrin, V. M. "Aprokrif ob Iosefě i Asenefě." Pages 146–99 in *Drevnosti: Trudy slavjanskoj kommissii imperatorskago moskovskago archeologičeskago obščestva*. Moscow: Lissner & Geschel, 1898.
Jacobson, Howard. "Artapanus Judaeus." *JJS* 57 (2006): 210–21.
Jastrow, Morris. *A Dictionary of the Targumim, the Talmud Babli and Yerushalmi, and the Midrashic Literature with an Index of Scriptural Quotations*. London: Luzac; New York: Putnam's Sons, 1903.
Johnson, Janet J., ed. *The Demotic Dictionary of the Oriental Institute of the University of Chicago*. Chicago: Oriental Institute of the University of Chicago, 2001.
Jokiranta, Jutta. "Conceptualizing *GER* in the Dead Sea Scrolls." Pages 659–77 in *In the Footsteps of Sherlock Holmes: Studies in the Biblical Text in Honour of Anneli Aejmelaeus*. Edited by Kristin De Troyer, T. M. Law, and Marketta Liljeström. CBET 72. Leuven: Peeters, 2014.
Joüon, Paul. *A Grammar of Biblical Hebrew*. Translated and revised by T. Muraoka. 2 vols. SubBi 14. Rome: Pontifical Biblical Institute, 1991.
Kasher, Aryeh. *The Jews in Hellenistic and Roman Egypt: The Struggle for Equal Rights*. TSAJ 7. Tübingen: Mohr, 1985.
Kasyan, Maria S. "The Bees of Artemis Ephesia and the Apocalyptic Scene in *Joseph and Aseneth*." Pages 251–71 in *Intende, Lector: Echoes of Myth, Religion and Ritual in the Ancient Novel*. Edited by Marília P. Futre Pinheiro, Anton Bierl, and Roger Beck. Berlin: de Gruyter, 2013.

Koenen, Ludwig. "The Ptolemaic King as a Religious Figure." Pages 25–115 in *Images and Ideologies: Self-definition in the Hellenistic World*. Edited by Anthony W. Bulloch, Erich S. Gruen, Anthony Arthur Long, and Andrew F. Stewart. HCS 12. Berkeley: University of California Press, 1993.

Koskenniemi, Erkki. "Greeks, Egyptians and Jews in the Fragments of Artapanus." *JSP* 13 (2002): 17–31.

Kraemer, Ross Shepard. *When Aseneth Met Joseph: A Late Antique Tale of the Biblical Patriarch and His Egyptian Wife, Reconsidered*. New York: Oxford University Press, 1998.

Kugel, James L. *In Potiphar's House: The Interpretive Life of Biblical Texts*. Cambridge: Harvard University Press, 1994.

Kugler, Robert A. "Dispelling an Illusion of Otherness? Juridical Practice in the Heracleopolis Papyri." Pages 457–70 in *The "Other" in Second Temple Judaism: Essays in Honor of John J. Collins*. Edited by Daniel C. Harlow, Karina Martin Hogan, Matthew Goff, and Joel S. Kaminsky. Grand Rapids: Eerdmans, 2011.

———. "Hearing the Story of Moses in Ptolemaic Egypt: Artapanus Accommodates the Tradition." Pages 67–80 in *The Wisdom of Egypt: Jewish, Early Christian, and Gnostic Essays in Honour of Gerard P. Luttikhuizen*. Edited by A. Hilhorst and Geurt Hendrik van Kooten. AGJU 59. Leiden: Brill, 2005.

La'da, Csaba A. "Ethnic Designations in Hellenistic Egypt." 2 vols. PhD diss., University of Cambridge, 1997.

———. *Foreign Ethnics in Hellenistic Egypt*. Studia Hellenistica 38. Leuven: Peeters, 2002.

———. "Who Were Those 'of the Epigone'?" Pages 563–69 in vol. 1 of *Akten des 21. Internationalen Papyrologenkongresses, Berlin, 13.–19.8 1995*. Edited by Bärbel Kramer, Wolfgang Luppe, Herwig Maehler, and Günter Poethke. 2 vols. APFB 3. Stuttgart: Teubner, 1997.

Landgráfová, Renata. "Ars Memoriae Aegyptiaca? Some Preliminary Remarks on the Egyptian Hieroglyphs and the Classical Art of Memory." Pages 133–53 in *Visualizing Knowledge and Creating Meaning in Ancient Writing Systems*. Edited by Shai Gordin. BBVO 23. Gladbeck: PeWe-Verlag, 2014.

LeClant, Jean. "Biene." Page 787 in vol. 1 of *Lexikon der Ägyptologie*. Edited by Wolfgang Helck, Otto Eberhard, and Wolfhart Westendorf. Wiesbaden: Harrassowitz, 1975.

Lewis, Naphtali. *Greeks in Ptolemaic Egypt: Case Studies in the Social History of the Hellenistic World*. Oakville, CT: American Society of Papyrologists, 2001.

———. "Notationes Legentis." *BASP* 34 (1997): 21–33.

Lincoln, Bruce. *Discourse and the Construction of Society: Comparative Studies of Myth, Ritual, and Classification*. New York: Oxford University Press, 1989.

———. *Theorizing Myth: Narrative, Ideology, and Scholarship*. Chicago: University of Chicago Press, 1999.

Lloyd, Alan B. *Herodotus, Book II: Commentary 99–182*. EPRO 43. 2nd ed. Leiden: Brill, 1993.

———. Review of *Diodorus Siculus Book I: A Commentary*, by Anne Burton. *JEA* 60 (1974): 287–90.

Lord, Albert. *The Singer of Tales*. HSCL 24. Cambridge: Harvard University Press, 1960.

Malaise, Michel. "Sésostris, Pharaon de légende et d'histoire." *CE* 41.82 (1966): 244–72.

Manning, J. G. "Coinage as 'Code' in Ptolemaic Egypt." Pages 84–111 in *The Monetary Systems of the Greeks and Romans*. Edited by William Harris. Oxford: Oxford University Press, 2008.

Mariette, Auguste. *Monuments divers recueillis en Égypte et en Nubie*. Paris: Franck, 1872.

Mason, Steve. "Jews, Judaeans, Judaizing, Judaism: Problems of Categorization in Ancient History." *JSJ* 38 (2007): 457–512.

McGing, Brian. "Population and Proselytism: How Many Jews Were There in the Ancient World?" Pages 88–106 in *Jews in the Hellenistic and Roman Cities*. Edited by John R. Bartlett. London: Routledge, 2002.

McKenzie, Judith S., Sheila Gibson, and A. T. Reyes. "Reconstructing the Serapeum in Alexandria from the Archaeological Evidence." *JRS* 94 (2004): 73–121.

Metzger, Bruce M. *A Textual Commentary on the Greek New Testament*. 2nd ed. London: United Bible Societies, 1994.

Metzger, Marcel. *Les constitutions apostoliques*. Vol. 1. SC 320. Paris: Cerf, 1985.

Milne, J. G. "Ptolemaic Seal Impressions." *JHS* 36 (1916): 87–101.

Minas, Martina. *Die Hieroglyphischen Ahnenreihen der Ptolemäischen Könige: Ein Vergleich mit den Titeln der eponymen Preister in den demotischen und griechischen Papyri*. Mainz: von Zabern, 2000.

Modrzejewski, Joseph Mélèze. *The Jews of Egypt: From Rameses II to Emperor Hadrian*. Translated by Robert Cornman. Princeton: Princeton University Press, 1995.

Moffitt, David M., and C. Jacob Butera. "P.Duk. Inv. 727r: New Evidence for the Meaning and Provenance of the Word Προσήλυτος." *JBL* 132 (2013): 159–78.

Monson, Andrew. *From the Ptolemies to the Romans: Political and Economic Change in Egypt*. Cambridge: Cambridge University Press, 2012.

Moore, Stewart. *Jewish Ethnic Identity and Relations in Hellenistic Egypt: With Walls of Iron?* JSJSup 171. Leiden: Brill, 2015.

Moreshet, Menahem. "The Predicate Preceding a Compound Subject in the Biblical Language" [Hebrew]. *Leshonenu* 31 (1967): 251–60.

Moyer, Ian. *Egypt and the Limits of Hellenism*. Cambridge: Cambridge University Press, 2011.

Mueller, Katja. *Settlements of the Ptolemies: City Foundations and New Settlement in the Hellenistic World*. Studia Hellenistica 43. Leuven: Peeters, 2006.

Müller, Maya. "Re and Re-Horakhty." *OEAE* 3:123–26.

Muntz, Charles E. "The Sources of Diodorus Siculus, Book 1." *ClQ* 61 (2011): 574–94.

Muraoka, Takamitsu. *A Greek-English Lexicon of the Septuagint*. Leuven: Peeters, 2009.

Murray, Oswyn. "Hecataeus of Abdera and Pharaonic Kingship." *JEA* 56 (1970): 141–71.

———. Review of *Book I: A Commentary by Diodorus Siculus*, by Anne Burton. *JHS* 95 (1975): 214–15.

Nickelsburg, George W. E. *Jewish Literature between the Bible and the Mishnah: A Historical and Literary Introduction*. 2nd ed. Minneapolis: Fortress, 2005.

Nir, Rivka. "It Is Not Right For a Man Who Worships God to Repay His Neighbor Evil for Evil": Christian Ethics in *Joseph and Aseneth* (Chapters 22–29)." *JHebS* 13 (2013): art. 5. http://dx.doi.org/10.5508/jhs.2013.v13.a5.

———. *Joseph and Aseneth: A Christian Book*. Hebrew Bible Monographs 42. Sheffield: Sheffield Phoenix, 2012.

Nisse, Ruth. *Jacob's Shipwreck: Diaspora, Translation, and Jewish-Christian Relations in Medieval England*. Ithaca, NY: Cornell University Press, 2017.

Noegel, Scott. "Apollonius' *Argonautika* and Egyptian Solar Mythology." *CW* 97 (2004): 123–36.

Orlov, Andrei A. "Unveiling the Face: The Heavenly Counterpart Traditions in *Joseph and Aseneth*." Pages 771–808 in *The Embroidered Bible: Studies in Biblical Apocrypha and Pseudepigrapha in Honour of Michael E. Stone*. Edited by Lorenzo DiTommaso, Matthias Henze, and William Adler. SVTP 26. Leiden: Brill, 2018.

Pfeiffer, Stefan. *Das Dekret von Kanopos (238 v. Chr.): Kommentar und historische Auswertung eines Dreisprachigen Synodaldekretes der Ägyptischen Priester zu Ehren Ptolemaios' III. und seiner Familie*. APFB 18. Munich: Saur, 2004.

———. "The God Serapis, His Cult and the Beginnings of the Ruler Cult in Ptolemaic Egypt." Pages 387–408 in *Ptolemy II Philadelphus and His World*. Edited by Paul McKechnie and Philippe Guillaume. Mnemosyne Supplementum 300. Leiden: Brill, 2008.

Philonenko, Marc. *Joseph et Aséneth: Introduction, texte critique, traduction et notes*. SPB 13. Leiden: Brill, 1968.

Pier, Garrett Chatfield. *Egyptian Antiquities in the Pier Collection*. Chicago: University of Chicago Press, 1906.

Plantzos, Dimitris. "Female Portrait Types from the Edfu Hoard of Clay Seal Impressions." Pages 307–13 and pls. 47–53 in *Archives et Sceaux du monde hellénistique*. Edited by Marie-Françoise Boussac and Antonio Invernizzi. BCHSup 29. Athens: Ecole Française d'Athènes, 1996.

Portier-Young, Anathea E. "Sweet Mercy Metropolis: Interpreting Aseneth's Honeycomb." *JSP* 14 (2005): 133–57.

Porten, Bezalel. *The Elephantine Papyri in English: Three Millennia of Cross-Cultural Continuity and Change*. 2nd ed. DMOA 22. Atlanta: Society of Biblical Literature, 2011.

Pratt, Mary Louise. *Imperial Eyes: Travel Writing and Transculturation*. New York: Routledge, 1992.

———. "Linguistic Utopias." Pages 48–66 in *The Linguistics of Writing: Argument between Writing and Literature*. Edited by Nigel Fabb, Derek Attridge, Alan Durant, and Colin MacCabe. New York: Methuen, 1987.

Putthoff, Tyson L. "Aseneth's Gastronomical Vision: Mystical Theophagy and the New Creation in *Joseph and Aseneth*." *JSP* 24 (2014): 96–117.

Quaegebeur, Jan. "Cleopatra VII and the Cults of the Ptolemaic Queens." Pages 41–54 in *Cleopatra's Egypt: Age of the Ptolemies*. Edited by Robert Bianchi and Richard Fazzini. Brooklyn: Brooklyn Museum, 1988.

———. "Documents Concerning a Cult of Arsinoe Philadelphos at Memphis." *JNES* 30 (1971): 239–70.

———. "Ptolémée II en adoration devant Arsinoè II divinisée." *BIFAO* 69 (1971): 191–217.

———. "Reines ptolémaïques et traditions égyptiennes." Pages 245–62 in *Das ptolemäische Ägypten: Akten des Internationalen Symposions 27.–29. September 1976 in Berlin*. Edited by Herwig Maehler and Volker Michael Strocka. Mainz: von Zabern, 1978.

Quirke, Stephen, and Carol Andrews. *The Rosetta Stone: Facsimile Drawing*. London: British Museum, 1988.

Reden, Sitta von. *Money in Ptolemaic Egypt: From the Macedonian Conquest to the End of the Third Century BC*. Cambridge: Cambridge University Press, 2007.

Reinhartz, Adele. "Jew and Judean: A Forum on Politics and Historiography in the Translation of Ancient Texts." *Marginalia*. https://marginalia.lareviewofbooks.org/jew-judean-forum/.

Reinhold, Meyer. *History of Purple as a Status Symbol in Antiquity*. Brussels: Latomus 1970.

Reinmuth, Eckart, ed. *Joseph und Aseneth*. SAPERE 15. Tübingen: Mohr Siebeck, 2009.

Reynolds, L. D., and N. G. Wilson. *Scribes and Scholars: A Guide to the Transmission of Greek and Latin Literature*. New York: Oxford University Press, 1991.

Richardson, Brian. "Unnatural Narrative Theory: A Paradoxical Paradigm." Pages 193–206 in *Emerging Vectors of Narratology*. Edited by Per Krogh Hansen, John Pier, Philippe Roussin, and Wolf Schmid. Narratologia 57. Berlin: de Gruyter, 2017.

Royse, James R. "The Oxyrhynchus Papyrus of Philo." *BASP* 17 (1980): 155–65.

Rowlandson, Jane. "Dissing the Egyptians: Legal, Ethnic, and Cultural Identities in Roman Egypt." Pages 213–47 in *Creating Ethnicities and Identities in the Roman World*. Edited by Andrew Gardner, Edward Herring, and Kathryn Lomas. Bulletin Supplement 120. London: Institute of Classical Studies, 2013.

Runia, David T. *Philo in Early Christian Literature: A Survey*. CRINT 3. Assen: Van Gorcum, 1993.

Ryholt, Kim. "A Sesostris Story in Demotic Egyptian and Demotic Literary Exercises (O. Leipzig UB 2217)." Pages 429–38 in *Honi Soit Qui Mal Y Pense: Studien zum pharaonischen, griechisch-römischen und spätantiken Ägypten zu Ehren von Heinz-Josef Thissen.* Edited by Hermann Knuf, Christian Leitz, and Daniel von Recklinghausen. OLA 194. Leuven: Peeters, 2010.

Sacks, Kenneth S. *Diodorus Siculus and the First Century.* Princeton: Princeton University Press, 1990.

Sänger, Dieter. *Antikes Judentum und die Mysterien: Religionsgeschichtliche Untersuchungen zu Joseph und Aseneth.* WUNT 2/5. Tübingen: Mohr, 1980.

———. "Bekehrung und Exodus: Zum jüdischen Traditionshintergrund von 'Joseph und Aseneth.'" *JSJ* 10 (1979): 11–36.

———. "Erwägungen zur historischen Einordnung und zur Datierung von 'Joseph und Aseneth.'" *ZNW* 76 (1985): 86–106.

Schwartz, Daniel R. "'Judaean' or 'Jew'? How Should We Translate *Ioudaios* in Josephus?" Pages 1–27 in *Jewish Identity in the Greco-Roman World.* Edited by Jörg Frey, Daniel R. Schwartz, and Stephanie Gripentrog. AGJU 71. Leiden: Brill, 2007.

Schwartz, Eduard. "Hekataeos von Teos." *Rheinisches Museum für Philologie* 40 (1885): 223–62.

Selden, Dan. "Alibis." *ClAnt* 17 (1998): 289–412.

Shafer, Byron E., ed. *Temples of Ancient Egypt.* Ithaca, NY: Cornell University Press, 1997.

Shklovsky, Viktor. "On the Connection between Devices of *Syuzhet* Construction and General Stylistic Devices (1919)." Pages 48–72 in *Russian Formalism: A Collection of Articles and Texts in Translation.* Edited by Stephen Bann and John E. Bowlt. Translated by Jane Knox. New York: Barnes & Noble, 1973.

Simpson, R. S. *Demotic Grammar in the Ptolemaic Sacerdotal Decrees.* Oxford: Griffith Institute, 1996.

Sirinian, Anna. "'Armenian Philo': A Survey of the Literature." Pages 7–44 in *Studies on the Ancient Armenian Version of Philo's Works.* Edited by Sara Mancini Lombardi and Paola Pontani. SPhA 6. Leiden: Brill, 2011.

Smith, E. W. Review of *Joseph et Aséneth*, by Marc Philonenko. *JBL* 89 (1970): 257–58.

Smith, J. Z. *To Take Place: Toward Theory in Ritual.* Chicago Studies in the History of Judaism. Chicago: University of Chicago Press, 1987.

Smith, R. R. R. *Hellenistic Royal Portraits.* Oxford Monographs on Classical Archaeology. Oxford: Clarendon, 1988.

Spalinger, Anthony J. "Calendars." *OEAE* 1:224–27.

Standhartinger, Angela. *Das Frauenbild im Judentum der hellenistischen Zeit: Ein Beitrag anhand von "Joseph und Aseneth."* AGJU 26. Leiden: Brill, 1995.

———. "From Fictional Text to Socio-historical Context: Some Considerations from a Text Critical Perspective on Joseph and Aseneth." Pages 303–18 in *Society of Biblical Literature 1996 Seminar Papers*. SBLSPS 35. Atlanta: Scholars Press, 1996.

———. "Humour in *Joseph and Aseneth*." *JSP* 24 (2015): 239–59.

———. "Recent Scholarship on *Joseph and Aseneth* (1988–2013)." *CurBR* 12 (2014): 353–406.

———. Review of *Joseph und Aseneth*, by Christoph Burchard. *JSP* 15 (2006): 151–55.

———. Review of *When Aseneth Met Joseph: A Late Antique Tale of the Biblical Patriarch and His Egyptian Wife, Reconsidered*, by Ross Shepard Kraemer. *JAOS* 120 (2000): 488–89.

Stanwick, Paul Edmund. *Portraits of the Ptolemies: Greek Kings as Egyptian Pharaohs*. Austin: University of Texas Press, 2002.

Stephens, Susan. *Seeing Double: Intercultural Poetics in Ptolemaic Alexandria*. HCS 37. Berkeley: University of California Press, 2003.

Sterling, Gregory E. *Historiography and Self-Definition: Josephos, Luke-Acts and Apologetic Historiography*. NovTSup 64. Leiden: Brill, 1992.

Stern, David. *Parables in Midrash: Narrative and Exegesis in Rabbinic Literature*. Cambridge: Harvard University Press, 1991.

Stern, Menahem. *Greek and Latin Authors on Jews and Judaism*. 3 vols. Jerusalem: Israel Academy of Sciences and Humanities, 1981.

Stol, Marten. *Women in the Ancient Near East*. Translated by Helen Richardson and Mervyn Richardson. Berlin: de Gruyter, 2016.

Stone, Michael E. "Armenian Canon Lists I: The Council of Partaw (768 C.E.)." *HTR* 66 (1973): 479–86.

———. "Armenian Canon Lists III: The Lists of Mechitar of AYRIVANK' (c. 1285 C.E.)." *HTR* 69 (1976): 289–300.

Stork, Peter. *Index of Verb Forms in Thucydides*. Leiden: Brill, 2008.

Strugnell, John. "General Introduction, with a Note on Alexander Polyhistor." *OTP* 2:777–79.

Svoronos, I. N. Τα νομίσματα του κράτους των Πτολεμαίων [The coins of the Ptolemaic state]. 4 vols. Athens, 1904–1908.

Tcherikover, Victor A., ed. *Corpus Papyrorum Judaicarum*. 3 vols. Cambridge: Harvard University Press, 1957–1964.

Thiessen, Matthew. "Aseneth's Eight-Day Transformation as Scriptural Justification for Conversion." *JSJ* 45 (2014): 229–49.

———. "Revisiting the προσήλυτος in 'the LXX.'" *JBL* 132 (2013): 333–50.

Thomas, Christine M. *The Acts of Peter, Gospel Literature, and the Ancient Novel: Rewriting the Past*. New York: Oxford University Press, 2003.

Thompson, Dorothy J. *Memphis under the Ptolemies*. 2nd ed. Princeton: Princeton University Press, 2012.

Thucydides. *History of the Peloponnesian War*. Translated by C. F. Smith. 4 vols. LCL. Cambridge: Harvard University Press, 1919–1923.

Thwaites, Edward. Τὰ τοῦ ὁσίου πατρὸς Ἐφραὶμ τοῦ Σύρου πρὸς τὴν Ἑλλάδα μεταβληθέντα. [The translated works of the holy father Ephraim the Syrian into Greek]. Oxford, 1709.

Tiede, David Lenz. *The Charismatic Figure as Miracle Worker*. SBLDS 1. Missoula, MT: Society of Biblical Literature, 1972.

Toorn, Karel van der. "Religious Practices of the Individual and Family: Introduction." Pages 423–29 in *Religions of the Ancient World: A Guide*. Edited by Sarah Iles Johnston. Cambridge: Harvard University Press, 2004.

Tomashevsky, Boris. "Thematics." Pages 61–95 in *Russian Formalist Criticism: Four Essays*. Translated by Lee T. Lemon and Marion J. Reis. Lincoln: University of Nebraska, 1965.

Tov, Emmanuel. "Renderings of Combinations of the Infinitive Absolute and Finite Verbs in the LXX—Their Nature and Distribution." Pages 64–73 in *Studien zur Septuaginta—Robert Hanhart zu Ehren: Aus Anlass seines 65. Geburtstages*. Edited by Detlef Fraenkel, Udo Quast, and John William Wevers. MSU 20. Göttingen: Vandenhoeck & Ruprecht, 1990.

Tromp, J. "Response to Ross Kraemer: On the Jewish Origin of Joseph and Aseneth." Pages 266–71 in *Recycling Biblical Figures: Papers Read at a NOSTER Colloquium in Amsterdam, 12–13 May 1997*. Edited by Athalya Brenner and J. W. van Henten. STAR 1. Leiden: Deo, 1999.

Turner, C. H. "The Latin Acts of Peter." *JTS* 32 (1931): 119–33.

Valantasis, Richard. "Narrative Strategies and Synoptic Quandaries: A Response to Dennis MacDonald's Reading of *Acts of Paul* and *Acts of Peter*." Pages 234–39 in *Society of Biblical Literature 1992 Seminar Papers*. SBLSPS 31. Atlanta: Scholars Press, 1992.

Van der Vorm-Croughs, Mirjam. *The Old Greek of Isaiah: An Analysis of Its Pluses and Minuses*. SCS 61. Atlanta: SBL Press, 2014.

Vandorpe, K. "Seals in and on the Papyri of Greco-Roman and Byzantine Egypt." Pages 231–91 and pls. 45–47 in *Archives et Sceaux du monde hellénistique*. Edited by Marie-Françoise Boussac and Antonio Invernizzi. BCHSup 29. Athens: Ecole Française d'Athènes, 1996.

Vasunia, Phiroze. *The Gift of the Nile: Hellenizing Egypt from Aeschylus to Alexander*. Classics and Contemporary Thought 8. Berkeley: University of California Press, 2001.

Verheyden, Joseph. "A Jewish King in Egypt? A Note on the So-called *History of Joseph*." Pages 449–61 in *Old Testament Pseudepigrapha and the Scriptures*. Edited by Eibert J. C. Tigchelaar. BETL 270. Leuven: Peeters, 2014.

Vikan, Gary K. "Illustrated Manuscripts of Pseudo-Ephraem's 'Life of Joseph' and the 'Romance of Aseneth.'" 3 vols. PhD diss., Princeton University, 1976.

Vos, R. L. *The Apis Embalming Ritual: P. Vindob. 3837*. OLA 50. Leuven: Peeters, 1993.

Waltke, Bruce K., and Michael O'Connor. *An Introduction to Biblical Hebrew Syntax*. Winona Lake, IN: Eisenbrauns, 1990.

Walsh, Richard. "Fabula and Fictionality in Narrative Theory." *Style* 35 (2001): 592–606.

Warren, Meredith. "A Robe Like Lightning: Clothing Changes and Identification in *Joseph and Aseneth*." Pages 137–53 in *Dressing Judeans and Christians in Antiquity*. Edited by Kristi Upson-Saia, Carly Daniel-Hughes, and Alicia J. Batten. Surrey: Ashgate, 2014.

Widmir, Ghislaine. "Pharaoh Maâ-Rê, Pharaoh Amenemhat and Sesostris: Three Figures from Egypt's Past as Seen in Sources of the Graeco-Roman Period." Pages 377–93 in *Acts of the Seventh International Conference of Demotic Studies*. Edited by Kim Ryholt. CNI 27. Copenhagen: Museum Tusculanum Press, 2002.

Wilson, N. G. *Scholars of Byzantium*. Baltimore: Johns Hopkins University Press, 1983.

Wright, Benjamin G., III. *The Letter of Aristeas: "Aristeas to Philocrates" or "On the Translation of the Law of the Jews."* CEJL. Berlin: de Gruyter, 2015.

Wright, Jonathan Stuart. "After Antiquity: *Joseph and Aseneth* in the Manuscript Transmission; a Case Study for Engaging with What Came After the Original Version of Jewish Pseudepigrapha." 2 vols. PhD diss., University of Oxford, 2018.

———. Review of *Joseph and Aseneth: A Christian Book*, by Rivka Nir. *JTS* 66 (2015): 330–32.

Zangenberg, Jürgen. "*Joseph und Aseneths* Ägypten, oder: Von der Domestikation einer 'gefährlichen' Kultur." Pages 159–86 in *Joseph und Aseneth*. Edited by Eckart Reinmuth. SAPERE 15. Tübingen: Mohr Siebeck, 2009.

Zellentin, Holgar M. "'Artapanus,' Edition, Translation, and Commentary." *BNJ* 726.

———. "The End of Jewish Egypt—Artapanus's Second Exodus." Pages 27–73 in *Antiquity in Antiquity: Jewish and Christian Pasts in the Greco-Roman Period*. Edited by Gregg Gardner and Kevin Lee Osterloh. TSAJ 123. Tübingen: Mohr Siebeck, 2008.

Zerbe, Gordon M. *Non-retaliation in Early Jewish and New Testament Texts: Ethical Themes in Social Contexts*. JSPSup 13. Sheffield: Sheffield Academic, 1993.

Ancient Sources Index

Septuagint			39:5	19
			39:6–41:36	168
Genesis			39:14	19
3:12		69	39:17	19
3:17		69	39:21	19
9:2		166	39:21–23	169
11:27–32		201	39:23	19
12:10–20		195	40:15	19
14:14		166	41–47	202
15		204	41:12	19
17:3		179	41:16	19
17:17		179	41:38–39	169
19:1		170	41:39	19
21:33		203	41:41	168
22:1		176	41:43	181
22:11		176	41:45	169, 195
22:15		176	41:46–49	168
24:61		85	41:47	167
30:1–13		171	41:50–52	169
30:3–13		172	41:53	167
31:14		85	41:53–57	168
31:36		166	41:53–42:2	169
32:27–30		61	42:6	170
33:7		84–85	42:43	168
34		211	43:26	170
34:14		173	43:32	19
34:30		173	45:4–8	169
35:5		166	45:4–11	19
35:25–26		172	47:25	167
37		195	47:13–26	195, 201
37–50	7–8, 19, 21, 167, 181		47:42–43	223
37:12–36		167	48:12	170
39–41		195	50:15	170–71
39:1–6		167	50:19–21	169
39:2–9		169		

Exodus		4:34	204
1–40	204	5:6	204
1:8–12	204	6:12	204
1:15–2:4	195	6:20–25	204
2:5–10	195	7:18–20	204
2:11–25	204	8:11–18	204
7–11	200	9:25–29	204
7–14	204	11:4	166
7:14–25	207	11:25	166
14:4	166	15:15	204
14:8–9	166	16:1–2	204
15:16	166	19:1–10	213
25:3	120	20:1	204
26:1	120	24:1–4	18
26:31	120	24:17–18	204
6:36	120	24:21–22	204
7:16	120	26:5–10	204
28:4–5	120	28:68	204
28:8	120	29:1–2	204
28:15	120		
34:1–40	68	Joshua	
35:6	120	2:5	166
35:25	120	2:7	166
		2:16	166
Leviticus		8:16–17	166–67
11:45	204	10:19	167
18:2	204	20	214
19:36	204	24:5–7	204
22:33	204	24:6	167
24:8	204		
26:45	204	Judges	
		1:6	167
Numbers		2:12	204
1:1	204	6:7–10	204
9:1–5	204	6:13	204
12:1	85	7:23	167
14:11–25	204	8:26	120, 223
15:41	204	13:3–5	58
22:31	170	13:3–7	57
30:3	18	13:3–20	59–62
35	214	13:15–16	58
35:9–15	213	13:17–18	58
		13:20	58, 179
Deuteronomy			
2:25	166		

Ancient Sources Index

1 Kingdoms (MT 1 Samuel)		29:9	162
2:8	176		
3:4	176	2 Chronicles	
12:6	204	13:8	167
17	211		
17:40	175	Ezra	
17:42	173	6:19–22	205
17:49	175		
17:51	176, 219	Nehemiah	
17:52	167	9:19–25	205
22:6	203	12:43	162
23:25	167		
23:28	167	Esther	
24:15	167	1:6	120
25:41	170	1:11 (MT)	228
26:18	167	8:15	120
30:8	167	8:16	223
31:13	203		
		Psalms	
2 Kingdoms (MT 2 Samuel)		2:11	166
2:19	167	18:8–11	233
2:24	167	29:12–14	69
2:28	167	54:6	166
4:6	89	78	205
7:11	89–90	80	205
14:33	170	81	205
17:1	167	105	205
18:28	170	106	205
20:6	167	114	205
24:20	170	118:97–104	233
		136	205
3 Kingdoms (MT 1 Kings)			
1:23	170	Proverbs	
1:40	162	8:30	70
9:9	204	24:13–14	233
12:28	204		
		Song of Songs	
4 Kingdoms (MT 2 Kings)		3:10	120
17:17	204	7:6	120
23:21–23	204		
		Isaiah	
1 Chronicles		3:21–24	120
10:1	167	19:16	166
15:23	89	39:2	162
21:21	170	43:16–21	205

Isaiah (cont.)		Hosea	
52:3–10	205	2:14–20	205
54:15	212	8:13	205
62:3 (MT)	228	9:3	205

Jeremiah		Amos	
2:4–19	205	2:10	205
7:21–26	205		
10:9	120	Jonah	
11:1–8	205	4:6	162
23:7–8	205		
27:5	212	Haggai	
31:32	205	2:2–9	205
42–44	205		
52:8	167	Zechariah	
		2:15	212
Ezekiel		2:17	228
1:28	179	8:15	228
3	233		
16:10	120	Deuterocanonical Books	
20	205		
23:6	120	Tobit	
27:7	120	1:22	203
27:24	120		
44:11	89–90	Judith	
		2:28	166
Daniel		10:21	120
3:2	203	14:7	170
5–6	8	15:2	166
5:7	120, 223		
5:15	120, 223	Wisdom of Solomon	
5:29	120, 223	5:16	228
6:4	120	8:16	70
8:17	179	9:10	70
9:15	205		
10	211	Sirach	
10–16	8	6:28	70
10:5	179	6:30	120
10:6	178	11:5	228
10:8	179	24:13–22	233
10:11–12	180	27:17	167
10:14–12:4	180	47:6	228
12:1	180		
		Epistle of Jeremiah	
		11	120

Ancient Sources Index 273

71	120	2:9	107
		2:11	98
1 Maccabees		2:12	51
1:9	228	3:3	31
4:23	120	3:5	98
4:38	120	5:3	30
6:15	228	5:5–6	31
7:18	166	6:1	31
8:14	120, 223, 228	6:2	48
10:20	120, 223	7:2–6	108
10:62	120, 223	7:4	114
10:64	120, 223	7:5	31
10:78	167	8:5	107
11:3	228	8:8	31
11:54	228	8:9	40
11:58	120, 223	9:1	29
12:30	167	9:2	31
12:39	228	10:2	31, 83–85, 89–92, 96, 98, 105–6, 111
13:32	228		
14:43	120, 223	10:11	51, 114
14:44	120, 223	10:11–12	50, 106
		10:13	51
1 Esdras		10:14	38
1:15	89–90	11:1–18	46, 53, 57, 62–63, 74, 111
3:6	120	11:3	69
7:9	89–90	11:15	69
		11:15–18	63
2 Esdras		11:19–13:15	62
8:36	203	11:4	31
18:6	170	11:9	31
		11:13	31
4 Maccabees		12:2	32
4:10	120	12:5	62, 69
		12:6	69
Pseudepigrapha		12:8	30–31
		12:14–15	46
Aseneth (Bu)		13:9	46
1:1	114	13:11	31
1:2	31	14:4	31
1:5	41–42	14:6	32
1:5–6	31	13:15	30
1:6	116	13:15–16:7	110
2:2	28	14:1–9	47
2:7	48–49, 51–52, 111–12	14:3	57
2:8	30	15:1	30

Aseneth (Bu) (cont.)

15:2	53
15:2–10	58
15:4–6	70
15:5	38, 109, 111
15:6	53, 67
15:7	57, 61, 69, 111
15:7–12	68
15:12	57–61, 74, 111
15:13–15	58
16:9	31
16:13	31
16:15	46, 69
16:16–17	31, 53
16:17	35
17:3–4	58
17:18	58
18:2–19:1	96
18:3–5	47
18:5	68
18:5–9	57, 65
18:7	47
18:9	57, 83, 95–96, 105, 111
18:9–11	47, 96
19:1	68
19:3–8	47
19:10	30
19:11	47
20:4	47
21:3	163
21:4	45
21:4–8	42, 46
21:8–9	47
21:10–21	29, 47
22:5	84
22:6–9	47
24:15	98
24:20	107
25:3–27:11	99
25:7	107
26:6	107
27:10–11	42
28:13	99

Aseneth (Bu/F)

1:1	160, 167
1:1–6	142
1:3–4	169
1:5	20
1:6	137
1:7	160, 167
1:7–9	142
2:1–12	143
2:3	20, 165
2:7	105
3:1	105, 113, 116, 160, 167
3:1–4	143
3:3	162–63
3:5–6	143, 220
3:6	143, 159, 181, 183, 220, 222
4:1	162–63
4:1–2	144
4:3–8	144
4:7	139, 168–69
4:9	20, 167
4:9–5:3	144
4:10	168
5:1	160
5:2	112
5:3	136–37
5:4	169
5:4–6	223
5:4–7	145
5:5	181
5:7	170
6:1	162–63
6:1–8	145
6:2	181–82, 223, 227
6:2–7	227
6:5–6	227
7:1	20
7:1–6	145
7:3	20
7:4	105, 115–16
7:7–8	145
7:8	162–63
8:1–7	146
8:5	105, 164
8:5–7	146, 213

8:8	165–66	18:1	160–61
8:8–9	146	18:1–11	149
8:9	164	18:2–19:1	135
9:1	162–63, 166	18:5–9	149
9:1–2	147	18:6	220, 222
9:3–10:1	147	18:9	93
10–17	239	18:11	163
10:1	162–63, 166	19–20	20
10:1–16	147	19:1	160–61
10:2	92, 123	19:1–20:5	150
10:11	105, 112, 116	20:6–10	150
11:1–13:15	147	20:9	139
11:10	20	20–29	20
12:9	160	21:1	146, 150
12:15	20, 160	21:2–8	150, 169
13:15	161, 176	21:3	163
14–15	20	21:4	164–65
14–17	212	21:5	165
14:1	160–61	21:6	164–65
14:1–10	147	21:7	165
14:2	160–61	21:9	151, 169
14:3	178	21:10–21	151
14:4	176	22:1	160
14:6–7	176, 178	22:1–2	20, 151, 169
14:8	177–78, 180	22:3–10	151
14:9	160, 178, 182	22:5	170
14:10	162–63	22:8	163, 170
14:11	166, 180	22:9	164–65
14:11–17:10	149	22:11	172–73
14:12–15:10	180	22:11–13	151
15:4	180, 234	23–28	20
15:5	105, 115	23–29	235
15:7	164, 181, 212	23:1	151, 160, 237
15:11	162–63	23:2–4	174
15:12	164	23:2–6	151, 235
15:13–16:18	229	23:3–7	151
15:13–17:4	233	23:6–13	174
16:7	161	23:7	174
16:13–29:9	140	23:8–9	174, 236
16:16–17:5	165	23:9	146
16:17	151	23:10–14	153, 220
16:19–22	149	23:10–17	236
17:4	165	23:12	146, 174
17:4–5	164	23:14	173, 181–82, 184, 218
17:8	182	23:15–17	153

Aseneth of Egypt

Aseneth (Bu/F) (cont.)			
23:16	166	28:9	170
24–27	219	28:9–17	237
24:1–2	153	28:10	146, 174, 236
24:1–14	237	28:12–17	157, 236
24:2	172–73	28:12–29:6	237
24:3–10	153	28:13	184
24:4–14	154	28:14	146, 157, 174, 181–83, 218, 236
24:5	162	28:15–29:5	219
24:8	172	29:1–4	157, 219
24:9	167–68, 171, 181–83, 218	29:1–6	236
24:15	172–73	29:2	175
24:15–20	154, 236	29:3	146, 174, 220, 236
25–28	173	29:5–6	158
25:1–4	154	29:6	170
25:3–27:11	161, 184	29:6–9	239
25:5	167–69	29:7	184
25:5–6	169	29:7–9	157–58, 170
25:5–8	154	29:8–9	159
26:1	165	29:9	20, 181, 183–84
26:1–5	154		
26:5	155, 236	Aseneth (Ph)	
26:6	166–67	1:7	39–42
26:6–8	155	1:8	38
26:7	160–61	1:14	38
27–28	216	2:12	49
27:1	166, 174	2:13	48, 51–52
27:1–5	155, 235	2:18	48
27:2	162–63, 174–75	6:2–7	227
27:4	175	7:1–7	108
27:6	155, 166–67, 172, 236	8:5	38
27:7–9	236	8:10	38
27:7–10	155, 237	8:11	39
27:11–28:4	156	9:1	38
28:1–4	170, 183, 237	10:3	85, 89
28:1–17	156–57	10:12–13	50–51, 106
28:2	170, 181	10:15	37–38
28:2–4	217	12:6	62, 64, 69
28:3	171, 183	14:1–8	47
28:4	181–83, 217	14:4	57
28:7	165–66, 170	14:7	58
28:7–8	156	15:2	52
28:8	172	15:2–5	69
28:8–11	157	15:2–11	58
28:8–17	218	15:4	38–39, 109

15:5	38, 52, 67	Greco-Roman Literature	
15:6–13	68, 72		
15:6–14	135	Aesop, *Fabulae Aphthonii rhetoris*	
15:7	38, 57, 69, 72, 111	13.6	88
15:10	67	13.9	88
15:13–14	58		
16:10–12	52	Apollonios Dyscolus, *De pronominibus*	
17:3	58	1.1.56	89
17:6	58		
18:3	68	Apollonius, *Argonautica*	
18:3–7	57, 65	3.233–34	224
18:6	68–69	3.309–311	224
19:1	68	3.1227–1230	224
20:3	48	4.220	224
21:1–8	42–45	4.595–626	224
21:2–7	42, 46, 135	4.727–729	224
21:3–7	46		
21:3	38	Diodorus Siculus, *Bibliotheca historica*	
21:8	46, 47	1.11–14	201
27:8	42	1.11.3–4	201
28:2	38	1.13.1–2	197
		1.13.2	225
Testament of Job		1.13.3	201
6:5–6	89	1.13.4	201
7:1	89	1.16	201
7:5	89	1.16.1–2	197
		1.21.1–2	201
New Testament		1.21.6	197
		1.21.7	197
Mark		1.21.9	197
13:34	89	1.21.10–11	197
		1.26.1	201, 225
John		1.28.1	201
10:3	89	1.43.6	197, 201
18:16–17	89	1.44.1	201
		1.44.2–5	201
Rabbinic Works		1.54.1	193, 196
		1.45–68	201
Lamentations Rabbah	73	1.46.7	201
		1.46.7–8	201
Ancient Jewish Writers		1.46.8	192
		1.47–49	201
Josephus, *Contra Apionem*		1.50.6–7	201
1.183	192	1.51.1–2	193
		1.51.4–6	193

Diodorus Siculus, Bibliotheca historica (*cont.*)		2.108	192–93
		2.109	193
1.52.3	201	2.110.1	193
1.53.1	191–92, 201		
1.53.5–6	193	Homer, *Odyssea*	
1.54.1–3	196	11.109	227
1.54.3	193, 201	12.323	227
1.54.4–5	196		
1.55.1–2	196	Hymn to Demeter	
1.55.1–4	193	62–89	224
1.55.11	193		
1.56.1	193, 196	Lysias, *Orationes pro milite*	
1.56.2	193	17	165
1.56.2–4	192		
1.56.5–6	201	Plato, *Respublica*	
1.57.2	193, 196	364e	196
1.57.2–4	193		
1.57.4	193	Early Christian Literature	
1.57.4–5	196		
1.57.5	193	Aeilius Herodianus and Pseudo-Herodianus, *De prosidia catholica*	
1.57.6–7	192		
1.57.8	193	3.1:200	88
1.58.1–3	193		
1.58.5	201	Clement, *Stromata*	
1.61.4	201	1.23.153–55	194
1.62.2–3	201		
1.63.5	201	Constitutiones apostolorum	
1.68.6	201	2.26.23	90
1.69.7	192, 201	2.28.15	90
1.96	201	2.57.40	90
4.25.1	196	3.11.2	90
		3.11.7	90
Diogenes Laertius, *Vitae philosophorum*		6.17.7	90
9.6	191		
		Eusebius, *Praeparatio evangelica*	
Euripides, *Iphigeneia at Tauris*		9.18.1	195, 201, 204
1153	89	9.23.1–2	195
		9.23.2	195, 201, 203–4
Herodotus, *Historiae*		9.23.3	204
2.37	188	9.26–28	194
2.77	188	9.27.3	195
2.102	193	9.27.3–4	196
2.102–106	192	9.27.4	196–97
2.102–109	189–90	9.27.5	200
2.107	192	9.27.6	197, 204

9.27.6–8	196
9.27.7	200
9.27.7–11	200
9.27.9	197
9.27.12	198
9.27.13–18	200
9.27.18–20	204
9.27.20	200
9.27.22–37	204
9.27.28	206

Heschyius, *Lexicon*
A. 2894	89

Johannes Moschus, *Pratum spirituale*
143:3005	89

Suda
A. 1146	89
EI. 66	89

Theognostus, *Canones sive De orthographia*
395.2	88

Greek Words Index

ἀκτίς 145, 181, 223
ἀλλογενής 144
ἄρχων 44, 137–39
ἄρουρα 93–96, 195, 203, 211
βασιλεύς, 137–39, 145, 216, 226, 231
βασιλεύω 181, 184, 227, 231
βασίλισσα 156, 181, 183, 216–17, 222
δέομαι 50–51, 106, 156, 181, 183, 216–17
διάδημα 118–19, 158–59, 183–84, 220, 227–28
διοικητής 195, 202–3, 211
ἥλιος 181–82, 223–24, 227
θέριστρον 65, 68, 143, 149
Ἰουδαῖα/Ἰουδαῖος 14, 16–21, 189, 194–95, 205, 234, 237–40
καταφυγή 61, 68, 148, 164, 180–82, 212–13, 215, 218–19, 244
καταφύγω 181–82, 212–13, 218–19
μιαίνω 173, 181
στεφάνη 43, 145, 149, 221–22, 228
ὕβρις/ὑβρίζω 156–57, 173, 181–83, 217–18
ὑπόμνημα 215, 237–38

Subject Index

Abraham, 19, 164, 176, 179, 195, 201, 204, 206
ancient Greek novel, 7–8
angel (character in *Aseneth*), 20, 53, 57–71, 109, 135, 147–49, 159, 165–66, 176–82, 212, 222, 229
Apis, 197–99, 230
Artanapus, 9–11, 13, 185, 187–88, 191, 194–207, 210–11, 226, 235, 240, 244
Aseneth (character), 3, 7–12, 14–15, 20, 37–38, 40–41, 48–51, 53–69, 72, 74, 85–87, 90–93, 95–96, 106–9, 111–12, 117–18, 125, 135, 137, 140, 142–51, 153–57, 159, 161, 163–76, 178–80, 182–83, 195, 210–20, 222–23, 227–29, 234, 236–37, 239, 240, 244
Benjamin, 155, 157–59, 165–66, 172, 174–76, 216–17, 219–20, 235–37
Bilhah and Zilpah, sons of, 151, 153–57, 159, 169–73, 181, 183, 215–19, 236–37
 Dan and Gad, 235
 Naphtali and Asher, 168, 235
bees (in *Aseneth*), 118–20, 148–49, 210–11, 223, 229–33
book of the living/life, 148, 180, 234
chariot (in *Aseneth*), 11, 144–46, 149, 154–55, 168–69, 181–82, 223–25, 227
chora (Egypt), 12, 187, 193, 202–5, 221, 226, 232
contact (linguistic studies), 209–10
Daniel, 8, 121, 147–48, 176, 178–81, 203, 205, 211, 223
David, 174–76, 219–20, 236
Dead Sea Scrolls, 214, 246

Diadem, 10, 118–19, 143, 149, 158–59, 183, 184, 220–23, 225, 227–29, 231
Dinah, 153, 173, 182, 218, 237
Egypt
 Pharaonic, 20, 187–210
 Hellenistic, 11, 187, 188, 210–41, 244
ethnicity, 14–16, 235
ethnos, 15–21, 187, 201, 206, 211, 236, 237, 239, 244
fabula, 3, 5–8, 11–14, 22, 79, 88, 123–85, 188, 212–13, 216–20, 222–23, 227, 229, 233–38, 243–44
Hecataeus of Abdera, 11, 187–94, 196–98, 200–204, 206–7, 210, 225, 227, 232, 240
Helios, 11–12, 145, 182, 223–27, 229, 244–45
Heracles, 189
Herakleopolis, 205, 227
Hermes, 196–97, 200, 224
Herodotus, 188–93, 196, 202, 232
hybris, 153, 156–57, 171, 173, 181–83, 217–19, 236–38, 244
Isis, 197–98, 200, 227
Joseph, 8–11, 13–16, 19–21, 27, 41, 58, 65, 67–69, 72, 79, 101–4, 107–8, 112–14, 125, 135–39, 142–54, 157–59, 161, 163–65, 167–74, 177–78, 180–84, 195, 201, 203–4, 206, 210, 211, 213, 217–20, 223, 227–29, 237, 239–40, 244–45
Judean, 14–15, 17–19, 21–22, 90, 185, 187–89, 193, 195, 198, 200, 202–6, 209–13, 221–22, 228–29, 232–41, 244–45

Leah, sons of, 151, 155–57, 159, 165–66, 170, 172–75, 216–18, 236–37
    Levi, 152–53, 158, 181–82, 219, 220, 235, 239
    Simeon, 152–53, 181, 220, 235
Life of Joseph, 27, 30–33, 79, 80, 83, 100–105, 248
Maat, 200–201
matriarchs, Hebrew, 41, 143
Memphis, 187, 192–93, 197–200, 205, 211, 216, 225–26, 230–31
Metanoia, 7, 69–73, 148
Moses, 27, 65–66, 68, 187, 195–201, 203–4, 206–7, 235
nswt-bjt (Egyptian throne name), 229–31, 233
numismatics, Ptolemaic, 11, 188, 207, 220–22, 224–29
Osiris, 197–99
Paul the apostle, 126–30
Pentephres, 71, 136–37, 139, 142–45, 150, 159, 169, 181, 223
Pharaoh (character in *Aseneth*), 137–39, 142, 144, 150, 154, 158–59, 163, 165, 168–71, 181, 183, 223, 227, 239
Pharaoh's son (in *Aseneth*), 142, 151–55, 157–61, 170–76, 183, 216, 218–20, 227, 235–37, 239
politeuma, 18, 205, 237–38
Ptolemies, 9–14, 16, 180, 187, 192, 198–201, 206–8, 210–41, 244
purple (clothing), 118–20, 144–45, 148–49, 181, 223, 227, 229
Re, 225–27, 229, 244
reconstructions of *Aseneth*
    Burchard, 35, 38, 40–42, 45–53, 57–63, 65, 67–69, 74, 83–85, 89–92, 95–96, 99, 105–12, 114, 116
    Fink, 20, 92–93, 105, 109, 112–13, 115–16, 123, 135–84, 212–13, 216–20, 222–23, 227, 229, 233–39
    Philonenko, 37–53, 57–58, 62, 64–69, 72, 85, 89, 106, 108–9, 135
Refuge, City of, 14, 148, 180, 182, 211–20
Russian formalism, 3, 134–35, 184

Serapis, 187, 199, 227
Sesostris, 189–94, 196, 200–201, 206, 235
sjuzhet, 132–35, 139
soldiers, Judean (under Ptolemies), 234–40
stemma, Fink, 29, 31, 61, 79, 80–83, 92–93, 95–96, 105, 107, 109, 112, 114, 116, 123, 137, 141
two-majuscule theory, Burchard, 21–22, 79, 83–84, 93, 97, 105–6, 113, 116–17, 137
veil, 65–66, 68, 143, 149, 221–22, 228
Zilpah, sons of. *See* Bilhah and Zilpah, sons of

Modern Authors Index

Adler, William 194
Ahearne-Kroll, Patricia 5, 7–11, 194, 198, 233
Aitken, James K. 211
Alberti, Giovanni B. 247
Allen, James P. 200, 225, 229
Allen, W. C. 214
Altenmüller, Hartwig 232
Andrews, Carol 231
Aptowitzer, Victor 245
Arnold, Dieter 230
Assemanus, Josephus S. 100
Azzoni, Annalisa 239–40
Bal, Mieke 133
Barclay, John M. G. 11, 16, 19, 21, 203, 213
Bar-Kochva, Bazalel 191, 192, 202, 204
Barth, Fredrik 9
Batiffol, Pierre 4, 22–23, 34, 48–49, 53, 67–68, 86, 107, 115, 138–40, 143, 145, 150, 159, 160–61, 164–66, 168, 170, 175, 177–80, 182
Bauschatz, John 215–16, 237
Bell, Lanny 229
Bernard, André 231
Bloch, René 5
Braginskaya, Nina 5
Bremmer, Jan 126
Bohak, Gideon 13, 120, 212
Boheeman, Christine van 133
Borgeaud, Philippe 199
Bosch-Puche Francisco 230
Bourdieu, Pierre 207–9
Brock, Sebastian P. 3, 37, 40
Brooke, George J. 10
Brooks, E. W. 4, 23, 68, 85, 107, 112, 139, 140, 143–44, 150, 152, 158, 160, 162–66, 168–71, 175, 182
Burchard, Christoph 2–6, 8, 11, 21–23, 25–57, 59, 60–68, 72–73, 75, 77–80, 82–121, 123–24, 135–52, 156–84, 212–13, 247–48
Burfeind, Carsten 3–4, 30, 102
Burrus, Virginia 132
Burstein, Stanley M. 191–92
Burton, Anne 191–93
Butera, C. Jacob 214
Capponi, Livia 13
Chesnutt, Randall D. 2, 10, 12, 34, 40, 213, 239
Clarysse, Willy 21, 205–6
Collins, John 1, 10, 178, 195, 203–4, 213, 239, 246
Cowe, S. Peter 103–4
Cowey, James M. S. 20, 205
Dain, Alphonse 83, 88
Delling, Gerhard 8, 161, 163–64, 166–67, 175, 178, 234
Detienne, Marcel 13
Di Bitonto Kasser, Ana 215–19, 238
Di Lella, Alexander A. 178
Dillery, John 202
Docherty, Susan 8
Doetsch–Amberger, Ellen 230
Èjxenbaum, Boris 133–34
Elder, Nicholas A. 5, 124
El-Masri, Yahia 232
Empereur, Jean-Yves 232
Eynde, Sabine van den 164

Fink, Uta B.   3–6, 20–22, 25–26, 28–29, 31–33, 37, 41, 47, 50, 52–53, 55–56, 59–61, 64, 73, 75, 78–121, 123–24, 137–50, 152, 156–84, 212, 248
Finkelberg, Margalit   98
Finnestad, Ragnhild Bjerre   232–33
Fischer-Bovet, Christelle   17, 205, 234–35
Fritz, Graf   16, 196
Freudenthal, J.   194
Fulińska, Agnieszka   222
Gauthier, Henri   229–30
Gera, Deborah Levine   162
Gibson, Sheila   199, 232
Gruen, Erich S.   194
Hacham, Noal   13
Hall, Jonathan M.   14–17, 19
Hartman, Louis Francis   178
Haslam, Michael   98
Hazzard, R. A.   226
Helbing, Robert   161
Hezser, Catherine   7–8
Hickey, Raymond   209
Hicks-Keeton, Jill   10, 13–14, 102, 174, 239
Hirschberger, Martina   11, 13
Höbl, Günther   230, 232–33
Hoffmann, Herbert   224
Holladay, Carl   203
Holtz, Traugott   3, 37
Horbury, William   21, 205
Hude, Karl   247
Inowlocki, Sabrina   12, 194
Iossif, Panagiotis   225–26
Istrin, V.M.   34
Jacobson, Howard   194, 198
Jacoby, Felix   191–92
Johnson, Janet J.   231
Jokiranta, Jutta   214
Jastrow, Marcus   214
Joüon, Paul   84
Kasher, Aryeh   235
Kasyan, Maria S.   5
Koenen, Ludwig   208–9
Koskenniemi, Erkki   198, 203
Kraemer, Ross S.   1–3, 5, 8–11, 21–22, 25–26, 33, 36, 53, 56–75, 100, 108, 121, 176, 182, 213, 244–45, 248
Kugel, James L.   131
Kugler, Robert A.   18, 194
Laďa, Csaba A.   235
Landgráfová, Renata   232
LeClant, Jean   229
Lewis, Naphtali   218, 226
Lincoln, Bruce   207
Lloyd, Alan B.   190, 192
Lorber, Catherine   225–26
Lord, Albert   131–32
Malaise, Michel   190
Manning, J.G.   221
Maresch, Klaus   20–21, 205
Mariette, Auguste   231
Mason, Steve   15–18, 21
McKenzie, Judith S.   199, 232
McGing, Brian   205
Metzger, Bruce M.   100
Milne, J.G.   222
Minas, Martina   231
Modrzejewski, Joseph Mélèze   205
Moffitt, David M.   214
Monson, Andrew   203, 205
Moore, Stewart   240
Moreshet, Menahem   84
Moyer, Ian   12, 189, 190
Mueller, Katja   234–35
Müller, Maya   225
Muntz, Charles M.   191–92
Muraoka, Takamitsu   164
Murray, Oswyn   191–93, 202
Nickelsburg, George W. E.   212
Nir, Rivka   6, 10, 244, 245
Nisse, Ruth   247
Noegel, Scott   207, 225
Noy, David   21, 205–6
O'Conner, M.   162
Orlov, Andrei   6
Pfeiffer, Stefan   198–199, 225, 231
Philonenko, Marc   2–5, 8, 10–12, 21, 25–26, 33, 35–42, 45–46, 49, 53–54, 56, 62, 72, 74, 100, 109, 121, 123, 136,

Modern Authors Index

138, 140, 143, 146, 150, 161, 164, 166, 168–70, 175, 177–80, 182, 213, 246
Pier, Garrett Chatfield 231
Plantzos, Dimitris 222
Porten, Bezalel 235
Portier-Young, Anathea E. 213, 233
Pratt, Mary Louise 208–10, 233
Putthoff, Tyson L. 6
Quaegebeur, Jan 208, 223
Quirke, Stephen 231
Reden, Sitta von 220–21
Reinhartz, Adele 18
Reinhold, Meyer 223
Reinmuth, Eckart 248
Reyes, A. T. 199, 232
Reynolds, L. D. 83–84, 97, 98
Richardson, Brian 134
Rowlandson, Jane 18
Royse, James R. 246
Runia, David T. 246
Ryholt, Kim 190
Sacks, Kenneth S. 191, 193
Sagan, Carl ix–x
Sänger, Dieter 12–13, 18
Shafer, Byron E. 207, 229, 232
Seldon, Dan 207
Shklovsky, Viktor 134
Schwartz, Daniel R. 17
Schwartz, Eduard 191
Simpson, R. S. 225
Smith, E. W. 3, 40
Smith, J. Z. 17
Smith, R. R. R. 221, 223, 226
Spalinger, Anthony J. 207
Standhartinger, Angela 2–3, 5, 8, 10–11, 13, 21–22, 25–26, 33, 36–42, 45–48, 50–51, 53–57, 59, 74–75, 87–88, 97, 100, 104, 109, 121, 174, 218, 234, 248
Stanwick, Paul Edmund 208, 232
Stephens, Susan 9, 12, 189, 190, 193, 202, 207, 209–10, 225
Sterling, Gregory E. 191, 194, 201
Stern, David 131
Stern, Menahem 17
Stol, Marten 171

Stone, Michael E. 103–4
Stork, Peter 247
Strugnell, John 194
Svoronos, I. N. 221–22, 225–26, 228
Tcherikover, Viktor 21, 237
Thiessen, Matthew 214, 239
Thissen, Heinz-Josef 232
Thomas, Christine 3, 127–34
Thompson, Dorothy J. 12, 21, 198–99, 206, 226, 230, 232
Thwaites, Edward 100
Tiede, David Lenz 196
Tomashevsky, Boris 134
Toorn, Karel van der 16
Tov, Emmanuel 162
Tromp, J. 10
Turner, C. W. 126
Valantasis, Richard 133
Van der Vorm-Croughs, Mirjam 162
Vandorpe, K. 222
Vasunia, Phiroze 189
Verheyden, Joseph 5
Volokhine, Youri 199
Walsh, Richard 134
Waltke, Bruce K. 162
Warren, Meredith 5, 8
Wevers, John Williams 162
Widmir, Ghislaine 190
Wilson, N. G. 83–84, 97, 98
Wright, Benjamin G. 235
Wright, Jonathon 10, 22, 23, 112, 139–40, 143–46, 150, 152, 158, 161, 163, 166, 168, 170, 175–76, 178–80, 182–83, 248
Zangenberg, Jürgen 11
Zellentin, Holger M. 191, 193–94, 202
Zerbe, Gordon 236

www.ingramcontent.com/pod-product-compliance
Lightning Source LLC
Chambersburg PA
CBHW030435300426
44112CB00009B/1015